The Harrowsmith
COOKBOOK
Volume Number 1
Classic & Creative Cuisine

By the Editors & Readers of Harrowsmith Magazine

Compiled from the private recipe collections of the Editors, Readers,
Contributors and Staff of *Harrowsmith*, Canada's National Award Winning Magazine
of Country Living and Alternatives

CAMDEN HOUSE

© 1981 by Camden House Publishing

Revised and reprinted 1982
Third printing 1983
Fourth printing 1985
Fifth printing 1987
Sixth printing 1988

ISBN 0-920656-18-8 (Hardcover)
        0-920656-19-6 (Softcover)

Trade distribution by Firefly Books, Toronto

Printed in Canada by
D.W. Friesen & Sons Ltd., Altona, Manitoba, for
Camden House Publishing
(a division of Telemedia Publishing Inc.)
7 Queen Victoria Road
Camden East, Ontario
K0K 1J0

Cover by Roger Hill

COOKBOOK

Volume Number 1

Editor
PAMELA CROSS

Associate Editors
JENNIFER BENNETT, JAMES LAWRENCE

Consultants
RUTH GEDDES, ALICE GIBSON

Photography
ERNIE SPARKS

Food Design
MARIELLA MORRIN

Drawings
LARRY TURNBULL

Copy Editors
MARY PATTON, CATHY DAVIS, ALICE O'CONNELL

Design & Layout
LARRY TURNBULL, JUDITH GOODWIN
LYNN DUMBLETON, PAMELA MCDONALD

Typesetting
JOHANNA TROYER, CAROL SCRUTTON

Photography Credits
PHOTOGRAPHIC PROPERTIES COURTESY OF:
KITCHEN CARGO, 86 BROCK ST., KINGSTON, ONTARIO
MCCALLUM'S CHINA AND GIFTS, 79 BROCK ST., KINGSTON, ONTARIO
THE ART OF COOKING, 209 FAIRWAY HILL CRES., KINGSTON, ONTARIO

Contents

Introductions

*That he may bring food out of the earth
and wine that maketh glad the heart of man
and oil to make him a cheerful countenance
and bread to strengthen man's heart.*

— **Prayer Book, 1662**

"The discovery of a new dish does more for the happiness of mankind than the discovery of a star," wrote the French politician and gourmet, Anthelme Brillat-Savarin in 1825.

While certainly at odds with the astronomers of the world, Brillat-Savarin seems to have struck a note of truth in this statement and we dedicate this cookbook to those who agree, the kindred spirits who take delight in encountering new foods and recipes, in continuously expanding their culinary repertoires and who like to keep things lively in the kitchen and on the dining table.

This is a cookbook that defies easy description, having been created with the gleanings from hundreds of private recipe collections, the very best dishes of north woods cooks, professional gourmet chefs and amateur cooks of every ilk: men, women, vegetarians, rare beef lovers, farmhouse grannies, *cordon bleu* amateurs and simply everyday good cooks.

Drawing upon such disparate resources, cooks united only by *Harrowsmith* magazine and the Canada Post, this might be described as a melting pot of a cookbook that does not fall into the common classifications of modern recipe collections. It resists being labelled as a gourmet cookbook; it is not an ethnic cookbook, or a health food cookbook and is not part of the Kraft Kookery School of food thought.

In selecting entries from the 848 cooks who opened their recipe boxes to share their time-tested wealth, the editors immediately rejected anything dependent on highly processed foods — Jell-O, Dream Whip, CheezWhiz and the like — that have become so pervasive in modern cooking. Next on the rejection list were those recipes replete with healthy ingredients but which relegated attractiveness and flavour to a low priority. What the editors sought was healthy food, but food that people would eat — and enjoy.

There is an old English proverb stating that, "God sends meat and the Devil sends cooks," but the multitudinous authors of this volume seem to have provided the raw ingredients and editorial seasonings for a recipe collection that is already passing the most important test of any cookbook: Is it used, or does it merely find its way onto a shelf or into the back of a cupboard?

The many *Harrowsmith* staff members and friends who helped test and evaluate the more than 4,000 recipes contributed have pushed the office photocopier to its limit, exposing their families to a multitude of new dishes and variations on old favourites. The verdict? Many of the photocopies have found permanent homes in staff recipe books and boxes, and virtually all of those who tested recipes report having adopted a number of new ideas into their regular meal plans.

If the final results appear gratifying, it must also

be reported that this book came within a few weeks of becoming a victim of the national postal strike which fell like a dam at high tide on the Bay of Fundy. Fortunately, the single call for entries, published in a spring issue of *Harrowsmith*, had brought thousands of recipes through the cubbyhole post office in Hartman's General Store in Camden East.

Just prior to the strike, the editors were receiving a hundred letters a day, and file folders began to bulge. Intermittent staff testing quickly became inadequate and was reorganized into weekly office luncheons in which each participant chose and prepared a contributed recipe. Around picnic tables under the century-old maples in *Harrowsmith's* front lawn, staff members sampled salads, breads, soyburgers and puddings as the early summer sun tempted us to continue testing rather than return to work. The failure rate was substantial, but the approved recipes piled up, the sun shone and the staff began to grow fat.

Pamela Cross, a compulsive cook and recipe tester and the former owner of a natural foods bistro, finally found herself compelled to spend entire days and numerous evenings testing recipes, with her patient husband and two small children bravely downing foods from unknown contributors in far-flung places. (Letters and new dishes came from every province and territory in Canada, as well as from the United States, Australia and New Zealand.)

Fuelled by these submissions, *The Harrowsmith Cookbook* began to take shape. While we would not label it quite as immodestly as did "A Lady" who titled her 1747 publication, *The Art of Cookery made Plain and Easy: which far exceeds any Thing of the Kind ever yet Published,* the book was revealing itself as unique in character, certainly one-of-kind, written by people who belonged to no common club or society and who did not necessarily subscribe to a common philosophy. They were simply people who knew how to cook, had the inclination and took the time to write.

The efforts of all who wrote were inspiring. Some recipes were painstakingly illustrated, some accompanied by photographs, some beautifully hand-lettered. Some came with letters that told a little about the food and philosophy of the contributor. There were even poems about food preparation.

What suited the book best were recipes that were at once simple and imaginative, reflecting an approach with which "A Lady" would have agreed: "The great Cooks have such a high Way of expressing themselves that the poor Girls are [at] a Loss to know what they mean: And in all Receipt Books yet printed there are such an off Jumble of Things as would quite spoil a good Dish; and indeed some Things so extravagant, that it would be almost a Shame to make Use of them, when a Dish can be made full as good or better without them."

Such recipes might be family favourites, even family heirlooms. Some had endured generations of batter stains, while others were created by the contributors themselves.

The book itself, then, is composed of both old and new recipes, but all are deemed worthy of becoming future heirlooms. But to say that what remains after all the filtering is the *crème de la crème* of the contributions would be to overstate the case: Pamela Cross is still holding on to 1,500 excellent recipes that did not make the book but may, if the response to this one encourages it, be included in *Harrowsmith's* next cookbook. All the contributions had some merit; some simply were the right recipes sent to the wrong cookbook (or vice versa, according to one's point of view). So to all who contributed recipes, hints, letters — in short, who contributed their time and energy — the staff extends sincere thanks from its collective heart and stomach.

And to you, the reader, we express our appreciation as well, and our wish that you may enjoy meals as pleasant as those the staff shared under the summer sun on *Harrowsmith's* front lawn, evaluating the contributions of those who cared enough to send the very best.

Eggs & Cheese

A hen is only an egg's way of making another egg.

— **Samuel Butler**
Life & Habit

If, as Clifton Fadiman quipped, cheese is "milk's leap toward immortality," then surely an egg is the hen's most pristine contribution to cordon bleu cookery. Aesthetically perfect in its natural, unbroken state, an egg can be transformed into some of man's most subtle culinary creations. Eggs and cheese, in fact, have a lot in common in this respect, being perfectly at home in the exacting galleys of Maxim's — but equally at ease and equally important in the humbler kitchens of the world.

Both foods are among the best sources of high-quality protein which can be had at a relatively low price — barring, of course, eggs such as those from the ostrich, each of which is said to serve 18 for brunch, and the rare and costly *Vacherin des Beauges* cheese.

Both foods are what might be called animal by-products. Just as each egg is not a potential chicken — few eggs nowadays are fertilized — so cows' milk is seldom bound for calves' stomachs. A top-ranking modern dairy cow has been known to produce 15 gallons of milk a day, while a factory hen weighing four and a half pounds can produce 33 pounds of eggs in its first year.

Eggs and cheese both appreciate gentle cooking; high temperatures shorten and toughen protein fibres, resulting in latex fried eggs and curdled cheese sauce. There is one exception — the hard-boiled egg. In this case, the cook should place the egg in cold water containing a bit of vinegar or salt, set it over high heat and, once it boils, time it for 15 minutes, after which the egg is plunged into cold water, the better to avoid a dark ring around the yolk. The cook is advised not to hard boil eggs less than three days from the hen — much of the white will come away with the shell. Nor should one try beating really fresh eggs. Or, for that matter, old eggs. Consumers tied to the supermarket supply may find them difficult to avoid, but old eggs are not as good as fresh eggs for anything at all. And, in beating egg whites of any sort, remember that the bowl must be absolutely free of fat for best results; that means that even a trace of yolk, which is quite high in fat, will sabotage the cook's efforts when beating the whites for a soufflé.

Small stock owners should keep in mind that the average hen's egg weighs 50 grams. In substituting duck or goose eggs in a recipe, consider that the former weighs about 70 grams, the latter, 144 grams, and adjust the recipe accordingly, or beat the egg first in a bowl and remove an appropriate amount before proceeding with the recipe. Since home produced chicken eggs are usually considerably larger than the supermarket "medium," on which measurements in most cookbooks are based, it may be necessary to increase the other ingredients in a given recipe slightly, or to use fewer eggs.

Brown and white eggs differ only aesthetically — there is no variation in nutritional value. Free-range eggs, however, do have a much yellower yolk and a fresher, fuller flavour than do large-scale commercially produced eggs.

While eggs do not age gracefully beyond a couple of weeks, the case is quite different with most cheeses, which, like wine, tend to improve and to mature with the passage of time, provided storage conditions are proper. As these conditions do not exist in the refrigerator, it is generally best not to buy cheese in bulk, but to purchase only amounts that can be used within a few days.

The flavours and textures of cheeses depend on whether the curd is formed with lactic acid or rennet, whether cow's, goat's or sheep's milk is used, the amount of moisture, salt and spices added, the temperature and conditions of ripening and the particular mould or bacteria present.

Both eggs and cheese are beloved of vegetarians — those not averse to all animal products — as foods that fill in the nutritional blanks left by grains, fruits and vegetables, as well as complementing them in dishes ranging from the rustic to the sublime. Since cheese contains less water than milk, it is a more concentrated source of nutrients than is its very mortal parent: One pound of cheese contains the same amount of protein and fat as one gallon of milk. It is

especially valued for its protein, calcium, vitamin A, riboflavin and other B vitamins. Soft cheeses such as Camembert are higher in water and vitamin content than hard cheeses such as Cheddar and Parmesan. For the record, "processed" cheeses contain up to 60 per cent moisture, while Cheddar, in Canada, must not contain over 34 per cent to deserve the name.

Eggs are a complete protein food, containing all eight amino acids in a pattern more closely approaching the ideal than any other high-protein food including meat. While it is true that eggs contain cholesterol, they are also a good source of lecithin which helps the body to utilize fats normally.

Egg yolk is a good source of fat, vitamins A, E, B_6 and B_{12}, and also has some thiamine and riboflavin, while the white is mainly a colloidal solution of protein, containing about 88 per cent water, and is a good source of potassium.

All of which is of intellectual, but little gustatorial interest. In fact, we might mention one more similarity between eggs and cheese, the obvious fact that both foods vary so much in quality that one's understanding of the very words "egg" and "cheese" may be quite different from that of one's neighbour. *Chacun à son goût* — or Gouda.

QUICHE LORRAINE

THIS QUICHE CAN ALSO BE MADE INTO INDIVIDUAL PIES IN MUFFIN TINS AND SERVED as hors d'oeuvres. Variations are almost endless — asparagus, shrimp, leeks, ham and mushrooms all make delicious additions.

Pastry for 9-inch pie shell
8 slices bacon
1 cup grated Swiss cheese
4 eggs

1½ cups milk or light cream
½ tsp. salt
⅛ tsp. pepper
⅛ tsp. nutmeg

Bake pie shell at 400 degrees F for 10 minutes. Remove from oven and reduce temperature to 350 degrees.

Chop bacon and fry until crisp. Drain and place in pie shell. Top with grated cheese. Beat eggs, milk and seasonings together. Pour into shell and bake 25 to 35 minutes or until firm and lightly browned.

— Mary Lou Ross
Tavistock, Ontario

CHEESE AND ONION PIE

THIS EGG PIE IS VERY DENSE, AND WITH ONLY A GREEN SALAD IS A MEAL IN ITSELF. Chopped cooked bacon or ham may be added for variety.

Pastry for 9-inch pie shell
3 medium onions
1 cup water

4 eggs
½ cup milk
1-1½ cups grated Cheddar cheese

Line pie plate with pastry, prick with a fork and bake at 350 degrees F for 10 minutes.

Peel and slice onions, place in saucepan and cover with 1 cup boiling water and boil, covered, for 5 to 10 minutes. Cool.

Beat together eggs and milk.

Alternate layers of onions and grated cheese in the pastry shell. Pour custard over all.

Bake at 350 degrees for 20 minutes or until set.

— Rae Anne Huth
Fauquier, B.C.

SPINACH QUICHE

SPINACH, SWISS CHARD OR BEET GREENS — WHATEVER YOUR GARDEN PROVIDES — are good in this quiche.

1 cup flour
½ tsp. salt
¼ cup oil
2 Tbsp. milk
1 lb. fresh spinach
1 small onion, chopped

2 Tbsp. oil
2 eggs
1 cup yogurt
½ cup dried milk
½ tsp. salt
⅓ cup grated Parmesan cheese

To prepare crust, combine flour and salt. Add oil and milk and mix with a fork. Roll out to fit a 9-inch pie plate, or simply spread dough in plate with your fingers.

Wash and cook spinach until just limp. Drain and chop well. Heat oil in a frying pan and add onion and spinach, cooking a few minutes until liquid has evaporated.

In a bowl, beat eggs and stir in yogurt, milk and salt. Add spinach and onions. Stir together and pour into the unbaked pie crust. Sprinkle with cheese and bake at 375 degrees F for 25 minutes or until firm and starting to brown.

— Mikell Billoki
Gore Bay, Ontario

TOFU MILLET QUICHE

1 cup millet
2½ cups boiling water
1 tsp. salt
1 tsp. butter
1½ cakes tofu
1 Tbsp. oil
1 onion, finely chopped
2 cloves garlic, minced

3 cups raw spinach, cleaned & stemmed
2 Tbsp. tamari sauce
2 Tbsp. arrowroot
Basil, thyme & paprika
½ tsp. nutmeg
Handful sliced mushrooms
¼ lb. medium Cheddar cheese, grated

Add millet to boiling water and add salt. Simmer for 25 to 30 minutes. Butter a 10-inch pie plate and pat in the cooked millet while still warm. Bake at 425 degrees F for 5 to 7 minutes.

Place tofu in colander, weight it and let sit 30 minutes to drain.

Sauté onion and garlic in oil until tender but not browned. Remove from heat.

Steam spinach until limp, chop coarsely and add to onion and garlic.

In 2 batches, using a blender, mix until smooth the tofu, tamari, seasonings (except paprika) and arrowroot. If mixture is too thick, add a little water. Add this to onion-spinach mixture.

Pour into crust and arrange sliced mushrooms on top. Sprinkle cheese and paprika over all.

Bake at 425 degrees F for 10 minutes, reduce heat to 325 degrees and bake 20 minutes longer.

Serves 6.

— Francine Watanabe
Ottawa, Ontario

TOMATO & BASIL TART

THIS FRAGRANT TART CAN BE SERVED HOT OR COLD, FOR BREAKFAST, LUNCH OR AS an opening course with dinner.

Pastry for 9-inch pie shell
3 Tbsp. sweet butter
2 medium onions, finely chopped
2 lbs. tomatoes, peeled, seeded & chopped
1 cup whipping cream

3 large eggs
1½ tsp. salt
½ tsp. pepper
2 tsp. dried basil
1½ tsp. finely sliced green peppers

Melt the butter in a frying pan. Add onions and cook until transparent. Strain the tomatoes and add to the onions. Cook over low heat until the tomatoes are reduced to a pulp. Remove from the heat and cool.

Beat together cream and eggs. Add cooled tomato mixture and season with salt, pepper, basil and green onions.

Line tart pan with pastry and bake at 350 degrees F for 5 minutes. Add filling and bake 30 to 35 minutes longer.

— Auberge du Petit Prince
London, Ontario

SALMON-LEEK QUICHE

WITH WINTER-STORED LEEKS AND FRESH PARSLEY FROM AN INDOOR HERB GARDEN, this makes a pleasant midwinter dinner.

Pastry for 9-inch pie shell
2 large leeks
1 Tbsp. butter
16-oz. can salmon
1 cup grated old Cheddar cheese

3 eggs
¾ cup milk
½ tsp. salt
Freshly ground pepper
Fresh parsley, chopped

Bake pie shell at 400 degrees F for 5 minutes. Remove from oven and lower heat to 375 degrees.

Slice leeks in half lengthwise, wash carefully, slice thinly and sauté in 1 Tbsp. butter.

Drain salmon, flake and distribute over the bottom of the pie shell. Sprinkle with leeks and grated cheese.

Beat eggs with milk, salt and pepper and pour over mixture in shell. Top with a handful of fresh chopped parsley.

Bake at 375 degrees F for 25 to 35 minutes.

— *Beth Hopkins*
Courtenay, B.C.

CORN MEAL QUICHE

THE ADDITION OF CORN MEAL TO THE CRUST AND KERNEL CORN TO THE FILLING GIVES this quiche an unusual but pleasant texture and flavour.

½ cup corn meal
¾ cup flour
½ tsp. salt
Pepper
⅓ cup shortening
3 Tbsp. cold water
1 cup shredded cheese

1 small onion, chopped
2 cups whole kernel corn, drained
⅓ cup milk
6 eggs
1 tsp. salt
¼ tsp. cayenne

For crust, mix corn meal, flour, salt and pepper in a bowl. Cut in shortening. Sprinkle water over while stirring with a fork. Roll out and fit loosely into a 9-inch pie plate. Flute edges.

Spread cheese in bottom of unbaked pie shell. Sauté onion, then add it and the corn to the cheese. Mix milk, eggs and seasonings together and pour into pie shell.

Bake at 400 degrees F until firm and slightly browned on top — 20 to 30 minutes.

— *Mikell Billoki*
Gore Bay, Ontario

SALMON SOUFFLE

A LIGHT YET FILLING SUPPER DISH, SALMON SOUFFLE IS NICELY COMPLEMENTED with hot biscuits and a tossed salad.

3 Tbsp. butter
3 Tbsp. flour
1 cup milk
1 tsp. salt

Pepper
6-oz. can salmon
3 eggs, separated

Melt the butter, add flour, milk, salt and pepper. Boil until thick, then remove from heat. Add salmon and slightly beaten yolks. Beat egg whites and fold in. Pour into well-greased soufflé dish or other deep baking dish.

Bake at 350 degrees F for 20 to 25 minutes, or until golden brown.

Serves 2 to 3.

— *Lynda Howson*
Peterborough, Ontario

ASPARAGUS & CHICKEN SOUFFLE

6 oz. fresh asparagus,
  cut into ¼-inch pieces
¼ cup butter
¼ cup flour
¼ tsp. thyme
¼ tsp. dry mustard
½ tsp. Tabasco sauce

¼ tsp. salt
1¼ cups milk
4 eggs, separated
½ cup cooked, shredded chicken
¾ cup grated Parmesan cheese
¼ tsp. cream of tartar

Prepare a 1½-quart straight-sided soufflé dish with collar. To do this, fold a 26-inch sheet of aluminum foil in half lengthwise; wrap it around the dish with a 3-inch rim extending above the top edge. Tape or tie in place.

In a medium saucepan, steam asparagus in 1 inch of boiling water for 6 minutes or until tender. Drain and set aside.

In the same pan, melt butter and blend in flour, thyme, mustard, Tabasco sauce and salt. Cook for 1 minute. Gradually stir in milk. Cook over medium heat, stirring constantly, until sauce thickens and boils. Reduce heat and simmer for 1 more minute.

In a medium-sized bowl, beat egg yolks, then quickly stir in sauce. Add chicken, cheese and asparagus and mix well. Cool slightly.

In large bowl of electric mixer, beat egg whites with cream of tartar until whites are stiff, but not dry. Gently fold in the sauce mixture. Turn into prepared soufflé dish. Bake at 375 degrees F for 45 to 50 minutes or until golden brown. Remove collar and serve immediately.

Serves 4.

— Gregg A. Collis
Burlington, Ontario

BROCCOLI CHEESE SOUFFLE

AN INTERESTING AND ATTRACTIVE DISH, THIS SOUFFLE IS GOOD SERVED WITH ROLLS and a green salad.

1 tsp. butter
1 Tbsp. Parmesan cheese
3 Tbsp. butter
3 Tbsp. flour
⅓ cup powdered milk
¾ cup boiling water
½ tsp. salt
⅛ tsp. pepper

Cayenne & nutmeg
4 egg yolks
⅔ cup grated Swiss, Parmesan or
  Cheddar cheese
⅔ cup cooked & chopped broccoli
1 egg white
Salt

Preheat oven to 400 degrees F.

Butter a 6-cup soufflé dish with 1 tsp. butter and sprinkle with 1 Tbsp. Parmesan cheese.

Melt the 3 Tbsp. of butter in a saucepan and stir in the flour. Cook for about 2 minutes without letting it brown. Remove from heat and add powdered milk mixed with boiling water. Beat with a wire whisk until well blended. Add seasonings and return to moderate heat. Remove from heat after 1 minute.

Add egg yolks to mixture, one at a time, beating well after each one. Correct the seasoning. Add cheese and broccoli.

Beat egg white with a pinch of salt until stiff. Blend one-quarter of the egg white into the cheese mixture, then carefully fold in the remaining egg whites.

Turn the mixture into the soufflé dish and smooth the top. Place on middle rack of oven and reduce heat to 375 degrees.

Do not open the oven door for at least 20 minutes. Bake 25-30 minutes (4-5 minutes longer if you like it quite firm). Serve immediately.

Serves 4 to 6.

— Olga Harrison
Peterborough, Ont.

CHEESE SOUFFLE

THIS IS A BASIC SOUFFLE RECIPE. ONCE MASTERED, ALMOST ENDLESS VARIATIONS are possible.

¼ cup butter
¼ cup flour
½ tsp. salt

1½ cups hot milk
½ lb. Cheddar cheese, grated
4 eggs, separated

Blend butter, flour and salt together in a saucepan. Add hot milk and cook, stirring, until the mixture thickens. Remove from heat and blend in cheese.

Stir a little of the cheese mixture into the egg yolks, then pour into the saucepan and mix thoroughly.

Beat egg whites until stiff and fold gently into the egg and cheese mixture.

Turn into a buttered soufflé dish and bake at 375 degrees F for 35 minutes. Serve immediately.

Serves 4.

— Shirley Thomlinson
Carp, Ontario

OVERNIGHT SOUFFLE

12 slices bread, trimmed & cubed
½ lb. sharp Cheddar cheese, grated
3¼ cups milk
7 eggs, beaten

¾ tsp. salt
1 tsp. Worcestershire sauce
¼ cup grated Parmesan cheese

In a buttered 9" x 13" casserole dish, layer the bread and cheese: first spread out half the bread, cover with half the cheese, then the rest of the bread and the rest of the cheese.

Mix milk, eggs and seasonings, and pour over bread and cheese. Cover and refrigerate overnight.

Sprinkle with Parmesan cheese and bake uncovered at 325 degrees F for 45 to 55 minutes, or until set. Serve immediately.

Serves 6.

— Joan Panaro
Jenner, California

NETTLE PIE

½ paper grocery bag of young nettles
3 Tbsp. butter
2 Tbsp. chopped onion
2 cloves garlic, chopped
2 Tbsp. flour
1 cup milk
Bay leaf

1 cup grated Cheddar cheese
2 eggs
⅔ cup flour
⅓ cup milk
⅓ cup water
¼ tsp. salt
½ cup Parmesan cheese

Wearing rubber gloves, remove central stem from nettles. Steam until tender, then place in a large greased casserole dish.

In a frying pan, melt butter, add onion and garlic and cook until limp. Mix in flour. Add milk and bay leaf and cook, stirring, until thickened. Pour this mixture over the nettles. Spread grated cheese over nettles and sauce.

Beat remaining ingredients together for 2 minutes and pour over the cheese. Sprinkle with Parmesan cheese. Bake at 400 degrees F for 20 minutes.

Serves 6.

— Dianne Radcliffe
Denman Island, B.C.

SPINACH PIE

SPINACH, EGGS AND FETA CHEESE COMBINED IN LAYERS WITH FILO PASTRY GIVE this dish a delectably rich flavour.

¼ cup olive oil
½ cup finely chopped onions
¼ cup finely chopped scallions
2 lbs. fresh spinach, washed,
 drained & finely chopped
¼ cup finely cut fresh dill leaves
 (2 Tbsp. dried)
¼ cup finely chopped parsley

½ tsp. salt
Freshly ground black pepper
⅓ cup milk
½ lb. feta cheese, finely crumbled
4 eggs, lightly beaten
½ lb. butter, melted
16 sheets filo pastry

Heat olive oil in a heavy skillet. Add onions and scallions and cook, stirring frequently, until soft but not brown. Stir in spinach, cover tightly and cook for 5 minutes. Add dill, parsley, salt and a few grindings of pepper while stirring and shaking pan. Cook uncovered for about 10 minutes — until most of the liquid has evaporated and spinach sticks slightly to the pan.

Transfer to a bowl, add milk and cool to room temperature. Add cheese and slowly beat in eggs. Taste for seasoning.

With a pastry brush, coat the bottom and sides of a 7" x 12" dish with melted butter. Line the dish with a sheet of filo, pressing the edges into the corners of the dish. Brush the surface of the pastry with 2 or 3 tsp. of butter. Lay another sheet on top. Again, spread with 2 to 3 tsp. of butter. Continue until there are 8 layers of filo in the pan.

Spread the spinach mixture on top of the filo. Place another layer of filo on top, coat with butter, and repeat, as before, until there are 8 layers. With scissors, trim the excess filo from around the edges of the dish. Brush top with remaining butter.

Bake at 300 degrees F for 1 hour or until pastry is golden brown. Cut into squares and serve hot or at room temperature.

— *Carol Gasken*
Winlaw, B.C.

SPINACH CREAM CHEESE PIE

ALTHOUGH THIS PIE HAS NO CRUST, THE WHEAT GERM BAKES TO A CRISPY texture, resulting in a quiche-like dish.

10 oz. spinach
8 oz. cream cheese
1 Tbsp. minced onion
Dash nutmeg
6 eggs

Wheat germ
¼ lb. Cheddar cheese, sliced
Paprika
1 Tbsp. flour
1 tsp. water

Cook spinach, drain and press out excess water. Soften cream cheese and add spinach, onion and nutmeg. Beat 5 of the eggs and stir into the spinach mixture.

Grease sides and bottom of a pie plate, sprinkle it with wheat germ and pour in spinach mixture. Cover with cheese slices and sprinkle with paprika.

Beat remaining egg with flour and water and pour over the cheese.
Bake at 350 degrees F for 35 to 45 minutes, until top is lightly browned.

Serves 4.

— *Laura Poitras*
Kemptville, Ontario

EGG AND CHEESE PUFFS

LIGHT, SATISFYING AND TASTY, THESE MAKE AN INTERESTING ADDITION TO A BRUNCH menu.

4 eggs
1 Tbsp. chopped onion
⅓ cup flour
½ tsp. salt

1 tsp. baking powder
⅓ cup sharp Cheddar cheese,
  cut into ¼-inch cubes
⅓ cup shortening

Beat eggs and combine with onion, flour, salt and baking powder. Add cheese.

Heat shortening in a frying pan. Drop batter into pan using a tablespoon and fry the puffs, turning them over until golden brown on both sides.

Serves 2.

— *Lew Harpelle*
Port Stanley, Ontario

SUMMER OMELETTE

AN OMELETTE CAN CONTAIN ALMOST ANY FILLING, INCLUDING COOKED MEATS and seafood. The two presented here make use of summer vegetables. Variations could include tomatoes, green pepper or other vegetables.

6 eggs
⅓ cup milk
Salt & pepper
¼-½ cup chopped celery

2-3 Tbsp. chopped onion
¼ cup sliced mushrooms
¼-½ cup grated Cheddar or
  Swiss cheese

Beat together eggs, milk, salt and pepper.

Lightly sauté celery, onion and mushrooms. Add to egg mixture along with the cheese. Mix well and pour into greased 8-inch square cake pan.

Bake at 350 degrees F for approximately 30 minutes or until knife comes out clean.

Serves 4.

ZUCCHINI OMELETTE

ZUCCHINI RECIPES ARE ALWAYS WELCOME. THIS ONE, AN ITALIAN STANDARD, IS A boon for those overburdened with both zucchini and eggs.

2 small zucchini
2 Tbsp. cooking oil
2 eggs

Salt & pepper
½ tsp. dried oregano
½ cup grated Romano or Parmesan cheese

Cut zucchini into ⅛-inch slices. Sauté in hot oil in a small cast-iron frying pan, stirring constantly, until golden brown. Reduce heat to medium low. Beat eggs with wire whisk until well blended but not frothy, and add to zucchini in pan. Sprinkle with remaining ingredients.

Cook, covered, until egg is set. Fold omelette in half, allow to cook a few seconds longer, then remove to warmed plate and cut into wedges.

Serves 2.

— *Dorothy Farmiloe*
Elk Lake, Ontario

CREPES

THE VARIETY OF FILLINGS FOR CREPES IS ALMOST UNLIMITED. A FEW suggestions follow the crêpe batter recipe. Crêpes may be served hot or cold, as a main course or as a dessert.

¾ cup flour
Salt
1 egg yolk
1 egg
1¼ cups milk
1 Tbsp. melted butter or light oil

Sift the flour into blender or mixing bowl. Add salt, egg yolk, whole egg and half the milk. Blend for 1 minute or stir with a wire whisk until smooth. Add the rest of the milk and the melted butter or oil.

Let rest, refrigerated, for 1 hour.

To cook, heat 1 Tbsp. butter in small, heavy frying pan. When bubbling, pour in a very small amount of batter and immediately swirl pan to coat. The thinner the crêpe the better.

Cook over high heat for approximately 1 minute, or until crêpe is lightly browned and firm enough to flip with a spatula. Brown other side and remove to a warmed plate. Continue cooking and stacking crêpes until batter is used up. No additional greasing should be necessary. The crêpes will not stick together when stacked. If the first few crêpes do not turn out, do not become discouraged — it often takes a little time to season the pan and to refine the swirling technique.

Makes 12 crêpes.

Cooked crêpes may be kept refrigerated for several days or frozen for several months. Crêpe batter may be refrigerated overnight, but it may need to be thinned with 1-2 Tbsp. milk when used.

— Jeanne Nugent
Perth, Ontario

Crêpe Filling Ideas

Meat
    Chicken in Cream Sauce
    Beef Stroganoff
    Boeuf Bourguignon
    Ham and Cheese
    Chicken Divan

Vegetable
    Broccoli in Cheese Sauce
    Creamed Spinach
    Green Beans Amandine
    Stir-Fried Snow Peas

Dessert
    Any fresh fruit topped with whipped cream or yogurt
    Vanilla ice cream topped with hot chocolate sauce
    Cottage cheese with fruit or nuts

Seafood
    Coquilles Saint Jacques
    Shrimp Curry
    Sole Amandine
    Lobster Newburg
    Seafood Creole

To serve, place a crêpe flat on a plate, put filling in centre and fold 2 sides over it.

PANCAKE MIX

THIS HOMEMADE PANCAKE MIX, AS WELL AS BEING CONVENIENT, HAS THE additional charm of flexibility — it can be tailor-made to suit individual tastes by using, for example, whole wheat flour, wheat germ or buttermilk flour.

12 cups flour
4 cups milk powder
¾ cup baking powder

¾ cup sugar
2 Tbsp. salt

Mix well and store in airtight containers.

Makes 16 cups mix.

To use: Combine 1½ cups mix, 1 cup water, 1 egg and 2 Tbsp. oil.

Makes 8 pancakes.

— Dawn Livingstone
Georgetown, Ontario

BRAN PANCAKES

1 cup bran
1 cup whole wheat flour
1 cup unbleached white flour
½ cup raisins (optional)
¼ cup brown sugar

1 Tbsp. baking powder
½ tsp. salt
2½ cups milk
2 eggs
¼ cup oil

In a large mixing bowl, combine flour, bran, raisins, sugar, baking powder and salt, and mix well.

In a small bowl, beat milk, eggs and oil until blended. Add to flour mixture and mix well.

Pour batter, using about ⅓ cup for each pancake, into a hot, greased frying pan. Cook, turning once, until both sides are golden brown.

Serves 5 to 6.

— Marnie Horton
Tweed, Ontario

POTATO PANCAKES

4 medium raw potatoes, shredded
Salt & pepper
3 Tbsp. flour
1 egg, beaten

¼ cup grated onion
½ cup grated Cheddar cheese
Heavy cream
Butter

Mix shredded potatoes with flour, egg, onion, cheese, salt and pepper. Add enough cream to make a moist but not wet batter.

Heat butter in a heavy skillet and drop batter by spoonfuls into the hot fat. Fry until both sides of pancakes are golden brown, then slide onto a cookie sheet. Bake at 400 degrees F for 4 minutes.

Serve hot with butter and maple syrup.

Serves 4 to 6.

— Pearl Lentz
Rama, Ontario

CURRIED EGGS

GOOD FOR BRUNCH, LUNCH OR DINNER, THIS ATTRACTIVE AND EASY-TO-PREPARE DISH hints at the exotic.

2 Tbsp. butter
2 Tbsp. flour
1 cup milk
1 tsp. curry powder

½ cup peas
4 hard-boiled eggs, chopped into
    bite-sized pieces

Melt butter and stir in flour. Add milk gradually, stirring constantly. Add curry powder and peas. Cook over low heat, still stirring, until peas are soft. Gently fold in eggs. Serve on toast points.

Serves 4.

— Mrs. L.H. Lowther
Harrowsmith, Ontario

A QUICK PANCAKE

A CROSS BETWEEN A PANCAKE AND AN OMELETTE, THIS HAS A LIGHT TEXTURE AND A pleasant, nutty flavour. Fresh fruit, chopped, sautéed in butter and brown sugar and placed in the bottom of the pan, can provide a delicious variation.

2 eggs, separated
1 cup yogurt
1 cup quick cooking oats
1 Tbsp. sugar

¼ tsp. baking soda
¼ tsp. baking powder
¼ tsp. salt
1 Tbsp. butter

Beat egg yolks well and stir in yogurt. Add dry ingredients and mix well. Beat egg whites until stiff, then gently fold into batter.

Melt butter in a large frying pan which can be used in the oven. Spoon batter into pan and bake for 20 minutes at 350 degrees F.

Serve with honey or jam.

— Carol Frost
Chilliwack, B.C.

EGG CASSEROLE

A HEARTY, SUBSTANTIAL CASSEROLE OF PARTICULAR INTEREST TO GARLIC LOVERS, this dish makes a good brunch when you have a lot of visitors.

12 eggs
½ lb. bacon
¼ cup butter
¼ cup flour
1 cup light cream
1 cup milk
1 lb. sharp Cheddar cheese, grated

2 small cloves garlic, crushed
¼ tsp. thyme
¼ tsp. marjoram
¼ tsp. basil
¼ tsp. chopped parsley
¾ cup bread crumbs

Hard boil the eggs, peel and slice them.

Broil the bacon until crisp, drain and crumble.

Melt butter, stir in flour and gradually mix in cream and milk. Heat, stirring constantly, until sauce thickens. Add cheese and seasonings.

Pour half the sauce into a well-greased casserole dish. Add the eggs as the next layer, then the bacon. Top with the rest of the sauce and sprinkle bread crumbs over it.

Bake at 350 degrees F for 30 minutes.

Serves 8 to 10.

— Jody Schwindt
Burlington, Ontario

EGGS KARIEL

TASTY, NUTRITIOUS AND QUICK TO PREPARE, THIS SERVE-IT-ANYTIME DISH CAN BE easily adjusted to suit the number of hungry people present.

1 lb. fresh spinach   1 cup Cheddar cheese
8 eggs

Clean and rinse spinach. Place in a wide saucepan containing enough water to cover bottom of the pan, cover and steam briefly – until spinach is wilted.

Make hollows in spinach and break eggs into them. Replace cover and continue to steam until eggs are poached. Sprinkle cheese over top, recover, and cook until cheese is melted.

Serves 4 for lunch, 8 for breakfast.

— N. Kariel
St. John's, Nfld.

BAKED EGGS

A HEARTY, TASTY BREAKFAST OR BRUNCH DISH, THIS CAN BE PREPARED THE NIGHT before, ready to pop into the oven in the morning.

1 lb. ground sausage meat or ham   2 slices bread, trimmed & cubed
6 eggs   1 tsp. dry mustard
2 cups milk   1 cup grated mild cheese

Brown sausage meat or ham and drain on towels. Beat eggs and combine all ingredients in a 9" x 13" baking dish.

Bake at 350 degrees F for 45 minutes or until lightly browned.

Serves 6.

— Mrs. J. Hall-Armstrong
Cochrane, Ontario

EGG McRIVERS

2 English muffins split, toasted & buttered   4 poached eggs
4 slices cooked ham   ½ cup Cheddar cheese, grated

Place English muffins on a cookie sheet. On each, place a slice of ham and a poached egg, and sprinkle Cheddar cheese on top. Broil until cheese is bubbly.

Serves 4.

— Deborah Rivers
Alliston, Ontario

EGGS MAYONNAISE

4 eggs   1 Tbsp. oil
Lettuce   Parsley
½ cup mayonnaise   Grated carrot
1 egg yolk   Dash cayenne pepper

Boil eggs until they are semi-hard (5 minutes). Shell and slice them in half lengthwise and place them yolk side down on crisp lettuce leaves.

Combine mayonnaise, egg yolk and oil. Mix well and spoon over the eggs. Sprinkle with parsley, carrot and cayenne pepper.

Serves 4.

— Sandra James-Mitchell
Pickering, Ontario

DEVILLED TOFU

IT'S NOT JUST HEALTHY, IT LOOKS PRETTY AND TASTES GOOD. TRY THIS SPREAD ON open-faced sandwiches with alfalfa sprouts, cucumber and tomato.

18 oz. (3 cakes) tofu
2 stalks celery, finely chopped
3-4 green onions, finely chopped
1 cup mayonnaise
3 Tbsp. vinegar

1 tsp. celery seed
¾ tsp. salt
1 tsp. garlic powder
½ tsp. dry mustard
1¼ tsp. turmeric

Slice tofu lengthwise and press with paper towels to remove water. Chop finely and mix with celery and onions.

Combine mayonnaise, vinegar and remaining ingredients, then stir into the tofu and vegetable mixture. Chill.

Makes 3 cups.

— *Sass'frass Saloon*
Victoria, B.C.

TICINI

THE SARDINES GIVE THIS DISH A DECIDEDLY SHARP AND SALTY FLAVOUR, BUT blend well with the eggs to make a tasty spread.

4 hard-boiled eggs
4-oz. tin sardines, drained
1½ Tbsp. mayonnaise

2 Tbsp. lemon juice
2 tsp. Worcestershire sauce
Salt & pepper

Chop eggs and sardines coarsely. Combine and add remaining ingredients. Chill.

Garnish with paprika and fresh parsley and serve with crackers or rye bread.

Makes 2 cups.

— *Nita Hunton*
Cambridge, Ontario

EGG SALAD

THIS COOL, REFRESHING SPREAD IS GOOD SERVED ON WHOLE WHEAT BREAD, PITA bread, sesame crackers, or wrapped in spinach or lettuce leaves.

5 hard-boiled eggs
⅓ cup finely chopped carrot
⅓ cup finely chopped celery
⅓ cup finely chopped onion
½ cup toasted sunflower seeds
½ cup toasted sesame seeds, ground

½ cup ricotta cheese
¼ cup yogurt
¼ cup mayonnaise
Salt
Paprika

Mash the eggs in a bowl. Add other ingredients and mix well. Refrigerate for several hours before serving.

Serves 4 to 6.

— *N. Burk*
St. Anne de la Rochelle, Quebec

SCOTCH EGGS

HOT OR COLD, THESE EGGS ARE DELICIOUS AS HORS D'OEUVRES, SNACKS OR accompaniments to salads.

12 hard-boiled eggs, peeled
½ cup flour
2 lbs. skinless sausage meat
1 egg

1 Tbsp. water
Fine bread crumbs
   or quick-cooking rolled oats

Roll cooked eggs in flour. With floured hands, coat each egg with sausage meat.

Combine raw egg and water and beat together. Dip sausage-covered eggs into egg mixture, then roll in bread crumbs.

Fry in deep fat until golden brown. If preferred, eggs can be cooked in shallow fat or baked at 350 degrees F until the bread crumbs are crisp and the meat is thoroughly cooked.

— *Sherri McMillan*
Uxbridge, Ontario

EGGS FLORENTINE

ANOTHER BRUNCH, LUNCH OR DINNER FAVOURITE, THIS IS A DELICIOUS AND attractive dish.

2 Tbsp. butter
1 Tbsp. minced onion
1½ tsp. flour
¼ tsp. salt
Pepper & nutmeg

1 cup milk
¼ cup Parmesan cheese
1 pkg. spinach
4 eggs
Parmesan cheese

Sauté onion in melted butter. Add flour, salt, pepper and nutmeg and stir until smooth. Blend in milk, bring to a boil, then reduce heat and simmer, stirring constantly, for 3 minutes. Add ¼ cup Parmesan cheese.

Cook and drain spinach and combine with milk mixture. Turn into a shallow baking dish.

Poach the eggs and arrange them on top of the spinach mixture. Sprinkle with Parmesan cheese and place under the broiler just long enough to melt the cheese.

Serves 4.

— *Brenda Eckstein*
Kamloops, B.C.

EGGS MOLIERE

4 eggs
4 tomatoes
2 Tbsp. oil
½ lb. mushrooms, thinly sliced

2 scallions, chopped
2 Tbsp. flour
1½ cups hot chicken stock
Salt & pepper

Boil eggs until they can be peeled but are not hard cooked, about 5 minutes. Peel and set aside.

Cut off the tops of the tomatoes and hollow them out with a spoon. Season with salt and pepper and place in an ovenproof baking dish. Bake for 10 minutes at 375 degrees F and set aside.

Heat the oil in a saucepan. Add the mushrooms and the scallions, season to taste and cook over medium heat for 3 to 4 minutes. Stir in the flour and continue to cook for 2 to 3 minutes. Add the hot chicken stock and correct seasoning. Cook over low heat for another 15 minutes.

Place 1 peeled egg inside each cooked tomato shell. Cover with the sauce and bake for 7 to 8 minutes. Garnish with parsley.

Serves 4.

— *Brenda Eckstein*
Kamloops, B.C.

TOFU PARMESAN

2 two-inch cubes tofu, thinly sliced
2 Tbsp. butter
2-4 Tbsp. tamari sauce
2 Tbsp. oil
2 cloves garlic

1 medium zucchini, sliced
½ lb. mushrooms, sliced
1 cup tomato sauce
½ lb. mozzarella cheese, thinly sliced
Parmesan cheese

Brown tofu slices in butter and tamari sauce. When crisp, line the bottom of a buttered shallow casserole dish.

Sauté garlic in oil, then discard garlic. Add zucchini and mushrooms to oil and lightly brown. Remove with a slotted spoon and spread over tofu.

Cover with tomato sauce and then mozzarella cheese. Sprinkle with Parmesan cheese and bake, covered, at 350 degrees F until bubbly — 10 to 15 minutes.

Serves 4.

— *Jane Pugh*
Toronto, Ontario

RAREBIT FONDUE ON TOAST

AN ADAPTATION OF A TRADITIONAL FONDUE RECIPE, THIS RAREBIT HAS A VERY satisfying and pleasantly garlicky flavour.

8 thick slices whole wheat bread
Butter
½ lb. mushrooms, sliced
½ cup finely chopped onion
2 cups dry white wine

½ clove garlic, chopped
½ lb. Gruyère cheese, grated
2 Tbsp. or more whole wheat flour
Freshly ground pepper

Butter bread on both sides and bake at 400 degrees F for 5 to 8 minutes — until golden brown on both sides.

Sauté mushrooms and onion in butter until the onion is soft. Add garlic and wine. Mix flour and cheese and add to the hot wine mixture, 1 handful at a time, stirring until each addition of cheese melts. Cook, stirring, over low heat until the sauce bubbles and thickens. Season with pepper.

Place the toast on individual serving plates and top with sauce.

Serves 4.

— *Janet Flewelling*
Toronto, Ontario

ZUCCHINI EGG FOO YUNG

4 medium unpeeled zucchini, grated
3 eggs, beaten
¼ cup flour or ½ cup wheat germ
¼ tsp. garlic powder
1 tsp. salt

1 onion, grated
1 cup vegetable stock
2 Tbsp. soya sauce
1 Tbsp. cornstarch

Mix together zucchini, egg, flour or wheat germ, garlic powder, salt and onion.

Drop by tablespoonfuls into hot oiled skillet and fry, turning once, until golden brown on both sides.

Combine remaining ingredients in a saucepan and cook, stirring, until thickened.

Arrange zucchini patties on a platter and top with sauce.

Serves 4 to 6.

— *Chris Nofziger*
Elmworth, Alberta

BAKED FONDUE

⅔ cup butter
2 cloves garlic
1 tsp. dry mustard
1 loaf French or Italian bread
3 cups grated Swiss cheese
3 Tbsp. grated onion

1½ tsp. salt
1 tsp. paprika
¼ cup flour
3 cups milk
1 cup dry white wine
3 eggs, beaten

In small bowl, cream ⅓ cup butter with garlic and ½ tsp. mustard until blended.

Remove ends of bread and cut loaf into ¼-inch slices. Spread with butter mixture and place, buttered side down, in bottom and along sides of heavy casserole dish.

In large bowl, combine cheese, onion, salt, paprika and remaining mustard. Toss until well blended.

Melt remaining butter in heavy saucepan. Remove from heat, stir in flour and return to heat. Gradually stir in milk and bring to a boil. Reduce heat and stir in wine. Add a little hot mixture to the eggs, stir and pour back into hot milk.

Arrange alternate layers of cheese mixture, egg mixture and remaining bread slices, ending with bread, buttered side up.

Refrigerate, covered, overnight or all day. Bake at 350 degrees F for 35 to 45 minutes, until puffy and golden brown.

— Dorothy Hurst
Nanaimo, B.C.

KAFKADES

THESE TRADITIONAL GREEK PATTIES ARE DELICIOUS AS WELL AS WHOLESOME.

2 cups cottage cheese
2 egg yolks
1 cup flour

2 cups loosely packed bite-sized spinach
Olive oil
Salt & pepper

Combine cottage cheese, egg yolks and flour. Mix well, if necessary, adding more flour, until mixture becomes a thick paste. Add spinach.

In a large skillet, heat oil to cover the bottom of the pan to a medium high temperature. For each patty, drop batter from a large spoon onto the pan. Cook until golden brown on one side, then turn carefully and cook until the other side is done. Season with salt and pepper.

Makes 10 to 12 patties.

—Susan Gammon
Glenburnie, Ontario

CHEESE SNACKS

THESE TASTY INSTANT CANAPES CAN BE PREPARED AHEAD OF TIME, FROZEN, brought out and baked as the need or the inclination arises.

1 loaf unsliced whole wheat bread
¾ cup butter, softened
2 egg whites

½ lb. old Cheddar cheese, grated
Salt
½ tsp. dry mustard

Cut bread into bite-sized pieces.

Beat butter, egg whites, cheese, salt and mustard together until creamy and smooth — about 5 minutes. Spread cheese mixture on bread.

Freeze on a cookie sheet, then pack into plastic bags to store.

To serve, bake at 350 degrees F for 8 to 10 minutes, until bubbly. Serve warm.

— Marie Blundell
Ste. Marguerite Station, Quebec

APPLE 'N' CHEESE NIBBLES

THIS IS AN UNUSUAL SNACK, TANGY AND FLAVOURFUL, WHICH CAN BE PREPARED ahead of time and simply heated when ready to serve.

2 McIntosh apples
2 Tbsp. sweet butter
1 tsp. lemon juice

1 cup grated Cheddar cheese
Freshly ground pepper
16 slices whole wheat bread

Peel, core and slice apples. Add, with lemon juice, to melted butter in a saucepan and simmer over medium heat until apples are soft — do not let them brown. Add cheese and pepper and stir just to mix. Cook until cheese melts.

Cut a 3- to 3½-inch round from each slice of bread and toast. Place on a cookie sheet and top with the apple and cheese mixture. Cover and keep cool until serving time.

To serve, run under broiler, 3 inches away from heat, until brown.

Makes 16 rounds.

— Shirley Hill
Picton, Onario

ONION CHEESE SQUARES

DELICIOUS AS A MAIN COURSE FOR LUNCH OR DINNER, THESE SQUARES ARE inexpensive and simple to make.

¾ cup chopped onion
2 Tbsp. butter
¾ cup scalded milk
2 eggs, beaten
1 cup grated Cheddar cheese
Salt & pepper

¼ cup pimento, diced
  or 1 tomato, chopped
2 Tbsp. chopped fresh parsley
2 Tbsp. wheat germ
2 Tbsp. (or more) bread crumbs
Sesame seeds

Sauté onion in butter until soft and golden. Remove from heat.

Combine milk and eggs and add to onion. Add all remaining ingredients except sesame seeds. If mixture seems very runny, add extra bread crumbs.

Pour into greased 8-inch pie plate. Sprinkle with sesame seeds.

Bake at 325 degrees F for 45 minutes, or until knife inserted into centre comes out clean.

— Pam Collacott
North Gower, Ontario

CHEESE & TOMATO BAKE

5 slices bacon
4 Tbsp. flour
3 cups tomato juice
1 tsp. salt

½ small onion, minced
1 cup grated Cheddar cheese
3 cups cooked whole wheat
¼ cup buttered bread crumbs

Fry bacon until lightly browned. Cut into ½-inch pieces and set aside. Reserve 1 Tbsp. of the fat.

Stir flour into reserved bacon fat. Add tomato juice, salt and onion and cook, stirring, until thickened. Remove from heat and add the bacon and three-quarters of the cheese.

Place wheat in a greased baking dish and pour the tomato mixture over it. Sprinkle with bread crumbs and remaining cheese. Bake at 350 degrees F for 45 minutes.

Serves 4 to 6.

— Joanne Ramsy
Aylmer, Ontario

CORN, CHEESE & CHILI PIE

2 tsp. shortening
3 large eggs
8½-oz. can creamed corn
1½ cups corn kernels
½ cup butter, melted
½ cup corn meal
1 cup sour cream

¼ lb. Monterey Jack cheese,
  cut in ½-inch cubes
¼ lb. sharp Cheddar cheese,
  cut in ½-inch cubes
Diced green chilies to taste
½ tsp. salt
¼ tsp. Worcestershire sauce

Grease 9-inch pie plate with shortening. In a large bowl, beat eggs. Add remaining ingredients and mix well. Pour into pie plate and bake at 350 degrees F for 1 hour, until pie is firm in centre.

Serves 6.

— Veronica Green
Winnipeg, Manitoba

POTATO CHEESE CASSEROLE

½ cup milk
2 large eggs, beaten
2 cups mashed potatoes

1-2 onions, chopped
½-¾ cup grated Parmesan cheese
4 Tbsp. wheat germ

Combine milk, eggs, potatoes and onions. Pour into a 9-inch square buttered pan and sprinkle with Parmesan cheese and wheat germ. Bake at 350 degrees F for 30 minutes, until top is golden brown.

Serves 4 to 6.

— Richard & Elaine Domsy
Ruthren, Ontario

SUNFLOWER SPECIAL

This childhood invention of John Travers, the owner of the Sunflower Restaurant, is the restaurant's most popular sandwich.

Coat one slice of lightly buttered whole wheat toast with mayonnaise. Layer, in order listed, all or any of chopped green onions, alfalfa sprouts, tomato slices, sliced old Cheddar cheese and a sprinkling of sunflower seeds.

Broil until cheese is melted and seeds are browned.

Serves 1.

— The Sunflower Restaurant
Kingston, Ontario

ALMOND CHEESE SPREAD

½ cup almonds, with skins
8 oz. cream cheese, softened
½ cup mayonnaise
5 slices bacon
1 Tbsp. chopped green onion

1 Tbsp. chopped celery
1 Tbsp. green pepper
½ tsp. dill weed
⅛ tsp. pepper

Place almonds on cookie sheet and bake at 350 degrees F for 20 to 25 minutes. Fry bacon until crisp; crumble.

Beat cream cheese, then gradually stir in mayonnaise. Add bacon, vegetables and seasonings. Mix well, cover and chill overnight.

When chilled, cover top surface with almonds. Serve with crackers and raw vegetables.

Makes about 1¼ cups.

— Genie & Peter Suffel
Sault Ste. Marie, Ontario

POTTED CHEESE

THIS CHEESE SPREAD HAS A DELICIOUS BLUE CHEESE FLAVOUR, AND IS BEST SERVED with crackers or as a dip for raw vegetables.

8 oz. cream cheese
½ cup soft margarine
1 tsp. Worcestershire sauce
2 cups finely shredded Gouda, Gruyère
  or Cheddar cheese

¼ tsp. garlic powder
¼ lb. crumbled blue cheese
¼ cup grated Parmesan cheese
Chopped pecans

Beat first 5 ingredients together until well blended. Work in remaining cheeses. Press into attractive serving dish and sprinkle with pecans. Cover well and keep chilled. Will keep refrigerated for up to 3 weeks.

— Pamela England
Central Butte, Sask.

CHEDDAR CHEESE BALL

½ lb. old Cheddar cheese, grated
½ cup ground pecans
½ small green pepper, finely chopped

1 stalk celery, finely chopped
2 green onions, finely chopped
4 oz. cream cheese, at room temperature

Combine Cheddar cheese, pecans and vegetables. Mix in cream cheese. If too dry to work with, add a small amount of milk, yogurt or beer. Form into a ball and sprinkle with chopped nuts or parsley.

Chill well before serving.

Makes 2 cups.

— Joan Hoepner
Norway House, Manitoba

GOUDA SESAME LOG

3 cups coarsely grated Gouda cheese
1 cup coarsely grated ice-cold butter
1 tsp. hot mustard

2 Tbsp. whiskey
¾ cup toasted sesame seeds

Cream cheese and butter together until well blended. Mix in mustard and whiskey. Shape into log and roll in sesame seeds. Refrigerate for 24 hours before serving.

Makes 3 to 4 cups.

— Kumari Campbell
Parkdale, P.E.I.

MRS. SHAVER'S CHEESE BALL

3 cups grated Cheddar cheese
8 oz. cream cheese
¼ cup sour cream

¼ cup chopped green onion
Dash Tabasco & Worcestershire sauce
Caraway seeds

Soften cream cheese and thoroughly blend in the rest of the ingredients except the caraway seeds. Shape into a ball, place on a serving dish and sprinkle with caraway seeds. Refrigerate.

Makes 4 to 5 cups.

— Laurie Shaver
Moose Jaw, Sask.

PARTY CHEESE BALL

½ lb. mild Cheddar cheese, grated
½ lb. Jack cheese, grated
8 oz. cream cheese
Salt & pepper

Nutmeg & paprika
¼ tsp. parsley
½ tsp. Worcestershire sauce
2 oz. chopped walnuts

Allow cheeses to reach room temperature. Blend together cream cheese, Cheddar cheese and Jack cheese. Add seasonings and blend well.

Form cheese into a ball on a serving dish and cover with walnuts. Refrigerate until 2 hours before serving.

Makes 3 cups.

— Johanna Vanderheyden
Strathroy, Ontario

HOT CHEESE DIP

2 cups light cream
2 tsp. dry mustard
1 Tbsp. Worcestershire sauce
1 clove garlic, cut in half
3 Tbsp. flour

6 cups coarsely grated
  sharp Cheddar cheese
¼ tsp. salt
2 Tbsp. sherry

In a glass or enamel saucepan, heat cream, mustard, Worcestershire sauce and garlic.

Mix cheese with flour, and drop, a handful at a time, into the hot cream. Cook over low heat, stirring with a wooden spoon, until cheese is melted and mixture is smooth.

Add salt and sherry. If only a mild hint of garlic is desired, remove it now from the dip.

Pour dip into a chafing dish or heavy fondue pot and serve with such dunking delights as raw vegetables, chunks of good fresh bread or cooked shrimp.

Makes 4 to 6 cups.

— Dorothy Hurst
Nanaimo, B.C.

CHEESE SPREAD

DEVISED AS A SUBSTITUTE FOR THE COMMERCIAL VARIETIES, THIS VERSATILE SPREAD can be used for anything from sandwiches to canapés. For variety, virtually any flavouring you like with cheese may be added: onion, garlic, parsley, oregano or curry to mention a few.

½ lb. sharp Cheddar cheese, grated
1 tsp. dry mustard
4 tsp. cornstarch
½ tsp. salt

1 cup water
⅓ cup powdered milk
1 tsp. Worcestershire sauce

Melt cheese in the top of a double boiler. Combine mustard, cornstarch and salt. Add a little water and mix into a paste. Gradually stir in the rest of the water, then add milk powder and Worcestershire sauce. Stir this mixture into the cheese and cook until thick. Pour into jars and refrigerate.

Makes 2 cups.

— Janet Caldwell
Meadow Lake, Sask.

BOURSIN

A HOMEMADE RECIPE FOR THIS DELICATE CHEESE SPREAD IS A BOON TO ADDICTS, since it is easy to make and considerably less expensive than the commercially produced versions.

16 oz. cream cheese
¼ cup mayonnaise
2 tsp. Dijon mustard

2 Tbsp. finely chopped chives
2 Tbsp. finely chopped dill
1 clove garlic, minced

Soften cheese, then, using an electric mixer, thoroughly blend in mayonnaise, mustard, chives, dill and garlic. Spoon into a small serving bowl, cover and refrigerate for 24 hours.

Serve with bagels, crackers, Melba toast, rye bread, pumpernickel bread, celery, mushrooms or other raw vegetables.

Makes 2½ cups.

— Shirley Hill
Picton, Ontario

HERBED CHEESE DIP

8 oz. cream cheese, softened
½ cup butter, softened
2 cloves garlic, minced

½ tsp. salt
¼ tsp. pepper
¼ cup chopped fresh parsley

Beat cream cheese and butter with electric mixer until well mixed and airy. Beat in remaining ingredients.

Spoon into a mould lined with plastic wrap and chill for several hours. Unmould and serve with raw vegetables or crackers.

Makes 1½ to 2 cups.

Soups & Chowders

Soup of the evening, beautiful soup!

— **Lewis Carroll**
Alice in Wonderland

One of the advantages of a wood stove is that, as long as the fire burns or has recently burned, there is always a spot at the back of the stove just the right temperature for keeping a big iron pot of soup or chowder simmering. It isn't a small advantage. After a winter's day of chopping wood or cross-country skiing, few pleasures can compare with the combination of an easy chair by the warm stove and a bowl of hot soup with muffins or homemade bread.

Soup does not link quite as naturally with electric or gas stoves, but it is still among the easiest and most satisfying of dishes, often nutritionally complete within the pot. What is most surprising is that the purchase of a few cans or packages of supermarket soup has become so taken for granted that few cooks today realize just how easy and inexpensive homemade soup can be, and that the result is often far superior to anything brought home in the grocery bag. Besides, what better way is there to use the chicken carcass, leftover meat bones, purchased soup bones, and old, tough garden produce?

Soup is both the practical and the adventuresome solution. For the stock pot is the only place in which overmature vegetables and older meat animals and meat bones are better than peak-of-perfection meats and vegetables. In the stock pot,

long, slow simmering extracts the greater — and sometimes surprising — flavour and hidden nutrients of foods otherwise too tough to use. There is nothing as suffused with the full taste of chicken as soup made from a hen whose laying days are over.

Cooks who do make their own stock should start with cold water covering washed vegetables and/or meat and bones — hold the potatoes, they make a starchy stock — gradually raising the temperature to simmer, where it will remain for anywhere from a few hours (for vegetables) to at least 12 hours (for soup bones).

The cook can best remove the grease by pouring the finished mixture through a colander to remove the big pieces, allowing it to cool, and then scooping off the solidified grease with a spoon. Grease that bubbles to the top of cooking soup can be removed with a meat baster. Or float a paper towel on the top, then immediately remove and discard it.

While having one's own stock will enhance both the flavour and economy of homemade soup, it is by no means a necessity. Beef and chicken soup powders or cubes, bought in the supermarket, are a reasonable substitute. Use less than the package dictates, or add them to taste. A few well-chosen herbs and vegetables will mask the distinctive

"soup powder" flavours of these commercial stocks.

Soups may be clear or they may be thickened with barley, oatmeal, soy or white flour, quick-cooking tapioca, grated raw potato, or beaten egg yolk — which must be mixed with a bit of hot soup before it is stirred into the soup pot. If one uses flour as a thickener, it should be combined with some cold water before it is added to the soup. Overthickened soups are more like stew, or as some call it, "stewp." To thin them, just add more stock, or, if appropriate, more milk or plain water. Soups that contain milk, egg or cream should not be allowed to boil, as they can curdle. It is quite difficult to go wrong with soup as long as the cook tastes it after each additional ingredient. Just keep adding until it tastes right. For colour, if desired, the cook may add a teaspoon or two of molasses or a dash of Worcestershire sauce.

Once the cook has done some experimentation with soup, he is likely to be unrestrained by mere recipes. Soups are such made-to-order resting places for leftovers and tired vegetables that they fairly cry out for innovation. Recipes such as those that follow are, however, guidelines and inspiration. Their ingredients have been found to complement each other well. Lunch may never be the same.

M.F.K. Fisher, a well-known gastronome and author of many cookbooks, including a penny-saving wartime guide called *How to Cook a Wolf* (1942), described her regard for soups in that book:

"The natural progression from boiling water to boiling water with something in it can hardly be avoided, and in most cases is heartily to be wished for. As a steady diet, plain water is inclined to make fairly thin fare, and even saints, of which there are an unexpected number these days, will gladly agree that a few herbs and perhaps a carrot or two and maybe a bit of meagre bone on feast days can mightily improve the somewhat monotonous fare of the hot liquid.

"Soup, in other words, is good."

BEEF STOCK

2 - 3 lbs. beef bones
8 cups water
1 onion, unpeeled
1 carrot, scrubbed & sliced
Celery leaves
2 - 3 sprigs parsley

5 - 6 whole peppercorns
3 whole cloves
Several basil leaves (1 tsp. crushed)
1 clove garlic
2 Tbsp. vinegar
2 tsp. salt

Brown bones slowly in a heavy pot. Add remaining ingredients and simmer, covered, for several hours. Strain broth and cool. Skim fat from top of stock.

— Jan Gilbert
Ashton, Ontario

TURKEY STOCK

1 turkey carcass
1 onion, halved
1 carrot, halved
1 - 2 celery stalks
2 - 3 sprigs parsley
5 - 6 peppercorns

1 - 2 bay leaves
1 tsp. savory
1 tsp. basil
4 whole cloves
2 tsp. salt
1 Tbsp. vinegar

Place all ingredients in a large pot and cover with cold water. Cover and simmer for several hours.

Strain and chill. Skim fat from top of stock.

— Jan Gilbert
Ashton, Ontario

POTATO PEEL BROTH

TO MAKE A VEGETABLE BROTH OR STOCK, USE ANY LEFTOVER OR OVER-RIPE vegetables, no matter how unusable they appear, in addition to the ingredients listed below. Strongly flavoured vegetables, such as cabbage or broccoli, will impart their own flavour to the stock.

Peel from 6 to 7 large
  brown-skinned potatoes
1 large onion, peeled
2 carrots, scrubbed but unpeeled
1 stalk celery
2 qts. water
1 large sprig parsley

1½ Tbsp. olive oil
Small bay leaf
¼ tsp. thyme
Pinch sage
1 clove garlic
Tabasco sauce
1 tsp. lemon juice

Combine all ingredients except Tabasco sauce and lemon juice in a large pot and simmer for 1½ to 2 hours.

Strain out the vegetables for a clear broth, sieve or purée in blender for a thicker broth, removing the garlic and bay leaf first.

Add a few drops of Tabasco sauce and lemon juice before serving to bring out the flavours.

Makes 6 cups.

— Cary Elizabeth Marshall
Thunder Bay, Ontario

CHICKEN & MUSHROOM SOUP

¼ cup minced shallots
¼ cup diced celery
¼ cup sliced mushrooms
1½ tsp. butter
6 cups chicken stock

¼ tsp. salt
Pepper
½ cup fine egg noodles
⅓ cup diced chicken
½ tsp. fresh parsley

Sauté vegetables in butter. Add chicken stock, salt and pepper and cook for 20 minutes.

Cook egg noodles separately in salted water. Drain and rinse well under cold water. Add to soup. Add chicken and parsley.

Serves 6.

— Nicole Chartrand
Aylmer, Quebec

COCK-A-LEEKIE

THIS SOUP ORIGINATED IN SCOTLAND IN THE DAYS WHEN COCK FIGHTS WERE popular. The loser in the fight was unceremoniously thrown into the soup pot.

3-lb. boiling chicken
1 bunch leeks, chopped
12 prunes

2 sprigs parsley
Salt & pepper

Simmer the chicken, covered with water, in a covered pot for 2 or 3 hours. Remove, separate meat from bones and return meat to pot.

Add the leeks along with the prunes, parsley and salt and pepper.

Simmer for another 45 minutes.

Serves 6.

— Cary Elizabeth Marshall
Thunder Bay, Ontario

CHICKEN VELVET SOUP

THE CREAM AND MILK IMPART A RICH, SMOOTH, VELVETY TEXTURE TO THIS SOUP.

6 Tbsp. butter
⅓ cup flour
½ cup milk
½ cup light cream

3 cups chicken broth
1 cup finely chopped cooked chicken
Pepper to taste
Parsley & pimento to garnish

Melt butter in saucepan and blend in flour. Add milk, cream and broth and cook, stirring, until mixture thickens and comes to a boil. Reduce heat.

Stir in chicken and pepper. Heat again to boiling. Serve at once, garnished with parsley and pimento.

Serves 4.

— Pam Collacott
North Gower, Ontario

TURKEY NOODLE SOUP

1 turkey carcass
1 onion, finely chopped
Small handful celery leaves,
  finely chopped
¼ tsp. each of savory, marjoram, thyme,
  sage & curry powder

Salt & pepper
2 tsp. soya sauce
2 cups fine egg noodles
Chopped parsley

Cover turkey carcass with cold water. Bring to a boil and simmer for several hours. Remove bones and meat from broth and chop meat. Return meat to the broth and chill. Skim off fat.

Reheat broth to boiling, add onion, celery leaves, seasonings and soya sauce. Simmer gently for 3 hours. Add egg noodles half an hour before serving. Top with chopped parsley.

Serves 6 to 8.

— *Ruth Anne Laverty*
Listowel, Ontario

SNAPPING TURTLE SOUP

4 cups turtle meat
Cold water
½ stalk celery
4 onions
1 carrot
4 cups peas
2 cups corn

4 hard-boiled eggs
4 potatoes
1 handful pickling spice in cheesecloth
Juice from 3 or 4 lemons
½ cup ketchup
Salt & pepper
½ cup flour

Cover turtle meat on bone with water and cook until meat falls off bone. Strain through cloth, reserving broth, and leave meat to cool.

Grind meat, celery, onions, carrot, peas, corn, eggs and potatoes.

Combine broth, spice bag, ground ingredients, lemon juice, ketchup and salt and pepper. Cook 1½ to 2 hours over medium heat, stirring often. Remove spice bag.

Brown flour in skillet and stir into soup to thicken.

Serves 8 to 10.

— *Mrs. H. G. Fetzer*
Mt. Brydges, Ontario

HABITANT PEA SOUP

CONSIDERED A NATIONAL DISH, THIS SOUP ORIGINATED IN QUEBEC AND IS SIMPLE, substantial and delicious.

1 lb. split yellow peas
2 qts. water
1 small carrot, grated
1 medium onion, diced
2 tsp. salt

2 sprigs parsley, minced
1 bay leaf
2 thick slices heavily smoked bacon
Pepper

Soak the peas in water overnight. In the morning, bring to a boil in a large saucepan and add carrot, onion and salt. Reduce heat to simmer.

Add parsley, bay leaf and chopped bacon to the soup and simmer for 3 to 4 hours, until thick, adding additional water as needed.

Remove bay leaf, adjust seasonings and serve.

Serves 6 to 8.

— *Cary Elizabeth Marshall*
Thunder Bay, Ontario

HEARTY WINTER SOUP

3 lbs. meaty soup bones
10 cups water
2 tsp. salt
3 slices onion
3 peppercorns
¾ lb. ground beef
1 egg
½ cup dry bread crumbs

⅓ cup tomato juice
¾ tsp. salt
¼ cup chopped onion
¼ tsp. garlic powder
1 cup egg noodles
15-oz. can tomatoes
2 cups mixed chopped vegetables

Cover bones with water and add salt, onion and peppercorns. Simmer, covered, for 3 hours. Remove bones and boil to reduce stock to 6 cups.

Meanwhile, combine ground beef, egg, bread crumbs, tomato juice, salt, onion and garlic powder. Shape into small balls and fry until a rich brown colour. Drain and set aside.

Cook noodles in salted water and drain.

Add vegetables and tomatoes to stock and cook until just tender. Add noodles and meatballs and boil gently for 15 minutes.

Serves 8.

— Shirley Hill
Picton, Ontario

BEEF LENTIL SOUP

1½ cups raw lentils
2-3 lbs. beef soup bones
2 onions, chopped
3 stalks celery, chopped
¼ lb. spinach, torn into bite-sized pieces

3 large tomatoes, chopped
Salt & pepper
Oregano & basil
2 cloves garlic, minced
2-3 bratwurst sausages, chopped

Soak lentils in water for 2 hours.

Brown soup bones, then cover with water and pressure cook for 1 hour. Remove bones and skim fat.

Sauté onions, celery, spinach and tomatoes and add to beef and stock. Add lentils, seasoning, garlic and sausages.

Simmer for several hours, adding water if necessary.

Serves 6 to 8.

— D. Parsons
Oshawa, Ontario

BEEF & BARLEY SOUP

2 cups stewing beef, browned
9 cups cold water
1 cup tomato juice
1 cup raw barley
½ cup finely chopped onion

½ cup carrots, cut in very thin strips
3 beef bouillon cubes (optional)
1 tsp. salt
⅓ cup finely chopped celery

Combine all ingredients in large pot and simmer, covered, for 3 hours or until barley is tender. Taste for salt and adjust if necessary.

— Wendy Neelin
Masset, British Columbia

VEGETABLE BEEF SOUP

THIS SOUP CAN BE STORED IN THE REFRIGERATOR AND REHEATED, WITH ADDITIONAL leftover vegetables, for several days running.

Beef bones
2 cups canned tomatoes or tomato juice
2 onions, chopped
Small handful celery leaves, chopped
3 large potatoes, peeled & diced
6 carrots, diced
2 cups leftover cooked vegetables & gravy

½ cup rice or barley
¼ tsp. each of savory, marjoram,
  thyme & cumin
1 bay leaf
Salt & pepper
1 tsp. Worcestershire sauce or soya sauce

Cover bones with cold water and bring to a boil. Simmer for several hours. Remove bones, cut off meat and return meat to stock. Chill and skim off fat. Reheat stock to boiling and add vegetables and seasonings. Simmer until vegetables are tender.

Serves 6 to 8.

— *Ruth Anne Laverty*
Listowel, Ontario

BEEF SOUP

2 Tbsp. butter
Beef bones
1½ cups chopped beef scraps
1 large onion, chopped

½ tsp. celery seed
6 cups water
Salt & pepper
Chopped vegetables

Melt butter in heavy pot. Add bones, chopped beef, onion and celery seed. Fry, stirring, until browned. Add water and salt and pepper.

Simmer, covered, for 2 to 3 hours. Remove bones. Add chopped vegetables.

Serves 4 to 6.

— *Velma Hughes*
Brantford, Ontario

MINESTRONE

1 clove garlic, minced
1 medium onion, chopped
½ cup chopped celery
1 Tbsp. oil
1 cup diced carrots
1 cup shredded cabbage
19-oz. can tomatoes
5 cups beef stock

½ cup chopped parsley
½ tsp. pepper
Salt
1 cup broken spaghetti noodles
1 cup thinly sliced zucchini
2-3 cups cooked kidney beans, undrained
2 cups cooked beef, finely chopped
Grated Parmesan cheese to garnish

In a heavy pot, sauté garlic, onion and celery in oil. Add carrots, cabbage, tomatoes, stock, parsley, pepper and salt. Cover and simmer for 20 minutes.

Add noodles, zucchini, beans and meat. Simmer 10 minutes longer or until spaghetti and vegetables are cooked. Add more salt if necessary.

Serve topped with freshly grated Parmesan cheese and accompanied by hot crusty bread.

Serves 6.

— *Jan Gilbert*
Ashton, Ontario

PORK HOCK & LIMA BEAN SOUP

1 lb. dry baby lima beans
2 pig's feet or pork hocks
2 bay leaves

1 Tbsp. salt
4 onions, coarsely chopped
Several stalks celery, chopped

Soak beans overnight in water to cover. Drain and combine with remaining ingredients, add water and cook until the beans are tender and meat falls away from the bones.

Serves 6.

— V. Alice Hughes
Mariatown, Ontario

BEAN & HAM SOUP

1½ cups dried lima beans
2 lbs. ham, with bone
1 large onion, quartered
1 large clove garlic, crushed
8¾ cups water

1 bouquet garni, consisting of 4 parsley
  sprigs, 1 spray thyme & 1 bay leaf
½ tsp. white pepper
20 large black olives, cut in half
3 Tbsp. chopped parsley to garnish

Put the beans in a bowl, cover with water and let soak overnight. Drain and place in a large saucepan with the ham, onion and garlic. Add water, place the pot on high heat and bring to a boil.

Add the bouquet garni and pepper to the pot and stir well. Lower the heat and simmer the soup for 1½ to 2 hours, or until the beans are cooked.

Remove the meat and cut into pieces. Remove the bouquet garni and discard. Purée some of the beans and return to soup to thicken. Stir in the ham pieces and the olives. Taste and add more salt and pepper if necessary. Pour the soup into bowls and garnish with parsley.

Serves 6 to 8.

— Dolores de Rosario
Hamilton, Ontario

PEA SOUP

1 ham bone
1 large onion, chopped
1 rib celery, chopped
1 cup chopped celery leaves
1 carrot, finely diced

1 bay leaf
1 lb. split peas
Salt & pepper
2 sprigs fresh parsley
1 cup sour cream

Place all ingredients except sour cream in large, heavy pot and cover with cold water. Bring to a boil, lower heat and simmer for several hours, until peas are very soft.

Remove bone and chop meat. Put soup through blender, 2 cups at a time, and return to pot with chopped ham. Add sour cream, stir and heat through.

Serves 12.

— Virginia Mitchell
Richelain, Quebec

GREEN PEA PUREE

1 large potato
2 large carrots
2 large onions
2 stalks celery, diced

4 stalks asparagus (optional)
2 qts. fresh peas
4 cups chicken stock
1 Tbsp. tarragon

Peel potato, carrots and onions and slice thinly. Combine with celery and asparagus and cover with water in a saucepan. Boil until soft — 10 to 15 minutes. Drain.

Meanwhile, cook peas until tender in chicken stock with tarragon.

Place 3 large spoonfuls of vegetables in blender and add 1½ cups of stock. Liquify. Continue until all the vegetables and stock are blended.

Makes 10 cups.

This pureé may be frozen and stored until needed for soup.

To make soup: to 1 cup of pureé, add 2 cups of milk and heat gently, adding salt and pepper to taste.

— John D. Perkins
Hillsburgh, Ontario

BORSCHT

6 medium beets
1 medium onion
1 medium potato
1 medium apple
2 carrots
½-1 lb. beef, tenderized & thinly sliced
2 Tbsp. butter

6-8 cups boiling water
½ small cabbage
Salt & pepper
1 tsp. dill weed
½ cup lemon juice
Sour cream to garnish

Peel vegetables and apple and grate coarsely. Brown meat in oil in large soup pot.

Melt butter, add vegetables except cabbage, and cook, covered, for 1 hour, stirring occasionally.

Add boiling water, cabbage, salt, pepper, dill weed and lemon juice. Cook 15 minutes longer. Adjust seasonings if necessary. Serve with sour cream.

Serves 8.

— Lois Pope
Whitehorse, Yukon

FRENCH ONION SOUP

2 medium onions, thinly sliced
1 Tbsp. butter
2 cups beef stock
2 Tbsp. lemon juice
¼ tsp. nutmeg

Worcestershire sauce
Salt & pepper
4-6 Tbsp. Parmesan cheese
¾ cup grated Swiss cheese
2 cups toasted croutons

Cook onions in butter over medium heat for 3 minutes. Add stock, lemon juice, nutmeg and a few drops of Worcestershire sauce. Cook gently until onions are tender. Season with salt, pepper and 2 Tbsp. Parmesan cheese.

To serve, place the Swiss cheese in 2 soup bowls. Ladle soup into bowls and top with croutons. Sprinkle with remaining Parmesan cheese.

Broil until cheese is lightly browned.

Serves 2.

— Christine Collis
Burlington, Ontario

NAVY BEAN SOUP

2 cups navy beans
6 cups water
1 large onion
1 large stalk celery

2 carrots
Bay leaf
Salt

Cook beans in water until tender — 45 minutes to 1 hour. Add remaining ingredients and cook until vegetables are tender — 1 to 2 hours.

Serves 6.

— Nel vanGeest
Weston, Ontario

FRESH TOMATO SOUP

½ cup chopped onion
¼ cup butter
¼ cup flour
1 cup water
6 medium tomatoes,
  peeled, seeded & diced

1 Tbsp. minced parsley
1¼ tsp. salt
½ tsp. thyme leaves
¼ tsp. pepper
1 bay leaf
Lemon slices to garnish

In a 3-quart saucepan over medium heat cook onion in butter until tender. Stir in flour until blended. Gradually stir in water.

Add tomatoes and remaining ingredients, except lemon slices, and heat mixture until boiling. Reduce heat to low, cover and simmer for 30 minutes, stirring frequently. Add more water if needed. Discard bay leaf. Serve with lemon slices.

Serves 3 to 4.

— Margaret Godbeer Houle
Dollard des Ormeaux, Quebec

TOMATO WINE SOUP

1 cup dry white wine
½ cup dry sherry
3 cups beef stock
4 cups tomato juice
½ cup sliced onion
2 sprigs parsley

2 stalks celery, chopped
1 Tbsp. honey
½ tsp. pepper
2 cloves
1 lemon, sliced

Combine all the ingredients in a saucepan and bring to a boil. Reduce the heat, cover and cook slowly for 20 minutes.

Strain the soup and return it to the saucepan. Adjust seasoning. Heat thoroughly and serve.

Serves 8 to 10.

— Janet Flewelling
Toronto, Ontario

FREEZER CREAM OF TOMATO SOUP

2 onions, chopped
2 carrots, diced
6 Tbsp. butter
½ cup flour
6 cups water
2 lbs. chicken backs or necks

6 cups ripe tomatoes
¼ tsp. thyme
Salt & pepper
Celery leaves
Parsley & basil

In a deep pot, sauté onions and carrots in butter. Slowly stir in flour, then gradually add water. Cook, stirring constantly, until thickened.

Add remaining ingredients, cover and simmer for 1 hour. Discard bones. Purée soup in blender. Freeze.

To serve, combine equal amounts of milk and tomato purée and heat thoroughly.

Makes 12 cups of purée.

— *Mrs. L.H. Lowther*
Harrowsmith, Ontario

TOMATO & CHEDDAR CHEESE SOUP

4 cups finely chopped onions
½ lb. butter
12 cups crushed tomatoes

12 cups water
18 cups grated Cheddar cheese
12 cups sour cream

Sauté onions in butter until soft. Add tomatoes, water and cheese and cook, stirring, until cheese is mostly melted.

Stir in sour cream.

Serves 50 to 70.

— *Terry Shoffner*
Toronto, Ontario

MUSHROOM BARLEY SOUP

½ cup raw barley
4 cups vegetable or chicken stock
½ cup chopped celery
½ cup diced carrots
3 Tbsp. butter

1 clove garlic
1 cup chopped mushrooms
½ cup chopped onion
Salt

Cook barley in stock over low heat for 45 minutes or until barley is tender.

Meanwhile, sauté celery and carrots in butter with garlic. After 10 minutes add mushrooms and onion. Cook until onion is soft. Remove garlic.

Add vegetables to barley and stock and cook for 5 minutes.

Serves 4.

— *Debbi Walsh*
Portland, Maine

CURRIED PEA SOUP

1 lb. garden peas
3 Tbsp. butter
3 Tbsp. flour

4 Tbsp. curry powder
4 cups vegetable stock
1 cup milk

Blend peas. Melt butter and stir in flour. Add peas, curry powder, milk and stock and mix well. Cook until slightly thickened.

Serves 4 to 6.

— *Mrs. A.E. Nehua-Cafe*
New South Wales, Australia

SPINACH SOUP

4 cups chicken stock
¾ lb. spinach

Hard-boiled eggs & sour cream to garnish

Bring stock to a boil. Wash spinach and tear into bite-sized pieces. Add to boiling stock and simmer briefly.

Place in individual bowls and garnish with sour cream and hard-boiled eggs.

Serves 4.

— Carole Peterson
Paradise, Nfld.

ARTICHOKE SOUP

6 medium artichokes
2 Tbsp. oil
4 cloves garlic, crushed
Salt
3 eggs

½-¾ cup grated Parmesan cheese
½-¾ cup bread crumbs
1 tsp. paprika
2 cups water

Wash artichokes and trim outer leaves. Cut into quarters, place in a pot and cover with water. Add oil, garlic and salt to taste. Cook over medium heat for 45 minutes.

Meanwhile, combine 1 egg with enough cheese and bread crumbs to make a moist paste. Stir in salt and paprika. Roll into tiny balls.

Add cheese balls to the soup and simmer gently for 15 minutes. Add water and salt to taste. Beat together remaining 2 eggs and slowly pour into soup, stirring gently. Simmer for 10 minutes.

Serves 4.

— Mary Andrasi
Acton Vale, Quebec

SHERRIED WILD RICE SOUP

2 Tbsp. butter
1 Tbsp.-½ cup minced onion
¼ cup flour
4-5 cups chicken stock
1-2 cups cooked wild rice

½ tsp. salt
1 cup light cream
¼ cup dry sherry
Parsley or chives, minced

Melt butter in saucepan, add onion and cook until onion is golden. Blend in flour and stock, stirring constantly until thickened. Stir in rice and salt and simmer 5 minutes.

Blend in cream and sherry and simmer until well heated. Garnish with minced parsley or chives.

Makes 6 cups.

— Anne Ulmer
Cannon Falls, Minn.

MISO SOUP

2 carrots
2 onions
Oil for frying
4 cups water

1 strip kombu (seaweed),
  chopped & soaked until soft
4 Tbsp. miso

Chop carrots and onions and fry in oil. Bring water to a boil, add vegetables and seaweed and simmer for 20 to 30 minutes.

Remove from heat and add miso. Stir.

Serves 4.

— Terry Bethune
Wardsville, Ontario

CREAM OF SHRIMP SOUP

¼ cup butter
2 tsp. chopped onion
¼ cup flour
1 Tbsp. chicken stock
1 cup light cream

2 cups milk
1 tin small shrimp, undrained
2 Tbsp. sherry
Parsley to garnish

Melt butter in top of double boiler, add onion and flour and blend well. Add stock, cream and 1 cup milk and cook, stirring constantly, until slightly thickened.

Stir in undrained shrimp and cook, covered, over boiling water for 10 minutes. Add sherry and remaining cup of milk. Heat through.

Serve garnished with parsley.

Serves 3.

— Shirley Hill
Picton, Ontario

MARITIME CLAM CHOWDER

4 large onions, chopped
¼ cup butter
8 medium potatoes, peeled & cubed
1 Tbsp. salt
½ tsp. pepper

4 cups milk
2 cups grated Cheddar cheese
2 cans clams
3 Tbsp. parsley

Sauté onions in butter in large, heavy saucepan until tender. Add potatoes, salt and pepper and cover with boiling water. Simmer, covered, for 20 minutes or until potatoes are tender.

Add milk and cheese, stirring until cheese is melted. Add clams. Heat through, but do not boil. Stir in parsley.

Serves 8.

— Debbie Walker
Delta, Ontario

MANHATTAN CLAM CHOWDER

¼ cup chopped onion
2 Tbsp. butter
1 cup diced potato
¼ cup chopped celery
2 cups boiling water
1 cup canned tomatoes

1 tsp. salt
Pepper
¼ tsp. thyme
1 cup chopped clams
1 cup clam liquor

Brown onion in butter. Add potato, celery and boiling water and cook for 10 minutes or until potato is tender.

Add remaining ingredients and simmer for 20 minutes.

Serves 4 to 6.

— Delia Schlesinger
Calgary, Alberta

FISH CHOWDER

2 slices bacon
1 medium onion, chopped
¼ green pepper, chopped
1 medium potato, peeled & sliced
½ pkg. frozen cod fillets, thawed
1 cup water

1 tsp. salt
1 bay leaf
⅛ tsp. basil, thyme or fennel
3 Tbsp. flour
1 cup milk
1 cup table cream

Fry bacon in large heavy saucepan until crisp. Lift out and crumble. Turn heat to low and fry onion and green pepper for 2 minutes. Drain and reserve bacon fat. Put potato, fish, water and seasonings in pot, bring to a boil and simmer gently, covered, for 10 minutes.

Remove fish, separate into large chunks and return to the pot. Blend together 3 Tbsp. reserved bacon fat, flour and milk. Add to pot, discarding bay leaf. Add cream and bacon bits. Reheat, without boiling, and stir gently as it thickens.

Serves 4 to 6.

— *Joan Graham*
Don Mills, Ontario

OYSTER CHOWDER

6 slices bacon, diced
1 cup chopped onion
1 pint fresh oysters
2 cups diced potatoes
¾ cup diced carrots

4 cups light cream
2 tsp. salt
Pepper
½ cup dry white wine
¼ cup chopped parsley

In a large frying pan, cook bacon until crisp. Remove, then sauté onion in fat until golden brown.

Simmer oysters in their liquor for 3 minutes. Drain and reserve liquid.

Add water to reserved oyster liquor to make 1 cup.

Add vegetables and liquid to onion, cover and simmer until vegetables are tender — about 15 minutes.

Stir in cream, salt and pepper and bring soup to a boil. Reduce heat, add oysters and wine and heat through.

Serves 8.

— *Carol Frost*
Chilliwack, B.C.

CREAM OF FIDDLEHEAD SOUP

3 cups fiddleheads
3 cups cream
2 Tbsp. butter

⅛ tsp. pepper
Marjoram
Chicken stock to thin

Cook fiddleheads in salted water for 15 to 20 minutes. Drain and chop.

To chopped fiddleheads, add cream, butter, pepper and marjoram to taste. Heat gently and add chicken stock, if desired, to thin soup. Simmer for 10 to 20 minutes.

Serves 4.

— *Trudy Mason*
Meaford, Ontario

CREAM OF CAULIFLOWER SOUP

½ cup butter
1 onion, finely chopped
2 stalks celery, finely chopped
1 apple, peeled & finely chopped
1 tsp. curry powder
¼ cup flour
4 cups chicken stock

1 small head cauliflower,
  cut into small flowerettes
1 egg yolk, lightly beaten
1 cup light cream
Salt & pepper
2 Tbsp. parsley, to garnish

Melt butter and sauté onions, celery and apple. Sprinkle with curry powder and flour. Cook, stirring, for 2 more minutes.

Gradually stir in stock. Bring to a boil and add the cauliflower. Cook, covered, for 10 minutes. Combine egg yolk and cream and gradually stir into mixture. Heat but do not boil.

Sprinkle each serving with parsley.

Serves 4.

— *Olga Harrison*
Peterborough, Ontario

CREAM OF SWISS CHARD SOUP

⅓ cup chopped onion
¼ cup melted butter
⅓ cup flour
2 tsp. salt

¼ tsp. pepper
⅛ tsp. nutmeg
6 cups milk
2 cups chopped, cooked Swiss chard

Sauté onion in butter until tender. Blend in flour, salt, pepper and nutmeg.

Cook slowly until mixture is smooth and bubbly. Gradually stir in milk and Swiss chard.

Bring to a boil, stirring constantly, and cook for 1 minute.

Serves 6 to 8.

— *Florence Graham*
Alberton, P.E.I.

POTATO SOUP

5 medium potatoes
Garlic salt
½ small onion, chopped
Celery salt

2 Tbsp. butter
¼ cup flour
3 cups milk

Peel and wash potatoes and cut into 1-inch pieces. Cover with water and bring to a boil. Add garlic salt, onion and celery salt and cook until potatoes are tender.

Remove from heat; do not drain. Mash well. Cover with a lid and set aside.

Melt butter in a small saucepan and slowly add flour to make a fine paste. Remove from heat.

Return potatoes to heat and add flour paste a little at a time. Bring to a boil, stirring constantly. Add milk slowly, stirring to avoid scorching, and cook until thoroughly heated.

Serves 4.

— *Deborah Exner*
Delisle, Sask.

LEEK & POTATO SOUP

THIS IS A HEARTY VARIATION OF THE COLD SOUP, VICHYSSOISE. IT CAN BE BLENDED immediately before serving for a smoother texture.

1 slice bacon	Salt & pepper
1 oz. butter	½ cup milk
1 lb. potatoes	½ cup grated cheese
2 large leeks	Parsley
1½ cups chicken stock	

Cut up the bacon and fry in butter. Peel and cut potatoes, and clean and cut up leeks. Add to the saucepan and fry for 5 minutes. Stir in stock, add salt and pepper to taste. Cover and simmer for 30 minutes until the vegetables are tender. Add milk and reheat but do not boil. If desired, blend for a few seconds. Serve with grated cheese and parsley.

Serves 4.

— *Mary Rogers*
Kitchener, Ontario

CHEESY ONION & POTATO SOUP

3 medium onions, chopped	¼ tsp. salt
2 Tbsp. butter	Pepper
4 medium potatoes, peeled & cubed	3 cups milk
2 cups chicken stock	1 cup shredded Cheddar cheese

Cook onions in butter until soft but not brown. Add potatoes, stock, salt and pepper. Cover, bring to a boil, then simmer until potatoes are tender, about 15 minutes.

Remove from heat and blend in parts in blender or food processor. Return to saucepan, add milk and cheese and reheat slowly until cheese melts. Do not boil.

Makes 6 servings.

— *Christine Steele*
Port Dover, Ontario

CHUNKY CORN CHOWDER

THIS SOUP TAKES ONLY MINUTES TO PUT TOGETHER — WITH INGREDIENTS which are usually on hand.

4 slices bacon, diced	¾ lb. kernel corn
1 small onion, chopped	1 tsp. salt
1 cup chopped celery	½ tsp. dried dill
2 large potatoes, peeled & cubed	Freshly ground pepper
1 qt. milk	¼ tsp. Tabasco sauce

Cook the bacon in a large saucepan just until it begins to brown. Add onion, celery and potatoes. Cook over medium heat, stirring occasionally, until the onion is soft — about 5 minutes.

Add the remaining ingredients. Cover and heat, but do not boil. Reduce heat and simmer 20 to 30 minutes or until potatoes are tender. Stir often.

Serves 6.

— *Shirley Hill*
Picton, Ontario

CHEESE SOUP

½ cup grated carrot
2 onions, chopped
4 Tbsp. oil
½ cup flour
4 cups vegetable stock
4 cups milk
2 Tbsp. soya sauce

1 tsp. dry mustard
1 tsp. paprika
1 lb. sharp Cheddar cheese, grated
¼-½ lb. Swiss cheese, grated
1 green pepper, chopped
4 stalks celery, chopped

Sauté grated carrot and one of the onions in oil in a frying pan. Gradually add the flour, then some of the vegetable stock, stirring and keeping the mixture consistently smooth. Pour into a large soup pot over low heat. Gradually add remaining stock, milk and seasonings. Add cheese slowly and stir constantly as it melts. Add remaining onion, green pepper and celery.

For variety, add any other chopped green vegetables and simmer until cooked.

Serves 8.

— Sandra Wozniak
Iona Station, Ontario

WILD COUNTRY CREAM SOUP

1 cup fiddlehead ferns
½ cup butter
¾ cup finely chopped wild leeks
¼ cup finely chopped green onions
1 cup sliced mushrooms
1 tsp. salt

Cayenne
¼ cup flour
1 cup chicken stock
3 cups milk
1 tsp. salt
1 tsp. lemon juice

Clean fiddleheads thoroughly. In a saucepan, cook ¼ cup of the butter, the leeks, onions, fiddleheads and mushrooms until tender but not browned. Add salt and cayenne.

Gradually add remaining butter, flour and chicken stock, stirring constantly, and bring to a boil. Add milk and cook on low heat for 1 hour. Allow to cool, then reheat to serve.

Serves 6.

— Janet Mayhew
Guelph, Ontario

TURNIP SOUP

1 medium turnip
1 onion
2 cups chicken stock
Pinch garlic salt

Pinch curry powder
1½ cups cream
Salt
Sour cream

Chop turnip and onion and boil with stock, garlic salt and curry powder until tender. Place in blender and purée. Cool and add cream.

Heat soup, adding salt to taste. Garnish generously with sour cream.

Serves 2 to 4.

— Michael Bruce-Lockhart
Paradise, Nfld.

FRESH VEGETABLE SOUP

2 cups diced unpeeled potatoes
1 cup diced carrots
1 cup diced kohlrabi
1 cup peas
1 cup sliced green beans
2-3 small onions

Parsley
Salt & pepper
2 cups milk
2 cups cream
2 Tbsp. butter

Cook potatoes, carrots and kohlrabi in 2 cups of water. Add remaining vegetables after 5 minutes and cook a further 7 minutes.

Add remaining ingredients, bring just to the boiling point and serve.

Serves 4 to 6.

— Jean Stewart
Rimbey, Alberta

PARSNIP CHOWDER

¼ lb. pork belly
2 slices lean bacon, cut into strips
1 large onion, diced
1 large leek, diced
4 parsnips, diced
3 potatoes, diced

2 cups chicken stock
Juice of ½ lemon
1 cup whipping cream
Salt & pepper
Chopped parsley or chives to garnish

Dice pork and fry slowly in heavy saucepan until well browned. Remove with slotted spoon and set aside.

In remaining fat, fry bacon, onion and leek until golden brown. Remove. Fry parsnips and potatoes until golden, adding butter if necessary.

Return onion and bacon to pan, add stock, bring to a boil and simmer until tender but not mushy — about 10 to 12 minutes. Add lemon juice.

Stir in cream, salt and pepper, and bring chowder back to a boil. Serve garnished with pork and chopped parsley or chives.

Serves 6.

— Sheila Bear
St. John's, Nfld.

SPRINGTIME SOUP

THIS SOUP IS A WONDERFUL WAY TO SERVE FRESH, YOUNG VEGETABLES — THEIR delicate flavours are preserved by the short cooking time. Vegetables may be varied according to season.

1 cup chopped green onions
1 cup chopped baby beets & tops
1 cup chopped new carrots & tops
1 cup chopped new potatoes
1 cup edible podded peas

1 cup sliced green beans
6 cups goat's milk (light cream may
  be substituted)
Salt

Cook vegetables until tender in just enough water to prevent scorching. Add milk or cream and salt to taste. Heat to serving temperature, but do not boil.

— Harvey Lyons
Gillies Bay, B.C.

SQUASH BLOSSOM SOUP

THIS SOUP PROVIDES A TASTY WAY TO THIN OUT THE GARDEN IN LATE JULY WHEN the squash looks as though it is going to overrun everything else.

3 Tbsp. butter
⅔ cup minced onion
36 squash blossoms, stems discarded
 & coarsely chopped

3 cups chicken stock
1 cup light cream
1 egg yolk
Salt, pepper & nutmeg

Melt butter in heavy saucepan over medium heat. Add onion and sauté until soft. Stir in blossoms and soften.

Add stock and bring to a boil, reduce heat, cover and simmer for 10 minutes.

Beat cream with egg yolk, then stir in a small amount of hot stock. Slowly add this mixture to the rest of the soup, stirring constantly. Heat through and season to taste.

Serves 3 to 4.

— *Ingrid Birker*
Toronto, Ontario

MUSHROOM SOUP

½ cup butter
¼ cup chopped onion
½ lb. mushrooms, chopped
¼ cup flour
1 tsp. salt

Pepper
1 cup chicken broth
3 cups milk
1 Tbsp. lemon juice
Parsley

Sauté onions in butter until tender. Remove and set aside. Sauté mushrooms until soft —about 10 minutes. Blend in flour, salt and pepper and gradually stir in broth and milk. Cook until mixture thickens and comes to a boil.

Add onions, lemon juice, salt and pepper and simmer 10 minutes. Serve with sprinkle of parsley.

Serves 6.

— *Mary VanderSchaaf*
Penetanguishene, Ont.

CARROT PUREE

3 cups diced carrots
½ cup chopped onion
1 stalk celery, diced
4 cups chicken stock

1 bay leaf
Nutmeg
⅔ cup milk or light cream

Combine carrots, onion, celery, chicken stock and bay leaf in a 1½-quart saucepan. Cover and simmer for 30 minutes or until carrots are soft. Remove bay leaf.

Process in a blender until smooth. Return to saucepan, add nutmeg and bring to a boil. Remove from heat and stir in milk. Reheat but do not boil.

Serves 6.

— *E.A. Desfossés*
Gagetown, N.B.

WON TON SOUP

2 water chestnuts, finely chopped
½ lb. ground pork
1 lb. won ton wrappers

6 cups chicken stock
1 small head chard or spinach, chopped
Chopped green onion to garnish

Mix water chestnuts with ground pork.

Place a small amount of the meat on one corner of each won ton wrapper. Fold up meat and roll toward the centre. Shape into a crescent. Boil the won ton in batches in boiling water and drain. Combine chicken stock and chard or spinach. Add won ton and heat thoroughly.

Serve sprinkled with green onion.

Serves 6.

— *Bryanna Clark*
Union Bay, B.C.

HEAVENLY EGG DROP SOUP

6 cups chicken stock
½ cup matchstick-cut bamboo shoots
4 dried forest mushrooms,
  soaked to soften & cut in matchsticks

2 eggs, beaten
2 Tbsp. chopped green onions or chives
½ tsp. Oriental sesame oil

Heat stock and add bamboo shoots and mushrooms. Simmer for 15 minutes, then bring to a boil. Reduce to a simmer and gradually add beaten eggs in a thin stream. Stir constantly.

Remove from heat, add onion or chives and sesame oil.

Serves 6.

— *Lois Pope*
Whitehorse, Yukon

PESTO SOUP

6-8 cups stock or water
1 onion, chopped
1 cup chopped potato
2 tsp. salt
4 Tbsp. olive oil
4 cups canned tomatoes
1 cup green beans,
  cut into 1-inch pieces

1 cup zucchini, finely chopped
Pepper
4 cloves garlic
¼ cup fresh or 1 Tbsp. dried basil
¼ cup grated Parmesan cheese

Combine in a large pot the stock or water, onion, potato, salt and 1 Tbsp. of olive oil. Boil gently until potatoes are tender — 15 to 20 minutes.

Add drained tomatoes, green beans, zucchini and pepper to taste. Cook until vegetables are tender.

Meanwhile, crush garlic in a small wooden bowl. Pound in basil and, when well blended, work in Parmesan cheese and remaining 3 Tbsp. of oil.

Blend a few tablespoons of hot soup into pesto sauce, then add sauce to soup. Blend well and heat through.

Serves 8 to 10.

— *Jan Post*
West River Stn., N.S.

SOUPE AU PISTOU

A FAVOURITE IN THIS LONDON RESTAURANT, SOUPE AU PISTOU TAKES SOME TIME TO cook, but is well worth the effort.

3 cups water
¾ cup dry navy beans
4 Tbsp. olive oil
1 cup diced onions
1 lb. tomatoes, peeled, seeded
  & finely chopped
3 qts. water
1½ cups diced carrots
1½ cups finely diced potatoes
1 cup chopped leeks
1 Tbsp. salt

Pepper
1½ cups sliced green beans
1½ cups diced zucchini
½ cup broken pasta
2 pinches saffron
3 cloves garlic
½ cup fresh or 3 Tbsp. dried basil
1 Tbsp. tomato paste
¼ cup Parmesan cheese
3 Tbsp. olive oil

Bring the 3 cups of water to a boil in a 1-quart saucepan. Drop in the dry beans and boil them for 2 minutes. Remove from heat and let the beans soak for 1 hour. Return to a low heat and simmer, uncovered, for 1 to 1½ hours, adding water if necessary, or until the beans are tender. Drain the beans and reserve cooking liquid.

Meanwhile, heat olive oil in a heavy soup pot. Stir in diced onions and cook over a moderate heat until transparent. Add the tomatoes and cook for 3 to 4 minutes. Pour in the 3 quarts of water and bring to a boil over high heat, stirring occasionally. Add the carrots, potatoes, leeks, salt and pepper. Reduce the heat and simmer, uncovered, for 15 minutes. Stir in the white beans and their liquid, the green beans, zucchini, pasta and saffron. Simmer for another 15 minutes.

To make the pistou, mince the garlic and basil into a paste, using a mortar, food processor or blender. Work in the tomato paste and the cheese. Finally, beat in the olive oil one tablespoon at a time.

Add the pistou to the soup, or serve the soup accompanied with bowls of pistou.

Serves 12 to 15.

— *Auberge du Petit Prince*
London, Ontario

NORWEGIAN SWEET SOUP

MORE COMMON IN OTHER CULTURES THAN IN OUR OWN, FRUIT SOUPS, WITH THEIR delicate, light flavours, are ideal first courses for heavy meals.

1 lb. dried fruits
½ cup tapioca
2 cups fruit juice

1 cup sugar
1 stick cinnamon
1 lemon, sliced

Cover fruit with water and bring to a boil. Stir in the tapioca and add the rest of the ingredients.

Cook over low heat for about 1 hour, stirring frequently. Serve hot.

Serves 4.

— *Cary Elizabeth Marshall*
Thunder Bay, Ontario

AVOGLIMONO

THIS GREEK LEMON SOUP HAS A SMOOTH TEXTURE AND IS SIMPLE TO ASSEMBLE.

2 eggs
1 lemon
6 cups chicken stock

Salt
4 slices lemon to garnish

Beat eggs until frothy. Squeeze juice from lemon into the eggs, drop by drop, beating the whole time.

Heat chicken stock and stir in the lemon and eggs, adding salt to taste. Beat while heating for 1 minute.

Serve each bowl with a thin slice of lemon floating on top.

Serves 4.

— Cary Elizabeth Marshall
Thunder Bay, Ontario

APPLE CURRY SOUP

1 tart apple, unpeeled & quartered
1 onion, peeled & halved
2 cups beef or miso stock
1 tsp. honey

1 tsp. curry powder
Salt
1 cup light cream

Combine apple, onion and stock in a heavy saucepan. Add honey and bring to a boil. Reduce heat and simmer until the apple and onion are soft.

Blend in a blender, return to saucepan and add spices. Stir in cream and slowly heat through.

Serves 4.

— Suezan Aikins
Prospect, Nova Scotia

FRUIT MOOS

FROZEN OR DRIED FRUITS ARE AS GOOD IN THIS SOUP AS FRESH ONES. IF YOU ARE using dried fruit, soften it first in water or juice.

1 cup plums
1 cup peaches
1 cup rhubarb
1 cup cherries, pitted

Water
1 cup sugar
3 Tbsp. flour

Slice plums and peaches and chop rhubarb into 1-inch pieces. Place in saucepan with cherries and water to cover. Cook until tender. Remove fruit.

Combine sugar and flour and blend with enough water to make a thick paste. Stir into the water in saucepan and cook, stirring, over low heat until the mixture resembles a white sauce.

Add fruit and heat through. Taste and add sugar if a sweeter soup is desired.

Serve with heavy sweet cream.

Serves 4 to 6.

— Valerie Lanctôt
San Josef, B.C.

CHUNKY GAZPACHO SUMMER SOUP

2 large tomatoes,
  peeled & coarsely chopped
1 small cucumber, chopped
3 green onions, finely chopped
1 small green pepper, chopped
1 cup tomato juice

4 Tbsp. olive oil
1 Tbsp. cider vinegar
½ tsp. salt
⅛ tsp. pepper
Tabasco sauce
1 clove garlic, crushed

Mix all ingredients well. If a smooth soup is desired, it may be blended. Cover and refrigerate for at least 2 hours until icy cold.

Serves 4.

— *Margaret Silverthorn*
Iona Station, Ontario

COLD CUCUMBER SOUP

2 Tbsp. butter
¼ cup chopped onion
2 cups diced, peeled cucumber
½ cup chopped celery leaves
1½ cups basic white sauce, page 92
1 large potato, cooked,
  peeled & finely diced

Salt & pepper
¼ tsp. dry mustard
¾ cup water
Parsley to garnish

Melt butter, add onion and cook until transparent. Add cucumber, celery leaves, white sauce, potato, salt, pepper, mustard and water. Bring to a boil, reduce heat and cook for 10 minutes.

Blend in a blender for 40 seconds. Chill for several hours. Serve garnished with parsley.

Serves 4 to 6.

— *Shirley Hill*
Picton, Ontario

COLD YOGURT CUCUMBER SOUP

2 medium-sized cucumbers
Olive oil
½ tsp. salt
1 tsp. minced garlic
2 Tbsp. chopped fresh dill

Pepper
2 cups yogurt
1 cup iced water
⅓ cup chopped walnuts or almonds

Peel cucumbers if necessary. Cut in quarters lengthwise, then slice. Toss with a little olive oil to glaze them lightly. Add salt, garlic, dill and pepper to taste.

Chill for 1 to 3 hours. Drain and combine with yogurt, iced water and nuts. Check seasoning and serve very cold.

Serves 4.

— *N. Burk*
Ste. Anne de la Rochelle, Quebec

COLD AVOCADO SOUP

3 avocados, peeled
1½ cucumbers, peeled & sliced
3 cups chicken stock
¾ cup sour cream

3 Tbsp. lemon juice
1½ tsp. salt
Tabasco sauce
Parsley to garnish

Chop avocados and cucumbers coarsely and purée in blender. Add stock, sour cream, lemon juice, salt and Tabasco sauce and mix well.

Chill thoroughly. Garnish with parsley and serve.

Serves 6 to 8.

— Joan Stevens
Buckhorn, Ontario

CHILLED ZUCCHINI SOUP

3 Tbsp. butter
2 cups sliced zucchini
1 slice onion
⅛ tsp. curry powder

2 cups chicken stock
½ cup light cream
Salt & pepper

Combine butter, zucchini, onion and curry powder in a heavy saucepan. Cook, stirring occasionally, until vegetables are tender.

Add chicken stock and bring to a boil. Reduce heat and simmer for 15 minutes. Process in blender until smooth. Add cream and seasonings.

Chill for at least 1 hour before serving.

Serves 2 to 4.

— Carol Frost
Chilliwack, B.C.

Salads & Vegetables

Ho! tis the time of salads.

— **Laurence Sterne**
Tristram Shandy

Vegetables may be our least understood foods. Corn, potatoes, tomatoes — each food was initially mistrusted by the Europeans before finally being accepted into the diet. New settlers in North America sometimes died because they refused to accept the unfamiliar but nourishing bean diet appreciated by native Indians. (Now, of course, baked beans are almost synonymous with Boston.) Somehow, the well-to-do British survived several generations with the conviction that raw vegetables were unwholesome, and even cooked ones were to be suffered in small measure. As late as 1915, an Ontario government pamphlet advised, "The fresh vegetables are composed chiefly of water, most of them containing over 80 per cent of it so, in so far as nutriment is concerned, they are of little value." And today, misconceptions remain: oranges are our best source of vitamin C, carrots are best for vitamin A, spinach for iron.

Oranges for vitamin C? Yes, but where most of us live, oranges are expensive imports. And the proportion of vitamin C is higher in many foods that can be grown locally — peppers, broccoli, Brussels sprouts, cauliflower, strawberries and spinach, all of which also offer more additional nutrients than do oranges. Consider the following statement from Agriculture Canada's food advisory division. "You can obtain at least 100 per cent of the vitamin C you need daily by eating a half cup serving of cooked broccoli, Brussels sprouts or cauliflower. The same amount of raw or cooked cabbage, potato cooked in the skin, rutabaga or canned tomato supplies at least 50 per cent of the needed vitamin C." To lessen the loss of vitamin C in cooking vegetables, stay away from copper pots, as this metal oxydizes the vitamin.

Are carrots the best source of vitamin A, the see-in-the-dark vitamin? All yellow or green leafy vegetables, as well as tomatoes and peppers, are good sources of vitamin A, which is produced in the body from carotenoids, the yellow pigments in many fruits and vegetables. A cup of grated carrots contains 12,100 International Units of vitamin A, a very respectable rating — an adult needs only 4,000 to 5,000 I.U. daily. But a cup of dandelion greens contains 21,060 I.U., a cup of canned pumpkin, 14,590, a cup of dried apricots, 16,350 and a cup of cooked spinach, 14,580.

On the subject of spinach, what about that Popeye-popping vegetable? In iron content, it has a good showing of 3.1 milligrams in 100 grams of raw leaves; Swiss chard has 3.2 mg, beet greens, 3.3 mg. And Lima beans, dried apricots and peaches, dates, prunes and raisins all contain proportionately more iron than does spinach.

When vegetables are cooked, some vitamins are

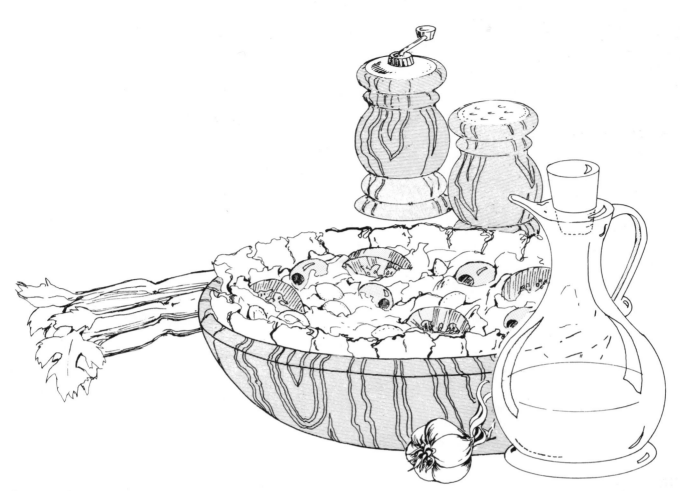

destroyed or lost into the cooking water, which is why one should save the liquid for soups and baking. Vitamins C and B are both water-soluble. Any cooking method that helps retain nutrients makes good sense, so steaming, baking and stir-frying are better than boiling. In any case, vegetables should never be overcooked. As that venerable tome *The Joy of Cooking* states, "It is probably true that more outrages are perpetrated against vegetables than against any other basic food." Most diners appreciate the slight crunch and bright colour of properly cooked vegetables.

Another way to ensure that vegetables are their most nutritious when they are served is to buy them fresh (or better yet, pick them fresh) when they are at their best. Prices are lowest, too, when produce is in season. One can make the best savings on the best foods by growing a garden or by visiting a pick-your-own operation in summer, canning and freezing anything that cannot be immediately used.

In the supermarket, the cook should look for the firmest, freshest produce, and buy what looks best, not necessarily what he had in mind when he arrived. In North America, where the home is often miles from a market, the notion of buying the finest available produce daily is a decidedly foreign one, but it has resulted in the highest of

culinary reputations for many European households and restaurants.

When choosing vegetables to be eaten fresh or cooked, keep the rest of the meal in mind; potatoes and cauliflower may be fine stir-fried with chicken, peppers, tomatoes, carrots and beans, but the meal will look colourless and unappealing if both are served with a baked chunk of chicken breast. The judicious use of salad dressings and sauces can add immeasurably to the flavours, textures and colours of the complete meal. But judicious is the important word – sauces can just as easily be gooey, insipid or overpowering as they can be subtly complementary.

Often, simplicity is the best course to follow. Wash all vegetables thoroughly just before cooking them, even if they look clean. Cook them until they are just tender, and then serve the carrots with a little butter, the tomato slices with mayonnaise, the tossed greens with olive oil, vinegar and salt – the word "salad," after all, is derived from the word "salt." Such a course, allowing the vegetables themselves to shine forth in all their flavour and colour, is the surest way to success with the bounty from market stall or vegetable garden.

STIR-FRIED GREEN BEANS

1 qt. fresh green beans
2 Tbsp. oil
½ tsp. ground ginger
3 drops Tabasco sauce
½ tsp. sugar

Salt
2 Tbsp. sesame seeds
2 Tbsp. vinegar
Chopped green onion

Wash beans and remove ends if desired. Heat oil in wok, add beans and cook quickly over high heat, tossing constantly, for 2 to 3 minutes.

Add remaining ingredients, toss and serve.

Serves 4.

— Billie Sheffield
North Gower, Ontario

GREEN BEAN CASSEROLE

THIS RECIPE PROVIDES A QUICK AND EASY WAY TO DRESS UP AN EVERYDAY vegetable.

1 lb. green beans, cooked
2 Tbsp. vinegar
2 tsp. honey

2 slices toast, cubed
2-4 Tbsp. Parmesan cheese

Place beans in greased baking dish. Stir in vinegar and drizzle with honey. Toss in toast. Sprinkle cheese on top.

Bake at 450 degrees F for 15 minutes, then broil 2 minutes to brown top.

— Sharon Steele
Burns Lake, B.C.

SWISS GREEN BEANS

2 Tbsp. butter
2 Tbsp. flour
1 tsp. salt
¼ tsp. pepper
½ tsp. grated onion

1 cup sour cream
4 cups green beans, cooked & drained
¼ lb. Swiss cheese, grated
1 cup bread crumbs
2 Tbsp. melted butter

Melt butter and stir in flour, salt, pepper and onion. Add sour cream gradually. Fold in green beans. Pour into greased casserole dish. Sprinkle cheese over beans. Mix bread crumbs with melted butter and sprinkle over cheese.

Bake at 400 degrees F for 20 minutes.

Serves 6.

— Jayne Campsall
Prescott, Ontario

GLAZED BEETS

Beets
Butter

Honey or maple syrup

Cook beets until tender. Drain, peel and, if beets are large, slice. Combine equal quantities of butter and honey or maple syrup in a saucepan. Add the beets and let simmer until the sauce is thickened and beets are shiny with the glaze, usually 10 to 20 minutes.

— Donna Jubb
Fenelon Falls, Ontario

BEET HOLUPTIS

THIS RICH DISH WRAPS A BREAD-LIKE DOUGH IN BEET LEAVES.

2 tsp. yeast
1½ cups warm water
1 Tbsp. honey
1 Tbsp. oil
3 cups whole wheat flour
3 cups white flour

36 beet leaves
4 green onions, chopped
2-3 Tbsp. butter
1 cup whipping cream
¼-½ cup fresh dill, chopped

Dissolve yeast in water and honey and let stand 5 minutes. Add oil. Combine two flours and add to water to form a bread dough. Knead for 10 minutes. Place in a bowl and let rise in warm place until doubled in size — 1 to 1½ hours. Punch down and set aside.

Wash beet leaves and cut out main vein if it is very large. Steam just until limp.

Pinch off pieces of dough large enough to wrap a leaf around. Roll leaves around dough, then place on greased cookie sheets and let rise until doubled in size. Bake at 350 degrees F until golden brown — 20 to 30 minutes.

Before serving, sauté onions briefly in butter. After about a minute, add the holuptis. Pour cream over them and add dill. Stir over low heat until holuptis are warm and have absorbed most of the cream. Serve warm.

Makes 36 holuptis.

— *Kay Chornook*
Burlington, Ontario

BEETS & GREENS IN SOUR CREAM

12 small beets
Honey
2 Tbsp. butter

1 small onion, minced
Salt & pepper
½ cup sour cream

Separate beet roots from greens. Cook the roots, drain, skin and slice them.

Rinse and chop the greens. Steam them briefly with a drop of honey, butter and onion. When greens are wilted, add the beet roots, salt and pepper and sour cream.

Serves 2-4.

— *Bryanna Clark*
Union Bay, B.C.

BROCCOLI MEDLEY

A PLEASANT AND UNUSUAL WAY TO SERVE EITHER FRESH OR FROZEN BROCCOLI, this dish can be made ahead and reheated at serving time.

2 heads fresh broccoli or
  2 10-oz. pkgs. frozen broccoli
1 cup chicken stock
¼ lb. bacon, cut in 1-inch pieces
2 cups mushrooms, sliced

1 can water chestnuts, drained & sliced
¼ cup slivered almonds
1 tsp. salt
⅛ tsp. pepper
Pimento strips

Cook broccoli in stock until crisp-tender, about 6 minutes. Drain, reserving ⅓ cup of cooking liquid. Cut broccoli into bite-sized pieces.

Fry bacon until slightly crisp, then add remaining ingredients except pimento, broccoli and cooking liquid. Cook and stir until bacon is crisp and mushrooms are tender, about 5 minutes. Add broccoli and reserved cooking liquid. Continue cooking until hot. Arrange on serving dish and garnish with pimento.

Serves 12.

— *Pam Collacott*
North Gower, Ontario

BROCCOLI CASSEROLE

2 heads broccoli, chopped
1½ cups cream of mushroom sauce,
  page 92
½ cup shredded Cheddar cheese
¼ cup milk

¼ cup mayonnaise
1 egg, beaten
¼ cup bread crumbs
1 Tbsp. butter

Cook broccoli and drain. Place in a casserole dish. Mix remaining ingredients together and pour over broccoli. Bake at 350 degrees F for 45 minutes.

Serves 6 to 8.

— Karen Brouwers
Campbellville, Ontario

RED CABBAGE & APPLES

2 lbs. red cabbage
¼ cup butter
½ cup chopped onion
1½ tsp. salt

¼ tsp. pepper
3 Tbsp. vinegar
1½ cups peeled & diced apples
Sour cream to garnish

Shred cabbage coarsely. Melt butter, add cabbage, onion, seasonings and vinegar. Cook, covered, for 20 minutes over low heat, stirring occasionally. Add apples, cover and cook a further 20 minutes or until tender, stirring every few minutes.

Serve with sour cream.

Serves 6.

— Florence Graham
Alberton, P.E.I.

CREAMY CABBAGE

2 lbs. cabbage, shredded
½ lb. cooked ham, cubed
Salt
1 Tbsp. dill seeds
4 Tbsp. oil

1 small onion, diced
2 Tbsp. flour
1 Tbsp. paprika
½ cup sour cream

Place shredded cabbage in a heavy saucepan with ½ inch of water. Add cubed ham, salt to taste and dill seed (in a cheesecloth bag). Simmer for 10 minutes.

Meanwhile, heat oil in a small saucepan. Add onion and cook slowly for 2 minutes. Add flour and paprika and cook over medium heat, stirring constantly, for 2 minutes. Add ½ cup hot water and stir until mixture thickens. Remove from heat.

Add this sauce to cabbage. Cook slowly until cabbage is tender — 10 minutes. Remove from heat and add sour cream.

Serves 6 to 8.

— Mary Andrasi
Acton Vale, Quebec

BAKED CARROTS

4 carrots
4 Tbsp. butter

Nutmeg

Grate carrots into a buttered casserole dish. Dot with butter and sprinkle with nutmeg. Bake at 350 degrees F for 20 to 30 minutes.

Serves 4.

— Jenny MacDonald
Dartmouth, N.S.

CARROT CASSEROLE

8 carrots
1 cup finely chopped celery
1 medium onion, finely chopped

1 Tbsp. prepared mustard
½ cup mayonnaise
½ cup buttered bread crumbs

Boil carrots until tender. Drain and mash. Combine celery, onion, mustard and mayonnaise and add to carrots. Spoon into buttered casserole dish and top with bread crumbs.

Bake at 300 degrees F for 1 hour.

— Grace Zomer
Ingersoll, Ontario

STIR-FRIED CAULIFLOWER

AN UNUSUAL AND ATTRACTIVE WAY TO COOK CAULIFLOWER, THIS DISH IS FAST AND simple to prepare.

2 Tbsp. oil
2 cloves garlic, minced
1 slice fresh ginger,
  the size of a quarter
1 head cauliflower,
  washed & broken into florets
1 red pepper, seeded & cut into strips

½ cup chicken stock
½ tsp. oregano
½ tsp. basil
3 tomatoes, peeled, seeded
  & cut into strips
1 cup peas, fresh or frozen

Heat oil in a large skillet. Add garlic, ginger and cauliflower. Stir-fry for 3 minutes. Stir in pepper and cook for 2 minutes. Add stock and herbs, cover and steam for 5 minutes. Remove cover, stir in tomatoes and peas and cook 3 to 4 more minutes or until vegetables are tender-crisp. Remove from heat and serve quickly.

— Ingrid Birker
Toronto, Ontario

CELERY CRUNCH WITH CHEESE-NUT PASTRY

⅔ cup flour
1 tsp. salt
6 Tbsp. butter
1 cup diced almonds, toasted
2¼ cups shredded Cheddar cheese

2-3 Tbsp. cold milk
2½ cups diced celery
¼ cup flour
1½ cups milk

Sift together flour and ½ tsp. salt. Cut in 3 Tbsp. butter until mixture is crumbly. Stir in ⅓ cup almonds and ¾ cup cheese. Sprinkle 2-3 Tbsp. milk over mixture, stirring with a fork until dough holds together. Flatten into a ½-inch-thick square. Roll out to fit top of baking dish. Set aside.

Cook diced celery in boiling water until tender, drain and add 3 Tbsp. butter. Stir in ¼ cup flour and ½ tsp. salt. Mix well. Gradually blend in 1½ cups milk. Cook over medium heat, stirring constantly, until thickened. Stir in remaining almonds and cheese.

Place in baking dish and top with pastry. Bake at 425 degrees F for 20 to 25 minutes.

Serves 8.

— Susan Gillespie
Comox, B.C.

CELERY WITH ALMONDS

½ cup slivered almonds
2 Tbsp. butter
4 cups diced celery

½ cup chopped onion
Pepper
2 Tbsp. dry white wine

In a skillet, cook the almonds in 1 Tbsp. butter, stirring constantly, until they are lightly browned. Drain on paper towels.

Sauté the diced celery and onion in the remaining butter. Season with pepper, if desired. Cook over low heat, stirring occasionally, for about 7 minutes.

Add the wine and cook, covered, for 2 minutes. Transfer to a serving dish and garnish with the almonds.

Serves 4 to 6.

— *Janet Flewelling*
Toronto, Ontario

CORN FRITTERS

DELICIOUS WITH MAPLE SYRUP AT BREAKFAST, CORN FRITTERS CAN ALSO BE SERVED as a vegetable with dinner.

15-oz. can creamed corn
2 eggs, beaten
2 Tbsp. melted butter
2 cups flour

2 tsp. baking powder
1 tsp. salt
½ tsp. curry powder
4-5 cups oil for deep frying

Combine corn, eggs and butter. Sift dry ingredients together and blend in corn mixture. Drop mixture by spoonfuls into hot oil (375 degrees F). Fry for approximately 4 minutes, turning once to cook evenly. Drain well.

Makes 15-18 fritters.

— *Janice Clynick*
Clinton, Ontario

EGGPLANT CREAM CHEESE CHEDDAR

3 eggplants
1 cup flour
1 tsp. salt
2 eggs
¼ cup milk
2 cups corn meal

½ tsp. oregano
½ tsp. basil
Salt & pepper
1 lb. Cheddar cheese, grated
4 cups tomato sauce, page 204
1 lb. cream cheese

Slice eggplants ¼-inch thick. Mix flour and salt together. Beat together eggs and milk. Sift together corn meal, oregano, basil, salt and pepper.

Dip slices first in flour mixture, then in egg-milk mixture and then in corn meal. Coat both sides.

Lightly grease 2 baking sheets and lay eggplant slices on them. Bake at 350 degrees F for 15 minutes, turn slices over and bake 15 minutes longer.

Place one-third of the eggplant in greased 9" x 13" baking pan. Sprinkle with one-third of the grated cheese and then add one-third of the tomato sauce. Repeat layers two more times. Top with sliced cream cheese. Bake at 350 degrees for 45 minutes.

Serves 6.

— *Donna Blair*
Victoria, B.C.

EGGPLANT PARMESAN

1 large eggplant
2 eggs
¼ cup milk
½ cup flour

¼ cup sesame seeds
1¼ cups grated Parmesan cheese
2-3 cups spaghetti sauce
2 cups grated mozzarella cheese

Slice eggplant into ¼-inch slices. Beat eggs with milk. Mix flour with sesame seeds and ¼ cup Parmesan cheese. Dip eggplant slices in egg mixture and then in flour mixture.

Heat oil in frying pan and fry slices until brown on both sides.

Arrange a layer of fried eggplant slices on the bottom of a greased casserole dish. Spoon some spaghetti sauce over these and then sprinkle with some of the Parmesan and mozzarella cheeses. Repeat layers twice.

Bake at 350 degrees F for 30 to 45 minutes.

Serves 6.

— *Mikell Billoki*
Gore Bay, Ontario

EGGPLANT CASSEROLE

2 medium-sized eggplants
4 strips bacon
1 onion
1 green pepper
2 cloves garlic

3 slices bread
1 cup milk
2 cups shrimp, minced clams or tuna
4 eggs, well beaten
Salt & pepper

Peel eggplants and boil until tender. Drain, mash and set aside. Fry bacon until crispy, remove from pan and crumble. Finely chop onion, pepper and garlic and fry in bacon fat until tender. Soak bread in milk then gently squeeze out excess.

Mix together eggplant, bacon, vegetables, shrimp and bread. Stir well. Add eggs and salt and pepper to taste.

Place in casserole dish and bake at 350 degrees F for 25 to 30 minutes.

Serves 6.

— *James R. Wilson*
Ludlow, N.B.

EGGPLANT ENTREE

1 large eggplant
2 Tbsp. olive oil
4 tomatoes
1 green pepper
½ lb. mushrooms
1 bunch shallots or ½ medium onion
½ tsp. salt

¼ tsp. pepper
¼ tsp. oregano
½ tsp. basil
¼ tsp. dry mustard
1 Tbsp. cider vinegar
1 Tbsp. honey

Slice eggplant and sauté in oil. Chop vegetables and add to eggplant with remaining ingredients. Simmer gently for 5 minutes.

Serves 4 to 6.

— *David Slabotsky*
Richmond, P.E.I.

FIDDLEHEAD HARMONY

2 cups fresh fiddleheads
1 lb. tofu
1-2 Tbsp. butter
3 large tomatoes, sliced

2 Tbsp. tamari sauce
Salt & pepper
5 wild leeks, chopped,
  or 1 Tbsp. garlic powder

Wash the fiddleheads and boil in water for 5 minutes. Change the water and boil another 3 to 4 minutes, until chewy-tender.

Cut the tofu into strips and sauté in butter until lightly browned on both sides. Add fiddleheads, sliced tomatoes, tamari sauce, seasonings and leeks or garlic powder. Heat thoroughly.

Serves 6.

— *Kay Chornook*
Burlington, Ontario

FIDDLEHEAD CASSEROLE

1-1½ cups steamed fiddleheads
7-oz. can tuna
½ cup mayonnaise, page 92
1 tsp. curry powder

2 cups cream of mushroom sauce,
  page 92
½ cup buttered bread crumbs

Combine fiddleheads and tuna in a casserole dish. Mix together mayonnaise, curry powder and mushroom sauce. Add to fiddlehead mixture and mix well. Top with bread crumbs.

Bake at 350 degrees F for 30 minutes.

Serves 4 to 6.

— *Jenny MacDonald*
Dartmouth, N.S.

GREENS CHINESE STYLE

THIS IS AN INTERESTING WAY TO PREPARE ALL KINDS OF GREEN, LEAFY vegetables, such as kale, Swiss chard or leaf lettuce.

Wash greens and pat dry. Plunge briefly into a pot of boiling water until wilted. Mix with a dressing of equal parts oil and tamari sauce.

Serve immediately.

— *Brigitte Wolf*
Lucknow, Ontario

MUSHROOM LOAF

3 Tbsp. butter
1 onion, finely chopped
1 lb. mushrooms, sliced
2 cups bread crumbs

1 egg, beaten
½ cup water or tomato juice
3 Tbsp. butter
Salt & pepper

Melt 3 Tbsp. butter in heavy pan, add onion and sliced mushrooms and cook for 10 minutes. Lift vegetables out with slotted spoon and add to bread crumbs. Mix well.

Add beaten egg, liquid, remaining butter and salt and pepper. Bake in a greased loaf pan at 375 degrees F for 25 to 30 minutes.

Serves 4.

— *Jacqueline Dysart*
Espanola, Ontario

STUFFED MUSHROOMS

12-20 large mushrooms
6-8 slices of bacon, fried & crumbled
Parsley
Salt & pepper
½ cup Cheddar cheese

1 egg
½ cup bread crumbs
¼ cup finely chopped green pepper
2 cloves garlic, finely chopped
1 onion, finely chopped

Remove mushroom stems and chop. Mix all ingredients except mushroom caps. Place a tablespoon of mixture in each mushroom cap. Bake at 425 degrees F for 30 minutes.

— Diane Adrian
Thunder Bay, Ontario

HERB STUFFED MUSHROOM CAPS

THIS DISH, EXCELLENT AS A VEGETABLE SIDE DISH OR AS AN APPETIZER, CAN BE assembled ahead of time, refrigerated and baked before serving.

24 very large fresh mushrooms (1½ lbs.)
½ cup butter
3 Tbsp. finely chopped green onion
1 cup fresh bread crumbs

½ cup chopped fresh parsley
⅛ tsp. powdered savory
⅛ tsp. pepper

Wipe mushrooms with a damp cloth. Remove stems and chop them finely. Melt ¼ cup butter in a large skillet and toss mushroom caps in this for 1 minute. Remove mushroom caps to a flat baking dish or a cookie sheet.

Melt remaining ¼ cup of butter in the same skillet. Sauté stems and onions briefly. Remove from heat and stir in bread crumbs, parsley, savory and pepper, tossing lightly. Spoon this mixture into caps.

Bake mushrooms at 350 degrees F for 10 minutes.

— Wendy Searcy
Minnedosa, Man.

MUSHROOM BAKE

½ lb. mushrooms
½ cup butter
1 lb. tomatoes
1 cup fresh bread crumbs

1 small onion, grated
¾ cup grated Cheddar cheese
Juice & rind of ½ lemon
Cheese sauce, page 92

Wash and slice mushrooms and fry in ¼ cup butter for 5 minutes. Slice tomatoes and set aside.

Blend together the bread crumbs, onion, cheese, remaining butter and lemon rind, and press half the mixture into a casserole dish.

Spread mushrooms on top of crumb layer and follow with sliced tomatoes. Season well and sprinkle with lemon juice. Press on remaining crumb mixture.

Bake at 375 degrees F for 30 minutes. Serve with cheese sauce.

Serves 2.

— Mrs. A.E. Nehua-Cafe
New South Wales, Australia

MUSHROOM PATTIES

4 eggs
2 cups chopped mushrooms
2-4 green onions, chopped
1½ cups grated Cheddar cheese
1 cup bread crumbs

½ tsp. salt
½ tsp. garlic powder
Pepper
¼ tsp. basil
¼ tsp. oregano

Beat eggs together. Add remaining ingredients and mix well. Shape into 6 patties and fry slowly in butter until crispy on both sides.

Makes 6 patties.

— *Carol Bomke*
Vancouver, B.C.

SCALLOPED ONIONS

A PLEASANT CHANGE FROM SIMPLE BAKED ONIONS, THIS CASSEROLE CAN BE quickly and easily assembled with ingredients which are usually on hand. The combination of cheese and onion provides a satisfying accompaniment to meat dishes.

6 medium onions
¼ cup butter
¼ cup flour

2 cups milk
½ tsp. salt
2 cups grated Cheddar cheese

Slice onions and separate into rings. Place in 1½-quart casserole dish.

Melt butter and blend in flour. Slowly stir in milk and cook, stirring, until thickened. Stir in salt and grated cheese. Pour over onions.

Bake, uncovered, at 375 degrees F for 1 hour.

Serves 6.

— *Wendy Fitzgerald*
Carp, Ontario

ORANGE GLAZED PARSNIPS

THIS GLAZE CAN QUICKLY TURN AN EVERYDAY VEGETABLE INTO AN ATTRACTIVE side dish.

3 lbs. parsnips
½ tsp. salt
¼ cup butter

½ cup orange marmalade
¼ tsp. ginger
1 large navel orange to garnish

Wash and peel parsnips and cut into 3-inch pieces. Cook in boiling salted water until tender.

Melt butter in skillet and stir in marmalade, ginger and ¼ cup water. Boil 5 minutes. Add parsnips and stir to glaze well. Place in serving dish. Spoon glaze over parsnips and garnish with orange slices.

Serves 6.

— *Brenda Eckstein*
Kamloops, B.C.

Salmon-Leek Quiche, page 12

Chunky Gazpacho Summer Soup, page 52

Shrimp and Avocado Salad, page 82

September Garden Zucchini, page 78

Manitoba Wild Rice Casserole, page 113

Coquilles St. Jacques, page 130

Sweet and Sour Orange Chicken, page 142

Rabbit Pâté Camille, page 159

MEDITERRANEAN POTATO PIE

2 small onions, chopped
3 large potatoes, peeled
1 cup flour
½ tsp. pepper
1 tsp. salt
¼ cup olive oil
3 Tbsp. butter
3 Tbsp. flour

3 large ripe tomatoes, chopped
½ green pepper, chopped
½ bay leaf
2 cloves
1 tsp. oregano
½ lb. mozzarella cheese, diced
¼ cup grated Parmesan cheese

Sauté chopped onion in a little oil. Boil the potatoes and mash until smooth. Blend in 1 cup flour, salt and pepper. Press mixture ½-inch thick in the bottom of a shallow baking dish. Spoon olive oil on top.

Melt butter in a skillet and stir in 3 Tbsp. flour. Add tomatoes, remaining onion, green pepper, bay leaf, cloves and oregano. Simmer for 20 minutes. Remove bay leaf and cloves.

Spoon sauce over potato mixture and top with cheeses.

Bake at 350 degrees F for 15 minutes.

Serves 4.

— Brenda Kennedy
Armstrong, B.C.

DUSTY POTATOES

¾ cup dry bread crumbs
1½ tsp. nutmeg
½ tsp. salt

¼ tsp. pepper
4 medium potatoes, pared & quartered
⅓ cup melted butter

Mix bread crumbs and seasonings. Dip potatoes in melted butter and then roll in crumb mixture. Place on greased baking sheet. Bake at 350 degrees F until crisp and brown — about 1 hour.

Serves 4.

— Pam Collacott
North Gower, Ontario

POTATO CASSEROLE

6 large potatoes,
  cooked until just tender
1½ cups cream of mushroom sauce,
  page 92
1 cup chopped onion
2 cups sour cream

½ cup butter
½ lb. old Cheddar cheese, grated
Salt & pepper
½ cup bread crumbs
4 Tbsp. Parmesan cheese

Pare and grate cooked potatoes. Combine with all remaining ingredients except bread crumbs and Parmesan cheese. Place in a 9" x 13" baking dish and top with bread crumb-Parmesan cheese mixture.

Bake at 375 degrees F for 1 hour.

Serves 12.

— Mrs. G. Fellows
Bayfield, Ontario

POTATO PUFF

THIS IS AN EASY AND DELICIOUS WAY TO USE UP LEFTOVER POTATOES.

3 cups mashed potatoes
2 Tbsp. butter
1 tsp. chopped parsley
¼ tsp. salt

Few grains cayenne
1 tsp. onion juice
3 eggs, separated

Mix potatoes with butter, parsley, salt, cayenne and onion juice. Beat egg yolks, add to potatoes and mix well. Beat egg whites until stiff and fold in. Place in greased baking dish and bake at 350 degrees F for 40 minutes or until golden brown.

— *Shirley Morrish*
Devlin, Ontario

TWICE-BAKED POTATOES

ALMOST ANY FILLING CAN BE MIXED WITH THE COOKED POTATOES. SOME suggestions are cooked bacon, ham, mushrooms, onions or other vegetables.

6 medium potatoes
½ tsp. salt
Pepper
4 Tbsp. butter

¼ cup sour cream
Shredded mozzarella cheese
Parsley

Wash potatoes and bake at 400 degrees F until done, about 1 hour. Remove from oven, split tops and scoop out insides. Place this in a bowl and mash, combining with all other ingredients except cheese and parsley.

When well blended, scoop mixture back into potato shells. Top with cheese, sprinkle with parsley. Put back into oven at 300 degrees. Serve when cheese has melted.

Serves 6.

— *Johanna Vanderheyden*
Strathroy, Ontario

SCALLOPED POTATOES

3 cups peeled & sliced potatoes
1 large onion, thinly sliced
1½ cups cream of mushroom sauce,
 page 92
4 Tbsp. flour

1½ tsp. salt
½ tsp. pepper
4 Tbsp. butter
3 cups milk

Place a layer of potatoes in a deep casserole dish and add a layer of sliced onion. Spread half the mushroom sauce over this, sprinkle with flour, salt and pepper and dot with butter. Repeat layers.

Pour milk around the potatoes until it reaches the top layer of potatoes.

Bake, covered, at 375 degrees F for 30 minutes. Uncover and bake another 30 to 45 minutes — until top is golden brown.

Serves 4.

— *Aurora Sugden*
Argenteuil, Quebec

DUM ARVI

THIS SPICY SWEET POTATO DISH OF INDIAN ORIGIN MAY BE EATEN AS A MEAL IN itself or as an accompanying vegetable to a meat meal.

1 lb. sweet potatoes
½ cup ghee (clarified butter)
1 small onion
½ tsp. ground ginger
1 tsp. coriander powder

½ tsp. garam masala (a mixed spice)
½ tsp. paprika
1 tsp. salt
2 green chilies, chopped

Peel sweet potatoes and chop into 1-inch cubes. Fry in ghee, remove and set aside.

Slice onion and fry in remaining ghee. Stir in ginger, coriander, garam masala, paprika, salt and green chilies.

Cover and bake at 375 degrees F for 30 to 45 minutes, until potatoes are tender.

— *Sheila Bear*
St. John's, Nfld.

SWEET POTATO CASHEW BAKE

½ cup brown sugar
⅓ cup broken cashews
¼ tsp. ground ginger
½ tsp. salt

2 lbs. sweet potatoes, cooked,
  peeled & sliced
8 peaches, peeled & halved
3 Tbsp. butter

Combine sugar, cashews, ginger and salt. In a shallow baking dish, layer half the potatoes, half the peaches and half the nut mixture. Repeat layers and dot with butter.

Bake, covered, at 350 degrees F for 30 minutes. Uncover and bake 10 minutes longer.

Serves 6 to 8.

— *Elizabeth Clayton*
Nepean, Ontario

SPAGHETTI SQUASH WITH TOMATO SAUCE

1 onion, finely chopped
1 clove garlic, minced
Butter or oil
1 lb. tomatoes, peeled
  seeded & chopped

Fresh parsley & basil
½ tsp. lemon juice
Salt & pepper
1 spaghetti squash

Sauté the onion and garlic in butter or oil. Add the chopped tomatoes and their juices, the herbs, lemon juice and salt and pepper. Simmer briefly.

Place the squash, whole, in a 325 degree F oven and bake 20 to 30 minutes, until tender. Pierce one end to test for tenderness. Cut the squash in half, gently remove the seeds, then lift out the flesh. Pile on a plate, toss with a bit of oil and pour the hot tomato sauce over it.

Serves 6.

— *Kathee Roy*
Toronto, Ontario

SPINACH PROVENÇALE

2 lbs. spinach
1 large onion, sliced
1 clove garlic, minced
Olive oil

Butter
2 eggs, beaten
1 cup grated Parmesan cheese
Salt & pepper

Wash and tear spinach. Sauté onion and garlic in olive oil until the onion is transparent. Add spinach, cover and cook until spinach is wilted – about 2 minutes. Remove from heat and cool slightly.

In a baking dish, combine spinach mixture, beaten eggs and half the cheese. Season, and sprinkle the remaining cheese on top. Dot with butter and bake at 375 degrees F for 10 to 15 minutes.

Serves 6 to 8.

— Jean Hally
Hartington, Ontario

SCALLOPED TOMATOES

3 cups canned tomatoes
¼ cup butter
3 cups bread crumbs

1 tsp. salt
⅛ tsp. pepper
Ground allspice

Heat tomatoes and butter in saucepan until butter melts. Mix in bread crumbs, salt and pepper.

Spoon into buttered 9-inch square baking dish and sprinkle ground allspice lightly over the top. Bake, uncovered, at 375 degrees F until the mixture is set and lightly browned.

Serves 4.

— Doris Cober
Collingwood, Ont.

TOMATOES PROVENÇALES

IN THE LATE SUMMER AND EARLY FALL, WHEN TOMATOES ARE RIPENING ALL TOO quickly, this dish is an appetizing complement to any meal.

4 large tomatoes
3 Tbsp. olive oil
½ tsp. salt
½ tsp. pepper
2 cloves garlic, crushed

1 Tbsp. chopped parsley
1 tsp. basil
½ tsp. oregano
2 Tbsp. coarse bread crumbs
2 Tbsp. Parmesan cheese

Halve tomatoes crosswise and remove seeds by pressing each half in your hand.

Heat the oil in a large frying pan. Place tomatoes in oil, cut side down, and cook over medium heat for 3 minutes. Turn, and sprinkle cut side with salt and pepper. Place crushed garlic in bottom of pan and cook another 2 minutes.

Place tomatoes on a cookie sheet and sprinkle with parsley and basil mixed together. Top with bread crumbs mixed with Parmesan cheese. Broil for 5 to 10 minutes – until tomatoes are golden brown on top but still firm.

Serves 4.

— Carolyn Hills
Sunderland, Ontario

SCALLOPED TURNIPS

4 cups cubed turnip
2 Tbsp. butter
2 Tbsp. flour
1 cup milk
½ tsp. salt

¼ tsp. pepper
Nutmeg
⅓ cup bread crumbs
2 Tbsp. melted butter

Cook turnip in salted water for 20 minutes. Mash.

Melt 2 Tbsp. butter, add flour and stir. Add milk slowly, stirring constantly. Stir in salt, pepper and nutmeg to taste. Cook until thick. Add turnip and spoon into buttered casserole dish.

Combine bread crumbs with melted butter and sprinkle on top of the turnip. Bake at 350 degrees F for 20 minutes.

— *Irene MacPhee*
Clarence Creek, Ont.

APPLE & TURNIP BAKE

2-3 turnips
2 apples, diced
6 Tbsp. butter
4 tsp. sugar
3 tsp. salt

¼ tsp. pepper
2 eggs
1¾ cups fine bread crumbs
2 Tbsp. melted butter

Peel and cut up turnip and cook in boiling salted water until tender. Drain and mash with electric mixer. Add apples, butter, sugar, salt, pepper, eggs and half the bread crumbs. Mix well.

Pour into greased 2-quart casserole dish and top with remaining bread crumbs that have been tossed in the melted butter. Cool, cover and refrigerate.

Remove from refrigerator 1 hour before dinner and heat at 350 degrees F for 30 minutes.

Serves 12.

— *William E. Nelson*
Dartmouth, N.S.

ZUCCHINI PARMESAN LOAF

¾ cup flour
2 tsp. salt
⅓ cup milk
2 lbs. zucchini, cut lengthwise
  into ¼-inch slices

Salad oil
1 cup tomato sauce, page 204
½ cup grated Parmesan cheese
1 cup grated mozzarella cheese

Combine flour and salt on a sheet of wax paper. Pour milk into pie plate. Dip the zucchini in milk, then coat with flour.

In a 12-inch skillet over medium-high heat, cook zucchini in oil, a few slices at a time, until golden. Drain on paper towels.

In a greased loaf pan arrange half the zucchini, spoon on half the tomato sauce and sprinkle with half the mozzarella and Parmesan cheeses. Repeat layers.

Bake at 350 degrees F for 40 minutes, until browned and bubbly.

Serves 4.

— *Margaret Orr*
Belwood, Ontario

SEPTEMBER GARDEN ZUCCHINI

THIS RECIPE CAN BE EASILY ADAPTED TO BARBECUE COOKING. WRAP LAYERED vegetables in a square of aluminum foil and cook on grill, turning three or four times.

4 Tbsp. oil
1 large onion, cut in rings
1 zucchini, sliced

1 stalk celery, sliced
1 green pepper, sliced
2 tomatoes, quartered

Heat oil in a heavy frying pan and sauté onion, zucchini, celery and green pepper. When onions are transparent, add tomatoes.

Cover and simmer until tomatoes are soft.

— *Donna Gordon*
Dorval, Quebec

ZUCCHINI BOATS

WHEN LARGE ZUCCHINI ARE IN ABUNDANCE, RECIPES SUCH AS THE FOLLOWING provide delightful meals. Almost any combination of vegetables and cheese, with or without meat, can be used in these "boats."

1 large zucchini (approx. 12")
1 green pepper, cut in small squares
½ cup dry bread crumbs

½ cup grated Cheddar cheese
Butter
Salt & pepper

Cut zucchini in half lengthwise and then crosswise. Remove centre, except for a piece at each end, to form a boat. Fill with green pepper. Dot with butter, add salt and pepper to taste. Sprinkle bread crumbs on top and cover with grated cheese.

Bake in covered baking dish at 350 degrees F for 20 minutes, then remove lid and bake 10 to 15 minutes longer.

— *Eleanor Bell*
Cayuga, Ontario

ZUCCHINI MEDLEY

2 small zucchini
2 slices eggplant, peeled
2 cooking onions

½ sweet red pepper
4 Tbsp. butter
Salt & pepper

Cut zucchini into ¼-inch slices, eggplant into ½-inch squares, onions into rings and pepper into 1-inch strips. Stir-fry in melted butter and season with salt and pepper.

— *Eleanor Bell*
Cayuga, Ontario

ZUCCHINI SUPREME

Small zucchini
Parmesan cheese

Butter

Wash zucchini and slice in half lengthwise. Spread with butter and sprinkle on cheese. Place on cookie sheet on bottom rack of oven. Broil for 10 minutes or until bubbly and brown on top and crisp inside.

— *Beth Hopkins*
Courtenay, B.C.

VEGETABLE PIE

Pastry for double 9-inch pie crust
½ cup each of 5 or 6 different cooked
   vegetables (mushrooms, corn, beans,
   celery, carrots, zucchini, peas, broccoli,
   cauliflower, etc.)
½ cup diced onion

1 clove garlic, minced
1 Tbsp. butter
5 tsp. flour
1 cup milk
¼ cup grated Cheddar cheese
Salt & pepper

Line pie plate with pastry.

Sauté onion and garlic in butter until garlic is browned. Add flour. Stir in milk. Cook and stir until thickened. Add cheese, salt and pepper and cook gently until cheese is melted.

Mix together vegetables and place in pastry shell. Pour cheese sauce over vegetables and top with remaining pastry.

Bake at 375 degrees F for 30 minutes.

Serves 4.

— Andra Hughes
Apsley, Ontario

TEMPURA

Batter:

1 cup brown rice flour
1 Tbsp. cornstarch
Salt

1 egg, beaten
½ cup cold water

Vegetables:

Use almost any vegetable that will cook quickly. When using long-cooking vegetables such as carrots, lightly steam first.

Dipping Sauce:

1 cup chicken stock
½ cup tamari sauce

⅓ cup honey
2 Tbsp. sherry

Mix flour with cornstarch, salt, egg and cold water to make a thin batter. Chill 15 minutes.

To prepare vegetables, wash and dry thoroughly. Cut into small pieces and chill well. Dredge in flour before dipping into batter.

For sauce, combine all ingredients and mix well.

To cook, heat several inches of oil in a wok. Dip each vegetable piece in batter, shake and fry briefly until golden, turning often. Drain and serve immediately with sauce.

— Bryanna Clark
Union Bay, B.C.

BAKED VEGETABLE LOAF

1½ cups diced raw potatoes
2 cups diced raw carrots
½ cup beef stock
¼ cup finely chopped green pepper
¼ cup finely chopped onion
1 cup wheat germ, toasted

¼ cup melted butter
2 eggs, beaten
1 tsp. salt
¼ tsp. pepper
½ tsp. savory
Cream of mushroom sauce, page 92

Cook potatoes and carrots in a small amount of boiling water until barely tender. Drain.

Combine all ingredients except mushroom sauce and spoon into greased loaf pan. Bake at 350 degrees F for 1 hour or until set. Slice thickly and serve with mushroom sauce.

Serves 4.

— Gerri Bazuin
Morin Heights, Quebec

ALMOND VEGETABLES MANDARIN

1 cup thinly sliced carrots
1 cup green beans, cut in 1-inch slices
2 Tbsp. salad oil
1 cup thinly sliced cauliflower
½ cup sliced green onion

1 cup chicken stock
2 tsp. cornstarch
Pinch garlic powder
½ cup unblanched whole almonds

Stir carrots and beans in oil over medium heat for 2 minutes. Add cauliflower and onion, and cook 1 minute longer. Add chicken stock, cornstarch and garlic. Cook and stir until thickened and vegetables are crispy tender. Add almonds.

Serves 4 to 6.

— *Katherine Dunster*
Golden, B.C.

MINESTRA

A RICE-VEGETABLE STEW, MINESTRA GETS ITS NAME FROM THE ITALIAN *minestrare*, meaning "to serve."

1 large onion, chopped
1-2 Tbsp. butter
1½ cups raw rice
2 carrots, coarsely grated
½ cup sliced mushrooms
½ head cabbage, shredded

Salt & pepper
Marjoram
3 cups chicken stock
Chopped parsley to garnish
Parmesan cheese to garnish

In a large, heavy casserole dish, cook the onion in butter until soft. Add rice and carrots, stirring until rice begins to turn yellow. Add mushrooms, cabbage and seasonings. Cook and stir for 1 minute. Add stock. When it boils, reduce heat, cover, and simmer for 20 to 30 minutes.

When rice is cooked and liquid absorbed, remove from heat. Sprinkle with parsley and cheese.

Serves 4 to 6.

— *Winifred Czerny*
Pointe Claire, Quebec

RATATOUILLE

FOR A SATISFYING MEAL WITH ITALIAN OVERTONES, THIS SUCCULENT VEGETABLE stew can make a complete meal when served with black olives and warm fresh bread.

½ cup salad oil
2 large onions, thinly sliced
2-3 cloves garlic, minced
1 eggplant, peeled & diced
4 tomatoes, peeled & diced
1 zucchini, peeled & diced

2 green peppers, cleaned & diced
3 stalks celery, diced
2 tsp. fresh basil
1 tsp. oregano
Salt & pepper

Heat oil in heavy saucepan and brown onion and garlic. Add eggplant and tomatoes and cook for a few minutes.

Add remaining ingredients, bring to a boil and lower heat. Simmer for at least 1 hour.

Serves 4 to 6.

— *Mrs. E. Imboden*
Uxbridge, Ontario

VEGETABLE MORSELS

AN EXCELLENT FILLING FOR PITA, THESE VEGETABLE BALLS TASTE DELICIOUS WITH yogurt and marinated tomatoes, cucumbers and onions.

3 eggs
2 tsp. seasoned salt
1 tsp. ground cumin
¼ tsp. pepper
3 Tbsp. sesame seeds
3 Tbsp. flour

3 Tbsp. wheat germ
2 carrots, shredded
1½ cups cooked, drained
 & chopped spinach
1½ cups chopped green beans

Combine all ingredients in order listed. Drop by spoonfuls onto greased cookie sheets and bake at 450 degrees F for 10 minutes.

Serves 6 to 8.

— *Bryanna Clark*
Union Bay, B.C.

VEGETABLE STEW

THE SPECIAL APPEAL OF THIS DISH IS THAT IT DOES NOT USE SALT BUT RATHER relies upon the subtle flavours of each vegetable for seasoning.

¼ cup butter
4 carrots, cut into ¼-inch slices
1 large turnip, cut into strips
1 celeriac root, cut into strips
4 potatoes, cubed
2 green peppers, cut into rings
4-6 tomatoes, chopped

6 small whole onions
4 tsp. chopped parsley
½ tsp. thyme
3 soya cubes mixed in 3 cups water or
 3 cups chicken stock
¼ cup arrowroot
½ cup water

Melt butter in stewing pot. Add carrots and turnip, cover and cook for 10 to 15 minutes.

Add celeriac, potatoes, peppers, tomatoes, onions, seasonings and broth. Simmer for 1 hour.

Mix arrowroot with water and add to stew when vegetables are tender. Simmer for 10 more minutes.

Serves 4.

— *Christine Taylor*
Norbertville, Quebec

VEGETARIAN EGG ROLLS

1 cup bean sprouts
1½ cups shredded cabbage
1 medium broccoli stalk, chopped
2 onions, chopped
2 stalks celery, thinly sliced
1 carrot, grated
2 Tbsp. oil

¾ cup cashews, chopped
½ cup tofu, mashed
1½ cups grated Cheddar cheese
Salt
Garlic powder
1 pkg. egg roll wrappers

Stir-fry vegetables in oil. Add nuts, tofu, cheese and salt and garlic powder to taste.

Fill egg roll wrappers with approximately ¼ cup of filling each, and wrap, following package directions.

Deep fry for approximately 3 minutes on each side or until lightly browned.

Serves 6.

— *Kristine Reid*
Floyd, Virginia

SHRIMP & AVOCADO SALAD

1 avocado, peeled & chopped
½ cup shrimp, cleaned & cooked
½ English cucumber, cubed
½ head Boston lettuce, broken
1 cup alfalfa sprouts

¼ cup mayonnaise, page 92
¼ cup sour cream
1-2 Tbsp. lemon juice
Salt & pepper

Combine avocado, shrimp, cucumber, lettuce and sprouts and toss. Mix remaining ingredients. Pour over salad and toss gently.

Serves 2.

— *Jane Pugh*
Toronto, Ontario

MARINATED ONION RINGS

4 medium onions
1 cup vinegar
1 cup water
½ cup sugar

½ tsp. salt
Pepper
1 cup sour cream
Poppy seeds

Slice and separate onions. Cover with boiling water and drain immediately.

Combine vinegar, water, sugar, salt and pepper in saucepan. Bring to a boil. Pour over onions and marinate, refrigerated, for 1 hour. Drain.

Add sour cream and poppy seeds. Toss gently.

Serves 4.

— *Mary Reid*
Georgeville, Quebec

TOSSED VEGETABLE SALAD

1 lb. broccoli, cauliflower,
  Brussels sprouts or combination
¼ lb. mushrooms
½ cup olive oil
¼ cup wine vinegar
1 clove garlic, minced
½ large red onion, chopped

1 tsp. dry parsley
½ tsp. salt
¼ tsp. basil
¼ tsp. pepper
6 slices bacon, cooked until crisp
1 cup croutons

Cut broccoli into bite-sized pieces and steam until cooked but still crunchy. Drain and cool. Slice mushrooms. Mix together oil, vinegar, garlic, onion and herbs. Marinate all together in refrigerator for at least 4 hours. Toss with croutons and crumbled bacon just before serving.

Serves 6.

— *Elizabeth Templeman*
Heffley Creek, B.C.

CELERY SALAD

¼ cup olive oil
Juice of ½ large lemon
1 tsp. dried mustard

Salt
1 bunch celery, washed & sliced

Combine olive oil, lemon juice, mustard and salt. Mix well. Pour over celery, toss and marinate for at least 24 hours.

Serves 6 to 8.

— *Dawn Hermann*
Faro, Yukon

SWEET PEPPER SALAD

THE RED AND GREEN OF THIS SALAD MAKE IT A COLOURFUL ADDITION TO CHRISTMAS dinner.

2 large red peppers, sliced
2 large green peppers, sliced
½ lb. mushrooms, sliced
3 green onions, chopped
½ tsp. salt

½ tsp. pepper
¾ cup olive oil
3 Tbsp. vinegar
½ tsp. dry mustard
1-2 cloves garlic

Place all vegetables in a large bowl. Combine remaining ingredients and whirl in a blender. Pour over vegetables. Refrigerate for at least 3 hours before serving.

Serves 6 to 8.

— Pam Collacott
North Gower, Ontario

BROCCOLI SALAD

1 head broccoli, broken into
  bite-sized pieces
1 onion, quartered & separated

6-8 slices bacon
⅓ cup vinegar
⅓ cup brown sugar

Fry bacon until crisp. Remove from pan and crumble into serving bowl with broccoli. Sauté onion in bacon fat and add to broccoli.

Add vinegar and brown sugar to remaining bacon fat and simmer for a few minutes.

Pour over the broccoli, toss and serve.

Serves 4.

— Margaret Robinson
Victoria, B.C.

MARINATED CUCUMBER SALAD

2 medium cucumbers,
  pared & thinly sliced
1 medium onion, thinly sliced
1 tsp. salt
3 Tbsp. vinegar

3 Tbsp. water
½ tsp. sugar
¼ tsp. paprika
¼ tsp. pepper
1-2 cloves garlic, crushed

Combine cucumbers and onion in a bowl and sprinkle with salt. Mix lightly and set aside for 1 hour.

Meanwhile, combine remaining ingredients. Drain cucumbers, pour dressing over them and toss until well mixed.

Chill for 1 to 2 hours, stirring occasionally. Discard garlic before serving and sprinkle with additional paprika.

Serves 6.

— Valerie Gillis
Gloucester, Ontario

CARROT SALAD

1 lb. carrots, sliced
½ Spanish onion, quartered & separated
½ green pepper, cut into rings
1 cup finely cut celery
¾ cup tomato sauce, page 204
¼ cup vinegar
½ cup granulated sugar
½ tsp. prepared mustard
½ tsp. dry mustard
½ tsp. salt
½ tsp. pepper
½ Tbsp. Worcestershire sauce
¼ cup salad oil

Boil carrots until tender, drain and cool. Add onion, green pepper and celery.

Combine tomato sauce, vinegar, sugar, mustards, salt, pepper and Worcestershire sauce in a blender. When well blended, slowly pour in oil and blend well.

Toss salad with dressing and refrigerate for at least 24 hours.

Serves 6.

— V.A. Charles
Calgary, Alberta

EGGPLANT SALAD

THIS TRADITIONAL JEWISH DISH IS A PLEASANT AND UNUSUAL WAY TO SERVE eggplant.

1 large eggplant
1 green pepper, diced
1 large onion, diced
2 tomatoes, chopped
2 Tbsp. oil
¼ cup vinegar
Salt

Bake eggplant at 375 degrees F until tender. Peel and chop in a bowl. Add remaining ingredients and mix well. Chill and serve.

— Arlene Pervin
Moyie, B.C.

ORANGE BEAN SALAD

THIS PUNGENT SALAD SERVES AS AN EXCELLENT ACCOMPANIMENT TO PORK OR LAMB.

¾ lb. fresh green beans, cut in half
½ cup honey
¼ cup cider vinegar
½ cup oil
½ cup water or chicken stock
Dash coriander
¼ cup fresh chopped parsley
2 cups cooked red kidney beans
½ cup red onion, chopped
3 oranges, peeled & sectioned

Cook green beans in boiling water for 4 minutes.

Mix together honey, vinegar, oil, water or stock, coriander and parsley.

Drain beans. Combine with kidney beans, chopped onion and orange sections in large bowl. Pour ⅓ cup dressing over all ingredients and mix well. The rest of the dressing will keep in the refrigerator.

Serves 6 to 8.

— Ingrid Birker
Toronto, Ontario

THREE BEAN SALAD

½ cup vinegar
¼ cup oil
1 tsp. salt
Dash pepper
Dash garlic powder
2 Tbsp. sugar
2 cups green beans,
  cooked, drained & chopped

2 cups wax beans,
  cooked, drained & chopped
2 cups red kidney beans,
  cooked & drained
¼ cup chopped green onions

Mix together vinegar, oil, salt, pepper, garlic powder and sugar. Add beans and onions. Toss well.

Cover and refrigerate for 3 hours or overnight, tossing occasionally.

— Wanda Gaitan
L'Annonciation, Quebec

POTATO SALAD

3-4 hard-boiled eggs
5 cooked potatoes
2-3 Tbsp. water
1 Tbsp. tarragon vinegar

1 onion, diced
1 tsp. celery seeds
1 tsp. salt
Mayonnaise, page 92

Peel and dice eggs and potatoes. Set aside.

Combine 2 to 3 Tbsp. water, vinegar, onion, celery seeds and salt in saucepan. Cook until onion is tender – about 5 minutes.

Pour over the potatoes and eggs, add mayonnaise to taste and toss gently.

Serves 4.

— Nancy McAskill
Burnaby, B.C.

CURRIED POTATO SALAD

2 Tbsp. butter
2 Tbsp. flour
2 tsp. curry powder
1 cup chicken stock
½ cup sour cream
½ cup mayonnaise, page 92
½ tsp. salt

½ cup sliced green onion
½ cup diced celery
½ cup sliced green olives
2 Tbsp. chopped parsley
2 Tbsp. chopped green pepper
4 cups diced cooked potatoes

Melt butter, stir in flour and curry powder. Add chicken stock and cook until thick and smooth. Stir in sour cream, mayonnaise and salt. Add remaining ingredients and combine gently.

Place in a greased baking dish and sprinkle with paprika. Bake at 375 degrees F until hot – 20 to 30 minutes. Serve hot.

Serves 6 to 8.

— Dorothy Hurst
Nanaimo, B.C.

DANDELION SALAD

2 slices bacon
½ cup unopened dandelion flower buds
2 cups young dandelion leaves
2 Tbsp. oil

1 Tbsp. vinegar
Salt & pepper
1 tsp. tarragon

Cook bacon until crisp. Remove from pan and drain.

Wash dandelion flowers and leaves and pat dry with paper towels. Cook flowers in bacon fat until the buds burst open. Drain. Crumble bacon into salad bowl. Add leaves and flowers.

Combine oil, vinegar and seasonings, pour over salad and toss.

Serves 4.

— *Shirley Morrish*
Devlin, Ontario

GREEK SALAD

LESS EXPENSIVE THAN RESTAURANT VERSIONS, THIS DELICIOUS SALAD MAY BE served as a meal with warm garlic bread, or as a side dish.

1 head romaine lettuce, shredded
½ Spanish onion, thinly sliced &
    separated into rings
1 green pepper, cut in ½-inch squares
4 tomatoes, cut in wedges
½ cucumber, cut into 4 lengthwise,
    then sliced

12 or more ripe black olives
½ lb. feta cheese, crumbled
2 cloves garlic, peeled & crushed
½ cup olive oil
1 Tbsp. wine vinegar
¼ tsp. salt
Dash black pepper

Place salad ingredients in large salad bowl. When ready to serve, place oil in a small container that has a lid. Drop crushed garlic clove into the oil, add vinegar, salt and pepper, cover and shake vigorously.

Pour over salad and serve immediately.

— *Don & Foley Boyd*
Likely, B.C.

CAESAR SALAD

1 head romaine lettuce
3 large cloves garlic
2 anchovy fillets
1 tsp. dry mustard
Juice of 1 lemon

1 egg yolk
2 Tbsp. blue cheese
Salt & pepper
¾ cup olive oil
4 Tbsp. Parmesan cheese

Wash, dry and tear up romaine lettuce. Set aside.

Crush garlic in a large wooden bowl, add anchovies, mustard, lemon juice, egg yolk and blue cheese. Stir, continuing to flatten cheese and anchovies against the bowl until a thick paste is formed. Add salt, pepper and olive oil, beating fast to make a thick and creamy dressing.

Toss in lettuce pieces and mix thoroughly. Sprinkle with Parmesan cheese.

Serves 4 to 6.

— *Julienne Tardif*
Toronto, Ontario

WILTED LETTUCE SALAD

2-3 strips bacon
2 Tbsp. vinegar
2 Tbsp. water

2 Tbsp. sugar
1 head lettuce

Cook bacon until crisp, remove from pan, drain and crumble. Reserve 2 Tbsp. fat.

To bacon fat, add vinegar, water and sugar. Bring to a boil.

Wash and tear lettuce, arrange on 4 plates and pour dressing over it. Toss and serve at once.

Serves 4.

— Mrs. Neil McAskill
Burnaby, B.C.

RUSSIAN SALAD

1 lb. pickled beets, diced
1 lb. fresh shelled peas
1 lb. mushrooms, diced
2 fillets of herring or anchovy, chopped

3 large potatoes, cooked & diced
2 hard-boiled eggs, diced
1 dill pickle, finely chopped
Mayonnaise

Mix all ingredients well, then stir in enough mayonnaise to coat. Chill well.

Serves 12.

— Chris Dickman
Holstein, Ontario

APRIL SALAD

1 cup dry chick peas
3 cups water
1 Tbsp. garlic powder
1½ tsp. celery seed

3-4 cups alfalfa sprouts
1-2 cups fenugreek sprouts
½ lb. feta cheese

Soak chick peas in 3 cups water for at least 4 hours. Add garlic powder, celery seed and more water, if necessary. Bring to a boil and simmer until chick peas are chewy-tender — about 1½ hours. Drain and cool.

Make a bed of alfalfa and fenugreek sprouts and crumble feta cheese over them. Top with chick peas.

Serves 8 to 10.

— Susan Ellenton
Whitehorse, Yukon

SPRING SALAD

2 cups watercress
2 cups dandelion leaves
3 wild leeks, chopped
¼ cup sunflower seeds
2-3 fresh basil leaves

¼ cup salad oil
¼ cup cider vinegar
1 Tbsp. lemon juice
2 tsp. sugar
½ tsp. Worcestershire sauce

Combine cleaned watercress and dandelion leaves. Add leeks, sunflower seeds and basil and toss.

Combine remaining ingredients, pour over salad and toss well.

Serves 6 to 8.

— Nora Jones
Toronto, Ontario

CHICK PEA SALAD

TASTY AND COLOURFUL, THIS IS A GOOD WINTER SALAD WHEN FRESH PRODUCE IS scarce.

16-oz. can chick peas
  or 2 cups home-cooked beans
½ cup sesame seeds
1 medium onion, finely chopped
2 carrots, finely chopped
¼ cup vegetable oil
¼ cup cider vinegar

1 Tbsp. brown sugar
½-1 tsp. salt
Ground pepper
¼ cup fresh chopped chives
  or green onions
1 large tomato

Drain chick peas. Mix together all ingredients except chives and tomato. Cover the bowl and chill for at least 2 hours. Just before serving chop the tomato into small pieces and mix in, along with the chives.

— Wendy Searcy
Minnedosa, Man.

HERBED CHERRY TOMATOES

12-15 cherry tomatoes
4 Tbsp. sunflower seed oil
2 tsp. vinegar
1 tsp. sugar
1 tsp. oregano leaves
  (about ½ tsp. powder)

1 tsp. salt
½ tsp. pepper
¼ tsp. sweet basil

Slice tomatoes in half and put in a serving bowl. Combine remaining ingredients and pour over the tomatoes.

Cover and refrigerate for at least 2 hours before serving.

Serves 6.

— Nicole Chartrand
Aylmer, Quebec

TOMATO CUCUMBER TOSS

THIS IS AN IDEAL SALAD FOR LATE SUMMER, WHEN GARDENS ABOUND WITH tomatoes and cucumbers.

3 ripe tomatoes
3 small cucumbers
¼ cup oil

¼ cup cider vinegar
Salt & pepper

Chop tomatoes and unpeeled cucumbers into chunks. Place in a shallow bowl and toss with the oil, vinegar and seasonings.

— Mikell Billoki
Gore Bay, Ontario

COLESLAW

1 large head cabbage
4 carrots
2-4 green onions, chopped
½ cup vinegar

⅔ cup oil
2 Tbsp. salt
3 Tbsp. sugar

Shred cabbage and carrots into a large bowl. Add green onion.

Place remaining ingredients in a saucepan and bring to a boil. Let cool and pour over cabbage and carrots. Toss gently.

Refrigerate for at least 24 hours, stirring occasionally.

— Helen Owen
The Pas, Manitoba

CABBAGE SALAD

WHEN FRESH GREENS ARE SCARCE, THIS TANGY CABBAGE SALAD WILL BRIGHTEN up winter meals. It can also be made with red cabbage for more colour.

1 large cabbage
1 green pepper
1 small onion
3-4 stalks celery
¾ cup white sugar

1 cup white vinegar
¾ cup cooking oil
½ tsp. celery seed
1 tsp. curry powder
1 Tbsp. salt

Shred cabbage and dice remaining vegetables. Combine. Mix remaining ingredients together and boil for 2 minutes. Pour over vegetables. Chill well.

— Rose MacLeod
Kemble, Ontario

ONION & MUSHROOM SALAD

½ cup olive oil
½ cup white wine
⅓ cup white wine vinegar
2 tsp. salt
2 tsp. thyme
1 tsp. pepper

1 small bay leaf
1 clove garlic, minced
1½ lbs. small pickling onions
1½ lbs. small mushrooms
1 head romaine lettuce
¼ cup chopped fresh parsley

In a large saucepan, combine oil, wine, vinegar, salt, thyme, pepper, bay leaf, garlic and onions. Simmer for 10 minutes, add mushrooms and continue simmering, covered, for 5 minutes or until onions are tender.

Refrigerate for at least 12 hours, drain and serve on a bed of lettuce garnished with parsley.

Serves 10.

— Jennifer McGuire
Calgary, Alberta

SPINACH, MUSHROOM & BACON SALAD

10 oz. fresh spinach, washed
1 tomato, cut into wedges
1 small red onion, thinly sliced
 & separated into rings
½ cup sliced mushrooms

⅓ cup chopped cooked bacon
⅓ cup olive oil
2 Tbsp. wine vinegar
¼ tsp. oregano
¼ tsp. pepper

Tear spinach into bite-sized pieces. Place spinach, tomato, onion rings, mushrooms and bacon in salad bowl. Toss gently.

Combine oil, vinegar, oregano and pepper in a jar. Cover and shake well. Pour over salad and toss.

Serves 10.

— Jane Cuthbert
Prescott, Ontario

SPINACH-SPROUT SALAD

1 pkg. fresh spinach, washed
2 cups bean sprouts
¼ cup olive oil
2 oz. slivered almonds
2 Tbsp. malt vinegar

2 Tbsp. soya sauce
¼ tsp. ginger
1 Tbsp. brown sugar
Paprika
Salt

Tear spinach into bite-sized pieces and toss with bean sprouts.

Brown almonds in olive oil and combine them, undrained, with remaining ingredients. Pour over salad and toss.

Serves 8 to 10.

— *Marilyn Fuller*
Stroud, Ontario

BEAN SPROUT SALAD

2 cups bean sprouts
1 clove garlic, crushed
¼ cup oil
2 Tbsp. vinegar

2 Tbsp. soya sauce
2 Tbsp. sesame seeds
Salt & pepper

Mix together all ingredients except sprouts. Pour over sprouts and toss gently.

Serves 4.

— *Dawn Hermann*
Faro, Yukon

RICE & SPROUT SALAD

USING HOME-GROWN SPROUTS, THIS CRUNCHY SALAD SATISFIES A WINTER LONGING for crispy salad greens.

2 cups cooked brown rice
2 cups bean sprouts (lentil or mung)
3 stalks celery, chopped
1 cup peas, briefly steamed
⅓ cup oil

⅓ cup vinegar
1 Tbsp. honey
½ tsp. salt
Dash pepper

Mix together rice, sprouts, celery and peas. Blend together oil, vinegar, honey, salt and pepper and add to salad. Toss well and chill before serving.

— *Mikell Billoki*
Gore Bay, Ontario

MARINATED MUSHROOMS

THIS IS AN ADDICTIVE APPETIZER, PERFECT FOR SCOOPING ON CRACKERS. THE LEMON gives it an unusual tangy flavour.

½ cup onions, very thinly sliced
Zest of 1 lemon, cut in
   julienne matchsticks
3 Tbsp. olive oil
⅛ tsp. mustard seed
⅛ tsp. cardamom
¼ tsp. thyme

¼ tsp. pepper
¼ tsp. salt
¼ tsp. coriander seeds
¾ cup water
2 Tbsp. lemon juice
1 Tbsp. minced parsley
½ lb. (3 cups) fresh mushrooms, quartered

Sauté onions and lemon zest in olive oil until translucent. Add remaining ingredients except mushrooms. Simmer for 5 minutes. Add mushrooms, toss to blend, cover and boil for 3 minutes. Strain mushroom mixture and boil down strained liquid until syrupy. Add to mushrooms, then refrigerate before serving.

— *Merilyn Mohr*
Astorville, Ontario

MUSHROOM PATE

2 lbs. unsalted butter
2½ lbs. mushrooms, sliced
1 lb. chicken livers
1½ Tbsp. salt
1½ Tbsp. pepper
1½ Tbsp. curry powder

In a skillet, sauté mushrooms and half the salt, pepper and curry powder in ½ lb. butter until mushrooms are limp.

In another skillet, sauté chicken livers and the remaining seasonings in ½ lb. butter until livers are thoroughly cooked.

Mix together livers and mushrooms and chop coarsely. Cream remaining 1 lb. butter and place in blender with chopped mixture and blend until smooth.

Place in 2 medium-sized moulds. Refrigerate for at least 12 hours.

To serve, unmould and leave at room temperature for 30 minutes.

— Liz Eder & Paul Jett
Baltimore, Maryland

FRUIT SALAD WITH VERMOUTH

SOME SUITABLE FRESH FRUIT COMBINATIONS FOR THIS SALAD ARE APPLES AND pears, peaches and melon or oranges, grapefruit and grapes. Toasted sesame or sunflower seeds can also make a tasty addition.

½ cup raisins
½ cup grated coconut
½ cup vermouth
Fruit, whatever is in season

Soak raisins and coconut in vermouth overnight. Slice up fruit, add to raisin mixture and toss. Refrigerate until time to serve.

— Kathe Lieber
Montreal, Quebec

TUTTI FRUITY SALAD

1 small head romaine lettuce
3-4 red onions, thinly sliced
2 ribs celery, sliced
2 navel oranges
1 tsp. celery seed
1 tsp. salt
1 tsp. dry mustard
1 tsp. paprika
⅓ cup lemon juice
½ cup sugar
¾ cup salad oil

Wash, dry and tear up lettuce. Add onion slices, separated into rings, celery and oranges, peeled, sliced crosswise into three and then segmented.

Combine celery seed, salt, dry mustard, paprika, lemon juice and sugar. Slowly add oil, beating with a whisk, until it thickens.

Pour ½ cup dressing over salad and toss. Remaining dressing will keep for several weeks if refrigerated.

Serves 6.

— Dorothy Malone
Nepean, Ontario

BASIC WHITE SAUCE

1 cup milk or light cream
Salt & pepper

2 Tbsp. butter
2 Tbsp. flour

Melt butter and stir in flour. Cook over low heat for 3 or 4 minutes, stirring constantly. Slowly stir in milk or cream and salt and pepper. Cook, stirring, until sauce has thickened.

Makes 1 cup.

CHEESE SAUCE

1 cup basic white sauce, above
½ cup grated Cheddar or Swiss cheese

1 tsp. lemon juice
Nutmeg

Warm the white sauce and gradually stir in grated cheese. Cheddar will give a tangy flavour while Swiss gives a milder, thicker sauce. Add lemon juice and nutmeg. Cook and stir until cheese is completely melted.

Makes 1¼ cups.

CREAM OF MUSHROOM SAUCE

1 cup basic white sauce, above
½ cup chopped mushrooms
2 Tbsp. butter

2 tsp. tamari sauce
½ tsp. thyme

Warm white sauce. Cook mushrooms in butter for 2 minutes. Add to white sauce with tamari sauce and thyme. Stir well and heat through.

Makes 1¼ cups.

BASIC MAYONNAISE

1 egg
1 tsp. salt
½ tsp. dry mustard

2 cloves garlic, peeled
2 Tbsp. vinegar
1 cup vegetable oil

Combine egg, salt, mustard, garlic, vinegar and ¼ cup oil in blender. Cover and whirl until ingredients are blended.

Remove lid and slowly pour in remaining oil, in a steady stream, until mixture has thickened. Keep refrigerated.

Makes 1¼ cups.

Herb Mayonnaise
To basic mayonnaise add:
2 Tbsp. chopped parsley
1 Tbsp. minced chives

¼ tsp. dried tarragon
1 tsp. chopped dill

Curry Mayonnaise
To basic mayonnaise add:
1 tsp. curry powder

½ clove garlic, chopped
1 tsp. lemon juice

Thousand Island Dressing
To basic mayonnaise add:
3 Tbsp. chili sauce
1 Tbsp. grated onion

2 Tbsp. finely chopped green pepper
2 Tbsp. chopped chives
⅓ hard-boiled egg, finely chopped

— Mrs. E. Louden
Port Coquitlam, B.C.

BOUQUET GARNI

1 clove garlic
1 Tbsp. dried parsley
1 tsp. dried basil
1 tsp. dried rosemary

1 tsp. oregano
2 bay leaves
6 whole peppercorns

Mix together and tie in 3 thicknesses of cheesecloth.

Makes 1 bag.

— Shirley Hill
Picton, Ontario

FRENCH DRESSING

12 Tbsp. olive oil
4 Tbsp. lemon juice
Salt & pepper

2 cloves garlic, peeled
½ tsp. dry mustard

Combine 2 Tbsp. of oil, 2 Tbsp. of lemon juice, salt, pepper and mustard and beat well with a whisk. When smooth, add 4 Tbsp. oil and beat well again. Add remaining lemon juice and oil.

Place in a jar, add garlic, cover and refrigerate.

Makes 1 cup.

OLGA'S SALAD DRESSING

½ cup oil
⅓ cup cider vinegar
2 Tbsp. honey

1 Tbsp. onion, grated
Salt & pepper
½ tsp. mustard

Combine all ingredients in a jar and shake until well blended. Let sit overnight at room temperature for best flavour.

OIL & VINEGAR DRESSING

⅔ cup oil
½ cup red wine vinegar
½ tsp. sugar
1 tsp. salt

¼ tsp. pepper
½ tsp. basil
½ tsp. tarragon
2 Tbsp. Parmesan cheese

Combine all ingredients, shake well and chill. This dressing is particularly tasty with a buttercrunch lettuce and mushroom salad.

— Beth Hopkins
Courtenay, B.C.

AFRICAN LEMON DRESSING

Grated peel of 2 lemons
¼ cup lemon juice
1½ tsp. salt
⅛ tsp. red pepper or Tabasco sauce
2 cloves garlic, chopped
⅔ - ¾ cup olive oil

½ tsp. ground coriander
½ tsp. ground cumin
½ tsp. dry mustard
½ tsp. honey
½ tsp. paprika

Combine all ingredients in a jar, shake well and refrigerate for several hours.

— Carol Gasken
Winlaw, B.C.

JAVANESE SALAD DRESSING

THIS DRESSING HAS AN UNUSUAL COMBINATION OF FLAVOURS — PEANUT AND VERY sharp lemon.

¾ cup lemon juice
½ cup crushed peanuts or
  3 Tbsp. peanut butter
1 tsp. salt

1 tsp. sugar
1 tsp. dill
¼ tsp. crushed red pepper

Combine all ingredients and mix well. Refrigerate until ready to use.

Makes 1 cup.

— *Susan Bates Eddy*
St. Andrews, N.B.

SESAME DRESSING

¼ cup olive oil
2 cloves garlic, diced
3 Tbsp. tamari sauce
3 Tbsp. lemon juice

1 tsp. honey
½ tsp. ginger
½ tsp. black pepper
3 Tbsp. toasted sesame seeds

Combine oil and garlic. Let sit at room temperature for 1 to 2 hours. Add tamari, lemon juice, honey, ginger and black pepper and shake well.

At serving time, add sesame seeds.

— *Shiela Alexandrovich*
Whitehorse, Yukon

TOMATO HERB DRESSING

1 cup salad oil
1 cup tomato sauce, page 204
⅓ cup vinegar
¼ cup sugar
2 cloves garlic, crushed

2 tsp. dry mustard
2 tsp. Worcestershire sauce
1 tsp. paprika
½ tsp. pepper
1 Tbsp. parsley

Place all ingredients in a blender and blend for 1 minute, or shake to blend in a large jar. Chill overnight before using.

Makes 2½ to 3 cups.

— *Valerie Gillis*
Gloucester, Ontario

BLUE CHEESE MARINATED SALAD DRESSING

FOR THOSE WHO ARE FOND OF BLUE CHEESE, THIS TANGY DRESSING IS AN IDEAL WAY to liven up winter greens.

½ cup salad oil
2 Tbsp. lemon juice
½ tsp. salt
½ tsp. sugar
Dash pepper

Dash paprika
1 cup blue cheese, crumbled
2 medium onions, thinly sliced
½ cup sliced mushrooms

Combine oil, lemon juice, salt, sugar, pepper and paprika and whisk together. Add cheese, onions and mushrooms, stirring gently. Cover and refrigerate for several hours.

Makes 2½ to 3 cups.

— *L. Anne Mallory*
Lac Ste. Marie, Quebec

BLUE CHEESE PROTEIN DRESSING

1 clove garlic, crushed
1 Tbsp. tahini
Crumbled blue cheese, to taste
2 Tbsp. lemon juice

Dash of curry powder
1 Tbsp. cottage cheese
1 tsp. yogurt
¼ cup oil

Combine all ingredients and whisk together to blend.

This is especially good on a spinach salad with hard-boiled eggs, or on sliced tomatoes and raw mushrooms.

— Kathe Lieber
Montreal, Quebec

CELERY SEED DR   ING

1 tsp. salt
1 tsp. dry mustard
1 tsp. celery seed
1 tsp. paprika

½ cup sugar
⅓ cup vinegar
1 cup oil

Place all ingredients in the blender. Purée until well combined.

Store in refrigerator. Shake well before using.

Makes 1½ cups.

— Joanne Bombard
Kingston, Ontario

POPPY SEED DRESSING

4 Tbsp. lemon juice
2 tsp. Dijon mustard
1 tsp. salt
Cayenne pepper

2 Tbsp. honey
6 Tbsp. olive oil
6 Tbsp. vegetable oil
1 Tbsp. poppy seeds

Combine all ingredients in a jar and shake well. Keep in refrigerator. Makes enough dressing for one large salad.

— Sherrie Dick
Quesnel, B.C.

PARSLEY PESTO SAUCE

THIS RICH SAUCE IS DELICIOUS TOSSED WITH HOT PASTA, OR MIXED WITH CREAM cheese as a spread. It can also be added to soups or stews.

2 cups firmly packed parsley
½ cup fresh basil
½ cup olive oil
2 cloves garlic, peeled & chopped

Salt & pepper
¼ cup chopped pine nuts or almonds
½ cup freshly grated Parmesan cheese

Place all ingredients except cheese in blender and blend at high speed until smooth, stopping occasionally to scrape side with a spatula. Mix in cheese.

Makes 2½ cups.

— Shirley Hill
Picton, Ontario

TARRAGON CREAM DRESSING

This unusual salad dressing has a tangy flavour which complements cool salad greens.

½ tsp. dry mustard
1 tsp. Dijon mustard
¼ tsp. sugar
1 tsp. lemon juice
1-2 tsp. crushed garlic
5 Tbsp. tarragon vinegar

2 Tbsp. olive oil
10 Tbsp. vegetable oil
1 egg, beaten
½ cup light cream
Salt & pepper

Blend all ingredients well and store in refrigerator.

— *Sheila Couture*
Trenton, Ontario

FRUIT SALAD DRESSING

1 egg, well beaten
¼ cup honey
Juice of 1 lemon

Juice of 1 orange
Sour cream

Mix together egg, honey, lemon and orange juice. Cook until thickened and let cool. Mix in sour cream until the dressing reaches the desired consistency. Pour over mixed fruits and toss gently.

Makes 1 cup.

— *Pat McCormack*
Whitehorse, Yukon

RAW VEGETABLE DIP

1½ cups mayonnaise, page 92
3 Tbsp. grated onion
3 Tbsp. honey

3 Tbsp. ketchup
1 Tbsp. curry powder
Dash lemon juice

Mix together all ingredients. Refrigerate for a few hours before serving.

— *Elizabeth Templeman*
Heffley Creek, B.C.

SOUR CREAM VEGETABLE DIP

Delicious with a variety of raw vegetables, fruit or crackers, this is an easy-to-make dip which will keep well.

1 cup sour cream
1 cup mayonnaise, page 92
1 Tbsp. parsley flakes

1 Tbsp. dill weed
1 Tbsp. minced onion
Dash lemon pepper

Mix together all ingredients and refrigerate for 2 hours.

— *Martha Brown*
Saskatoon, Sask.

YOGURT & BACON DIP

10 slices bacon
1 cup plain yogurt
¼ cup mayonnaise, page 92

1 Tbsp. chopped green onion
1 Tbsp. chopped parsley
½ tsp. salt

Chop bacon and cook until crisp. Drain well and set aside, reserving 1 Tbsp. of drippings.

Combine drippings with yogurt, mayonnaise, onion, parsley and salt. Add bacon.

Mix well, cover and refrigerate for several hours.

Makes 1½ cups.

— Christine Steele
Port Dover, Ontario

CURRY DIP

1 cup mayonnaise, page 92
2 tsp. horseradish
2 tsp. diced raw onion

1 tsp. curry powder
1 tsp. salt

Combine all ingredients and mix well. Serve with raw vegetables.

Makes 1¼ cups.

— Karen Moller
Nakusp, B.C.

GUACAMOLE

2 ripe avocados
Juice of 1 lemon

2 cloves garlic, minced
2 Tbsp. chili powder

Peel avocados and then mash with a fork or purée in a food processor. Add remaining ingredients and mix well. Keep covered and refrigerated until ready to serve.

Makes 1½ cups.

— Bryanna Clark
Union Bay, B.C.

Beans & Grains

Full o' beans and benevolence.

— **Robert Smith Surtees**
Handley Cross

In the nursery story, *Jack and the Beanstalk,* Jack was sent off with the family cow and his mother's instruction to sell it and return home with the money. He came back, instead, with a handful of beans, "magic beans." The transaction that took place gives Jack little credit as a skillful financier, but it does have nutritional significance. Next to meat or a meat by-product such as the milk given by Jack's bartered cow, his best food investment was indeed beans. (Those particular beans, of course, provided little sustenance other than food for thoughts of generations of youngsters.)

Beans, "the poor man's beef," have the highest proportion of protein of any food other than meat or animal by-products. Like grains, beans are seeds, storehouses of nutrients designed to get a plant off to a good start in life. No wonder cereals are our traditional food of choice for getting ourselves off to a good start each day.

Although they are high in protein, beans on their own (except soybeans) are not an adequate protein source for the human body, which requires eight different protein components, amino acids, all within the same meal, for the protein to be most useful. But as it happens, beans and grains eaten together do form complete proteins, the type that come with animal products; while beans are high in lysine and deficient in sulphur-containing amino acids, for instance, grains are deficient in lysine and high in sulphur-containing compounds. The result, "complementary proteins," is of great interest to vegetarians, who regularly team beans with grains to ensure that their meatless meals do not lack protein. Such combinations include brown rice with tamari sauce, corn bread with baked beans, and muffins made with a combination of wheat and soy flours.

While a diet based upon beans and grains may sound tediously restrictive to those accustomed to eating meat, the variety of both grains and beans —there are nine of the former, 24 of the latter (including peas and lentils) available to most North Americans — ensures that the imaginative cook with access to a good natural food outlet need not have or serve a monotonous diet. Those who are not vegetarian should also be acquainted with the notion of complementary proteins. Most North Americans eat far more meat than nutritional requirements alone dictate. And all that meat is expensive, far more so than a comparable amount of protein consumed as a beans-and-grains combination. Meat is regarded as a luxury food in most of the world, and so it is; a great deal of vegetable protein must be used as animal feed to produce a relatively tiny amount of animal protein. The average steer reduces 16 pounds of grain and soy to one pound of meat.

The cook who is fairly new to cooking with beans other than Libby's and with grain products other than all-purpose flour may find the explanation of a few relevant terms useful in finding his way around recipes and natural food stores. And he should remember that beans and grains are living foods; they should be stored in a cool, dry place, packaged to prevent the entry of pests. Fresh beans should, of course, be stored in the refrigerator or freezer.

Bulgur is parched, cracked or ground wheat, which can be prepared much like rice.

Groats usually refer to hulled buckwheat, a grain that is especially rich in potassium and phosphorus. Cracked wheat or oats may also be called groats.

Triticale is a man-made cross between wheat and rye, and may be used wherever those grains are requested.

Wheat germ is the nutrient-rich heart of the wheat grain which, especially if purchased raw (untoasted), should be stored in the refrigerator, as it can quickly become rancid.

Bran is the outer, fibrous coating of the wheat grain.

Millet is a term that may designate any of several Oriental or African grains. Very nutritious, millet may be available whole or pearled — that is, with the hard outer covering removed.

Pearl barley is free of its outer hull, and appears polished. Pot barley is less refined, so it is more nutritious but takes a little longer to cook.

Rice — parboiled, "converted" rice contains more B vitamins than white rice, but fewer nutrients than brown rice, which is available in either short or long grains.

Tofu or soybean curd is a very nutritious custard-like product of cooked, strained soybeans. It can be stored for a few days in the refrigerator.

Miso is a fermented soybean paste, especially popular in soups but also useful as a flavour enhancer in stews and dressings.

Soya sauce — the "real thing," tamari, is a fermented soya product and is available primarily in Oriental and natural food stores, under brand names such as Kikkoman. The "soya sauce" sold in most grocery stores is simply coloured, hydrolyzed vegetable protein.

BANDERSNATCH BARLEY

1 cup uncooked barley
2 cups stock
4 oz. cream cheese
1 egg
½ cup sour cream

¼ tsp. salt
Pepper
3 tsp. dill
½ cup Parmesan cheese

Cook barley in stock. Bring to a boil, then simmer for 25 minutes. Mix remaining ingredients except Parmesan cheese into barley.

Put into a greased casserole dish and sprinkle with cheese.

Bake at 350 degrees F for 20 to 25 minutes, then broil for 2 minutes.

Serves 4.

— Dee Lowe
Meacham, Sask.

MUSHROOM BARLEY CASSEROLE

½ lb. mushrooms
1 large onion, chopped
1 cup pot barley
¼ cup butter

½ tsp. salt
⅛ tsp. pepper
4 cups chicken stock

Sauté mushrooms, onion and barley in melted butter. Place in a casserole dish and add remaining ingredients. Mix well.

Bake, covered, 1½ hours at 350 degrees F. If there is too much liquid, remove lid for last 20 minutes.

Serves 6 to 8.

— Eileen Deeley
Kamloops, B.C.

ZUCCHINI & BARLEY CASSEROLE

2 medium zucchini, sliced
1 small onion, chopped
1 clove garlic, crushed
½ tsp. oregano
½ tsp. basil
2 Tbsp. butter
1 cup pot barley, cooked & cooled

1 apple, cored & diced
1 green pepper, chopped
½ lb. mushrooms, sliced
2 stalks celery, sliced
10-oz. can tomatoes
1 cup grated Cheddar cheese

In a casserole dish combine zucchini, onion, garlic, oregano, basil and butter. Bake, covered, at 350 degrees F for 15 minutes.

Remove from oven and add cooked barley, apple, green pepper, mushrooms and celery. Partially drain tomatoes, then chop them. Stir into casserole.

Bake at 350 degrees for 45 minutes. Top with cheese and return to oven for 5 minutes.

Serves 4 to 6.

— Diane Schoemperlen
Banff, Alberta

BARLEY PILAF

2 Tbsp. butter
2 Tbsp. oil
¼ cup chopped onions
6 mushrooms, sliced
¾ cup uncooked barley

2½ cups stock
¼ cup diced salami or fried bacon
¼ cup finely chopped parsley
Salt & pepper

Heat butter and oil in frying pan. Add onions and cook for 5 minutes over low heat, stirring constantly. Add mushrooms and cook for 3 minutes longer.

Remove vegetables, leaving 1½ Tbsp. drippings in pan. Add barley and cook over low heat for 10 minutes or until well browned, stirring often. Place barley in casserole dish. Stir in onions, mushrooms, salt, pepper and stock. Cover and bake at 350 degrees F for 45 minutes. Add salami or bacon, cover and bake for another 25 minutes. Toss with parsley and serve.

Serves 3 to 4.

— *Jo Belicek*
Edmonton, Alberta

QUILTER'S STEW

1 cup lentils
6 cups water
1 cup tomato sauce, page 204
1 bay leaf
2 tsp. salt
1 tsp. pepper

1 potato, chopped
2 stalks celery, chopped
1 tsp. basil
2 Tbsp. brown sugar
1 cup uncooked small noodles

Combine all ingredients except noodles in a stew pot and cook for 30 minutes over medium heat.

Add noodles and cook for 10 minutes longer.

Serves 8.

— *Marie Yoder Dyck*
Pandora, Ohio

LENTIL SALAD

½ lb. green lentils
3 Tbsp. red wine or vinegar
2 Tbsp. oil
½ tsp. salt
Freshly ground black pepper

1 clove garlic, chopped
½ medium onion, chopped
Chopped green pepper
Cayenne pepper

Drop lentils into several cups of boiling water, reduce heat and simmer, partly covered, for 25 to 30 minutes until tender but not mushy. Drain and cool under cold water.

Combine remaining ingredients and add lentils. Allow to marinate at room temperature for 1 hour, stirring occasionally. Chill.

Serves 4.

— *Water St. Co-op*
Halifax, N.S.

SOYBEAN PIZZA CASSEROLE

1½ cups dry soybeans
Water to cover
2 Tbsp. oil

1 cup tomato sauce, page 204
½ cup grated mozzarella cheese
⅓ cup raw wheat germ

Soak soybeans in water overnight. With oil, cook in a pressure cooker with water to cover for 40 minutes or until tender. Drain.

Mix with tomato sauce and place in a casserole dish. Bake, covered, at 375 degrees F for 20 minutes.

Combine cheese and wheat germ, pour over casserole and bake 10 minutes longer.

Serves 4.

— *Kristine Reid*
Floyd, Virginia

SOYBEAN CASSEROLE

1 onion, sliced
1 clove garlic, crushed
1 green pepper, sliced
1 cup chopped celery
1 lb. fresh mushrooms, sliced
1 tomato, chopped
Safflower oil as needed
1 Tbsp. brewer's yeast
¼ cup wheat germ

6-oz. can tomato paste
1 cup stock
Cayenne pepper
½ tsp. thyme
½ tsp. basil
1 cup cooked soybeans
⅓ cup grated Cheddar cheese
2 Tbsp. sesame seeds

Lightly sauté onion, garlic, pepper, celery, mushrooms and tomato in oil for approximately 5 minutes. Remove from heat, add yeast and wheat germ and mix lightly.

In a separate bowl, mix the tomato paste with the stock and seasonings.

In a casserole dish, layer soybeans and vegetables. Pour tomato stock over the casserole and top with grated cheese. Sprinkle with sesame seeds.

Bake at 350 degrees F for 30 minutes.

— *Dena Ross Reuben*
Roxboro, Quebec

REFRIED BEANS

2 Tbsp. oil
5 cups cooked kidney beans
1½ Tbsp. oregano

1½ Tbsp. minced garlic
1 Tbsp. crushed chili peppers
½ lb. Cheddar cheese, grated

Place oil, beans, oregano, garlic and chili peppers in a heavy, deep frying pan. Simmer for 10 minutes. Mash until all the beans are broken up.

Stir in cheese and cook until it melts. Serve in tortillas.

Serves 6 to 8.

— *Donna Schedler*
Lyndhurst, Ontario

POLENTA

THIS VARIATION OF A TRADITIONAL ITALIAN DISH, POLENTA, WITH A MUSH-LIKE consistency, is good topped with cheese and stew.

5 cups water
1 tsp. salt

3 cups cold water
3 cups corn meal

Bring 5 cups of salted water to a boil. Combine cold water with corn meal and add to boiling water. Cook, stirring, over medium heat for 30 minutes — until mixture thickens.

Serves 4.

— *Anne Erb Panciera*
State College, Pennsylvania

BROCCOLI & CHICK PEAS

½ cup water
½ tsp. salt
1 lb. broccoli, cut into 1-inch pieces
2 cups cooked & drained chick peas
2 Tbsp. chopped red pepper

1 tsp. lemon juice
½ tsp. basil
Salt & pepper
Artichoke hearts (optional)

In medium-sized saucepan, bring water and salt to boil. Add broccoli and cook for 4 minutes. Add remaining ingredients.

Toss gently and cook until heated through. Serve hot or cold.

Serves 4.

— *Ingrid Birker*
Toronto, Ontario

FELAFEL

THIS TRADITIONAL MIDDLE EASTERN "HAMBURGER" CAN BE MADE MORE OR LESS spicy to taste, depending on the amount of garlic, cumin and coriander used. For those who really like hot food, crushed chili peppers may be added. Garlic may also be added to the yogurt topping.

1 lb. uncooked chick peas
4 onions, sliced
4 cloves garlic
½ cup chopped parsley
2 tsp. cumin

2 tsp. coriander
1 tsp. baking powder
Salt & pepper
Cayenne

Cook chick peas in water to cover, adding more water as needed, until just tender but not soft. Grind with onions and garlic.

Mix in a bowl with remaining ingredients. Chill for 1 hour, form into small balls and deep fry. Serve in pita bread (page 265) with chopped lettuce and yogurt.

Serves 8.

— *Bryanna Clark*
Union Bay, B.C.

CREAMY BULGUR & CHEESE CASSEROLE

1 medium onion, chopped
1 clove garlic, minced
2 Tbsp. oil
1 cup uncooked bulgur
2 cups water
Salt & pepper

1 large tomato, peeled & thinly sliced
1 cup cottage cheese
1 egg, beaten with ½ cup water
2 Tbsp. fresh parsley, chopped
½ cup grated Cheddar cheese

Sauté onion and garlic in oil until onion is translucent. Add bulgur and cook, stirring, for 2 minutes. Add water, bring to a boil, cover and simmer for 15 minutes.

Place two-thirds of the bulgur in a greased casserole dish. Add salt and pepper to taste, and cover with sliced tomato. Mix cottage cheese with egg and stir in parsley. Pour over tomato and top with remaining bulgur. Cover with grated cheese. Bake for 30 minutes at 350 degrees F.

— Carol Bomke
Vancouver, B.C.

BULGUR-NUT PILAF

THIS IS ONE OF MANY VARIATIONS OF TRADITIONAL RICE PILAF. OTHER POSSIBILITIES include the addition of meat or seafood, or, for a fancier meal, a topping of grated cheese.

1 cup uncooked bulgur
1 onion, chopped
1 Tbsp. butter
2 cups broth

2 medium carrots, shredded
½ tsp. salt
½ cup chopped almonds

Sauté bulgur and onion in butter for 5 minutes. Stir in broth, carrots and salt. Cover and bake at 350 degrees F for 25 minutes. Stir in nuts.

Serves 4.

— Marva Blackmore
Vancouver, B.C.

SPANISH BULGUR

BULGUR, WHICH IS CRACKED WHEAT, CAN BE SUBSTITUTED FOR RICE IN MANY recipes, including this one which is generally thought of as a rice dish. It cooks very quickly and has a pleasant nutty flavour.

1 clove garlic, minced
½ cup green onions, chopped
½ green pepper, diced
1¼ cups uncooked bulgur wheat
2 Tbsp. cooking oil
1 cup cooked lima beans

1 tsp. paprika
1 tsp. salt
⅛ tsp. ground pepper
Dash of cayenne pepper
28-oz. can tomatoes

Sauté garlic, onions, pepper and bulgur in oil for 5 minutes. Add remaining ingredients, cover and bring to a boil. Simmer 15 minutes or until liquid is absorbed and bulgur is tender. If necessary, add more liquid.

Serves 4 to 6.

— Laura Poitras
Kemptville, Ontario

TABOULEH

Of Middle Eastern origin, tabouleh makes a delicious light lunch in the heat of summer.

1 cup uncooked bulgur
4 bunches parsley, chopped
2 medium tomatoes, chopped
1 medium onion, chopped
1 cucumber, diced

1 green pepper, diced
2 green onions, chopped
Juice of 1 lemon
¾ cup olive oil
Salt

Cover bulgur with boiling water and soak until softened. Drain, add remaining ingredients and toss. Chill well.

Serves 6.

— Glenn Countryman
Victoria, B.C.

BETTY'S BAKED BEANS

1 cup navy beans
1 tsp. dry mustard
1 tsp. salt
¼ tsp. pepper
¾ cup brown sugar

2 cups tomato juice
½ cup chopped onion
1 cup bacon pieces
3 medium-sized apples

Cook beans in boiling water until tender. Add mustard, salt, pepper, brown sugar, tomato juice, onion, bacon and apples.

Place in bean pot or casserole dish, cover and bake at 300 degrees F for 1 hour.

Serves 4.

— Catherine Rupke
Kettleby, Ontario

PICKLED WHITE BEANS

16 oz. navy beans
Pinch baking soda
¾ cup sugar
1 tsp. salt
½ tsp. pepper

⅔ cup vinegar
⅓ cup vegetable oil
1 green pepper, chopped
1 onion, chopped
Parsley

Soak beans in water overnight. Bring beans and baking soda to a boil (add more water if necessary), and then simmer until beans are soft. Cool.

Mix together remaining ingredients and combine well. Chill overnight.

BEAN FILLING FOR PITA BREAD

4 cups cooked white navy beans
5 Tbsp. oil
2 Tbsp. lemon juice
1 tsp. oregano
½ tsp. salt
½ tsp. cumin

¼ tsp. ground pepper
4 oz. cream cheese, cubed
2 medium tomatoes, chopped
1 medium cucumber, diced
2 Tbsp. chopped parsley
Pita bread for 4 (page 265)

Toss beans, oil, lemon juice and spices in a large bowl. Gently stir in cheese, tomato and cucumber. Cover and chill for 2 hours.

Cut bread in half and fill with bean mixture. Sprinkle with parsley.

Serves 4.

— Margaret Silverthorn
Iona Station, Ontario

HUMMUS

A CHICK PEA PATE OF MIDDLE EASTERN ORIGIN, HUMMUS MAKES A FLAVOURFUL AND protein-rich sandwich spread or appetizer dip.

2 cups cooked chick peas
⅓ cup water
Juice of 2 lemons
½ cup tahini (ground sesame seeds)

2 cloves garlic, crushed
½ tsp. salt
Cayenne pepper

Whir all ingredients in a blender until smooth. Serve as a dip for pita bread or raw vegetables.

Makes 2½ cups.

— Sandra James-Mitchell
Pickering, Ontario

VEGI-BURGERS

THERE ARE MANY GOOD RECIPES FOR MEATLESS BURGERS. MOST GRAINS CAN BE used, but it is important to add sufficient seasoning, otherwise the finished product will be bland and pasty. Toppings can include regular hamburger sauces, sprouts, yogurt, chili sauce and so on.

1 cup grated Cheddar cheese
1 cup sunflower seeds
2 cups bread crumbs
¼ cup bran
¼ cup wheat germ

¼ cup oats
1 cup onion, finely chopped
1 tsp. salt
1 tsp. sage
6 eggs

Mix all ingredients together and form into patties. Fry on both sides in vegetable oil. Makes 12 patties.

— Brenda Kennedy
Armstrong, B.C.

LENTIL BURGERS

1 cup uncooked lentils, rinsed
½ cup uncooked rice
3 cups water
1½ Tbsp. salt
1 cup bread crumbs
½ cup wheat germ
1 large onion, chopped

½ tsp. celery seed
½ tsp. marjoram
¼ tsp. thyme
1 tsp. salt
½ tsp. pepper
1 Tbsp. chopped fresh parsley
Wheat germ

Combine lentils, rice, water and salt in a saucepan. Bring to a boil, lower heat, cover and simmer for 35 to 45 minutes or until rice is tender. Remove from heat, let stand 10 minutes and then mash together with any remaining liquid in pan.

Place in a large bowl with bread crumbs, wheat germ, onion, celery seed, marjoram, thyme, salt, pepper and parsley. Mix well and shape into patties.

Coat with wheat germ and fry in vegetable oil until golden brown on both sides.

Makes 24 patties.

— Barbara J. Spangler
Sylacanga, Alabama

SOY MILLET PATTIES

THESE PATTIES ARE GOOD SERVED HOT AS A HAMBURGER SUBSTITUTE, OR COLD IN A sandwich with alfalfa sprouts and mayonnaise.

2 cups cooked soybeans
2 Tbsp. oil
½ cup water
2 Tbsp. chopped onion
1½ tsp. celery seed
1½ tsp. oregano
1 tsp. salt
3 Tbsp. soya sauce
1½ cups cooked millet
¼ cup raw ground cashews
¼ cup raw ground sunflower seeds
1 cup bread crumbs

Blend in a mixing bowl, soybeans, oil, water, onion, celery seed, oregano, salt and soya sauce. Add remaining ingredients. Mix well and form into patties.

Fry in butter until cooked through and lightly browned, about 20 minutes.

Serves 6.

— *Andrea Stuart*
Winnipeg, Manitoba

CHEESE NUT LOAF

1 medium onion, chopped
1 clove garlic, chopped
3 Tbsp. oil
1 cup cooked rice
½ cup wheat germ
½ cup chopped walnuts or cashews
½ cup thinly sliced mushrooms
¼ tsp. salt
¼ tsp. pepper
½ lb. Cheddar cheese, grated
2 eggs, beaten

Sauté onion and garlic in oil. Combine with rice, wheat germ, nuts, mushrooms, salt, pepper and all but half a cup of cheese. Mix well, add eggs and mix again.

Place in a greased loaf pan and bake at 350 degrees F for 50 minutes. Sprinkle with remaining cheese after 30 minutes.

Serves 4.

— *Carol Bomke*
Vancouver, B.C.

SUNFLOWER-SPROUT LOAF

1½ cups stale bread crumbs
1½ cups milk
½ green pepper, chopped
1 stalk celery, chopped
1 small onion, chopped
2 cloves garlic, minced
2 Tbsp. oil
2 cups bean sprouts
¼ cup sunflower seeds
1 cup grated cheese
½ cup powdered milk
2 eggs
1-2 Tbsp. tamari sauce
Tarragon
Pepper

Soak the bread crumbs in milk until softened. Lightly sauté pepper, celery, onion and garlic in oil. Combine with remaining ingredients in a mixing bowl.

Bake in a greased loaf pan at 350 degrees F for 1 hour, or until firmly set and bubbly.

Serves 4 to 6.

— *Anna Lee*
Sault Ste. Marie, Ont.

SOYA-SEED LOAF

¼ cup roasted sesame seeds
¼ cup roasted sunflower seeds
⅓ cup roasted wheat germ
1 onion, chopped
1 clove garlic, minced
1 Tbsp. oil

½ tsp. sage
½ tsp. oregano
2 cups cooked soybeans
1 egg
1 tsp. salt
1 cup grated zucchini

Grind seeds and wheat germ into a fine meal.

Sauté onion and garlic in oil until onion is translucent. Add sage and oregano and cook for 1 minute. Remove from heat.

Place soybeans in a blender with a small amount of liquid and blend until a thick paste is formed.

Mix all ingredients together and place in greased loaf pan. Bake at 350 degrees F for 50 minutes.

Serves 4 to 5.

— Shan Simpson
Leslieville, Alberta

NUT LOAF

2 cups uncooked red river cereal
1 cup boiling water
1 cup light cream
1 small onion, chopped
1 cup Cheddar cheese, cubed

1 cup walnuts. chopped
3 Tbsp. Worcestershire sauce
1 tsp. sage
1 egg

Pour boiling water over the cereal, stir in the cream and let stand.

Combine remaining ingredients, add to cereal mixture, and pack into a loaf pan coated with ⅛-inch of vegetable oil.

Bake at 350 degrees F for 1 hour.

Serves 4.

— Norma Stellings
Waterdown, Ontario

MEATLESS STUFFED CABBAGE ROLLS

1½ lbs. mushrooms
1 medium onion, chopped
2 Tbsp. cooking oil
½ tsp. salt
¼ tsp. pepper
½ tsp. marjoram
1 cup cooked rice

¼ cup grated Cheddar cheese
1 head cabbage
Boiling water
2 cups tomato sauce, page 204
1 Tbsp. lemon juice
¼ cup brown sugar
1 cup water

Sauté mushrooms and onions in oil. Add salt, pepper, marjoram, rice and cheese. Blend well. Cut core out of cabbage and pour in boiling water to separate the leaves. Divide rice mixture into 6 portions and roll in 6 large outside leaves. Chop rest of cabbage and add to the remaining ingredients in a large saucepan. Place cabbage rolls on top and simmer, covered, for 30 minutes, or until tender.

Makes 6 cabbage rolls.

— Merilyn Mohr
Astorville, Ontario

CHEESE, BROCCOLI & RICE CASSEROLE

1 cup chopped onion
1 Tbsp. butter
1½ cups white sauce, page 92
½ cup sliced mushrooms
Salt & pepper
2 tsp. tamari sauce

1 cup grated Cheddar cheese
1 cup cooked rice
½ tsp. dry mustard
4 hard-boiled eggs, quartered
1 bunch broccoli, cooked

Sauté onion in butter until soft, then gradually stir in white sauce, mushrooms, salt, pepper and tamari sauce. Add cheese, rice and mustard and cook, stirring, until cheese is melted. Fold in quartered eggs.

Place broccoli in greased 2-quart baking dish and pour sauce over it.

Bake at 350 degrees F for 20 minutes.

Serves 6 to 8.

— Signe Nickerson
Grand Forks, B.C.

RICE-SPINACH-CHEESE BAKE

2 cups cooked brown rice
1 cup cottage cheese
2 eggs, beaten
10 oz. spinach
½ cup chopped green pepper

2 cups grated Cheddar cheese
1 tsp. salt
⅛ tsp. pepper
3 Tbsp. bread crumbs
Melted butter or olive oil

Combine all ingredients except bread crumbs and butter. Pour into a buttered baking dish. Sprinkle top with bread crumbs, then drizzle with butter or olive oil.

Bake at 350 degrees F for 30 minutes, or until bubbly hot.

Serves 4 to 6.

— Jacqueline L. Dysart
Espanola, Ontario

CHEESY RICE CASSEROLE

1¼ cups uncooked rice
2 Tbsp. soy grits
2 Tbsp. butter
2 small onions, chopped
2 stalks celery, diced
1 green pepper, diced
1 large carrot, chopped

¼ cup sunflower seeds
6 mushrooms, sliced
½ tsp. thyme
Dash cayenne
½ cup grated Cheddar cheese
¼ cup grated Parmesan cheese

Cook the rice and soy grits in simmering water for about 25 minutes. Drain.

Melt butter in a frying pan. Sauté the onion, celery, green pepper, carrot and sunflower seeds until the onion softens. Add the mushrooms and seasonings and sauté a few minutes longer. Add the drained rice and soy grits and mix thoroughly. Stir in the Cheddar cheese.

Turn the mixture into a greased casserole dish and top with Parmesan cheese. Bake at 350 degrees F for 30 minutes, or until heated through.

Serves 4 to 6.

— Janet Flewelling
Toronto, Ontario

RICE WITH SOUR CREAM & GREEN CHILIES

1 cup uncooked rice
4-oz. can green chilies,
  chopped & drained
8 oz. sour cream

Salt & pepper
½ lb. Cheddar cheese, grated
2 Tbsp. butter

Cook rice and combine it with the green chilies, sour cream, salt, pepper and three-quarters of the cheese.

Place in a 2-quart casserole dish, sprinkle with remaining cheese and dot with butter.

Bake, uncovered, at 350 degrees F for 30 minutes.

Serves 2 to 4.

— Liz Eder and Paul Jett
Baltimore, Maryland

BEAN & RICE CASSEROLE

4 cups cooked kidney or pinto beans
4 cups cooked rice
3 cups tomato sauce, page 204
1 large onion, finely chopped
1 cup corn meal
1⅔ cups boiling water
⅔ cup powdered milk

5 Tbsp. vegetable oil
5 Tbsp. honey
1 egg, beaten
1¼ cups flour
4 tsp. baking powder
½ tsp. salt
1 cup grated Cheddar cheese

Combine beans, rice, tomato sauce and onion, mix well and place in a 9" x 13" casserole dish. The mixture should be quite liquidy — add additional tomato sauce if necessary. Bake at 375 degrees F for 25 minutes or until bubbly.

Meanwhile, combine corn meal, boiling water and powdered milk and let sit 10 minutes. Stir in oil, honey and egg.

Combine flour, baking powder, salt and cheese and add to corn meal mixture. Stir until just mixed.

Remove beans from oven and raise heat to 400 degrees. Top casserole with corn meal mixture and bake for 20 minutes.

Serves 6 to 8.

— Sandy McCallum
Bancroft, Ontario

BUSTER'S RED BEANS & RICE

1 smoked pork hock
Oil for frying
4 cups uncooked small red beans
Cold water to cover
4 large onions, sliced

1 bulb garlic, broken into cloves
  & chopped
Salt
4 cups raw rice, cooked

Cut pork hock in half, fry in oil and place in a large pot. Add beans and cold water to cover.

Fry onions in oil, add to pot and bring mixture to a boil. Simmer, covered, for 5 to 6 hours or until beans are tender. Let cool.

Remove pork hock from pot, discard bone and fat and return meat to pot. Add garlic and simmer 1 more hour. Add salt to taste.

Serve over a bed of rice.

Serves 10.

— Cathy Reed
Kamloops, B.C.

GARDEN RICE

1½ cups green beans, cut in 1-inch lengths
1 cup shelled green peas
1 small bunch broccoli, cut up
2 small zucchini, thickly sliced
½ cup rice
1 cup water
3 ripe tomatoes, cubed
8 Tbsp. butter

2 cloves garlic, crushed
¼ lb. sliced mushrooms
1 tsp. dried basil
Salt & pepper
¼ tsp. crushed chili peppers
¼ cup chopped parsley
½ cup cream
⅓ cup Parmesan cheese

Place 1 inch of water in a large saucepan and add peas and beans. Place vegetable steamer on top and add broccoli and zucchini. Cook until vegetables are crispy-tender. Meanwhile, cook rice in 1 cup of water.

In a large frying pan, sauté tomatoes in 6 Tbsp. of butter. Add garlic, mushrooms, basil, salt, pepper, chilies and parsley. When mushrooms are done, add the cooked vegetables and simmer while making the sauce.

To make sauce, melt remaining 2 Tbsp. butter in small saucepan, add cream and cheese and cook over medium heat until cheese melts and sauce is smooth.

Add rice and sauce to vegetables and mix well. Cook over low heat until everything is heated through.

Serves 2 to 3.

— *Kynda Fenton*
Cowansville, Quebec.

SWISS BROWN RICE

2 cups sliced onion
3 stalks celery, sliced
½ lb. mushrooms, sliced
½ cup chopped parsley
2 Tbsp. oil
1 clove garlic, minced
1½ tsp. paprika

1 tsp. salt
½ tsp. black pepper
½ tsp. ginger
3 cups cooked rice
1 lb. Swiss cheese, grated
Chopped parsley to garnish

Sauté onion, celery, mushrooms and parsley in oil. Add garlic and seasonings and mix well.

Layer the rice, vegetables and cheese in a shallow casserole dish and bake at 350 degrees F for 20 to 25 minutes. Garnish with parsley.

Serves 8 to 10.

— *Water St. Co-op*
Halifax, Nova Scotia

BROWNED RICE

2 cups uncooked rice
¼ cup butter
1 cup sliced mushrooms

¼ cup chopped green onions
½ lb. slivered almonds
3 cups chicken stock

Brown rice in butter in large saucepan. Sauté mushrooms, onion and almonds in butter in a frying pan. Boil stock and pour over rice. Boil again, reduce heat, cover and cook for 15 minutes.

Add mushrooms, onions and almonds and leave on low heat until ready to serve.

Serves 8 to 10.

— *Jacquie Gibson*
Ottawa, Ontario

MUSHROOM BROWN RICE

1 cup bread crumbs
1½ cups melted butter
2 cups mushrooms, sliced
6 cups cooked brown rice

Salt & pepper
1 cup grated Cheddar cheese
¼ cup minced parsley

Sauté bread crumbs in ½ cup melted butter. Remove crumbs from pan, then sauté mushrooms.

Place rice in a casserole dish and toss lightly with remaining butter. Add mushrooms, bread crumbs and salt and pepper to taste. Mix well and top with cheese and parsley.

Bake at 350 degrees F for 20 to 30 minutes.

Serves 8 to 10.

— Winona Heasman
Powassan, Ontario

SPANISH RICE

QUICKLY AND EASILY ASSEMBLED, THIS DISH CAN BE SERVED AS A MEATLESS MAIN dish or as a side dish.

1 cup uncooked brown rice
2 cups water
1 onion
1 green pepper
3 stalks celery
3 cloves garlic

4 Tbsp. oil
28-oz. can tomatoes
1 tsp. salt
Dash of pepper
3 whole cloves or ½ tsp. ground cloves
1 cup grated Cheddar cheese

Cook rice in boiling water for 45 minutes. Meanwhile, chop onion, green pepper and celery and sauté with garlic in oil until onion becomes translucent. Add tomatoes and seasonings to vegetables and simmer for 10 minutes.

Combine with cooked rice in casserole dish and top with grated cheese. Bake at 350 degrees F for 15 to 20 minutes.

Serves 4.

— Rae Anne Huth
Fauquier, B.C.

HERBED RICE

3 Tbsp. butter
¼ cup finely chopped chives
  or green onions
1 cup uncooked rice

½ tsp. marjoram
½ tsp. rosemary
½ tsp. salt
2 cups chicken stock

In a heavy saucepan, melt butter and sauté chives or onions until softened. Add rice and cook, stirring constantly, until the rice is lightly browned. Add the herbs, salt and chicken stock.

Cover tightly and bring to a boil, then lower heat and simmer until rice is tender.

Makes 3 cups.

— Kathy Christie
Singhampton, Ontario

DONNA'S RICE PILAF

2 cups beef stock
1 cup rice
½ tsp. salt
1 onion, chopped

1 stalk celery, chopped
¼-½ cup chopped mushrooms
1 small green pepper, chopped

Bring stock to a boil and add rice and salt. Stir, cover, return to a boil, then reduce heat to minimum. Simmer until rice is cooked.

Sauté onion, celery, mushrooms and pepper in a frying pan. When rice is cooked, add vegetables, stir, and replace lid. Turn heat off but leave pot on warm burner for another 5 minutes.

Serves 4.

— *Donna Gordon*
Dorval, Quebec

CURRIED RICE & FRIED EGGS

1 cup uncooked rice
½ tsp. salt
1 Tbsp. curry powder
¼ tsp. ground Jamaican ginger
1 onion, coarsely chopped

½ cup slivered almonds
5-6 mushrooms, thinly sliced
4 eggs
Pepper

Cook rice in 2 cups boiling water with curry powder, salt and ginger. When rice is cooked, remove from heat, stir in onion, almonds and mushrooms, replace lid and let sit.

While rice is sitting, gently fry eggs.

To serve, place rice on plate, top with eggs and sprinkle with pepper.

Serves 2.

— *Steve Pitt*
Toronto, Ontario

MANITOBA WILD RICE CASSEROLE

1 cup wild rice
¼ tsp. basil
½ tsp. pepper
½ tsp. salt
1 tsp. thyme

1 tsp. sage
3 cups beef stock
8 slices bacon
1 onion, chopped
½ lb. mushrooms, sliced

Soak rice overnight, wash and drain. Place rice, basil, salt, pepper, thyme, sage and beef stock in the top of a double boiler and cook, covered, over boiling water for 45 minutes or until tender.

Meanwhile, chop and fry bacon. Add onion and mushrooms, and stir until cooked.

Combine rice and bacon mixtures in a greased casserole dish. Bake at 350 degrees F for 20 to 25 minutes.

Serves 6.

— *Joan Hoepner*
Norway House, Manitoba

RICE CAKES

2 eggs, well beaten
3 cups cooked brown rice
3 Tbsp. flour
2-3 Tbsp. finely chopped onion

½ cup milk
1 tsp. salt
1-2 tsp. parsley

Blend eggs into cooled rice. Add flour, onion, milk and seasonings. Mix well.

Drop by spoonfuls onto hot frying pan. Flatten, brown and flip.

— Pat Dicer
Mission, B.C.

PARMESAN RICE CRUST

1 egg, beaten
¼ cup Parmesan cheese
Juice of 1 lemon
Pepper

2 cups cooked rice
2 Tbsp. melted butter
¼ cup sesame meal

Mix together egg, cheese, lemon juice and pepper. Toss rice with butter and sesame meal and stir into egg-cheese mixture.

Press into 9-inch pie pan and bake at 350 degrees F until it becomes crusty — about 15 minutes. Use for quiches.

— Kathie Reid
Downsview, Ontario

RICE SALAD

2 small onions
1 green pepper
3 cups chilled cooked rice
1 cup uncooked peas

1 cup mayonnaise, page 92
Salt
Green onions, radishes &
  parsley to garnish

Dice onions and green pepper. Add to rice along with peas, mayonnaise and salt. Mix well. Garnish with sliced green onions, radishes and chopped parsley.

Serves 6.

— Carolyn Somerton
Prince George, B.C.

CURRIED RICE SALAD

1½ cups uncooked rice
2 Tbsp. diced green pepper
2 Tbsp. raisins
1 small onion, finely chopped
2 Tbsp. snipped parsley
⅔ cup olive oil
⅓ cup wine vinegar

Salt & pepper
½ tsp. dry mustard
1 clove garlic, mashed
1 Tbsp. curry powder
Green pepper rings & tomato wedges to
garnish

Cook rice and cool. Add green pepper, raisins, onion and parsley and mix well.

Combine oil, vinegar, salt, pepper, mustard and garlic in a small bowl.

When ready to serve, pour dressing over salad, add curry powder and mix well. Garnish with green pepper rings and tomato wedges.

Serves 6.

— Sandra Kapral
Prince George, B.C.

CHINESE RICE SALAD

1 cup cold cooked rice
1 cup cooked peas
¼ cup chopped green onion
½ cup shrimp
1½ cups chopped celery
1 tsp. salt

1 Tbsp. soya sauce
3 Tbsp. vinegar
1 tsp. curry powder
⅓ cup oil
½ tsp. sugar

Combine rice, peas, onion, shrimp and celery.

Combine remaining ingredients to make a dressing and pour over rice mixture. Mix well and refrigerate for several hours.

Serves 6 to 8.

— Beth Hopkins
Courtenay, B.C.

CINNAMON GRANOLA

1½ tsp. vanilla
¾ cup oil
1 cup honey
1 cup rolled oats
1 cup bran
1 cup wheat flakes
½ cup wheat germ
½ cup sesame seeds
½ cup coconut

½ cup sunflower seeds
½ cup cashews
½ cup rye flakes
1 cup powdered milk
1 tsp. cinnamon
½ tsp. nutmeg
2 cups raisins
¾ cup chopped dried apricots

Combine vanilla, oil and honey and heat.

Mix oats, bran, wheat flakes, wheat germ, sesame seeds, coconut, sunflower seeds, cashews, rye flakes, powdered milk, cinnamon and nutmeg. Add honey mixture and blend thoroughly with fingers.

Place in two 9" x 13" pans and bake at 325 degrees F for 30 to 45 minutes.

Remove from oven and add raisins and apricots. Store in refrigerator.

Makes 9 cups.

— Shirley Thomlinson
Carp, Ontario

CRUNCHY GRANOLA

1 cup butter
½ cup honey
1 Tbsp. milk
1 tsp. salt
4 cups rolled oats

1 cup wheat germ
1 cup coconut
¼ cup sesame seeds
½ cup sunflower seeds
½ cup raisins

Heat butter, honey, milk and salt. Combine rolled oats, wheat germ, coconut, sesame seeds and sunflower seeds. Mix in honey-butter mixture until well combined.

Place in a large shallow pan and bake at 350 degrees F for 20 minutes, stirring from time to time.

Stir in raisins and cool.

Makes 7 cups.

— Carol Frost
Chilliwack, B.C.

AL TAYLOR'S GRANOLA

½ cup oil
½ cup honey
1 Tbsp. milk
4 cups rolled oats
1 cup rolled wheat flakes
1½ cups wheat germ
1 cup sesame seeds

1 cup sunflower seeds
1 cup coconut
¼ cup flax seeds
¼ cup poppy seeds
½-1 cup chopped almonds or cashews
1 tsp. salt
1 cup raisins

Combine and heat oil, honey and milk.

Mix remaining ingredients, except raisins, and spread in a large shallow pan. Dribble oil-honey mixture over cereal and mix in.

Bake at 350 degrees F for 15 minutes, stir well and bake another 15 minutes.

Remove from oven and stir in raisins. Cool and store in airtight containers.

Makes 11 to 12 cups.

— Paddy & Daryl Taylor
Estevan, Sask.

HOT CEREAL

1 heaping Tbsp. buckwheat groats
1 heaping Tbsp. hulled millet
1 Tbsp. sesame seeds
1 Tbsp. safflower oil
Raisins

¼ tsp. kelp
1¼-1½ cups water
1 Tbsp. brewer's yeast
1 Tbsp. lecithin granules

Place all ingredients in top of double boiler and soak for at least 12 hours.

Using only top of double boiler, bring cereal to a boil, reduce heat and cook gently, stirring frequently, for 8 to 10 minutes.

Meanwhile, heat water in the bottom of the boiler. Place top over bottom, cover and let stand until ready to serve, about 10 minutes.

Just before serving, stir in brewer's yeast and lecithin granules. Serve with milk.

Serves 2.

— John Osborne
Markdale, Ontario

CINNAMON OAT WHEAT CEREAL

3½ cups water
½ tsp. salt
2 Tbsp. cinnamon
¾ cup raisins

4 Tbsp. soy grits
1⅓ cups rolled wheat
1⅓ cups rolled oats
2 cups milk

Bring water, salt, cinnamon and raisins to a boil. Add soy grits and rolled oats, stirring well.

Cook over low heat, uncovered, until water is absorbed and oats are tender. Serve with milk and honey.

Serves 6.

WHEAT BERRY MUESLI

SERVED WITH MILK, MUESLI MAKES AN UNUSUAL AND WHOLESOME BREAKFAST.

¼ cup oatmeal
½ cup water
1 cup raisins
1 cup steamed wheat
1 cup yogurt

3-4 Tbsp. honey
1 tsp. lemon juice
1 apple, unpeeled & chopped
1 banana, sliced

Soak oatmeal in ½ cup water for 30 minutes. Simmer raisins until tender, then drain. Combine oatmeal, raisins and remaining ingredients and chill. Muesli will keep for several days, refrigerated, in a glass container.

Serves 4.

— *Joanne Ramsy*
Aylmer, Ontario

WHEAT AND RAISINS

A HEARTY, SATISFYING DISH, THIS IS GOOD SERVED HOT OR COLD, AS A DESSERT OR a cereal. Dried apricots, prunes or peaches can be substituted for raisins.

1 cup raisins
2 cups water
1 Tbsp. vinegar
3 Tbsp. honey

1 Tbsp. butter
2 Tbsp. cornstarch
4 cups cooked whole wheat

Simmer raisins in water until soft. Add vinegar, honey and butter. Add cornstarch and cook, stirring, until thickened. Add wheat and serve.

Serves 6.

— *Joanne Ramsy*
Aylmer, Ontario

SESAME CEREAL

1½ cups water
¼ tsp. salt
1 Tbsp. soy grits

1 cup rolled wheat
2 Tbsp. roasted & ground sesame seeds

Bring water to a boil, add salt, soy grits and wheat. Cook over low heat until thick. Stir in sesame seeds.

Serves 2.

Fish & Seafood

This dish of meat is too good for any but anglers, or very honest men.

— **Izaak Walton**
The Compleat Angler

The oyster is one of those foods that divides humanity into two opposing camps: those who consider raw oysters food of the gods, letting the morsels slide unobstructed from shell to stomach, "like swallowing a baby," in William Thackeray's words, and those whose innards turn at the very idea. *De gustibus non disputandum est* − there's no accounting for taste. Fortunately, there is a middle ground in all of this, occupied not only by those innocuous hors d'oeuvres, smoked oysters, but also by vast amounts of seafoods from lox to caviar to fast food fishburgers, some of which appeal to just about everyone.

We have only to observe the endless disputes over off-shore rights and inshore fisheries to be aware of the importance of seafoods in the human diet. In most Oriental countries they are more important than meat, which is due not only to those countries' long sea coasts, seagoing traditions and lack of land for raising livestock, but also to the fact that fish is high in lysine and contains adequate amounts of isoleucine, two amino acids deficient in rice. A serving of just a quarter of a pound of fish can satisfy up to one half of an adult's daily protein requirement. Pound for pound, halibut contains more protein than chicken, ground beef, veal or lamb; salmon rates about the same as chicken. And all this produced on less food than livestock requires. It is no wonder that aquaculture, the intensive, controlled rearing of fish in ponds, is now foreseen as a partial answer to the world's protein requirements.

Fish are divided into two culinary categories, "oily" and "white." The former, including herring, mackerel, salmon and sardines, is especially high in vitamins A and D. The "white" fishes such as cod and halibut are very low in fat. high in protein, a combination that makes them a stand-by in many weight reduction diets.

Fish can be purchased or caught fresh or bought frozen or canned. While processed fish can scarcely be compared in flavour or texture with its fresh counterpart, the cook must be far more careful in purchasing fresh fish. Those who live near the water will, of course, have the best chance of obtaining high quality fresh seafood. But everyone visiting a fish market should keep in mind the characteristics of really fresh fish.

To test fish for freshness, check that the scales are shiny and adhere tightly to the skin, the eyes bulge, the gills are rose coloured and the flesh is firm when pressed − no identation should remain. At home, the shopper can discover whether the fish is truly fresh, or has previously been frozen. A fresh fish will float in cold water, while one that is not will sink. Such thawed fish, if still sound, is

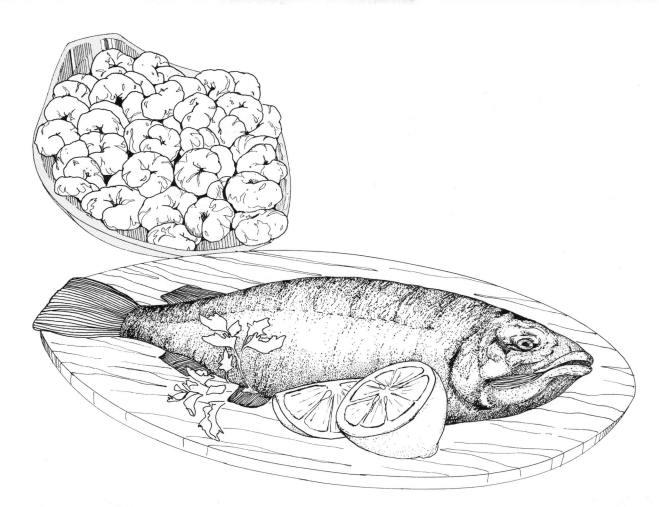

perfectly good to eat, but should not be refrozen. All fresh seafoods are highly perishable; for best results, cook them the day they are caught or bought.

Fish is adaptable to any cooking method, although the one the cook chooses should suit the texture and flavour of the variety. It may be deep-fried, sautéed, fried, broiled, baked, poached, steamed — or eaten raw, as is often done by the Japanese. Some, too, can be salted, marinated or smoked; Pacific Coast Indians were able to preserve salmon for months by first drying and smoking the fillets.

Be sure not to overcook fish, which dries out and loses flavour when overdone. Because fish has less connective tissue than meat, and no elastin, it does not require long cooking to become tender, and its protein is more easily digested than is that of meat. Fish is done when the interior temperature reaches 140 degrees F. A meat thermometer can be inserted into the flesh behind the gills, in the thickest part of the meat. Or test the fish by inserting a knife into the thickest part — it is done when the flesh flakes easily and is no longer translucent.

Unless otherwise requested by the recipe, shellfish should be cooked over low heat, and for as short a time as possible. Containing as much

iron as pork or beef kidney, shellfish such as oysters or clams also provide calcium, vitamin A and niacin, as well as traces of many other nutrients. Raw clams also contain vitamin C.

For most of us, fish are not simply a source of valuable nutrients, but a welcome addition to a diet that is already richly gifted with foods from out of season and out of place, thanks to technological advances that can bring lobster to Edmonton, Chinook salmon to Montreal, and tuna sandwiches to the lunch buckets of Whitehorse school children.

SALMON MEDITERRANEAN

1 qt. tomatoes
¼ cup olive oil
4-6 cloves garlic, minced
1 Tbsp. basil
1 tsp. oregano
Salt & pepper

Large bunch parsley, chopped
4 lbs. salmon,
  cut into 1½-inch steaks
2 onions, thinly sliced
1 large lemon, thinly sliced

Combine tomatoes, olive oil, garlic, basil, oregano, salt, pepper and parsley in a saucepan and cook for 15 minutes. Transfer to a baking dish.

Place salmon steaks in baking dish so that at least half of each steak is submerged in sauce. Arrange onion and lemon slices among the steaks. Cover and bake at 325 degrees F for 30 minutes, uncover and bake a further 30 minutes.

Serves 6 to 8.

— Chris Ferris
Lasqueti Island, B.C.

SPRING SALMON WITH CREAM & CHIVE SAUCE

1 large head romaine lettuce
2-3 stalks celery
1-2 carrots
1 leek
2 Tbsp. butter
3 cups fish stock
1 cup white wine

Salt & white pepper
1 onion, chopped
Juice of ½ lemon
4 slices fresh salmon fillets
1 bunch chives
2 cups light cream
¼ cup butter

Dip lettuce leaves in boiling water and rinse in cold water.

Cut celery, carrots and leek in julienne style. Blanch for 2 minutes in boiling water, then sauté in 2 Tbsp. butter for 3 or 4 minutes. Combine stock, wine, salt, pepper, onion and lemon juice.

Spread out lettuce leaves, grouping 3 or 4 together to form one serving. Salt and pepper salmon and place on lettuce leaves. Spread vegetables on top and fold as for cabbage rolls. Simmer in fish stock for 10 to 15 minutes.

Remove rolls from stock and keep warm. Reduce stock to one-third, add chives and cream and heat until slightly thickened. Whisk in butter and pour sauce around salmon. Garnish with parsley.

Serves 4.

— Ascona Place Restaurant
Gravenhurst, Ontario

CANADIAN SMOKED SALMON

1 lb. smoked salmon
Juice of 1 lemon
2 Tbsp. mayonnaise, page 92
1 dill pickle, finely chopped
1 large green onion, finely chopped

Salt & pepper
Salad greens
Tomato, radishes, cucumbers &
  green peppers to garnish.

Slice salmon thinly, removing bones and skin. This is most easily done if the salmon has been placed in the freezer for a few hours first.

Toss in lemon juice and mayonnaise. Add dill pickle, onion, salt and pepper. Toss again and refrigerate.

Serve on a bed of greens, garnished with raw vegetables.

Serves 6 as an appetizer.

— Nita Hunton
Cambridge, Ontario

SALMON A LA KING

2 cups cooked salmon
⅓ cup chopped green pepper
1 tsp. grated onion
¼ cup chopped pimento or red pepper
¼ cup butter
¼ cup flour

1 tsp. salt
Dash pepper
2 cups milk
2 beaten egg yolks
1½ cups sliced mushrooms

Drain fish and flake. Sauté green pepper, onion and pimento in butter until tender. Blend in flour, salt and pepper. Add milk and cook until thick and smooth, stirring constantly. Stir a little of this mixture into the beaten egg yolks, then pour egg yolks into sauce, stirring constantly. Add the fish and mushrooms and heat thoroughly. Serve over rice, noodles or puff pastry.

Serves 6.

— Ken Parejko
Holcombe, Wisconsin

SALMON LOAF

15-oz. can salmon
1 egg, beaten
½ cup cottage cheese
1 cup cracker crumbs
2 or 3 chopped green onions
½ cup green peas

1 Tbsp. Worcestershire sauce
1 Tbsp. lemon juice
½ tsp. paprika
Salt & pepper
¼ cup milk

Drain salmon, remove bones and break into small pieces. Add remaining ingredients and blend well. Pack lightly into a buttered baking dish and bake at 350 degrees F for 30 minutes.

Serves 4.

— Dawn Hermann
Faro, Yukon

SALMON SUPPER CASSEROLE

2 cups cooked salmon
1 large onion
4 medium potatoes

Salt & pepper
1 cup milk
Flour

Remove bones and flake the salmon. Spread one half in buttered casserole, cover with thin slices of onions and a generous layer of sliced raw potatoes. Sprinkle with salt, pepper and flour. Repeat these layers, then pour milk over all.

Dot with butter and bake at 400 degrees F for about 50 minutes, or until potatoes are tender.

Serves 4.

— Mrs. Fred Smith
Mountain Grove, Ont.

BAKED SALMON CAKES

7-oz. can salmon
4 green onions, finely chopped
½ tsp. salt

¼ tsp. pepper
6 boiled potatoes, mashed
Breadcrumbs

Mix all ingredients together, adding a little salmon juice, if necessary, and form into patties. Cover patties with bread crumbs. Leave in a cool place overnight.

Bake in shallow dish at 350 degrees F for 15 minutes.

Makes 10 to 12 cakes.

— F. Rosati
Agincourt, Ontario

SALMON CAKES

2 cups cooked salmon
1 medium onion, chopped & sautéed
1 egg
¼ cup chopped parsley

1 tsp. dry dill weed
½ tsp. sweet basil
4 Tbsp. flour

Combine all ingredients except flour in a bowl and shape into patties. Coat well with flour. Fry, turning once, until crisp and golden.

Makes 8 large patties.

— Chris Ferris
Lasqueti Island, B.C.

POACHED COD

1 lb. fish fillets
1¼ cups milk
½ tsp. salt
1 small bay leaf
3 peppercorns
1 whole clove

2 Tbsp. butter
3 Tbsp. chopped green onion
2 Tbsp. flour
⅛ tsp. pepper
2-3 Tbsp. lemon juice

Cut fish into serving-sized pieces. Heat milk, salt, bay leaf, peppercorns and clove to boiling in a large skillet. Add fish, bring just to a boil, lower heat, cover and simmer until flaky — 5 to 10 minutes. Lift fish out and keep warm.

Meanwhile, melt butter and add onion. Cook, stirring, for 3 minutes. Sprinkle in flour and pepper, stirring to blend. Remove from heat and stir into fish liquid.

Return pan to heat and stir sauce until boiling, thickened and smooth. Add lemon juice. Pour the sauce over the fish and garnish with more green onion.

Serves 4.

— Sharron Jansen
Pembroke, Ontario

BREADED COD FILLETS

1 lb. cod fillets
1 egg
¼ cup milk
8-10 crushed crackers
¼ tsp. sea salt

Pinch of pepper
¼ tsp. garlic powder
¼ tsp. sweet basil
¼ tsp. dill weed

Dip fillets in egg and milk beaten together. Combine remaining ingredients and coat fillets with this mixture.

Fry fillets in oil for about 5 minutes on each side.

Serves 4.

— Diane Schoemperlen
Banff, Alberta

BAKED COD WITH VEGETABLES

2 lbs. frozen cod fillets
2 cups finely chopped tomatoes
½ cup finely chopped onion
¼ cup finely chopped green pepper
1 tsp. salt

⅛ tsp. pepper
½ tsp. basil
¼ tsp. thyme
¼ tsp. tarragon
¼ cup corn oil

Thaw fish until fillets can be separated, and arrange in a shallow greased baking dish. Combine tomatoes, onion, green pepper, seasonings and oil, and spread on top of fish. Bake 10 to 15 minutes at 475 degrees F or until fish flakes when tested with a fork.

Serves 6.

— Shirley Gilbert
Calgary, Alberta

SOLE AMANDINE

WITH ITS SUBTLE FLAVOURS AND CONTRASTING TEXTURES, THIS SIMPLE BUT elegant dish can only be described as delectable.

½ cup flour
1 tsp. salt
¼ tsp. pepper
1 tsp. paprika
2 lbs. sole fillets
3 Tbsp. butter

3 Tbsp. slivered almonds
3 Tbsp. lemon juice
1 tsp. grated lemon rind
3 Tbsp. chopped chives
⅓ cup salad oil

Combine flour, salt, pepper and paprika in a flat dish. Cut fish into serving-sized pieces and dip into flour mixture to coat both sides.

Heat butter in a small skillet. Add almonds and cook gently, stirring, until golden. Stir in lemon juice, lemon rind and chives.

Heat oil in large heavy skillet and fry fish quickly on both sides until golden. Lift out onto a hot platter and pour almond mixture over fish. Serve immediately.

Serves 6.

— Patricia Burley
Elliot Lake, Ontario

CAPERS' SOLE

1 lb. sole, thinly sliced
1 cup sour cream
1 green onion, chopped

¼ lb. baby shrimp
6 oz. orange juice
Grated Parmesan cheese to garnish

Place half the sole in a greased baking dish. Cover with half the sour cream and half the green onion. Sprinkle with all of the shrimp. Repeat layers of sole, sour cream and green onion. Pour orange juice over all and sprinkle with Parmesan cheese.

Bake at 350 degrees F for 30 minutes.

Serves 2.

— Capers Restaurant
Prince George, B.C.

SOLE FLORENTINE

1½ lbs. spinach, cooked,
   drained & chopped
2 lbs. sole fillets, wiped dry
3-4 green onions, chopped
2 cups sliced mushrooms

4 Tbsp. butter
½ cup butter
½ cup flour
2 cups milk
Salt & pepper

Place spinach in buttered casserole dish and lay fish fillets on top.

Sauté mushrooms in 4 Tbsp. butter. Sprinkle green onion and mushrooms on top of fish.

Melt remaining ½ cup butter in heavy saucepan. Stir in flour and cook for about 2 minutes. Gradually add milk, stirring constantly. Bring to a boil and cook for 1 to 2 minutes or until thick. Add salt and pepper to taste.

Pour over fish and bake at 425 degrees F for 15 to 20 minutes.

Serves 6.

— Sheila Bear
St. John's, Nfld.

HADDOCK FILLETS WITH MUSHROOM SAUCE

2½ lbs. haddock fillets
1 tsp. salt
Pinch pepper
Pinch cayenne
5 Tbsp. flour
5 Tbsp. butter

1 Tbsp. oil
Pinch white pepper
2 cups milk
½ cup finely chopped mushrooms
1 tsp. chopped fresh dill

Pat fillets dry with a paper towel, season on both sides with ½ tsp. salt, pepper and cayenne, and dust lightly with 1 Tbsp. flour.

Place 1 Tbsp. butter and oil in a heavy frying pan, heat and brown fillets, one at a time, on both sides. Place on a heated serving platter to keep warm.

Melt 4 Tbsp. butter in heavy saucepan and stir in 4 Tbsp. flour, white pepper and remaining salt. Slowly stir in milk until sauce is smooth and creamy. Add mushrooms.

Pour mushroom sauce over fish and garnish with dill.

Serves 4 to 6.

— *Brenda Eckstein*
Kamloops, B.C.

FISH IN BEER BATTER

12-14 oz. flat beer
3 Tbsp. Thousand Island dressing
Whole wheat flour
White flour
1 tsp. baking powder
¼ tsp. tarragon

¼ tsp. paprika
¼ tsp. parsley
¼ tsp. dill
Salt & pepper
9 fillets fish (bass, perch, pickerel)

Pour beer into a large mixing bowl, add the dressing and beat until it breaks into tiny particles.

Slowly mix in flour, using white and whole wheat in proportion to suit your taste, breaking up lumps until batter is thick, not runny, and adheres to a wooden spoon. Add baking powder and seasonings and let sit for 30 minutes.

Dip fillets in batter and fry or deep fry until golden brown and crisp. Drain well and serve.

Serves 4.

— *Roly Kleer*
Pickle Lake, Ontario

TUNA CASSEROLE

3 Tbsp. butter
3 Tbsp. flour
1 cup milk
Pinch each: celery salt,
  dry mustard, paprika
¼ tsp. garlic powder
¼ tsp. basil

½ cup grated Cheddar cheese
1 cup uncooked macaroni
1 small onion, chopped
1 green pepper, chopped
2 stalks celery, chopped
½ cup chopped mushrooms
1 large tin tuna

Melt butter, blend in flour and cook on low heat for 5 minutes. Slowly blend in milk and seasonings. Add cheese and cook, stirring, until thick and smooth. Remove from heat and set aside.

Cook macaroni in boiling water until tender.

In a casserole dish, mix together the vegetables, macaroni, cheese sauce and tuna. Bake at 350 degrees F for 45 minutes.

Serves 6.

— *Diane Schoemperlen*
Banff, Alberta

BAKED FISH ALASKA

2 lbs. fish fillets
1 cup sour cream
½ cup chopped green onion tops

Salt
⅓ cup grated Parmesan cheese
Paprika

Place fillets in well greased baking pan. Combine cream, onion tops, salt and cheese, and spread over fillets. Bake at 350 degrees F for 20 to 25 minutes or until fish flakes easily when tested with a fork. Sprinkle with paprika and serve.

Serves 4.

— *J. Bertrand*
High Level, Alberta

BAKED FISH

2-3 lbs. fish fillets
1 cup milk
1 tsp. salt
Pepper
Paprika

1 Tbsp. lemon juice
3 Tbsp. butter
4 slices bacon
Fine dry bread crumbs

Cut fillets into serving-sized pieces and arrange in a greased casserole dish. Pour milk over fish. Add salt, pepper, paprika and lemon juice. Dot with butter. Arrange bacon slices on fish, cutting them in half if necessary. Sprinkle with bread crumbs. Bake at 425 degrees F until fish flakes easily when tested with a fork — 15 to 20 minutes.

Serves 4 to 6.

— *Johanna Vanderheyden*
Strathroy, Ontario

STIR-FRIED FISH

Safflower oil or unsalted butter
1 onion, diced
1 green pepper, diced
½ lb. mushrooms, diced
1½ lbs. fish, boned
1½ cups hot water with 1 soya cube added
  or 1½ cups vegetable stock

4 tsp. flour
1 tsp. soya sauce
½ tsp. ginger
2 Tbsp. sherry (optional)

Coat wok with oil or butter. Sauté vegetables quickly in the order listed, placing each new vegetable in centre of wok.

Cut fish into bite-sized pieces and sauté quickly. Add remaining ingredients and stir together.

Serves 4.

— *Trish Hines*
Wyebridge, Ontario

OVEN-FRIED FILLETS

½ cup fine dry bread crumbs
½ tsp. salt
⅛ tsp. pepper
1 Tbsp. parsley flakes

1 tsp. paprika
2 Tbsp. vegetable oil
2 lbs. sole or perch fillets

Combine bread crumbs, salt, pepper, parsley flakes and paprika in a bowl. Add oil and blend with fork until thoroughly combined. Spread on wax paper.

Separate fish fillets carefully. Press into crumb mixture to coat both sides. Place on greased cookie sheet and bake at 450 degrees F for 12 minutes, or until fish flakes easily.

Serves 6.

— *Helen Potts*
Tilden Lake, Ontario

FILLETS AU GRATIN

2 Tbsp. butter
2 Tbsp. flour
½ tsp. salt
1 cup milk

1 cup grated cheese
1 lb. fish fillets
1 cup bread crumbs tossed with
   4 Tbsp. melted butter

Melt butter, remove from heat, blend in flour and salt. Add milk slowly. Return to heat when well blended. Cook until smooth and thickened. Add cheese and remove from heat.

Meanwhile, steam the fillets gently for about 5 minutes. Break them up into a baking dish. Pour cheese sauce over fish. Sprinkle with bread crumbs. Bake at 350 degrees F for 20 minutes.

Serves 4.

— Anne White
Stirling, Ontario

BOATMAN'S STEW

2 lbs. white fish
Salt
2 Tbsp. butter
2 medium onions, sliced
6-oz. can tomato paste

3 cups water
¼ tsp. red pepper
¼ tsp. black pepper
1 cup chopped fresh parsley
⅓ cup dry white wine (optional)

Cut fish into 2-inch chunks. Sprinkle with salt and let stand for 1 hour.

Melt butter in a heavy saucepan and brown onions. Pour off fat and stir in tomato paste, water, pepper, parsley and wine. Simmer for 30 minutes.

Drain fish and add to onion/tomato paste mixture. Simmer for 10 minutes.

Serves 6.

— Wendy Searcy
Minnedosa, Manitoba

SWEET & SOUR FISH

2 lbs. fish fillets
2 Tbsp. cornstarch
2 Tbsp. oil
1 small onion, chopped
1 clove garlic, minced
1 slice ginger

3 Tbsp. soya sauce
2 Tbsp. sherry (optional)
½ cup honey
4 Tbsp. vinegar
½ tsp. sesame oil (optional)
1 cup chicken stock

Cut fish into 2-inch chunks and shake in cornstarch to coat. Heat oil in wok and fry fish until golden brown, stirring frequently. Remove from pan.

Add chopped onion, garlic and ginger and fry until golden brown.

Combine remaining ingredients, add to wok and bring to a boil. Lower heat and cook until thickened. Add fish and simmer 1 minute.

Serves 6.

— Brigitte Wolf
Lucknow, Ontario

CREAMY TUNA FILLING

1 cup cottage cheese
½ cup mayonnaise, page 92
1 small can tuna, drained & flaked

¼ cup sliced stuffed olives
Few drops Tabasco sauce

Combine cottage cheese and mayonnaise and blend until smooth. Add tuna, olives and Tabasco sauce. Combine thoroughly.

Chill and use for sandwiches.

Makes 2 cups.

— Donna Jubb
Fenelon Falls, Ontario

ANCHOVY DIP

8 oz. cream cheese
1 cup sour cream
1 can anchovies

¼ cup sweet pickled cocktail onions
2 cloves garlic

Cream together cheese and sour cream. Mince anchovies, onions and garlic finely. Stir into cheese mixture. Serve with fresh raw vegetables.

Makes 2 cups.

—Maureen Johnson
Pembroke, Ontario

SALMON CHEESE BALL

2 6½-oz. cans salmon
8 oz. cream cheese, softened
1 Tbsp. lemon juice
2 tsp. grated onion

¼ tsp. salt
Dash Worcestershire sauce
6 Tbsp. mayonnaise, page 92
3 Tbsp. snipped fresh parsley

Drain and flake salmon, removing bones. Mix all ingredients thoroughly except the parsley. Chill several hours. Shape into a ball or log, roll in parsley and chill.

Makes 2½ cups.

— Marva Blackmore
Vancouver, B.C.

KIPPER PATE

1 lb. kipper fillets
4 Tbsp. butter

1 onion, peeled & finely chopped
Black pepper

Cook kippers by gently poaching in water.

Melt butter in pan and fry onion until very soft but not brown. Add kippers. Flake and mix well with onion and pepper to taste.

Remove from heat. Mash well with fork until quite smooth.

Put into earthenware dish or other container suitable for serving. Press down. Cover and refrigerate until served.

— Sheila Bear
St. John's, Nfld.

HOT SEAFOOD COCKTAIL SPREAD

8 oz. cream cheese
1 Tbsp. milk
7½-oz. tin shrimp

2 tsp. Worcestershire sauce
2 Tbsp. green onion

Soften cream cheese and combine with milk. Crumble shrimp and add to cheese mixture. Add Worcestershire sauce and green onion and mix well.

Turn into greased 8-inch pie plate and bake at 350 degrees F for 15 minutes. Spread on crackers and serve hot.

Makes 1½ cups.

— Olga Harrison
Peterborough, Ontario

CRAB DELIGHT

8 oz. cream cheese, softened
1 Tbsp. milk
6 oz. cooked crabmeat

1 Tbsp. finely chopped green onion
Pinch Dijon mustard
Pinch salt

Cream cheese with milk until soft and smooth. Add crabmeat, onion, mustard and salt. Blend well.

Refrigerate 3 to 4 hours. Serve with crackers or bite-sized fresh vegetables.

— Brenda Watts
Surrey, B.C.

SHRIMP DIP

8 oz. cream cheese
Juice of 1 lemon
½ cup mayonnaise, page 92
2 Tbsp. ketchup

1 small onion, grated
Dash Worcestershire sauce
Dash salt
1 cup chopped shrimp

Cream cheese with lemon juice and add remaining ingredients. Chill well before serving.

Makes 2 cups.

— A.H. McInnis
Fredericton, New Brunswick

BETHANY PEPPERS

4 large green peppers
2 Tbsp. butter
1 onion, chopped
1 clove garlic, minced
1 tsp. minced parsley
2 cups canned tomatoes, drained

¼ cup wheat germ or fine bread crumbs
Salt & pepper
1 egg, beaten
1 cup cooked shrimp
½ cup bread crumbs tossed with
  3 Tbsp. butter

Split in half and seed green peppers. Steam for 5 minutes and set aside.

Sauté onion in melted butter. Add garlic, parsley, tomatoes and wheat germ or bread crumbs. Cook, stirring, until soft and well mixed. Season with salt and pepper, then stir in egg and shrimp.

Stuff peppers with this mixture and sprinkle with bread crumbs. Bake at 350 degrees F for 20 minutes.

Serves 4.

— Bryanna Clark
Union Bay, B.C.

SCALLOPED CRAB

2 Tbsp. butter
2 Tbsp. flour
1 cup light cream
Salt & pepper
½ tsp. paprika

2 cups crabmeat
⅔ cup bread crumbs
2 Tbsp. melted butter
Paprika

Melt the butter, add flour and cook a few minutes. Add cream and cook, stirring, until smooth and thick. Season with salt, pepper and paprika.

In an ovenproof dish place half the sauce, the crabmeat, the rest of the sauce, then the bread crumbs. Drizzle the melted butter over all and dust with paprika. Bake for about 25 minutes at 350 degrees F.

Serves 4.

— *Irene Louden*
Port Coquitlam, B.C.

CRAB TARTS

2 loaves thin sandwich bread
½ cup melted butter
3 Tbsp. butter
¼ cup flour
1½ cups milk
1 cup grated Cheddar cheese
6-oz. can crabmeat, drained & flaked

1 Tbsp. green onion, finely chopped
1 Tbsp. lemon juice
2 Tbsp. minced parsley
1 tsp. Worcestershire sauce
1 tsp. prepared mustard
½ tsp. salt
Dash Tabasco sauce

To make toasted shells, cut circle out of bread using a medium-sized cup. Brush melted butter on both sides of the bread circles. Press bread gently into muffin tins to form a shell. Bake at 425 degrees F for 5 minutes, or until edges are crisp and golden brown.

To make filling, melt butter in medium saucepan over medium heat. Let butter bubble, then stir in flour to form a smooth paste. Let bubble and add milk. Bring to a boil, stirring frequently, then turn heat to low. When mixture forms a thick, creamy sauce, add the cheese, stirring until melted.

Add the remaining ingredients one at a time, stirring after each addition. Remove from heat. Spoon filling into toasted shells and place on a cookie sheet. Bake at 350 degrees F for 15 minutes.

Makes 3 dozen.

— *Cathy Davis*
Kingston, Ontario

BAKED SCALLOPS

1 cup bread crumbs
Salt & pepper

1 lb. scallops
½ cup melted butter

Butter a casserole dish and layer the crumbs, seasoned with salt and pepper, and scallops, finishing with a layer of crumbs. Pour melted butter over all and bake at 375 degrees F for 15 to 20 minutes.

Serves 2.

— *Audrey Moroso*
Puslinch, Ontario

SHRIMP TARTS

Pastry for 9-inch pie crust
1½ cups shrimp
½ cup chopped green onion
½ lb. Swiss cheese, grated
1 cup mayonnaise, page 92

4 eggs
1 cup milk
½ tsp. salt
½ tsp. dill weed

Roll out pastry and cut into six 4-inch circles. Place in muffin tins. Combine shrimp, green onion and cheese and place in pastry shells. Beat together mayonnaise, eggs, milk, salt and dill weed. Pour over mixture in shells.

Bake at 400 degrees F for 15 to 20 minutes.

Makes 6 tarts.

— Linda Fahie
Tangier, Nova Scotia

CLAM CRISP

1¼ cups flour
1 tsp. baking powder
¼ tsp. cayenne
2 eggs
½ cup milk

2 cans minced clams
1 green onion, chopped
Parsley
1 celery stalk, chopped
Salt & pepper

Mix flour, baking powder and cayenne in a bowl. Beat eggs and milk together, then beat in flour mixture until smooth. Let stand for 30 minutes.

Add clams, onion, parsley, celery, salt and pepper. Drop by spoonfuls into hot oil and cook until golden brown.

— Jane Guigueno
Victoria, B.C.

COQUILLES ST. JACQUES

1 lb. scallops
½ cup white wine
¼ cup water
1 small onion, chopped
Salt & pepper
Bouquet garni (small cheesecloth bag
  containing 1 bay leaf, 6 sprigs parsley,
  chopped celery stalk & 6 peppercorns)
¼ lb. mushrooms

Juice of 1 lemon
3 Tbsp. butter
3 Tbsp. flour
1 cup light cream
1 egg yolk
¼ cup bread crumbs
2 Tbsp. melted butter
2 Tbsp. Parmesan cheese

Wash scallops and simmer slowly in wine and water with onion, salt, pepper and bouquet garni. Drain, reserving liquid. Place liquid back on stove, boil down to ½ cup and set aside.

Slice mushrooms, combine with lemon juice and cook 4 minutes. Set aside.

Melt butter, stir in flour and cook until smooth. Stir in cream and cook slowly, stirring constantly, until mixture thickens. Stir in scallop liquid. Beat egg yolk and pour sauce over it slowly, stirring constantly.

Combine scallops, drained mushrooms and sauce. Pour into a casserole dish or scallop shells. Sprinkle with bread crumbs, melted butter and Parmesan cheese. Brown under broiler and serve immediately.

Serves 6 as an appetizer.

— Margaret Silverthorn
Iona Station, Ontario

SEAFOOD CASSEROLE

1 lb. scallops
2 cups milk
¼ cup butter
¼ cup flour
½ tsp. salt

Pepper
1 tsp. curry powder
1 can cream of shrimp soup
½ cup shrimp

Cover scallops with milk and simmer for 10 minutes. Drain and reserve 1½ cups of milk.

Meanwhile, melt butter and stir in flour and seasonings. Add reserved milk and cook, stirring, until thickened. Stir in curry powder and shrimp soup.

Pour into serving dish and add shrimp and scallops.

Serves 4.

— J.E. Riendl
Grand Bay, N.B.

SHRIMP CURRY

1 stalk celery, finely chopped
½ green pepper, finely diced
2 green onions, finely chopped
¼ cup butter
1 lb. shrimp, cleaned & deveined

¼ cup flour
2 cups light cream
Salt & pepper
2 Tbsp. curry powder

Sauté celery, green pepper and onions in butter. When celery is slightly softened, stir in shrimp and continue to sauté, stirring constantly, until shrimp is bright pink. Remove shrimp and vegetables from pan.

Stir flour into remaining liquid, adding butter, if needed, to make a roux. Slowly stir in cream to make a thick cream sauce. Add salt, pepper and curry powder. Return shrimp and vegetables to sauce and heat through.

Serves 2.

SHRIMP IN BEER CREOLE

½ cup sliced blanched almonds
3 Tbsp. butter
1 Tbsp. oil
Salt
2 lbs. shrimp, shelled & deveined
¼ cup butter
¼ cup minced scallions

1 green pepper, cut into strips
½ lb. small mushrooms, cleaned
1 Tbsp. paprika
Salt & pepper
1 tsp. tomato paste
1 cup light beer
¾ cup heavy cream

In a small skillet, sauté the almonds in 1 Tbsp. of butter and the oil until golden. Drain on paper towels, sprinkle with salt and set aside.

Cook the shrimp in ¼ cup butter over medium heat, stirring, until they turn pink. Transfer the shrimp and pan juices to a bowl and reserve.

Add 2 Tbsp. butter to saucepan and sauté scallions and green pepper until softened. Add mushrooms, paprika, salt and pepper and cook until mushrooms are tender. Stir in tomato paste, beer and pan juices and reduce liquid over high heat to ½ cup. Reduce heat to low, add cream and shrimp and simmer until hot.

Serve over rice pilaf and garnish with almonds.

Serves 4.

— Veronica Green
Winnipeg, Manitoba

SHRIMP & SCALLOP TILSIT

12 oz. scallops
1½ tsp. lemon juice
1 tsp. salt
⅓ lb. small mushrooms, halved
1 Tbsp. diced green pepper
7 Tbsp. butter
6 Tbsp. flour
1½ cups milk
8 oz. Tilsit cheese, diced

¼ tsp. garlic powder
¼ tsp. white pepper
¼ tsp. dry mustard
1 tsp. ketchup
8 oz. cooked shrimp
2 Tbsp. sherry
Patty shells or
  homemade cream puff shells

Cover scallops with water, add ½ tsp. lemon juice and ¼ tsp. salt and simmer 10 minutes. Drain, reserving ¼ cup of the stock.

Cook mushrooms and green peppers in 2 Tbsp. butter for 5 minutes. Add remaining butter, stir in flour, then slowly add milk and stock. Stir in cheese until melted, add remaining lemon juice and seasonings. Add scallops, shrimp and sherry. Heat through and serve in patty shells.

Serves 4.

— *Dorothy Hurst*
Nanaimo, B.C.

TURKEY OYSTER PIE

1 onion, diced
2 stalks celery, diced
1 small green pepper, diced
2 Tbsp. butter
2 cups diced cooked turkey
2 cups fresh oysters, lightly poached

1½ cups cream of mushroom sauce,
  page 92
Dash Worcestershire sauce
Pepper
3-4 cups mashed potatoes

Sauté onion, celery and green pepper in butter. Place in casserole dish and add turkey, oysters, mushroom sauce, Worcestershire sauce and pepper. Combine well and top with mashed potatoes.

Bake at 350 degrees F for 30 to 40 minutes.

Serves 6.

— *The Sword Restaurant*
Consecon, Ontario

SCALLOPS MORNAY

2 lbs. scallops, cut in half
1 onion
Bouquet garni of bay leaf,
  parsley & thyme
1-2 cups white wine

Salt & pepper
¼ cup butter
¼ cup flour
1 cup cream
½ cup grated Swiss cheese

Combine scallops, onion, bouquet garni, salt and pepper in saucepan and add enough white wine to cover. Gently bring to a boil and simmer for 2 minutes. Drain and reserve 1 cup stock.

In a separate pan, melt butter, add flour and cook for 2 minutes. Slowly add cream, stirring constantly. Add stock, bring to a boil and cook gently for 2 minutes. Add Swiss cheese and cook until melted. Add scallops and stir well.

Pour into greased casserole dish and top with a sprinkling of bread crumbs, grated Swiss cheese and a drizzle of melted butter. Brown in oven and serve.

Serves 6.

— *Sheila Bear*
St. John's, Nfld.

SEAFOOD IN FILO PASTRY

2 Tbsp. butter
½ cup thinly sliced celery
½ cup chopped onions
1 cup sliced mushrooms
4 Tbsp. flour
1 tsp. salt
1½ cups milk
½ cup white wine
2 Tbsp. lemon juice
¼ cup grated Parmesan cheese
½ lb. cooked shrimp
½ lb. cooked sole
1 lb. cooked salmon
8 sheets filo pastry
¾ cup melted butter

Melt butter in large, heavy saucepan. Add celery and onion and cook until tender. Add mushrooms and continue cooking. Stir in flour and salt. Add milk slowly, stirring constantly, and cook until slightly thickened. Stir in wine, lemon juice and cheese. Cook until thickened, stirring constantly. Remove from heat and add seafood.

Grease a 9" x 13" baking dish. Brush each sheet of pastry with melted butter and layer in dish. When all 8 sheets are buttered and in dish, spoon a row of filling down the middle of pastry.

Fold both sides in, so they overlap. Flip gently so seam is facing down. Tuck ends under and brush top with remaining butter.

Bake at 375 degrees F for 45 minutes or until crisp and golden brown.

Serves 8.

— Susan Gillespie
Comox, B.C.

CRAB LOUIS

2 tsp. chili sauce
2 tsp. chopped green onion
1 tsp. vinegar
1 tsp. horseradish
1 tsp. mustard
½ tsp. sugar
¼ tsp. paprika
Salt & pepper
½ cup mayonnaise
½ cup sour cream
1 lb. crabmeat,
  cooked & cut into chunks
1 head lettuce
2-3 hard-boiled eggs, sliced
1 cucumber, sliced

Combine chili sauce, green onion, vinegar, horseradish, mustard, sugar, paprika, salt, pepper, mayonnaise and sour cream. Toss with crabmeat.

Shred lettuce and line serving bowl with it. Top with crabmeat mixture and surround with egg and cucumber slices.

Serves 6.

— J. Bertrand
High Level, Alberta

CRABMEAT MOUSSE

2 tsp. gelatin
¼ cup cold water
¼ cup boiling water
¾ cup mayonnaise, page 92
1 cup flaked crabmeat
½ cup chopped celery
2 Tbsp. chopped parsley
½ cup chopped cucumber
2 Tbsp. chopped olives
1-2 Tbsp. lemon juice
Shredded lettuce

Soften gelatin in cold water and then dissolve in boiling water. Add mayonnaise, then crabmeat, celery, parsley, cucumber, olives and lemon juice and mix well.

Place in a wet mould and chill until firm. Unmould onto lettuce.

Serves 6.

SHRIMP SALAD

1½ cups cooked rice
1½ cups raw peas
1½ cups chopped celery
¼ cup chopped green onion
1 cup shrimp
½ cup salad oil

1 Tbsp. soya sauce
1 tsp. celery seed
2 Tbsp. cider vinegar
Salt
½ Tbsp. sugar

Combine rice, peas, celery, onion and shrimp. For dressing, blend remaining ingredients well. Pour over shrimp mixture. Toss and chill.

Serves 4.

— *Trudy Mason*
Meaford, Ontario

LOBSTER MOULD

1 lb. cooked lobster
1 Tbsp. capers
⅓ small onion
3 Tbsp. whipping cream
⅓ cup butter, softened

2 Tbsp. anisette
Dash Tabasco sauce
1 tsp. salt
1 tsp. fresh tarragon
Whipped cream & grapes to garnish

Grind together the lobster, capers and onion. Add whipping cream, butter, anisette, Tabasco sauce, salt and tarragon. Mix well and pack into a mould. Refrigerate for several hours before unmoulding.

Place unmoulded salad on a bed of lettuce, cover with whipped cream and garnish with green grapes.

Serves 4.

SEAFOOD SALAD

EQUALLY GOOD HOT OR COLD, THIS DISH CAN BE MADE WITH FRESH, FROZEN OR canned seafood.

¼ cup butter
¼ cup chopped onion
¼ cup chopped green & red peppers
2 cups crabmeat,
  drained & rinsed if canned
10 oz. large shrimp,
  drained & rinsed if canned

1 cup mayonnaise, page 92
1 tsp. Worcestershire sauce
2 tsp. mustard
Salt & pepper
Parsley
Lemon wedges

In a small skillet, melt butter, add onions and peppers, and cook until onions are translucent. Pour into lightly greased baking dish. Add remaining ingredients except parsley and lemon. Mix well. Bake at 350 degrees F for 20 minutes, sprinkle with parsley, layer lemon over top and serve.

Serves 4.

— *C. Majewski*
Pansy, Manitoba

SALAD NIÇOISE

2 cloves garlic, peeled
6 anchovy fillets, coarsely chopped
6-oz. can tuna, drained
2 tomatoes, peeled & quartered
1 cucumber, peeled & finely chopped

12 black olives, pitted & chopped
1 cup Bibb lettuce, torn up
1 cup romaine lettuce, torn up
French dressing, page 93

Rub salad bowl with garlic and discard garlic. Combine anchovy fillets, tuna, tomatoes, cucumber, olives and lettuces. Toss gently with dressing to coat. Chill well before serving.

Serves 2 as a main course, 4 as a salad.

HERRING SALAD

HERRING IS A TRADITIONAL YULETIME DISH FOR MANY, AND THIS SALAD PROVIDES A colourful and flavourful method of serving it. Milter herring are the male fish during breeding season.

6 milter herring
1 cup dry red wine
2 hard-boiled eggs, cubed
1 cup cooked veal, cubed
2 cups pickled beets, cubed
½ cup chopped onion
2 stalks celery, chopped

½ cup chopped boiled potatoes
3 cups diced apples
1 cup shredded almonds
1 cup sugar
2 Tbsp. horseradish
2 Tbsp. parsley
Olives to garnish

Soak the herring in water for 12 hours. Skin them and remove the milt and bones. Rub the milt through sieve with wine.

Cube the herring and mix with eggs, veal, beets, onion, celery, potatoes, apples and almonds.

Combine milt mixture with sugar, horseradish and parsley. Pour over salad and mix well. Shape into mound and garnish with olives.

Serves 12.

CHINESE TUNA SALAD

2 6½-oz. cans tuna
2 cups coarsely shredded lettuce
¼ cup chopped onion
½ cup chopped parsley or watercress
¼ tsp. grated lemon rind
½ tsp. ground coriander

¼ cup sesame seeds
¼ cup toasted slivered almonds
3-oz. pkg. chow mein noodles
1 Tbsp. lemon juice
3 Tbsp. soya sauce
1 Tbsp. oil

Combine all but last 3 ingredients. Mix together lemon juice, soya sauce and oil, pour over salad and toss.

Serves 6.

— Anna J. Lee
Sault Ste. Marie, Ontario

Poultry & Game

Not to presume to dictate,
but broiled fowl and
mushrooms — capital thing!

— Charles Dickens
Pickwick Papers

"**W**hat is sauce for the goose may be sauce for the gander, but it is not necessarily sauce for the chicken, the duck, the turkey or the Guinea hen," said Alice B. Toklas, whose intent was undoubtedly philosophical, not merely culinary. Nevertheless, having visited many a greasy spoon that serves canned beef-flavoured gravy over everything from french fries to open-faced turkey sandwiches, we have to attest to the truth of Toklas' words, even in the kitchen.

Turkeys are not simply big chickens or land-bound ducks; Guinea fowl are not just little turkeys with spots. As omni-gravy does justice to nothing, so each type of poultry has its own peculiarities and pluses, and responds best to certain ways of cooking and serving. Goose, for instance, is usually so greasy it must be roasted on a rack over a pan that has to be periodically emptied, while roast turkey needs occasional basting — moistening with its own juices — to prevent it from becoming too dry.

Poultry meat, especially chicken, has escalated in popularity as its reputation as a lean meat of relatively low price has spread. Poultry, excepting wild bird, tends to have a delicate flavour that adapts pleasantly to the flavours of many herbs and most vegetables and fruits. As the birds are

hardy and quite inexpensive to raise, most of the world's various cuisines include chicken, providing examples of just how versatile the meat can be, flavoured with everything from soya sauce to curry to tomatoes and cheese and hot chilies.

As is the case with all fresh poultry, fresh turkey is tastier and better in texture than frozen, but it is not always available to city buyers. Those who depend on the frozen turkey supply must remember to begin thawing the bird several hours or even days ahead of roasting time; calculate the time so that the bird will be thawed just an hour or two before it is to go into the oven.

Leave the frozen bird in its wrapper. Placed in the refrigerator it will take about two hours per pound (4 hours per kilo) to thaw. Immersed in a sink filled with cold water, it will thaw in about an hour per pound; at room temperature, allow about one and a half hours per pound.

Do not stuff poultry until it is almost time to begin roasting, as a stuffed bird is easy prey for spoilage organisms. Pack the stuffing loosely to allow the oven heat to penetrate it more quickly. A roasted, stuffed bird is done when a meat thermometer extended into the centre of the stuffing reads 165 degrees F; an unstuffed bird will be 185 degrees F in the thickest part of the thigh. Or use a pre-

meat-thermometer method; any roasted bird is done when the thigh joint is loose and limber.

Poultry is often served in pieces or chunks, which increases its adaptability to various dishes. To divide a whole bird, first remove the legs and wings from the body, twisting them back so they can be cut away cleanly. Then snip along the centre and breast bone with poultry shears or clean pruning shears and, pulling from the centre outward, cut along between the ribs and the back, leaving the neck and back as a single section that can be used as is or simmered for soup stock. The remaining pieces — two legs, two wings and two breasts — can be left whole for frying, baking, broiling or barbecuing.

The cook who wants even smaller chunks of meat — for stir-frying, for example — should cook the whole bird or entire pieces before removing the meat, to minimize meat loss. And when almost all the meat has been removed from a whole carcass, half-submerge it in a big pot, let it simmer until the meat and gristle fall from the bones, pour it through a colander, add to the broth any bits of remaining meat as well as herbs, seasonings and vegetables, and have excellent afternoon-after soup.

Especially suited to soups and stews are older birds, whose meat is just as nutritious as that of the young, tender and more expensive ones. Old birds, however, must be cooked in a way that takes their toughness into consideration; not for nothing are old hens called "stewing fowl." Their meat is tasty, however, and very tender after hours of slow cooking in liquid.

Rabbits have the most poultry-like flesh of all domestic animals, and like chickens, they are quite easily and profitably kept by smallholders. Although domesticated, they are usually called "game," a word whose meaning was described by French gastronome Brillat-Savarin in his classic of 1825, *The Physiology of Taste:*

"By game we mean those animals which live in the woods and fields in a state of natural freedom and which are still good to eat. We say 'good to eat' because some of these creatures are not properly covered by the title of game, like the foxes, badgers, crows, magpies, screech owls and others: they are called vermin, *bêtes puantes.*"

What Brillat-Savarin thought of groundhog or raccoon for dinner he didn't say — no doubt one man's game is another man's *bête puante* — but there is little argument about the tastiness of some of the better accepted game animals such as rabbit, deer or moose.

CHICKEN BREASTS IN MAPLE SYRUP

4 chicken breasts, boned
Seasoned flour
3 large mushrooms, finely chopped
½ cup finely diced ham
½ tsp. dried chives

2 Tbsp. butter
¼ cup butter
1 cup thinly sliced onion
Savory
4 Tbsp. maple syrup

Roll each breast in seasoned flour. Fry mushrooms, ham and chives in 2 Tbsp. butter for 2 to 3 minutes or until mushrooms are tender.

Slit thick portion of each breast and insert spoonful of ham mixture. Pinch edges together to seal. Brown stuffed breasts in ¼ cup butter. Remove from pan, add onion to pan and fry until golden brown.

Arrange breasts in casserole dish. Top with onion and sprinkle with savory. Spoon maple syrup over chicken breasts. Rinse frying pan with ½ cup water, then pour over chicken.

Bake, uncovered, at 350 degrees F for 30 minutes.

Serves 4.

— Mary Rogers
Kitchener, Ontario

PARMESAN CHICKEN

1 cup bread crumbs
1½ cups grated Parmesan cheese
3 Tbsp. parsley
¼ tsp. salt
1 tsp. dry mustard

½ tsp. Worcestershire sauce
¼ tsp. garlic salt
½ cup melted butter
8-10 boned chicken breasts

Combine bread crumbs, cheese, parsley and salt and set aside. Combine remaining ingredients except chicken. Dip chicken, one piece at a time, into butter mixture, then into bread crumbs.

Place in shallow baking pan and bake at 350 degrees F for 40 to 50 minutes. Garnish with pitted, sliced black olives and sliced mushrooms.

Serves 4 to 5.

—Barbara Johnson
Prince George, B.C.

CHICKEN BREASTS ALFREDO

3 eggs, beaten
3 tsp. water
½ cup grated Romano cheese
¼ cup snipped parsley
½ tsp. salt
3 whole chicken breasts, split & boned
½ cup flour
1 cup fine dry bread crumbs

3 Tbsp. butter
3 tsp. oil
1 cup whipping cream
¼ cup water
¼ cup butter
½ cup grated Romano cheese
¼ cup snipped parsley
6 slices mozzarella cheese

Mix together eggs, water, Romano cheese, parsley and salt. Dip chicken in flour, then egg mixture and then bread crumbs.

Melt butter and oil in large skillet. Cook chicken over medium heat until brown — about 15 minutes. Remove to baking dish.

Heat cream, water and butter in 1-quart saucepan until butter melts. Add cheese, cook and stir over medium heat for 5 minutes. Stir in parsley. Pour over chicken.

Top each piece with a slice of mozzarella cheese. Bake at 425 degrees F until cheese melts and chicken is tender, about 8 minutes.

Serves 4 to 6.

— Pam Collacott
North Gower, Ontario

CREAMY BREAST OF CHICKEN WITH SHRIMP

2 large chicken breasts
Salt
Pepper
Nutmeg
1 clove garlic, minced
½ cup flour
¼ cup butter

½ cup celery
1½ cups fresh mushrooms, sliced
½ cup chopped onions
¾ cup dry white wine
1½ cups shrimp
2 Tbsp. chopped parsley
½ cup sour cream

Cut each breast into bite-sized pieces. Sprinkle with seasonings and garlic and let sit for half an hour. Coat chicken pieces with flour and brown in half the butter until crisp. Add celery, mushrooms, onions and white wine. Simmer, covered, for 30 minutes.

Sauté shrimp in remaining butter for 5 minutes and add to chicken mixture. Add parsley and sour cream and bring to a boil.

Serve over rice.

Serves 4.

— *Shirley Gilbert*
Calgary, Alberta

ROLLED CHICKEN WASHINGTON

½ cup finely chopped fresh mushrooms
2 Tbsp. butter
2 Tbsp. flour
½ cup light cream
1¼ cups shredded sharp Cheddar cheese
¼ tsp. salt

Cayenne pepper
6 chicken breasts
Flour
2 eggs, slightly beaten
¾ cup fine dry bread crumbs

Cook mushrooms in butter for 5 minutes. Blend in flour and stir in cream and cheese. Add salt and cayenne pepper. Cook over low heat, stirring constantly, until cheese is melted. Turn mixture into pie plate and cover. Chill until cheese is very firm and then cut into 6 equal portions.

Remove skin and bones from chicken breasts. Pound to a thickness of ¼-inch. Sprinkle with salt. Place piece of cheese mixture on each breast and roll up, tucking in sides. Press to seal well.

Dust chicken rolls with flour. Dip in slightly beaten egg, then roll in bread crumbs. Cover and chill for at least 1 hour.

Fry in butter at 350 degrees F, turning occasionally, until golden brown on the outside and meat is cooked through.

Serves 6.

— *Martha Brown*
Saskatoon, Sask.

COATED CHICKEN BREASTS

¾ cup sour cream
¼ tsp. sage
½ tsp. salt
¼ tsp. thyme
¼ tsp. basil
Freshly ground pepper
2 tsp. grated onion

½ tsp. lemon juice
1 cup fine bread crumbs
½ cup grated Cheddar cheese
½ tsp. paprika
12 chicken breasts, boned
½-1 cup flour

Combine sour cream, seasonings, onion and lemon juice in a bowl. Combine crumbs, cheese and paprika in a flat dish. Dip chicken in flour to coat both sides, then in sour cream mixture, then in crumb mixture. Place in greased baking dish. Cover with foil and bake at 350 degrees F for 30 minutes. Uncover and bake until tender, about 15 minutes more.

Serves 6 to 8.

— *Shirley Hill*
Picton, Ontario

CHICKEN DIVAN

1 cup white sauce, page 92
1 egg yolk
2 Tbsp. cream
2 Tbsp. grated Parmesan cheese
2 Tbsp. grated Gruyère cheese

3 Tbsp. sherry
3-4 lbs. chicken breasts, skinned & boned
2 lbs. broccoli
Parmesan cheese to garnish

Warm the white sauce. Beat together the egg yolk and cream until well blended. Add a little of the warm sauce to the egg and cream, stir, then return mixture to the rest of the sauce. Heat through, then add cheeses and sherry and continue cooking and stirring until sauce thickens. Set aside.

Poach chicken breasts until tender but still juicy. Cook broccoli until crispy-tender. Drain.

Arrange broccoli on a heatproof platter. Place chicken pieces on top of the broccoli and pour the sauce over it all. Sprinkle with Parmesan cheese.

Bake at 350 degrees F for 20 minutes, or until bubbly.

Serves 6.

— *Cary Elizabeth Marshall*
Thunder Bay, Ontario

CHICKEN KIEV

½ cup soft butter
2 Tbsp. chopped parsley
1 clove garlic, chopped
2 Tbsp. lemon juice
¼ tsp. cayenne pepper

6 chicken breasts, skinned & boned
½ cup flour
2 eggs, beaten
½ cup bread crumbs

Combine butter, parsley, garlic, lemon juice and pepper. Mix well and chill until firm.

Halve chicken breasts and flatten. Salt and pepper lightly. Place a piece of butter mixture on each chicken breast, roll and secure with toothpicks. Coat each roll with flour, dip in beaten eggs and then bread crumbs.

Chill for 1 hour, then deep fry until golden — 15 minutes.

Serves 6.

— *Marney Allen*
Edmonton, Alberta

CHICKEN ROYALE

2 chicken breasts, boned
2 pork sausages
¼ cup oil
3 potatoes, thinly sliced
2 cups broccoli pieces

Stuff boned chicken breasts with sausages, roll and fasten with a toothpick. Heat oil in an electric frying pan and brown breasts. Lower heat, add vegetables and cook for 20 minutes.

Serves 4.

— *Hazel R. Baker*
Coombs, B.C.

CHICKEN IN BACON ROLL WITH CHEESE

4 whole chicken breasts,
  skinned & boned
4 slices ham
4 2-inch cubes mozzarella cheese
12 slices bacon

Pound chicken breasts between sheets of wax paper until quite thin — ¼ inch.

Wrap each piece of cheese in a slice of ham and place in the centre of each breast. Fold edges of chicken over ham and cheese. Wrap 3 slices of bacon around each breast.

Place on a baking sheet and bake at 375 degrees F for 30 minutes.

Serves 4.

— Kathee Roy
Toronto, Ontario

CRANBERRY GLAZED CHICKEN

3 lbs. frying chicken, cut into pieces
1 cup flour
2 tsp. paprika
Garlic salt
Pinch rosemary, thyme & sage
2 Tbsp. brown sugar

¼ tsp. ginger powder
½ cup cranberry jelly
¼ cup orange juice
1 Tbsp. Worcestershire sauce
1 tsp. grated orange rind

Rinse and pat dry chicken. Coat with flour, mixed with paprika, garlic salt, rosemary, thyme and sage. Bake at 400 degrees F for 35 minutes.

Combine sugar, ginger, cranberry jelly, orange juice, Worcestershire sauce and orange rind in small saucepan. Bring to a boil, stirring constantly. Spoon over chicken and bake 10 to 15 minutes longer until chicken is tender.

— Mrs. K. Love
Cobble Hill, B.C.

Serves 4.

BAKED CHICKEN WITH APPLES

3 lbs. chicken pieces
Seasoned flour
2 Tbsp. butter
2 Tbsp. oil
1 clove garlic, crushed
3 apples, cored & quartered

2 Tbsp. brown sugar
½ tsp. ginger
1½ cups unsweetened apple juice
½ cup water or dry sherry
2 Tbsp. cornstarch
¼ cup cold water

Dredge chicken in flour. Brown in butter and oil with garlic. Remove chicken and discard garlic. Add apples to drippings. Sprinkle with brown sugar and brown the apples.

Place chicken and apples in a casserole dish, sprinkle with ginger and pour drippings, apple juice and water or sherry over them. Cover and bake for 45 minutes at 350 degrees F.

Remove chicken from sauce and keep warm. Blend cornstarch with water and stir into pan juices. Cook over high heat, stirring until thickened. Pour over chicken and serve.

Serves 4 to 6.

— Bryanna Clark
Union Bay, B.C.

YOGURT MARINATED CHICKEN

THE MARINADE FOR THIS DISH PRODUCES PLEASANTLY MILD FLAVOURED CHICKEN which remains moist after baking. The chicken is delicious cold as well as warm.

1 broiler chicken,
  cut into serving-sized pieces
2 Tbsp. lemon juice
1 cup yogurt
¼ inch fresh ginger, minced

2 cloves garlic, minced
½ tsp. ground cardamom
½ tsp. chili powder
½ tsp. cinnamon

Combine all ingredients except chicken. Marinate chicken in yogurt mixture overnight. Bake at 375 degrees F for 30 to 45 minutes, basting occasionally.

Serves 6.

— *Ingrid Birker*
Toronto, Ontario

LEMON CHICKEN

THIS DISH MAY BE ASSEMBLED UP TO ONE DAY AHEAD AND REFRIGERATED UNTIL ready to cook.

2 lbs. chicken pieces
¼ cup lemon juice
2 Tbsp. melted butter
1 small onion, chopped
½ tsp. salt

½ tsp. celery salt
½ tsp. pepper
½ tsp. rosemary
¼ tsp. thyme

Arrange chicken in a baking dish. Mix together remaining ingredients and pour over chicken. Marinate for three hours, then bake at 325 degrees F, covered, for 45 minutes to 1 hour.

Serves 4.

— *Gena Hughes*
Belleville, Ontario

SWEET & SOUR ORANGE CHICKEN

5-6 lb. chicken, cut up
1 cup flour
6 Tbsp. oil
1½ cups orange juice
3 medium onions, thinly sliced
4 cloves garlic, crushed

⅓ cup soya sauce
⅓ cup cider vinegar
3 Tbsp. honey
2 Tbsp. water
1 large green pepper, sliced

Dredge chicken pieces in flour. Heat oil in deep frying pan and brown chicken slowly over medium heat.

Transfer to a casserole dish. Add orange juice, onions and garlic. Cover and cook at 350 degrees F for 20 minutes. Mix together soya sauce, vinegar, honey and water and pour over chicken. Add sliced pepper. Cover and continue cooking for 25 minutes.

Serves 6.

— *Ingrid Birker*
Toronto, Ontario

CHICKEN WITH PINEAPPLE

THE DELIGHTFUL IDEA OF COMBINING PINEAPPLE WITH MEAT IS POPULAR IN MANY parts of the world — even in areas where only the tinned variety is regularly available.

8-oz. can pineapple tidbits
¼ cup brown sugar
2 Tbsp. cornstarch
½ cup water

1 Tbsp. cider vinegar
1 Tbsp. soya sauce
4 lbs. chicken pieces

Drain pineapple and reserve syrup. Combine sugar, cornstarch and syrup in medium saucepan. Blend in water, vinegar and soya sauce.

Cook over low heat until thick and bubbly, stirring occasionally.

Place chicken pieces in a baking dish and cover with sauce. Add the pineapple tidbits. Bake at 350 degrees F for 40 to 45 minutes, basting chicken with sauce at 10 minute intervals.

Serves 4.

— Christine Collis
Burlington, Ontario

ORANGE-GINGER CHICKEN

4 Tbsp. frozen orange juice
  concentrate, thawed
4 tsp. soya sauce
Salt
1 tsp. powdered ginger
4 chicken breasts

Combine juice, soya sauce, salt and ginger. Place chicken breasts in a shallow pan and brush with sauce. Bake at 350 degrees F, basting frequently, until tender — 30 to 40 minutes.

Serves 4.

— Pat Bredin
Winnipeg, Manitoba

HAWAIIAN CHICKEN

1 Tbsp. oil
1 cup uncooked rice
2 cups chicken stock
1 cup coarsely chopped onion
½ cup chopped green pepper
2 cups chopped celery

1½ cups cooked chicken
1 Tbsp. soya sauce
1 cup pineapple juice
Salt & pepper
1 cup pineapple chunks

In a heavy frying pan, brown rice in oil, stirring frequently, for about 12 minutes. Add chicken stock, cover and cook for about 3 minutes.

Add remaining ingredients, except pineapple chunks, mix well and spoon into casserole dish. Top with pineapple chunks.

Bake at 350 degrees F for 30 to 35 minutes.

Serves 4.

— A.H. McInnis
Fredericton, N.B.

CHICKEN WITH OLIVES & LEMON

1 large onion, thinly sliced
1 clove garlic, minced
1 Tbsp. minced parsley
1 Tbsp. ground coriander
1 tsp. salt
½ tsp. pepper
⅛ tsp. turmeric
2-3 Tbsp. olive oil
2½-3 lbs. chicken pieces
1 lemon, thinly sliced
⅓ cup sliced green olives

Sauté onion, garlic, parsley, coriander, salt, pepper and turmeric in olive oil. Add chicken and brown. Place lemon slices on top of chicken. Cover and simmer for 30 minutes. Stir in olives.

Remove chicken to a platter and keep warm. Boil down juices and pour over chicken.

Serves 4 to 6.

— *Bryanna Clark*
Union Bay, B.C.

CHICKEN WITH WHITE WINE

3 lbs. chicken pieces
Salt & pepper
3 Tbsp. cooking oil
Few pinches basil
½ cup dry white wine
4 cups cooked rice

Season chicken pieces with salt and pepper and brown in oil in large skillet. Sprinkle with basil. Cover and cook for 30 minutes on low heat. Pour wine over chicken and cook, covered, until chicken is very tender.

Remove chicken and keep warm. Reduce pan juices and stir in rice, scraping bottom of pan. Add chicken and mix well.

Serves 4 to 6.

— *Bryanna Clark*
Union Bay, B.C.

CHICKEN MARENGO

3 lbs. chicken pieces
1 cup flour
Salt & pepper
¼ cup olive oil
1 clove garlic, crushed
1 small onion, chopped
4 tomatoes, quartered
1 cup dry white wine
1 bay leaf
Pinch thyme
1 Tbsp. minced parsley
¼ lb. mushrooms, sliced
2 Tbsp. butter
½ cup sliced olives
2 Tbsp. flour
½ cup cold broth

Dredge chicken in flour seasoned with salt and pepper. Brown in oil. Add garlic, onion, tomatoes, wine, bay leaf, thyme and parsley. Cover and simmer for 30 minutes.

Meanwhile, sauté mushrooms in butter. Add to chicken after 30 minutes along with olives. Discard bay leaf and remove chicken mixture to warm platter. Keep warm.

Thicken liquid with flour mixed with broth. Boil for 3 to 5 minutes, stirring, until thickened. Return chicken to sauce and simmer for 10 minutes.

Serves 4 to 6.

— *Bryanna Clark*
Union Bay, B.C.

CHICKEN CACCIATORE

4-lb. chicken, cut up
3 Tbsp. flour
2 Tbsp. chopped onion
1 clove garlic, mineed
¼ cup olive oil
¼ cup tomato paste
½ cup white wine
1 tsp. salt
¼ tsp. pepper

¾ cup chicken stock
1 bay leaf
⅛ tsp. thyme
½ tsp. basil
⅛ tsp. marjoram
½ tsp. oregano
2 Tbsp. chopped parsley
Parmesan cheese

Dredge chicken pieces with flour and brown with onion and garlic in oil. Add remaining ingredients except cheese. Simmer, covered, for 1 to 2 hours.

Serve over spaghetti or baby potatoes and top with grated Parmesan cheese.

Serves 6.

— *Carolyn Hills*
Sunderland, Ontario

CHICKEN WITH SOUR CREAM

¼ cup flour
1 tsp. salt
Pepper
1 tsp. paprika
½ tsp. poultry seasoning
1½ lbs. boned chicken,
  cut into bite-sized pieces
Cooking oil

1 cup soft bread crumbs
2 Tbsp. butter
½ cup grated Parmesan cheese
¼ cup sesame seeds
½ cup hot water
1½ cups cream of mushroom sauce,
  page 92
1 cup sour cream

Mix flour, salt, pepper, paprika and poultry seasoning. Dredge meat in this mixture and brown slowly in hot oil. Arrange meat in baking dish. Combine bread crumbs, butter, cheese and sesame seeds. Spoon over meat. Stir water into meat drippings. Pour around meat. Bake at 350 degrees F until tender — 45 to 50 minutes.

Heat mushroom sauce and blend in sour cream. Serve with chicken.

Serves 4.

— *Elizabeth Clayton*
Nepean, Ontario

HONEY MUSTARD CHICKEN

QUICK AND EASY TO PREPARE, THIS CHICKEN DISH HAS A SLIGHTLY SWEET-AND-SOUR flavour.

¼ cup butter
½ cup honey
¼ cup prepared mustard
10 chicken drumsticks
Salt & pepper

Melt butter, honey and mustard together. Dip chicken pieces into the mixture, then bake in a shallow casserole dish at 350 degrees F for 35 minutes.

Serves 5.

— *Ingrid Birker*
Toronto, Ontario

PAPRIKA CHICKEN

4 Tbsp. butter
1 large onion, chopped
2 Tbsp. paprika
2½-3 lbs. chicken pieces
Salt

2 green peppers, chopped
2 tomatoes, chopped
2 Tbsp. flour
½ cup cold water
½ cup sour cream

Heat butter in casserole dish, add onion and fry until translucent. Sprinkle with paprika and stir. Add a few tablespoons of water and cook until liquid is almost evaporated.

Add the chicken and salt and cook for 5 minutes, stirring frequently. Add a little water and cover. Continue cooking over low heat. Add peppers and tomatoes after 20 minutes. Continue cooking until chicken is tender, about 20 minutes.

Stir flour into ½ cup cold water and mix with sour cream. Add to chicken and stir until smooth. Cook for 5 more minutes.

Serves 6.

— Anton Gross
North Augusta, Ontario

CHICKEN EGG FOO YUNG

3 Tbsp. oil
1 lb. chopped chicken meat
2½ Tbsp. soya sauce
1 tsp. sugar
Salt
½ cup chopped celery
½ cup chopped onion

½ cup peas
1 lb. bean sprouts
½ cup chopped mushrooms
½ tsp. pepper
12 eggs
2-3 green onions, diced

Heat 2 Tbsp. oil in a skillet. Add the chicken when oil smokes. Sauté for a few seconds, then add ½ Tbsp. soya sauce, sugar and salt. Sauté for a few more seconds. Add celery, onion, peas, sprouts and mushrooms. Mix well and stir in 2 Tbsp. soya sauce and pepper. Cover and cook until it boils for 30 seconds.

Beat eggs, add green onions and combine with cooked mixture. Mix well.

To a clean, hot skillet over medium-high heat, add 1 Tbsp. oil. Place large spoonfuls of mixture in hot oil and fry patties until well cooked.

Serves 6.

— Brenda Watts
Surrey, B.C.

CHICKEN CASSEROLE

1 large chicken
6 onions, chopped
1 bunch celery, chopped
1 lb. mushrooms, chopped
1 green pepper, chopped

1 can pimento
¼ lb. butter
3 cups tomato sauce, page 204
Salt, pepper & any other seasoning desired
8-oz. package egg noodles (medium-sized)

Boil chicken, half-covered with water, until tender. Cool slightly, remove meat from the bones and cut into bite-sized pieces. Reserve broth.

Sauté onions, celery, mushrooms, green pepper and pimento in butter until vegetables are tender. Add tomato sauce, seasonings and chicken. Cook noodles in boiling salted water, drain and add to mixture.

Bake at 375 degrees F until hot and bubbling — 20 to 30 minutes.

Serves 6.

— J. Elizabeth Fraser
Sackville, N.B.

CHICKEN-ARTICHOKE CASSEROLE

1½ tsp. salt
¼ tsp. pepper
½ tsp. paprika
3-lb. fryer, cut up
6 Tbsp. butter
¼ lb. chopped mushrooms

2 Tbsp. flour
⅔ cup chicken stock
3 Tbsp. sherry
12- or 15-oz. jar marinated artichoke
　hearts, drained

Sprinkle salt, pepper and paprika over chicken pieces. Brown in 4 Tbsp. of the butter, then place in a large casserole dish.

In the remaining 2 Tbsp. of butter, sauté the mushrooms for 5 minutes. Sprinkle flour over them and mix it in. Add chicken stock and sherry and stir. Cook for 5 minutes.

Arrange artichoke hearts among the chicken pieces. Pour the mushroom-sherry sauce over them and bake, covered, at 375 degrees F for 40 minutes.

Serves 4 to 6.

— Carrie Spencer
Maple Ridge, B.C.

FLORIDA FRIED CHICKEN

THIS RECIPE PRODUCES GOLDEN DELICIOUS PIECES OF HONEY FRIED CHICKEN. JUST make sure that the oven is not too hot after the sauce is added or the honey will burn.

½ cup flour
1 tsp. salt
¼ tsp. pepper
2 tsp. paprika
4-6 lb. frying chicken, cut up

⅓ cup butter
¼ cup butter
¼ cup orange blossom honey
　(or any pure honey)
¼ cup orange juice

Combine flour, salt, pepper and paprika in a clean paper bag. Add chicken 1 piece at a time and shake to coat well. Melt ⅓ cup butter in a large shallow baking dish in the oven at 400 degrees F. Remove from oven and roll coated chicken pieces in butter. Leave in pan, skin side down. Bake for 30 minutes at 400 degrees, then cool oven to 300 degrees while making sauce.

In a small saucepan, melt ¼ cup butter, stir in honey and orange juice. Remove chicken from oven, turn pieces of chicken skin side up and pour sauce over all. Continue cooking another 30 minutes or until chicken is done.

Serves 6.

— Cheryl Suckling
Athens, Georgia

SOYA BUTTER BAKED CHICKEN

3 Tbsp. soya sauce
1 tsp. crushed chili peppers
⅛ tsp. pepper
1½ tsp. lemon juice

½ cup butter
⅓ cup water
½ tsp. salt
3 lbs. chicken, cut up

Combine all ingredients except the chicken in saucepan, bring to a boil, reduce heat and simmer for 10 minutes.

Place chicken in single layer in baking dish. Pour sauce over chicken and bake at 400 degrees F for 45 to 55 minutes, basting occasionally and turning chicken once.

Serves 4 to 6.

— June Plamondon
Sept-Iles, Quebec

JAMBALAYA

3-lb. roasting chicken, cut up
1 onion, finely chopped
1 green pepper, finely chopped
1 clove garlic, finely chopped
1 carrot, thinly sliced
19-oz. can tomatoes, cut up

½ tsp. oregano
½ tsp. basil
1 tsp. salt
½ tsp. pepper
8-oz. tin of shrimp
2 cups cooked rice

Combine chicken, onion, green pepper, garlic, carrot, tomatoes, oregano, basil, salt and pepper in a slow cooker. Cover and cook on low for 8 hours.

Approximately 1 hour before serving, add shrimp and rice. Cover and continue cooking for 1 hour or until heated through.

Serves 4.

— Ruth Faux
Hagersville, Ontario

FRENCH POTTED CHICKEN

4-6 lb. stewing chicken
¼ cup drippings
1 onion, chopped
1 cup chopped celery
1 cup sliced peeled carrots

2-3 cups chicken stock
2 whole cloves
1 tsp. salt
¼ tsp. thyme
Parsley

Brown chicken in drippings in heavy saucepan and remove from pan. Briefly sauté onions, celery and carrots.

Return chicken to pan. Add stock, cloves, salt and thyme. Cover and simmer 3 to 4 hours, adding more stock or water as needed.

Garnish with parsley before serving.

Serves 6 to 8.

— Jean Stewart
Rimbey, Alberta

CHICKEN, RICE & DUMPLINGS

1½ cups cooked rice
2 cups diced cooked vegetables
2 cups chicken broth or gravy
1 cup diced cooked chicken
1 cup flour
2 tsp. baking powder

½ tsp. salt
1 egg
¼ cup cold milk
Parsley
Pepper

Combine rice and vegetables with broth. Simmer for 5 minutes. Add chicken.

To make dumplings, mix flour, baking powder and salt together. Beat egg, mix with milk and add to dry ingredients. Stir until all the flour is moistened.

Dip a spoon into the broth, then take a spoonful of the batter and drop it onto the top of the broth. Repeat, leaving a small space between each dumpling, until the batter is gone.

Cover and simmer for 10 to 15 minutes, or until dumplings are cooked. Sprinkle with parsley and pepper and serve.

Serves 4.

— Joan Southworth
Tahsis, B.C.

CHICKEN CURRY

AN EXCELLENT AUTHENTIC INDIAN RECIPE FOR AN EASY POPULAR DISH, THIS CAN be made with leftover chicken meat, chicken pieces or a whole chicken.

4-lb. stewing chicken
1½ cups ghee (clarified butter)
1½ lbs. onions, sliced
1 cup chopped fresh ginger
1 head garlic (7 or 8 cloves)
2½ cups water
2 tsp. turmeric
2 tsp. garam masala
1 Tbsp. salt

1 Tbsp. cumin
½ tsp. ground black pepper
1 tsp. hot chili powder
10 cardamoms
10 cloves
4 bay leaves
5 sticks cinnamon
1¼ cups yogurt

Skin chicken and cut into pieces.

Melt ghee in large heavy saucepan, add half the onions. While they are frying on low heat, liquidize in a blender the ginger, garlic and remaining onions with water. When the onions are fried to golden brown, add spice mixture and stir over low heat for 10 minutes.

Add turmeric, garam masala, salt, cumin, pepper, chili powder, cardamoms, cloves, bay leaves and cinnamon. Cook, stirring, for a further 10 minutes.

Add chicken pieces and yogurt. Cover the pan and cook on low heat for 3 hours.

Serves 6 to 8.

— *Sheila Bear*
St. John's, Nfld.

CRISPY CHICKEN

½ cup flour
¼ cup corn meal
2 Tbsp. soy flour
2-3 Tbsp. wheat germ
½ tsp. sage
½ tsp. thyme

Curry powder
Pepper
1 egg, beaten
½ cup milk
1 chicken, cut up

Combine dry ingredients and liquid ingredients separately. Dip chicken pieces in liquid then coat with flour mixture. Place on a cookie sheet and bake at 375 degrees F for 45 minutes to 1 hour.

Serves 4 to 6.

— *Karen Armour*
Canoe, B.C.

BLANKETED CHICKEN

4-6 lbs. chicken, cut up
2 Tbsp. finely chopped green pepper
Salt & pepper
1 Tbsp. finely chopped chives

6 strips bacon
4 Tbsp. flour
1½ cups light cream

Place chicken pieces in roasting pan and add green pepper, salt, pepper and chives. Cover with bacon. Bake at 400 degrees F for 40 to 50 minutes.

Combine 3 Tbsp. fat from roasting pan, flour and cream and cook slowly until thickened. Season with salt and pepper.

Place chicken in serving dish and cover with sauce.

Serves 6.

— *Judy Bell*
Aldergrove, B.C.

COUNTRY CHICKEN

¾ cup sour cream
1 Tbsp. lemon juice
1 tsp. salt
1 tsp. paprika
½ tsp. Worcestershire sauce

Garlic powder
2½-3 lb. chicken, cut up
1 cup fine dry bread crumbs
¼ cup butter

Combine sour cream, lemon juice, salt, paprika, Worcestershire sauce and garlic powder.

Dip chicken in mixture, roll in bread crumbs and place in shallow baking dish. Dot with butter.

Bake, covered, at 350 degrees F for 45 minutes. Remove cover and cook 45 to 50 minutes longer.

Serves 5 to 6.

— *Donna Jubb*
Fenelon Falls, Ontario

CHICKEN HEARTS WITH MUSHROOMS

¼ cup uncooked rice
¼ cup uncooked bulgur
4 Tbsp. oil
1 cup boiling water
Salt to taste
2 Tbsp. soya grits
½ lb. mushrooms, chopped

1 lb. chicken hearts
2 cloves garlic, minced
1 cup cottage cheese
½ cup yogurt
1 stalk leafy celery, chopped
Pinch thyme & sage
Flour

Sauté rice and bulgur in oil until browned. Combine with boiling water, salt and soya grits in a saucepan. Simmer, covered, over low heat for 15 to 20 minutes, or until cooked. Set aside and keep warm.

Meanwhile, sauté mushrooms, hearts and garlic in oil until hearts turn pink. Remove from heat and keep warm.

Combine and heat cottage cheese, yogurt, celery and herbs. If necessary, thicken with a little flour. Add hearts, mushrooms and garlic.

Serve over rice-bulgur mixture.

Serves 3.

— *Nicol Séguin*
La Sarre, Quebec

POULET AUX TOMATES

1 or 2 chickens, cut up
Flour, salt & pepper to coat chicken
¼ cup butter
1 cup finely chopped onion
1 green pepper, cut in strips
1 clove garlic, minced
½ cup celery, finely chopped

½ lb. mushrooms, chopped
5 cups canned tomatoes
2 tsp. salt
½ tsp. pepper
½ tsp. thyme
1 Tbsp. parsley

Coat chicken with seasoned flour. Brown in melted butter. Add onion, green pepper, garlic, celery and mushrooms and sauté for 5 minutes. Add remaining ingredients and simmer for 10 minutes.

Place in a Dutch oven or casserole dish and bake at 350 degrees F for 1 hour.

Serves 6 to 8.

— *Jolaine Wright*
Warner, Alberta

OLD-FASHIONED CHICKEN POT PIE

3-lb. chicken
3 cups water
2 tsp. salt
½ tsp. peppercorns
1 medium onion, chopped
⅓ cup butter
¼ cup flour
¼ tsp. celery salt
⅛ tsp. pepper
1 cup cooked peas
1 cup cooked carrots
2 cups mashed potatoes

Cut chicken into pieces. Place in a large pot with water, 1 tsp. of salt and peppercorns. Bring to a boil, then simmer for 45 minutes, or until tender.

Remove chicken. Strain broth and discard peppercorns. Cool the chicken, remove skin and bones and cut up the large pieces.

Sauté onion in butter in a medium saucepan until tender. Add flour and blend well. Cook for 1 minute. Gradually add 2 cups of broth, stirring until smooth. Cook over low heat, stirring constantly until thickened and bubbly. Add 1 tsp. salt, celery salt and pepper. Remove from heat.

Arrange chicken, peas and carrots in a 2½-quart casserole dish. Spoon sauce over and top with mashed potatoes.

Bake at 425 degrees F for 20 minutes.

Serves 4.

— *Sharron Jansen*
Pembroke, Ontario

CRUSTY CHICKEN PIE

¼ cup butter
2¼ cups flour
1⅔ cups milk
1 cup chicken stock
2 cups diced cooked chicken
½ cup diced celery
1 cup cooked carrots
½ cup chopped mushrooms
¾ tsp. salt
4 tsp. baking powder
½ tsp. salt
⅓ cup cold butter
1 cup grated Cheddar cheese

Melt ¼ cup butter and stir in ¼ cup flour. Add 1 cup milk and chicken stock. Cook until thick, stirring constantly. Add meat, vegetables and ¾ tsp. salt and heat thoroughly. Place in casserole dish and keep warm.

Sift 2 cups flour, baking powder and ½ tsp. salt into bowl. Cut in butter until it is the size of peas.

Pour ⅔ cup milk into centre of flour mixture and stir until mixture comes away from sides of bowl. Knead gently on floured surface for 1 minute then roll out to ¼-inch thickness. Sprinkle with grated cheese. Roll as for jelly roll and cut in ½-inch slices. Place on top of hot chicken.

Bake at 425 degrees F for 20 minutes.

Serves 6.

— *Shirley Thomlinson*
Carp, Ontario

CHICKEN BEER BARBECUE

3 lbs. chicken pieces
12 oz. beer
1 tsp. salt
¼ tsp. pepper
2 Tbsp. lemon juice
½ tsp. orange extract
1 tsp. grated orange rind
1 Tbsp. brown sugar
1 Tbsp. dark molasses
Generous dash Tabasco sauce

Place chicken in large bowl. Mix together remaining ingredients. Pour over chicken and marinate for several hours or overnight.

Barbecue over hot coals, brushing frequently with marinade.

Serves 4 to 6.

— *Cynthia Stewart*
Pickle Lake, Ontario

BARBECUED CHICKEN

¼ cup vegetable oil
1 tsp. minced garlic
2 medium onions, finely chopped
6-oz. can tomato paste
¼ cup white vinegar
1 tsp. salt
1 tsp. basil or thyme
¼ cup honey

½ cup beef stock
½ cup Worcestershire sauce
1 tsp. dry mustard
1 chicken, cut up
Salt & pepper
2 Tbsp. oil
1 clove garlic, crushed

Heat oil in a 12-inch skillet. Add minced garlic and onions and cook, stirring frequently, until onion is soft. Lower heat and add remaining ingredients, except chicken, salt, pepper, garlic and oil. Simmer, uncovered, for 15 minutes.

Season chicken with salt, pepper and garlic. Brown in oil at a high temperature. Remove to a large deep, cast-iron frying pan. Pour barbecue sauce over the chicken, cover and cook over medium heat until sauce is lightly boiling. Reduce heat and simmer for 1½ to 2 hours.

Makes 2½ cups.

— Marilyn & Patricia Picco
Terrace, B.C.

COLD BARBECUED CHICKEN

4-lb. broiler, cut in pieces
4 Tbsp. salad oil or shortening
1 large onion, sliced
3 Tbsp. brown sugar
3 Tbsp. cider vinegar
¼ cup lemon juice
1 cup ketchup or tomato sauce

3 Tbsp. Worcestershire sauce
1 Tbsp. prepared mustard
½ cup diced celery
1¼ cups water
½ tsp. salt
½ tsp. oregano
¼ tsp. pepper

In a large frying pan, brown the chicken in salad oil. As pieces are done, place them in a 3-quart casserole dish.

Add remaining ingredients to pan and bring to a boil. Pour sauce over chicken. Cover and bake for 1 hour at 350 degrees F. Cool. Uncover and refrigerate until needed. Serve at room temperature.

Serves 4.

— Mrs. J. Hall-Armstrong
Cochrane, Ontario

CANTONESE CHICKEN WINGS

3 lbs. chicken wings
1 Tbsp. cooking oil
1 Tbsp. soya sauce
½ tsp. salt
¼ cup brown sugar

1 tsp. chili powder
¾ tsp. celery seed
¼ cup vinegar
1 cup tomato sauce, page 204

Pat chicken wings dry. Place on broiler pan. Mix oil and soya sauce and brush over each wing. Mix salt, sugar, chili powder and celery seed and sprinkle over top. Place 5 inches below broiler and cook for approximately 10 minutes.

Remove from oven, place in a casserole dish. Combine vinegar with tomato sauce and pour over casserole.

Bake at 350 degrees F for 1 hour.

Serves 4.

— Irene MacPhee
Clarence Creek, Ontario

PAULINE'S CHICKEN WINGS

4 lbs. chicken wings
½ tsp. salt
½ tsp. garlic powder
¼ tsp. pepper
½ cup brown sugar

½ tsp. cornstarch
¼ cup vinegar
2 Tbsp. ketchup or tomato paste
½ cup chicken stock
1 Tbsp. soya sauce

Combine all ingredients but chicken and pour over wings. Bake, uncovered, at 400 degrees F for 35 to 40 minutes, glazing every 10 minutes.

Serves 4.

— Mary Anne Vanner
Pembroke, Ontario

CHICKEN WINGS IN BEER

36 chicken wings
¼ cup sugar
2 Tbsp. minced onion
1 clove garlic, minced

½ tsp. ginger
1 cup beer
1 cup pineapple or orange juice
¼ cup vegetable oil

Cut tips off wings and discard. Wash wings well. Marinate, refrigerated, in remaining ingredients overnight, turning a few times.

Place in baking pan with marinade and bake, uncovered, for 2 hours at 350 degrees F.

Serves 8.

— Anne Lawrence
Binghamton, New York

CHICKEN WINGS

5 lbs. chicken wings
2 Tbsp. vegetable oil
1 medium onion, chopped
2 cloves garlic, minced
½ cup brown sugar

1 cup chili sauce
1 Tbsp. Worcestershire sauce
½ cup lemon juice
½ cup water
2 Tbsp. vinegar

Cook wings in oil in casserole dish at 350 degrees F for 30 minutes. Remove wings from oven. Combine remaining ingredients and pour over wings. Return to oven for 1 to 1½ hours.

Serves 4 to 6.

— Reo Belhumeur
Gatineau, Quebec

CHICKEN CHOW MEIN

2 Tbsp. butter
¼ cup chopped onion
½ cup celery
4 cups bean sprouts

1 cup diced cooked chicken
½ cup water
4 cups Chinese noodles
Salt & pepper

Melt butter in a large pot and add onion and celery. Sauté for 3 to 5 minutes. Add bean sprouts, chicken, water, noodles and seasonings. Stir.

Place in casserole dish and bake at 325 degrees F for 30 minutes.

Serves 2.

ALMOND CHICKEN

½ cup whole almonds
2-3 Tbsp. butter
3-4 stalks celery, thinly sliced
1 onion, sliced
1 green pepper, cut in strips
1½ cups peas
1 cup sliced mushrooms

2 cups cooked chicken,
 cut into bite-sized pieces
1 tsp. sugar
2 Tbsp. cornstarch
1½ cups chicken stock
1 tsp. soya sauce

Brown almonds in butter and set aside. To the remaining butter, add celery, onion and green pepper and brown slightly. Add peas. Cook about 1 minute, then stir in mushrooms and chicken. Blend sugar, constarch and stock. Add to pan, cooking until clear. At the last moment before serving, add soya sauce and almonds. Serve with rice.

Serves 4 to 6.

— *Adele Dueck*
Lucky Lake, Sask.

CHICKEN ENCHILADAS

12 tortillas
3 cups chopped cooked chicken
¾ cup sliced almonds
2 cups shredded Jack cheese
3 cups chicken stock

2 Tbsp. cornstarch
½ tsp. chili powder
¼ tsp. garlic powder
¼ tsp. cumin

Fry tortillas quickly on both sides in hot oil. Stack and keep warm. Combine chicken, almonds and ½ cup cheese.

To make sauce, bring chicken stock to a boil. Mix cornstarch with a little cold water and stir into stock. Add seasonings and boil for 1 minute.

Add ½ cup of sauce to chicken mixture. Dip each tortilla in sauce to soften, put some chicken mixture on it and roll up. Place tortillas in greased casserole dish in a single layer. Top with remaining 1½ cups cheese and pour remaining sauce around tortillas.

Bake at 350 degrees F for 20 to 25 minutes.

Serves 4.

— *Linda Townsend*
Nanaimo, B.C.

CHICKEN TETRAZZINI

1 cup sliced mushrooms
1 cup chopped celery
½ cup chopped green pepper
1½ cups slivered almonds
¼ cup butter
¼ cup flour
1 cup chicken stock

2 cups light cream
Salt & pepper
1 cup grated Swiss cheese
3-4 cups cooked chicken,
 cut into bite-sized pieces
12 oz. spaghetti, cooked
½ cup Parmesan cheese

Sauté mushrooms, celery, green pepper and 1 cup almonds in butter for 5 minutes. Remove with slotted spoon. To butter in frying pan, add flour and stir until smooth. Slowly add chicken stock and cream, stirring constantly. Cook until slightly thickened. Add salt, pepper and cheese.

When sauce has thickened, remove from heat. In large casserole dish, combine cooked spaghetti, vegetables, chicken and sauce. Mix well and top with Parmesan cheese and remaining almonds.

Bake at 350 degrees F for 20 to 30 minutes.

Serves 8 to 10.

CHICKEN CANTALOUPE SALAD

2 cups diced cooked chicken
1 cup sliced celery
¼ cup chopped green pepper
1½ Tbsp. lemon juice
2 Tbsp. French dressing, page 93

2 Tbsp. mayonnaise, page 92
½ tsp. salt
1 cantaloupe
Lettuce
⅓ cup slivered almonds

Combine chicken, celery and green pepper with lemon juice, French dressing, mayonnaise and salt. Chill.

Halve cantaloupe, place on lettuce leaf and fill with chicken mixture. Garnish with almonds.

Serves 2.

— *Laura Wilson*
Burlington, Ontario

CHICKEN SALAD

½ cup mayonnaise, page 92
1 Tbsp. fresh lemon juice
¼ tsp. salt
⅛ tsp. pepper
⅛ tsp. diced marjoram

2 Tbsp. heavy cream
3 cups chopped chicken, in large pieces
Ripe olives
Tomato slices

Combine mayonnaise with lemon juice, salt, pepper, marjoram and cream, mix chicken into dressing. Arrange on plate with olives and tomatoes.

Serves 4.

— *Winona Heasman*
Powassan, Ontario

TURKEY SQUARES

1 onion, chopped
2 Tbsp. oil
2 cups cooked rice
2 cups diced leftover turkey
¾ cup gravy

2 eggs, well beaten
1 tsp. salt
½ cup chopped celery
½-1 cup grated cheese

Sauté onion in oil. Combine with all remaining ingredients, except cheese, in a casserole dish. Bake for 40 minutes at 350 degrees F. Top with cheese and return to oven for another 5 minutes.

Serves 4.

— *Louise Jackson*
Arthur, Ontario

RICE TURKEY DRESSING

⅔ cup butter
¾ cup chopped onion
1 cup chopped celery
4 oz. mushrooms, sliced
4 oz. raisins (optional)

6-8 slices bread, cubed
1 cup uncooked brown or wild rice
1 Tbsp. savory
1½ Tbsp. chopped parsley
1½ cups hot water

Heat butter in skillet, add onion and celery and sauté over low heat for 15 minutes. Add mushrooms and raisins. Pour mixture over bread cubes, rice and seasonings. Add hot water and mix. Spoon into turkey using just enough to fill. Because stuffing swells during baking or roasting, pack it very loosely. (Extra stuffing can be added during the last half hour of cooking the turkey, or cooked separately in a covered casserole dish.) Pull flap of neck skin gently over stuffing and fasten with a skewer, then truss the legs of the bird.

Bake at 350 degrees F for 15 minutes per pound plus 15 minutes more. Grease skin thoroughly with butter before baking, place in a shallow pan, and cover loosely with foil. Do not allow the foil to touch the skin and remove for the last 15 minutes.

— *Trish Hines*
Wyebridge, Ontario

SAGE DRESSING

4 cups dry bread crumbs
2 cups mashed potatoes
½ cup melted butter
½ cup minced onion

1 tsp. salt
4 Tbsp. powdered sage
½ tsp. pepper

Mix all ingredients in bowl.

Makes enough dressing to stuff a 15-lb. bird.

— Barb Curtis
Bowmanville, Ontario

RUSSIAN TURKEY DRESSING

WITH THE CONSISTENCY OF A VERY FIRM PATE, THIS RICH STUFFING IS THICK enough to be sliced and makes fine leftover sandwich fare.

3 medium onions, chopped
3 stalks celery, chopped
½ cup butter
½ tsp. pepper
2 Tbsp. salt
2 Tbsp. poultry seasoning

10 cups bread crumbs
12 eggs
1 lb. chopped chicken livers
2 Tbsp. dried parsley
Milk to moisten dressing

Sauté onions and celery in butter and let cool. Mix remaining ingredients together and moisten with milk. Add onions and celery.

Makes enough stuffing for a 12- to 14-lb. turkey.

— Anne Lawrence
Binghamton, New York

OYSTER DRESSING

2 dozen large oysters, shucked
Seasoned flour
2 eggs, beaten with 1 Tbsp. oil &
  ½ tsp. Tabasco sauce
Cracker crumbs
¾ cup butter
1 cup chopped onion

¼ cup oil
¼ cup chopped celery
2 cups dry bread crumbs
1½ tsp. salt
½ tsp. thyme
⅛ tsp. each pepper & rosemary
1 Tbsp. chopped parsley

Dip the oysters into the seasoned flour, then into the egg mixture. Roll in cracker crumbs and let stand about 10 minutes. Melt 3 to 4 Tbsp. butter until bubbling and fry the oysters until golden brown – about 1 minute on each side. Drain.

Sauté the onion in oil and remaining butter until brown. Add the celery and cook for about 3 minutes more. Add all remaining ingredients except oysters, and toss thoroughly.

Stuff bird alternately with the crumb mixture and the fried oysters.

Makes about 8 cups.

— Nina Kenzie
Homer, Alaska

SAUSAGE DRESSING

1 lb. sausage meat
3 Tbsp. minced onion
4 Tbsp. minced parsley
4 Tbsp. minced celery

3 Tbsp. melted butter
Salt & pepper
5-6 cups bread crumbs

Fry sausage meat just until it loses the pink colour, and drain. Combine with remaining ingredients and mix well.

Makes enough dressing to stuff a 14- to 17-pound bird.

— Mary Reid
Georgeville, Quebec

MUSHROOM SAUSAGE DRESSING

¾ cup chopped mushrooms
¾ cup chopped onion
⅓ cup chopped celery
⅓ cup butter
½-¾ cup crumbled cooked sausage meat
4 cups dry bread cubes

1 Tbsp. parsley
1 tsp. salt
Pepper
Savory
Thyme
Chicken stock to moisten dressing

Sauté vegetables in butter. Add sausage meat, bread cubes and seasonings. Taste and adjust seasoning if necessary. Add enough stock to moisten.

Makes enough dressing to stuff a 10- to 12-lb. bird.

— Lynn Shelley
Sprucedale, Ontario

RICE DRESSING

2 cups cooked rice
2-3 green onions, chopped
1 cup mushrooms, chopped
½ tsp. thyme
½ tsp. sage

Combine all ingredients and place in an ovenproof dish. When poultry is nearly cooked, take 2 Tbsp. of drippings from roasting pan and add to dressing to moisten. Cover and bake for 30 minutes.

Serves 4.

— Lydia Nederhoff
Rouleau, Sask.

ORANGE CRANBERRY DRESSING

10-12 cups coarse bread crumbs
1 Tbsp. grated orange rind
2 oranges in segments
1 cup thick cranberry sauce
1 cup finely chopped celery

1 cup finely chopped onion
2 tsp. salt
½ tsp. pepper
½ cup soft butter

Toss all ingredients together lightly.

Sufficient to stuff a 10- to 12-lb. turkey.

— Sherri Dick
Quesnel, B.C.

BREADING FOR FRIED CHICKEN

2 cups flour
1 tsp. salt
1 Tbsp. celery salt
1 Tbsp. pepper
2 Tbsp. dry mustard
2 Tbsp. paprika

2 Tbsp. garlic powder
1 tsp. ginger
½ tsp. thyme
½ tsp. sweet basil
½ tsp. oregano

Mix thoroughly and store tightly sealed. Coat chicken pieces before frying.

Makes 2½ cups.

— Shirley Morrish
Devlin, Ontario

CHICKEN LIVER PATE

1 cup chicken livers
1 medium onion, chopped
2 Tbsp. Worcestershire sauce
1 Tbsp. lemon juice

2-4 cloves garlic, crushed
Salt & pepper
Pinch nutmeg
1 cup bread crumbs

Place all ingredients, except bread crumbs, in a small saucepan and add approximately ¼ cup water. Bring to a boil, then simmer for 10 minutes. Allow to cool slightly.

Add bread crumbs and place mixture in blender or food processor. Blend to a smooth paste. Refrigerate to chill and serve with crackers.

Makes 2 cups.

— *Nicolle de Grauw*
Dunedin, N.Z.

CHICKEN LIVER PATE CASANOVA

½ cup butter
4 oz. cream cheese
½ lb. chicken livers
1 small onion, quartered
6 Tbsp. chicken broth

2 Tbsp. brandy or cognac
½ tsp. paprika
½ tsp. salt
Cayenne pepper

Remove butter and cream cheese from refrigerator about 1 hour before starting.

Clean and quarter livers, sauté in skillet or saucepan with the onion, chicken broth and brandy for 5 minutes.

Empty mixture, including liquid, into blender container. Add paprika, salt and cayenne. Cover and blend on high speed. Slice in butter and cream cheese, scraping down mixture with rubber scraper if necessary.

Pour into small crock and chill for at least 2 hours. Serve with garnish of chopped hard-boiled eggs.

Makes 2½ cups.

— *Erika Johnston*
Toronto, Ontario

CHICKEN LIVER MOUSSE

THIS RICH PATE MAY BE UNMOULDED AND SERVED WITH CRACKERS OR dark rye bread as an appetizer or sliced for sandwiches.

1 lb. chicken livers
2 Tbsp. minced shallots
2 Tbsp. butter
⅓ cup Madeira or cognac
¼ cup whipping cream

½ tsp. salt
⅛ tsp. allspice
⅛ tsp. thyme
⅛ tsp. pepper
¼ cup butter

Cut livers into ½-inch pieces. Sauté with shallots in 2 Tbsp. butter until rosy. Scrape into blender.

Boil down Madeira or cognac rapidly and add to liver. Add cream and seasonings and blend to a smooth paste.

Melt ¼ cup butter, add and blend. Force through a fine sieve with a wooden spoon. Correct seasoning.

Spoon into a mould, cover and chill for 2 to 3 hours.

Makes 2 cups.

— *Susan Bates Eddy*
St. Andrews, N.B.

GOOSE LIVER PATE

2 Tbsp. bread crumbs
1 Tbsp. white flour
1 cup whipping cream
1 goose liver

1 egg
1 Tbsp. chopped onion
Salt & pepper
1 Tbsp. butter, melted & cooled

Mix bread crumbs and flour and soak them in the cream. Scrape the liver. Add to liver, egg, onion, salt and pepper. Stir in bread crumb mixture. Force through a sieve, or put through a food processor. Add cooled butter. Taste for seasoning.

Pour mixture into a greased ovenproof dish or pan. Cover with aluminum foil and cook in a water bath at 350 degrees F for about 40 minutes.

Serves 4.

— Sherrie Dick
Quesnel, B.C.

LIVER PATE

1 medium onion, chopped
1 clove garlic, chopped
2 eggs
1 lb. chicken livers
¼ cup flour
½ tsp. ginger

½ tsp. allspice
1 cup heavy cream
1 Tbsp. salt
1 tsp. pepper
¼ cup butter

Blend onion, garlic and eggs in a blender for 1 minute. Add liver and blend for 2 more minutes. Remove to a large bowl. Combine remaining ingredients, then add to liver mixture.

Place in greased loaf pan and cover with butter. Butter aluminum foil and cover pan with it. Set in a larger pan of water and bake at 325 degrees F for 3 hours.

Remove pâté from pan and cool. Wrap and refrigerate.

— Lisa Brownstone
Avonhurst, Sask.

RABBIT PATE CAMILLE

2-lb. rabbit with liver reserved
1 Tbsp. butter
1 tsp. salt
½ tsp. pepper
4 slices bacon
2 chicken livers
1 large shallot, finely chopped

⅛ tsp. allspice
¼ cup bread crumbs
2 large egg yolks
4 Tbsp. brandy
Fatback slices to line small casserole dish
¼ tsp. thyme
1 bay leaf

Cut rabbit meat from the bones in chunks. Coarsely chop and sauté in butter for a few minutes. Lightly salt and pepper then set aside.

Cut bacon into small pieces. Finely chop rabbit and chicken livers. Combine livers and bacon in bowl with shallots, salt, pepper, allspice, bread crumbs, egg yolks, brandy and rabbit meat. Mix thoroughly.

Line 3-cup terrine or small casserole dish with fatback. Spoon in pâté mixture and press down well. Sprinkle with salt, pepper and thyme. Place bay leaf on top, cover with more fatback and cover casserole dish.

Cook in a water bath at 300 degrees F for 3 hours. After removing from oven, put a weight on top of the pâté to compress and allow to cool. Refrigerate overnight.

Makes 3 cups.

— Sheila Bear
St. John's, Nfld.

SIDNEY BAY RABBIT

¼ cup butter
¼ cup honey
1 Tbsp. soya sauce

3-4 lbs. rabbit, cut up
2 Tbsp. chopped ginger root

Melt butter, honey and soya sauce together. Spread half this mixture over rabbit in a roasting pan.

Cover with foil and bake for 45 minutes at 375 degrees F. Remove foil, add ginger root, turn rabbit over and add remaining sauce.

Bake for 1 more hour, basting frequently, until rabbit is tender and sauce is thick and shiny.

Serves 4 to 6.

— *Helen Campbell*
Loughborough Inlet, B.C.

RABBIT WITH DRESSING

2-3 lbs. rabbit meat, cut up
1 onion, sliced
5-6 cups chicken stock
3 peppercorns
¼ cup minced onion
⅓ cup butter, melted

6 cups dry bread cubes
½ tsp. sage
Salt & pepper
4 Tbsp. butter
¾ cup flour
4 egg yolks, well beaten

Place rabbit pieces, onion slices, chicken stock and peppercorns in heavy saucepan. Simmer, covered, for 1½ hours, or until rabbit is tender. Remove rabbit from broth and cool. Set broth aside. Bone meat, cut up and arrange in a 3-quart casserole dish.

Sauté minced onion in melted butter. Combine with bread cubes, sage, salt and pepper and mix lightly. Sprinkle over rabbit pieces.

Strain broth. Heat 4 Tbsp. butter in skillet, stir in flour and blend in broth. Cook, stirring constantly, until thickened. Pour a little sauce into the egg yolks, then stir yolks back into the hot mixture. Cook for 1 minute, then pour over casserole.

Bake at 375 degrees F for 35 minutes or until dressing is set and golden brown.

Serves 8.

— *Charlene Bloomberg*
Englehart, Ontario

RABBIT IN SOUR CREAM & MUSTARD

2 medium onions, chopped
Olive oil
2-3 lb. rabbit, cut up into serving pieces

Dijon mustard
Water
1 cup sour cream

Sauté the onions in 2 Tbsp. olive oil, then put in a heavy saucepan. Coat the rabbit pieces generously with the mustard and fry gently in olive oil, being careful not to burn them. Place the meat on top of the onions. To drippings in pan, add just enough water to simmer the rabbit. Pour over rabbit and cook gently until it is done — about 2 hours.

Meanwhile, fry the liver and kidney. Add them to the rabbit mixture 10 minutes before it is done.

When the rabbit is cooked, remove the meat from the sauce and arrange on a serving dish. Keep warm. Add sour cream to the sauce and mix well while heating it, but do not let it boil. Pour sauce over meat and serve immediately.

Serves 4.

— *Eila Belton*
Warkworth, Ontario

ROAST RABBIT

Soak rabbit overnight in salted water. Drain and wipe dry. Rub shortening all over it and season with salt and pepper. Sprinkle rosemary and a sliced clove of garlic into the cavity.

Bake in a roasting pan at 300 degrees F for 2 hours. Increase the temperature to 350 degrees and roast for 1 more hour. Turn the rabbit over for the last 30 minutes, so that both sides will be brown and crisp.

Serves 4.

— F. Rosati
Agincourt, Ontario

RABBIT SAUSAGE CASSEROLE

1 rabbit	1 cup chicken stock
Flour	1 cup browned bread crumbs
4 Tbsp. oil	1 tsp. caraway seeds
1 lb. pork sausage	1 tsp. grated lemon peel
1 cup beer	1 tsp. brown sugar
¼ cup cider vinegar	Salt & pepper

Skin, clean and cut up the rabbit. Dust with flour and brown in hot oil. Place in a large, deep pot and add remaining ingredients.

Bring to a boil, reduce heat, cover and simmer gently for 2 hours.

If a thicker sauce is desired, blend 2 Tbsp. flour into a little water and stir into sauce.

Serves 6.

— Carolyn Hills
Sunderland, Ontario

RABBIT CASSEROLE

2 rabbits, cut up	1 green pepper, chopped
½ cup flour	½ lb. mushrooms
1 Tbsp. salt	Thyme
1 tsp. pepper	Cayenne
½ cup oil	Bay leaf
1 clove garlic, chopped	4 large tomatoes, quartered
1 cup chopped onion	1 cup dry white wine
1 cup chopped celery	½ lb. shrimp

Coat rabbit in mixture of flour, salt and pepper. Brown in oil, then place in a casserole dish. Sauté garlic and onion, then stir in celery, green pepper and mushrooms. Cook, stirring, over medium heat for 5 minutes. Add what is left of the flour mixture, thyme, cayenne, bay leaf, tomatoes and wine. Bring to a boil. Pour over rabbit and bake at 350 degrees F for 40 minutes. Add shrimp, cover and cook for another 20 minutes.

— Gail Cool
Assiniboia, Sask.

Serves 6 to 8

BARBECUED WILD DUCK

¾ cup oil	1 tsp. salt
½ cup vinegar	¼ tsp. pepper
¼ cup soya sauce	4 small wild ducks, cleaned,
1 sprig rosemary	dressed & cut up
1 Tbsp. celery seed	

Combine all ingredients except ducks and simmer for 10 minutes. Put duck pieces in sauce and simmer for another 10 minutes, turning so that all sides are covered. Place in roasting pan and roast, uncovered, at 350 degrees F for 50 to 60 minutes, basting often.

Serves 4

— Adele Moore
Baltimore, Ontario

ROAST DUCK OR GOOSE

Stuff duck or goose with whole apples. Place on rack in roaster and keep about half an inch of water in bottom of roaster while baking, to prevent fat drippings from burning.

Bake at 400 degrees F, uncovered, until done, turning every half hour or so. After the first half hour, prick the skin liberally with a fork to let the fat run out. Skim off excess fat. Sprinkle with salt, pepper and caraway seeds.

Simmer the heart and gizzard separately in water until tender and add to the roasting pan, along with the liver, during the last hour of baking.

When done, cut the bird into serving-sized portions with poultry shears and serve with the apples that were baked in it.

If gravy is desired, separate the fat from the broth in the roasting pan and thicken the broth with cornstarch mixed with a little cold water. Season with salt and pepper.

— Tonya Bassler
St. Joseph's, Nfld.

Serves 4.

GLAZED DUCK

½ cup butter
½ cup lemon juice or wine vinegar
2 cups hot water
1 duck

Flour
2 Tbsp. cranberry jelly
Water
Salt & pepper

Combine butter, lemon juice and hot water. Pour over duck in roasting pan. Cover and bake at 350 degrees F for 20 minutes per pound, basting several times.

For gravy, cool drippings and remove fat. Blend remaining juices with flour to make a paste, then add cranberry jelly and water until desired consistency is reached. Add salt and pepper to taste.

— Goldie Connell
Prescott, Ontario

Serves 4.

GROUSE A LA DAVID

8 grouse breasts
Flour
Salt & pepper
Oil
¼ cup red wine

Remove breast meat from bone. Pound each breast and coat with flour. Sprinkle with salt and pepper. Fry pieces in cooking oil until golden brown on both sides, about 5 minutes. Pour wine over meat. Cover and cook for 5 more minutes.

Serves 4.

— Ronald Manuel
Takla Landing, B.C.

GROUSE FRIED RICE

4 grouse, cut into bite-sized pieces
Garlic powder
Ginger
Salt & pepper
1 large onion, chopped

4 carrots, thinly sliced diagonally
1 bunch celery stalks & leaves, sliced
3 cups cooked rice
Curry powder
3 tomatoes, cut in wedges

In large frying pan, sauté grouse in oil over medium-high heat. Season with garlic powder, ginger, salt and pepper.

When meat is browned, add onion and carrots. Stir-fry until onions are almost soft, about 5 minutes, then add celery and cook for another 2 minutes.

Add ½ cup water and simmer, covered, for 20 minutes. Add rice, curry powder and tomato wedges and cook, stirring constantly, until heated through.

Serves 6 to 8.

— Lois Pope
Whitehorse, Yukon

ROAST CANADA GOOSE

Cut off the oil sack, then wash and dry the goose. Brush the cavity with lemon juice. Insert stuffing and close cavity.

Brush 2 Tbsp. seasoned melted butter over skin of goose. Pour water into base of roasting pan and place goose on tray. Bake at 450 degrees F for 15 minutes, reduce heat to 350 degrees and roast 20 minutes per pound.

If the goose is very fatty, pierce the flesh several times during roasting to drain excess fat.

— Goldie Connell
Prescott, Ontario

SMOTHERED PHEASANT

Salt
Pepper
Thyme
Basil
Seasoned salt
½ cup flour

2 or 3 pheasants, cut up
Oil
1 cup sliced onions
1 cup chopped mushrooms
1½ cups cream of mushroom sauce, page 92
1 pint sour cream

Add seasonings to flour and coat pheasant. Brown in oil. Put in roaster and top with onions, mushrooms and mushroom sauce. Cook for 1 hour at 350 degrees F. Add sour cream and cook for another 30 minutes.

— Gail Cool
Assiniboia, Sask.

GOURMET VENISON CHOPS

6 venison chops
½ cup brandy
½ cup olive oil
1 clove garlic, crushed
Freshly ground pepper

Marinate chops in brandy for 2 to 3 hours, turning once so brandy has a chance to soak into both sides. Combine olive oil and garlic and let sit while the meat is marinating.

Discard garlic and heat olive oil in a large frying pan. Sprinkle chops with pepper and brown in oil at a high temperature. Turn heat down to medium-low and cook, covered, for 5 minutes on each side. Serve immediately.

Serves 6.

— Nancy Russell
Saskatoon, Sask.

ROAST VENISON

Be sure the meat has been properly hung and aged. Wipe the roast with a damp cloth. Make several cuts in the top and insert pieces of salt pork, bacon or fat.

Bake in roasting pan in moderate oven, allowing 40 minutes per pound. Baste occasionally. Sprinkle with salt and pepper 30 minutes before time is up. To brown, raise the temperature to 450 degrees F for the last 10 minutes of cooking time.

— Goldie Connell
Prescott, Ontario

CURRIED MOOSE

2 Tbsp. butter
1 medium onion, chopped
2 cups beef stock
2-lb. moose roast, cubed while
  still partly frozen

12 oz. tomato paste
3 Tbsp. curry powder
Handful dark raisins
2 medium potatoes, cubed

Melt butter in skillet, sauté onion in it, then combine onion with beef stock in a large saucepan.

Sear meat in skillet until brown on all sides, about 10 minutes, then add to stock and onion in saucepan, leaving juices in skillet.

Combine tomato paste and curry powder in skillet. Cook briefly, stirring, over medium heat, then add to contents of saucepan.

Stir in raisins and simmer for 2 to 3 hours. Add potatoes, and continue to simmer for another 1½ hours.

Serves 2 to 4.

— John Mortimer
Dease Lake, B.C.

CORNED MOOSE

4 qts. hot water
2 cups coarse salt
¼ cup sugar
2 Tbsp. mixed pickling spice
3 cloves garlic
5 lbs. moose meat

Combine hot water, salt, sugar and pickling spice. When cool, add garlic and pour mixture over meat. Cure in refrigerator or cool place for 3 weeks. Cook in boiling water until tender (5 to 8 hours).

Serves 10.

— *Pat McCormack*
Whitehorse, Yukon

MOOSE STEAK ROAST

½ cup flour
Salt & pepper
2 medium-sized moose steaks
2 eggs, beaten
1 cup bread crumbs
Oil

1 cup tomato juice
2 onions, chopped
Dash soya sauce
Stalk of celery, chopped
½ green pepper, chopped

Combine flour, salt and pepper and sprinkle on both sides of meat. Pound with a meat hammer. Continue to sprinkle and pound until flour mixture is used up.

Brush both sides of meat with eggs, then coat in bread crumbs. Sear gently in oil.

Place meat in roasting pan and pour tomato juice over it. Sprinkle remaining ingredients on top.

Roast at 350 degrees F until tender. Baste frequently and add more tomato juice if necessary.

Serves 2 to 4.

— *H. Miller*
Thunder Bay, Ontario

MOOSE PEPPER STEAK

Cooking oil
1 onion, chopped
1 stalk celery, thinly sliced diagonally
2 lbs. moose meat
3 or 4 carrots, thinly sliced diagonally

1 potato, diced
Salt & pepper
1 cup chopped mushrooms
2 cups snow peas
2 Tbsp. tapioca, softened in 2 Tbsp. water

Pour a few teaspoons of oil into a heated wok. Add onions and celery, and stir until the onions are transparent. Add the meat and stir until browned. Stir in carrots, potato, salt and pepper.

Add about ½ cup water and cover until steam rises around edges of lid. Stir in mushrooms and snow peas, then tapioca. Cook, stirring, only until vegetables are glossy and sauce thickens. Serve immediately over cooked rice.

Serves 4.

— *Angela Denholm*
Agassiz, B.C.

MOOSE HEART & TONGUE CREOLE

1 moose heart
1 moose tongue
Salt & pepper
2 onions, chopped
4 Tbsp. butter
2 cloves garlic, minced
28-oz. can tomatoes
1 green pepper, chopped

1 bay leaf
2 Tbsp. chopped parsley
2 Tbsp. sherry or wine
Pinch thyme
2 Tbsp. sugar
1 cup sliced mushrooms
¼ cup chili sauce

Wash heart and tongue well. Place in pot, cover with water, add salt, pepper and 1 onion. Bring to a boil, lower heat and simmer until very tender — 3 to 5 hours. Peel tongue. Cut tongue and heart into thick slices. Set aside.

Melt butter, add remaining onion and garlic and cook, covered, for 2 minutes.

Add remaining ingredients and cook for approximately 1 hour. Add meat and heat through.

Serves 6 to 8.

— *Mrs. T. Cushman*
Wells, British Columbia

MOOSE RIBS

1 clove garlic
3 Tbsp. cooking oil
3 lbs. moose ribs,
  cut into serving-sized pieces
3 medium onions, sliced
1 cup tomato paste or ketchup
½ cup vinegar
1 tsp. curry powder

1 tsp. paprika
¼ tsp. chili powder
1 Tbsp. brown sugar
1 cup beef stock
½ tsp. salt
Pinch of pepper
½ tsp. dry mustard

Brown garlic in oil in a heavy frying pan. Remove garlic from oil and reserve. Brown ribs quickly in oil.

Place meat and garlic in a 2-quart baking dish. Layer onions on top. Combine remaining ingredients and pour over meat.

Cover and bake at 350 degrees F for 1 hour. Remove lid and continue baking at 300 degrees for another hour, or until meat is tender. Serve over rice.

Serves 4 to 6.

— *Florence Hutchison*
Clearbrook, B.C.

SADDLE OF ELK

6-lb. saddle of elk
Salted pork, cut into 2-inch strips
Garlic, peeled & cut in half
Butter

Preheat oven to 550 degrees F.

Lard the elk with pork strips — draw through meat surface with a larding needle, or make slits with a knife and insert pork.

Rub elk with garlic and then butter. Place, fat side up, in a roasting pan in oven, reduce heat to 350 degrees F and bake for 20 minutes per pound.

Serve with wild rice and gravy.

Serves 8.

ROAST WILD BOAR

THE PREPARATION OF YOUNG WILD BOAR IS VERY SIMILAR TO THAT OF SUCKLING PIG. Properly presented, with head intact and garnished, it makes a spectacular Christmas or New Year's dinner.

Flour
2 cups boiling chicken stock
Apple, cranberries & watercress
  to garnish

1 dressed boar, approximately 12 pounds
3 qts. stuffing, page 156
Butter

Stuff boar with dressings and sew it up. Place a block of wood in the mouth to hold it open. Skewer legs into position.

Rub with butter and dredge with flour. Cover tail and ears with foil and bake, uncovered, at 450 degrees F for 15 minutes. Reduce heat to 325 degrees and bake a further 25 minutes per pound. Baste every 15 minutes with the stock and pan drippings.

To serve: Remove foil and place boar on a platter. Remove wood from boar's mouth and replace with an apple. Place cranberries in eyes and garnish neck and platter with watercress.

Serves 12.

STEWED BEAVER

Remove as much fat as possible, especially the little kernels, then sear and brown the meat in a deep iron skillet. Season as you would rabbit or chicken. Add a little water and simmer until the meat falls from the bones, adding more water as required. Cook it as dry and brown as possible without burning. Serve hot.

— *Goldie Connell*
Prescott, Ontario

WILD CHILI

6 cups water
2 lbs. chicken necks
2 bay leaves
¾ tsp. rosemary
Freshly ground pepper
1 cup chopped celery & leaves
2 medium carrots, cut in half
¾ cup cubed turnip
1-1½ lbs. ground moose meat
1½ medium onions, chopped
2 cloves garlic, minced

½ lb. mushrooms, in thick slices
20-oz. can tomatoes
6-oz. can tomato paste
1½ cups cooked chick peas
  or kidney beans
2 cups cranberries
3 Tbsp. chili powder
Salt
½ cup uncooked bulgur
1 medium zucchini, sliced

In water, simmer chicken necks, bay leaves, rosemary, pepper, celery, carrots and turnip for about 2½ hours or until chicken comes away from the bone. Remove bay leaves and necks and let broth cook in refrigerator overnight. Remove excess fat and put broth and vegetables through blender.

Cook ground moose meat, onion, garlic and mushrooms in large casserole dish. Add broth and remaining ingredients. Simmer for 1½ to 2 hours.

Serves 8.

— *Nicol Seguin*
La Sarre, Quebec

Meat

When mighty roast beef was the Englishman's food
It ennobled our hearts and enriched our blood,
Our soldiers were brave and our courtiers were good
Oh! the roast beef of old England!

— **Richard Leveridge**

With this chapter, we leave behind the vegetarian, who will probably agree with Edna Ferber's sentiment that " 'Roast Beef Medium ' is not only a food. It's a philosophy." Meat-eating may seem unconscionable to some, but to most North Americans it is a way of life; indeed, a rare filet or a properly done joint of lamb with mint sauce is one of those things that seems to some to make life worth living. Clifton Fadiman wrote, "I have yet to meet the man who, with a good *tournedos Rossini* inside him, was not the finer for it, the more open to virtuous influences."

Meat gives the consumer the most expensive protein in the supermarket, but it is high quality protein; all eight of the amino acids needed by the human body are present in meat, dairy products and eggs. Meats are also good sources of most minerals and vitamins. The world's arctic natives subsisted for generations on a diet almost totally comprised of meat by including the vitamin-rich organs. A comparable weight of beef liver, for instance, contains three times as much vitamin A as fresh carrots, and brain, heart, liver and kidney all contain some vitamin C.

Liver is also the best dietary source of iron, a nutrient whose lack was "marked and widespread" amongst Canadian children and adolescents during the Nutrition Canada survey published in 1973. "Almost one half the infants and toddlers and a third of older children in the populations surveyed have dietary iron intakes below adequate levels." Nutritionists generally recommend that, to ensure adequate iron, liver be included in the diet once a week.

Most meats are also good sources of B vitamins, the exception being folic acid, but this is present in liver and kidney. As B vitamins are water-soluble, the juices produced as meat cooks should be saved whenever possible. Gravy is not simply flavour and decoration, it is an intelligent way to use vitamin-rich pan juices.

Buying meat in bulk may or may not save the shopper money. If the animal was raised at home, or bought "on the hoof," chances are good that one's freezer beef will be a good buy. But the hind quarter offered by a city butcher may not. Ask him, before ordering the meat, for a listing of the number, size and types of cuts that will be included, and compare the prices with those offered at supermarket specials. If a freezer is to be bought just for this purpose, the shopper should include its cost, which may be spread out over its expected lifespan. Include additional power costs as well. If the freezer can also be used for garden produce, soup stock and other bulk perishables, its value will be most assured.

A local health food or natural food outlet may be

able to advise a shopper about sources of meats that are free from chemicals and antibiotics. The quality of any meat, however, will depend upon the animal's age, what it was fed, and whether it was properly hung: aging meat for a specified duration ripens it, enhancing the flavour and quality. The true worth of any bulk purchase will be in the eating.

Those who buy meat in bulk will have to contend with a number of tough cuts. The more muscles are used, the tougher the meat, so while the underbelly contains choice cuts, the neck and leg meat is less desirable. Soup bones are easy to use; they are simply covered with cold water and simmered for hours and hours to make stock, which can be frozen for later use. Other tough cuts (which may comprise the entire animal if it was old; even hamburger can be tough) can be tenderized by pounding, scoring, marinating or long, slow, moist cooking. Marinades that include an acid such as wine or lemon juice will soften the connective tissue, the collagen.

As it cooks, muscle fibre proteins in the meat coagulate, and the meat shrinks. Collagen is converted into gelatin, causing the meat to soften, especially if it is cooked with moisture. Most or all food poisoning organisms and parasites are killed. This is especially important with pork. While most beef can actually be safely eaten raw

— *steak tartare,* a specialty at some expensive restaurants, is raw, spiced ground beef — pork is occasionally host to a round worm *Trichinella spiralis* which can infect man, causing trichinosis. An outbreak of trichinosis occurred as recently as 1979/80 in Quebec. Any danger of trichinosis can be avoided if the cook freezes or thoroughly cooks pork. When done, pork will have an internal temperature of 167 − 175 degrees F and will have no pink coloration.

Fresh meat keeps only about two days in the refrigerator, so cook it, if possible, the day it is bought or thawed. Cooked meat keeps a little better and may be frozen for longer storage. One way to prevent losses with a large roast is to cook the entire joint for supper, and then, saving some for lunches or stews, slice the rest into meal-sized portions, marking and freezing them for future sandwiches or cold plates. Freezing does cause some deterioration in texture and flavour, but most nutrients are maintained.

As we mentioned in an earlier chapter, most North Americans tend to overindulge in meat, which probably causes them to take this most energy-consumptive of foods for granted, while giving them more protein than they require. The cook who serves meat three or four days a week instead of seven can not only save money, but can make room for some variety in the menu as well.

SAUTE OF VEAL WITH HERBS

2 lbs. veal, cut into 1½" cubes
Salt & pepper
2 Tbsp. butter
2 Tbsp. oil
½ lb. mushrooms, sliced
1 medium onion, chopped
¾ cup chopped celery
1 clove garlic, minced

½ cup dry white wine
¼ cup flour
1½ cups chicken stock
1 cup crushed tomatoes
½ tsp. dried rosemary
2 sprigs parsley
1 bay leaf
2 medium onions, quartered

Sprinkle meat with salt and pepper, heat butter and oil in skillet and brown meat, a few pieces at a time. Set aside.

Add mushrooms, chopped onion, celery and garlic to skillet and cook until onion is soft. Add wine, and cook to evaporate.

Return meat to skillet and sprinkle with flour. Gradually add the stock, stirring to blend. Add the tomatoes, rosemary, parsley and bay leaf and cover. Cook over low heat for about 1 hour. Add the quartered onions and cook 45 minutes longer. Serve sprinkled with parsley.

Serves 4 to 6.

— Shirley Hill
Picton, Ontario

VEAL MARENGO

½ cup flour
1 tsp. salt
½ tsp. pepper
1 tsp. tarragon
3 lbs. veal, in thin slices or cutlets
½ cup olive oil

1 cup dry red wine
2 cups canned tomatoes
1 clove garlic, crushed
8 mushrooms, sliced
Snipped fresh parsley

Combine flour, salt, pepper and tarragon and dredge meat in it. Save leftover flour. Brown meat in oil in large skillet, then remove to a casserole dish.

Add reserved flour to pan juices, stirring quickly. Add the wine. Cook until sauce is thick and smooth, then pour it over the meat. Add tomatoes, garlic and mushrooms.

Cover and bake at 350 degrees F for 45 minutes, or until tender. Garnish with parsley.

Serves 6.

— Cary Elizabeth Marshall
Thunder Bay, Ontario

VEAL PARMESAN

3 Tbsp. butter
½ cup fine bread crumbs
¼ cup grated Parmesan cheese
½ tsp. salt
Dash pepper

1 lb. veal cutlets
1 egg, slightly beaten
1 cup tomato sauce, page 204
1 cup grated mozzarella cheese

Melt butter in 8-inch square baking dish. Combine crumbs, Parmesan cheese, salt and pepper. Cut veal into serving-sized pieces. Dip first into egg and then into crumb mixture.

Place in baking dish and bake at 400 degrees F for 20 minutes, turn and bake for another 15 minutes.

Pour tomato sauce over meat and top with mozzarella cheese. Return to oven to melt cheese — about 3 minutes.

Serves 4.

— Mrs. W. Atkins
Agincourt, Ontario

JELLIED VEAL LOAF

3 lbs. lean veal with bones
1 qt. water
1 medium onion
1 carrot
1 stalk celery
1 bay leaf

½ tsp. salt
Pepper
2 envelopes unflavoured gelatin
1 Tbsp. lemon juice
1 Tbsp. parsley

In a heavy saucepan, place veal, water, onion, carrot, celery, bay leaf, salt and pepper. Simmer until tender – 2 hours. Strain. Cool stock and set aside.

Remove fat and skin from meat and discard. Put meat through food processor or meat grinder.

Soften gelatin in cold stock, then simmer, stirring. Remove from heat and add lemon juice. Add meat and parsley. Pour into a mould which has been lightly greased with vegetable oil. Refrigerate until set.

— Margaret Burrow Robbins
Creemore, Ontario

BOEUF EN DAUBE

IN THIS RECIPE, THE BEEF IS COOKED IN ONE PIECE SURROUNDED BY VEGETABLES, BUT the final result is essentially a stew.

2½ lbs. rump of beef
2 Tbsp. butter
2 Tbsp. cooking oil
½ lb. onions, finely sliced
1 lb. carrots, finely sliced
½ lb. salt pork, cubed
1 cup dry white wine

½ cup beef stock
1 tsp. dried basil
½ tsp. dried rosemary
1 bay leaf
½ tsp. curry powder
Salt & pepper
6 black olives

Wrap string around beef to prevent it from falling apart. Brown quickly in butter and oil to seal. Drain and place in a casserole dish.

Fry onions, carrots and salt pork until golden brown. Drain and place around beef.

Pour wine and stock over everything in the casserole and add seasonings. Bring to a boil, cover, then bake at 325 degrees F for 2½ to 3 hours or until tender. Add olives 30 minutes before serving.

Serves 4 to 6.

— Sheila Bear
St. John's. Nfld.

OVEN STEW

THIS STEW CAN BE ASSEMBLED IN A MATTER OF MINUTES EARLY IN THE DAY AND left to simmer, unwatched, until dinner time. To use a slow cooker, start stew 10 to 12 hours before serving time.

2 lbs. stewing beef, cut into bite-sized
  pieces
1 onion, chopped
4 carrots, chopped
4 celery stalks, chopped
½ green pepper, chopped
¼ cup quick-cooking tapioca

¼ cup dry bread crumbs
1 cup mushrooms, chopped
Salt
28-oz. can tomatoes
¼ cup water
½ cup red wine

Combine ingredients, cover and cook for 4 hours at 300 degrees F.

Serves 4 to 6.

BEEF WELLINGTON

5 lb. fillet of beef
1 tsp. dry mustard
Fat back to cover beef
4 chicken livers
½ lb. mushrooms
¼ lb. cooked ham

1 small clove garlic
2 Tbsp. butter
⅓ cup sherry
1 Tbsp. meat extract
1 Tbsp. tomato purée
Puff pastry

Sprinkle beef with mustard and cover with fat back. Roast at 400 degrees F for 25 minutes. Cool and remove fat.

Sauté chicken livers, chop finely and set aside.

Finely mince mushrooms, ham and garlic and sauté for 5 minutes in butter. Add chicken livers, sherry, meat extract and tomato purée. Mix well and remove from heat.

Roll out puff pastry in a large enough sheet to enclose the fillet.

Lay the fillet in centre of pastry and spoon mushroom mixture over and around it. Carefully wrap pastry around fillet, turning in the ends and pressing all the seams together firmly. Lay fillet seam-side down in a baking dish.

Bake at 350 degrees F for 30 to 35 minutes, until crust is lightly browned.

Serves 8 to 10.

— *Cary Elizabeth Marshall*
Thunder Bay, Ontario

LAZY MAN'S ROAST

THIS RECIPE IS ALSO EASILY ADAPTED TO A SLOW COOKER — SIMPLY ALLOW 2 HOURS more cooking time.

3-4 lb. rump roast
1 cup red wine
1½ tsp. salt
10 whole peppercorns

1½ Tbsp. brown sugar
2 bay leaves
½ tsp. dried sage

Trim most of fat from roast and place meat in a casserole dish. Add wine, salt, peppercorns, sugar and herbs. Cover tightly and cook for 4 hours at 275 degrees F. Remove pan from heat and let meat sit in its liquid for 1 hour before serving.

Serves 6.

— *Kathleen Fitzgerald*
Fort McMurray, Alberta

YORKSHIRE PUDDING

THIS TRADITIONAL BRITISH ACCOMPANIMENT TO ROAST BEEF CAN BE PREPARED AS the roast cooks and baked while the roast rests before carving.

¼ cup hot drippings from roast
1 egg, well beaten
½ cup milk

½ cup flour
¼ tsp. salt

Divide drippings among 6 large muffin tins.

Beat egg and milk together until light. Gradually beat in flour and salt, and continue beating until batter is smooth.

Pour into muffin tins and let stand for 30 minutes. Bake at 450 degrees F for 15 to 20 minutes.

Serves 6.

— *Mrs. W. Atkins*
Agincourt, Ontario

CORNED BEEF

4-lb. rump roast
8 cups water
4 Tbsp. sugar
2 bay leaves

10 peppercorns
4 tsp. mixed pickling spice
2 cloves garlic, minced
1 cup salt

Place meat in a crock. Combine the remaining ingredients and pour over meat. Weight the meat down in the brine and cover. Let stand in a cool place for 5 to 7 days.

Remove meat from brine and place in cold water. Bring to a boil. Remove scum from the surface. Cover and simmer for 5 hours.

Serves 6.

— Pam McFeeters
Woodville, Ontario

NEW ENGLAND BOILED DINNER

4 lbs. corned beef brisket
Salt to taste
6 medium-sized carrots, diced

1 turnip, halved
1 small cabbage, quartered
6 medium potatoes, diced

Cover meat with cold water, bring to a boil, then lower heat and simmer gently for 2 hours.

Skim off fat. Add salt, carrots, turnip, cabbage and potatoes. Continue to cook for 1 more hour.

Serves 6 to 8.

— Shirley Morrish
Devlin, Ontario

MARINATED BEEF

½ cup soya sauce
½ cup lemon juice
2 cloves garlic, crushed

1 lb. chuck, blade or round steak
   cut into thin strips

Mix soya sauce, lemon juice and garlic. Pour over beef and marinate for 4 hours, turning once. Drain and dry beef, reserving marinade. Fry or broil beef at a high temperature, so that it cooks quickly.

Serve with rice, using marinade as a sauce.

Serves 3 to 4.

— Judy Wuest
Cross Creek, N.B.

STIR-FRIED MEAT & VEGETABLES

1 green pepper, cut in strips
2 stalks celery, cut in strips
1 cup thinly sliced onions
1 cup sliced mushrooms
4 Tbsp. butter
2 cups green beans, cut in pieces

½ cup leftover gravy
⅛ tsp. pepper
3 cups cooked meat, cut in 1-inch pieces
3 Tbsp. soya sauce
2 cups fresh bean sprouts

Brown green pepper, celery, onions and mushrooms in butter. Add green beans and stir gently. Then add remaining ingredients except for the bean sprouts and stir. Heat thoroughly. Stir in bean sprouts when ready to serve.

Serves 6.

— Ruth Anne Laverty
Listowel, Ontario

WINE BEEF STEW

THE FLAVOUR OF BEEF SIMMERED SLOWLY IN RED WINE IS DIFFICULT TO SURPASS. This recipe adds potatoes and carrots to provide a complete meal in one dish.

6 Tbsp. oil
3 lbs. beef chuck,
  cut into 1½-inch cubes
1 cup chopped onion
1 cup sliced celery
2 Tbsp. parsley
1 clove garlic, finely chopped
1½ Tbsp. salt
¼ tsp. pepper

⅛ tsp. thyme
1 bay leaf
1 cup tomato sauce, page 204
2 cups beef stock
1 cup dry red wine
6 medium potatoes, diced
6 medium carrots, sliced
1-2 Tbsp. flour
2 Tbsp. cold water

In hot oil, brown beef well on all sides. Remove and set aside.

Add onion and celery and sauté until tender — about 8 minutes. Return beef to pan.

Add parsley, garlic, salt, pepper, thyme, bay leaf, tomato sauce, beef stock and wine. Bring to a boil. Reduce heat and simmer, covered, for 1¼ hours.

Add potatoes and carrots. Simmer, covered, 1 hour longer, or until tender.

Remove from heat and skim off fat. Mix flour with cold water and stir into beef mixture. Return to stove and simmer, covered, for 10 minutes.

Serves 6.

— *Myrna Henderson*
Whitecourt, Alberta

STEAK & KIDNEY PIE

FOR AN UNUSUAL VERSION OF THIS TRADITIONAL DISH, ADD A PINT OF FRESH OYSTERS and a bay leaf.

Pastry for double 9-inch pie crust
1½ lbs. sirloin or round steak
1 lb. kidneys
2 tsp. salt
1 tsp. pepper
¼ cup flour
3 Tbsp. butter & 1 Tbsp. oil

1 cup sliced mushrooms
½ cup chopped onion
1½ cups water
¼ cup dry red wine
1 Tbsp. chopped parsley
¼ tsp. thyme
¼ tsp. Worcestershire sauce

Cut steak and kidney into cubes and dry with paper towels. Sprinkle with 1 tsp. salt and ½ tsp. pepper. Toss in a bowl with the flour.

Melt the butter and oil in a pan. Brown a few of the meat cubes at a time and transfer to a large casserole dish.

Stir the mushrooms and onion in the same pan for 2 to 3 minutes, then add to the meat.

Pour the water into the frying pan, bring to a boil, stirring to pick up the residues, and pour into casserole dish. Add wine, parsley, thyme, Worcestershire sauce and the rest of the salt and pepper. Stir gently.

Cover with pastry. Brush with water and bake at 425 degrees F for 30 minutes, reduce heat to 350 degrees and bake for 30 minutes longer.

— *Carolyn Hills*
Sunderland, Ontario

BARBECUED BEEF BRAISING RIBS

3½ lbs. beef braising ribs
3 Tbsp. oil
1 clove garlic, minced
¼ cup white vinegar
1 cup tomato paste
1 cup water

1 Tbsp. Worcestershire sauce
¼ cup brown sugar
½ cup minced onion
½ tsp. salt
¼ tsp. pepper
1 Tbsp. butter

Brown ribs in oil with garlic. Transfer ribs and drippings to roasting pan.

Combine remaining ingredients in a saucepan and simmer for 15 minutes. Pour over ribs and bake, covered, at 350 degrees F for 1½ to 2 hours, stirring after 1 hour.

Serves 6.

— *Diane Cane*
Baltimore, Ontario •

CORNISH PASTIES

INDIVIDUAL, MOON-SHAPED MEAT AND VEGETABLE PIES, PASTIES ARE EQUALLY delicious hot or cold.

Enough pastry for 2-crust pie
1 lb. stewing beef, cut in small cubes
Salt & pepper
2 medium onions, thinly sliced

4 small carrots, thinly sliced
4 small potatoes, thinly sliced
2 cups sliced turnip

Roll pastry into 4 circles with 7-inch diameters.

On one half of each piece of pastry, place meat, then sprinkle with salt and pepper. Place onions on top of the meat and the other vegetables on top of the onions.

Fold the other half of the pastry over filling and press edges down. Trim with a knife to within ½ inch of the contents. Moisten edges slightly with water and turn over to seal.

Make a small hole in the top and pour in 2 teaspoons of water.

Bake at 450 degrees F for 15 minutes. Reduce heat to 375 degrees and continue baking for another 45 minutes.

Serves 4.

— *Elizabeth Mitchell*
Belleville, Ontario

SWISS STEAK

¼ cup flour
1 tsp. salt
1 lb. round steak
3 Tbsp. oil
1½ cups tomato sauce
1½ cups water
1 medium onion, sliced

1½ cups sliced carrots
1½ cups Brussels sprouts
1 tsp. salt
1 tsp. parsley
1 tsp. Worcestershire sauce
Dash pepper & garlic powder

Combine flour and salt. Cut meat into serving-sized pieces and coat with flour mixture. Brown in oil in large frying pan.

Reduce heat and add remaining ingredients. Cover and simmer for 1½ hours or until meat is tender.

Serves 4.

— *Helen Eagles*
New Minas, N.S.

BEEF CURRY

3 lbs. stewing beef, in 1-inch cubes
1 cup chopped onion
1 cup chopped apple
3 cloves garlic, minced
½ cup butter
1 Tbsp. turmeric
2 bay leaves, crumbled
1 inch fresh ginger, minced
2 tsp. coriander

2 tsp. cumin
½ tsp. cardamom
½ tsp. ground mustard seed
½ tsp. cinnamon
½ tsp. ground fenugreek
4 hot chilies, crushed
Salt & pepper
3 cups coconut milk

Sauté meat, onion, apple and garlic in the butter. Combine spices and add to meat when well browned. Cook briefly, stirring.

Add coconut milk and simmer until meat is very tender — 3 to 6 hours.

Serve over rice with any or all of: fresh fruit, nuts, chopped celery, green peppers, coconut, raisins and yogurt.

Serves 8 to 10.

— *Ingrid Birker*
Toronto, Ontario

BOEUF AU VIN

¼ lb. bacon, finely chopped
1 clove garlic, finely chopped
1 onion, chopped
6 carrots, cut in spears
1 lb. round, chuck or blade steak, cubed

1 tsp. thyme
1 bay leaf
1 cup dry red wine
Parsley, finely chopped
½ lb. mushrooms, sliced

Cook bacon in a heavy frying pan until crisp. Remove with slotted spoon and reserve. Sauté garlic, onion and carrots in bacon fat until slightly browned. Remove and set aside.

Brown beef in remaining bacon fat. Add garlic, onion, carrots and bacon. Sprinkle with thyme and crumbled bay leaf. Add wine. Cover and simmer for 1½ hours. If necessary, add water during cooking. Add mushrooms and parsley and cook for another 10 minutes.

Serves 3 to 4.

— *Judy Wuest*
Cross Creek, N.B.

BOEUF BOURBONNAIS

Seasoned flour
2½ lbs. round steak, cubed
2 Tbsp. oil
2 cups beef stock
1 cup red wine
1 bay leaf

1 Tbsp. tomato paste
10-15 small onions
½ lb. mushrooms, halved
1-2 Tbsp. flour
2 Tbsp. water

Place seasoned flour in small bag. Add meat in small amounts and shake to coat. Brown meat in oil.

Add all remaining ingredients except mushrooms, flour and water. Bring to a boil, then turn heat low and cover. Simmer for 1½ hours, or until meat is tender. Cool quickly, uncovered, in the refrigerator.

An hour or so before serving, skim fat from top and heat mixture to a boil. Add mushrooms and thicken with flour mixed with cold water. Cook and stir until thickened.

Serves 8.

— *Donna Gordon*
Dorval, Quebec

RED EYE STEW

3 lbs. stewing beef, cut into 1-inch pieces
¼ cup flour
2 Tbsp. salt
1 tsp. pepper
¼ cup oil
4 large onions, sliced
1 clove garlic
12 oz. beer

1 Tbsp. soya sauce
1 Tbsp. Worcestershire sauce
1 Tbsp. tomato paste
½ tsp. thyme
2 bay leaves
2-3 cups tomato juice
3 potatoes, peeled & diced
2 cups peas

Dredge meat in flour mixed with salt and pepper. Brown in hot oil.

Add onions and garlic and cook until onions are transparent. Add beer, soya sauce, Worcestershire sauce, tomato paste, thyme and bay leaves. Bring to a boil, then reduce heat and simmer for 1 hour.

Add tomato juice and simmer for 30 minutes. Add potatoes, cook 20 minutes, then peas, and cook until tender. Remove bay leaves and serve.

Serves 10 to 12.

— Barbara Smith
Thunder Bay, Ontario

BOEUF A LA CREOLE

THIS BEEF DISH IS DELICIOUS WITH SAFFRON RICE AND A TOSSED GREEN SALAD.

4 Tbsp. olive oil
2 onions, peeled & sliced
1½ lbs. stewing beef
1 Tbsp. tomato sauce, page 204

1 clove garlic, sliced
1 sprig thyme
1 sprig parsley
Few pinches saffron

Pour olive oil into heavy casserole dish and top with onions. Cut beef into serving-sized pieces and place on top of onions. Add remaining ingredients, cover and simmer for 3 to 4 hours.

Serves 4.

HUNGARIAN GOULASH

ALMOST ANY MEAT CAN BE USED IN GOULASH; VEGETABLES OR RED WINE MAY BE added. The one constant is sweet paprika, available from specialty stores.

2 lbs. round steak
¼ cup butter
1½ cups chopped onion
1 cup boiling tomato juice

1 tsp. salt
½ tsp. Hungarian paprika
Cornstarch
6 cups cooked noodles

Cut beef into 1-inch cubes. Melt butter and brown meat on both sides. Add onion and sauté.

Add tomato juice, salt and paprika. Cover and simmer for 1½ to 2 hours. Remove meat from pot and keep warm.

To thicken gravy, mix cornstarch with a small amount of cold water and stir rapidly into hot gravy. Bring to a boil and cook until desired consistency is reached.

Place meat on noodles and pour thickened gravy over all.

Serves 6.

CHINESE BEEF & BROCCOLI IN OYSTER SAUCE

1 lb. round steak
2 Tbsp. soya sauce
1 tsp. cornstarch
1 large onion
1 head broccoli
3 Tbsp. oil
1 clove garlic

1 thin slice ginger
3-4 Tbsp. bottled oyster sauce
Brown sugar
Salt
½ cup cold water
1 Tbsp. cornstarch

Slice steak very thinly. Place in a bowl with soya sauce, cornstarch and a few drops of water. Mix well and set aside.

Slice onion very thinly. Cut broccoli into small pieces and steam until partly cooked. Drain and set aside.

Heat oil in skillet until very hot. Add garlic and ginger. Cook 1 minute, then remove. Add meat and fry until meat sweats, then add onion and broccoli. Stir-fry until vegetables are crispy-tender.

Stir in oyster sauce, a pinch of brown sugar, salt and ½ cup cold water with 1 Tbsp. cornstarch dissolved in it. Stir and cook until sauce is thickened. Serve with rice.

Serves 4.

— Bryanna Clark
Union Bay, B.C.

BEEF STROGANOFF

1½ lbs. round steak, cut in narrow strips
¼ cup flour
4 Tbsp. butter
1 onion, diced
½ cup dry red wine

½ lb. mushrooms, sliced
2 green onions, chopped
1 tsp. salt
¼ tsp. chervil
1 cup sour cream

Dredge meat in flour and brown in butter. Add onion and cook until translucent. Add wine and simmer, covered, for 30 minutes.

Add mushrooms, green onions, salt and chervil. Cook 2 to 3 minutes. Stir in sour cream and heat through but do not boil.

Serves 4.

ITALIAN STEAK

2 lbs. round steak
1 cup bread crumbs
1 cup Parmesan cheese
2 eggs, beaten
4 Tbsp. cooking oil
¾ cup chopped onion

2 cups tomato sauce, page 204
¼ cup water
¼ tsp. salt
⅛ tsp. pepper
1 tsp. oregano
¼ lb. mozzarella cheese, grated

Trim fat from meat and cut into serving-sized pieces. Combine bread crumbs and Parmesan cheese. Dip meat in egg and then in cheese mixture. Brown on both sides in 2 Tbsp. oil.

Sauté onion in remaining oil until tender — about 3 minutes. Stir in tomato sauce, water, seasonings and bring to a boil. Reduce heat and simmer for 10 minutes, stirring occasionally.

Arrange meat in a shallow baking dish, cover with three-quarters of sauce, spread with mozzarella and add remaining sauce.

Bake at 300 degrees F for 30 to 45 minutes, until meat is tender.

Serves 6.

— John & Leone Lackey
Smiths Falls, Ontario

ROUND STEAK WITH ORANGE SLICES

3 Tbsp. soya sauce
1 clove garlic, minced
1½ lbs. round steak

2 Tbsp. oil
2 onions, sliced & separated into rings
1 large orange, peeled & cut into slices

Blend soya sauce and garlic in large flat baking dish, add steak, cover and marinate in refrigerator several hours or overnight, turning a few times.

Heat oil in large skillet and cook steak for 4 minutes on each side, or until browned. Remove to warm platter.

Add onion and any remaining marinade to skillet and sauté for a few minutes. Cover and simmer for 5 minutes. Add orange slices and heat through. Cut steak crosswise in thin slices and top with orange and onion mixture.

Serves 6.

— Shirley Gilbert
Calgary, Alberta

CHILI FOR TWENTY

3-3½ lbs. lean ground beef
2 medium onions, chopped
2 medium green peppers, chopped
5 stalks celery, chopped

Salt & pepper
Crushed chilies to taste
15 cups cooked kidney beans
2 28-oz. cans tomatoes

Brown meat, onions, green peppers and celery. Add salt, pepper and chilies and cook for a few minutes. Add kidney beans and tomatoes and simmer for 3 hours.

The flavour of this dish improves with 1 or 2 days of ageing.

Serves 20.

— Janice Touesnard
River Bourgeois, N.S.

SPOONBREAD CHILI PIE

THIS RECIPE TOPS A BASIC CHILI WITH A CORN MEAL CHEESE BISCUIT.

½ lb. ground beef
1 medium onion, chopped
¼ green pepper, chopped
1 clove garlic, minced
1 tsp. chili powder
1¼ cups canned tomatoes
1½ cups kernel corn
1 tsp. salt

Pepper
2 cups cooked kidney beans
1¼ cups milk
1 Tbsp. butter
½ tsp. salt
¼ cup corn meal
½ cup grated Cheddar cheese
1 egg, beaten

Cook ground beef, onion, green pepper and garlic over medium heat for 8 minutes. Stir in chili powder and cook for another minute.

Stir in tomatoes, corn, salt and pepper. Cover and simmer for 5 minutes. Add kidney beans and cook for another 5 minutes. Turn into casserole dish and set aside.

Scald milk with butter and salt. Gradually add corn meal while stirring. Cook until thickened — 4 minutes. Remove from heat and stir in cheese and egg.

Spread topping over casserole. Bake at 375 degrees F for 35 minutes or until topping has set.

Serves 6.

— Nel vanGeest
Weston, Ontario

BEEF & POTATO PIE

1 partially baked pie shell
1 large onion, chopped
1 clove garlic, minced
1 stalk celery, chopped
½ cup minced celery leaves
4 Tbsp. oil
2 lbs. ground beef
1½ cups beef stock
2 Tbsp. cornstarch
1 tsp. salt

Dash pepper
Dash Worcestershire sauce
Dash Tabasco sauce
½ tsp. chili powder
1½ cups grated Cheddar cheese
8 potatoes, boiled
1 egg, beaten
½ cup milk
⅛ tsp. salt
1 tsp. butter

Cook onion, garlic, celery and leaves in oil until tender. Remove from pan. Cook ground beef until browned and drain.

Combine beef, vegetables, stock, cornstarch, salt, pepper, Worcestershire sauce, Tabasco sauce, chili powder and cheese. Simmer until thick, then place in pie shell.

Whip potatoes until fluffy. Add remaining ingredients and spread over pie.

Bake at 350 degrees F for 30 minutes.

Serves 4 to 6.

— Jaine Fraser
Elliotvale, P.E.I.

ABERDEEN ROLL

THIS CHILLED ROLL HAS THE TEXTURE OF A ROUGH PATE. THE COMBINATION OF bacon and ground beef gives an attractive marbled look to the completed dish.

½ lb. ground beef
½ lb. bacon, minced
1 large egg, beaten
1½ cups coarse bread crumbs
Salt & pepper

Pinch dry mustard
Pinch garlic powder
1 shake Tabasco sauce
2 small onions, finely chopped

Blend all ingredients together and shape into a roll. Cover tightly with tin foil. Boil for 2 hours. Chill and serve sliced.

— Wendy Wallace
Lakefield, Ontario

MEAT LOAF

2 eggs, slightly beaten
¼ cup milk
¼ cup ketchup
¾ cup onion, minced

¾ tsp. dry mustard
2 tsp. salt
2 cups soft bread crumbs
2 lbs. ground beef

Combine eggs, milk, ketchup, onion, mustard, salt and bread crumbs. Let stand for 10 minutes. Add beef and mix well. Place in loaf pan.

Bake at 350 degrees F for 35 minutes, then lower heat to 325 degrees and bake 1 hour longer.

Serves 8.

— Joanne Ramsy
Aylmer, Ontario

TOMATO MEAT LOAF

1½ lbs. ground beef
1 egg, beaten
1 cup fresh bread crumbs or wheat germ
1 medium onion, chopped
1¼ tsp. salt

¼ tsp. pepper
1 cup tomato sauce, page 204
2 Tbsp. vinegar
1 cup water
2 Tbsp. brown sugar

Combine beef, egg, bread crumbs, onion, salt, pepper and ½ cup tomato sauce and mix well. Place in loaf pan and bake at 350 degrees F.

Meanwhile, combine remaining tomato sauce, vinegar, water and brown sugar. Pour over meat loaf after it has cooked for 30 minutes, then bake 1 hour more.

Serves 6.

— *Laura Poitras*
Kemptville, Ontario

SWEDISH MEATBALLS

1 lb. ground beef
1 cup soft bread crumbs
½ cup milk
1 egg, well beaten
2 medium onions, finely chopped
2 tsp. salt

⅛ tsp. pepper
½ tsp. nutmeg
Oil
1 cup hot water
1 Tbsp. flour
2 Tbsp. cold water

Mix beef, bread crumbs, milk, egg, onions, salt, pepper and nutmeg. Form into 1-inch balls. Heat a little oil in skillet and brown balls on all sides. Remove and keep warm.

Add hot water to meat drippings and stir. Mix flour and cold water well and add to drippings. Bring to a boil, stirring until thick. Return meatballs to skillet, cover and cook for 30 minutes, adding more water if necessary.

Serves 4 as a main course, 12 as hors d'oeuvres.

— *Peter Suffel*
Sault Ste. Marie, Ont.

SWEET & SOUR MEATBALLS WITH SAUSAGES

2 onions, chopped
1-2 Tbsp. cooking oil
1 lb. ground beef
1½ cups water
Salt & pepper

1 lb. sausages
1 cup ketchup
4 Tbsp. brown sugar
4 Tbsp. cider vinegar
1-2 tsp. Worcestershire sauce

Sauté onions in oil over low heat until transparent. Remove from pan. Mix one-quarter of onions with ground beef, ½ cup water, 1 tsp. salt and pepper. Shape into 1-inch meatballs and brown in pan used for onions. Place in casserole dish. Deglaze pan with 1 cup water, reducing liquid to ⅓ cup. Set aside.

Cut sausages in half crosswise. Brown and place in casserole dish with meatballs.

Combine remaining onions, liquid from pan, ketchup, brown sugar, vinegar, Worcestershire sauce, ½ tsp. salt and pepper. Pour over meat.

Bake at 325 degrees F, covered, for 45 minutes. Remove lid and continue baking for another 15 minutes.

Serves 6 to 8.

— *Mrs. Garnet Baker*
Toledo, Ontario

PITA TACOS

Pita bread for 4
½ lb. ground beef
1 small onion, chopped
½ cup kidney or pinto beans, mashed
½ tsp. ground pepper
Salt

2-3 Tbsp. chili powder
Dash Tabasco sauce
6-oz. can tomato paste
½ lb. grated Cheddar cheese
Lettuce & tomato

Slit bread to form a pocket and warm in oven.

Sauté beef and onion until brown. Drain. Add remaining ingredients except lettuce and tomato. Stuff into bread.

Garnish with lettuce and tomato.

Serves 4.

— Melody Scott
Bramalea, Ontario

BEEF ENCHILADAS

Olive oil
1 lb. ground beef
1 onion, chopped
1 green pepper, chopped
1 tsp. parsley flakes
2 cloves garlic, crushed
¾ tsp. chili powder
½ tsp. cumin
½ tsp. dried chilies
Salt & pepper
½ cup kernel corn

1 tomato, chopped
2-4 Tbsp. sour cream
3½ cups tomato sauce, page 204
1 Tbsp. white vinegar
½ tsp. oregano
½ tsp. basil
½ tsp. rosemary
½ tsp. garlic powder
1 tsp. brown sugar
6 tortillas
2 cups grated Cheddar cheese

In olive oil, fry ground beef, onion and green pepper. Season with ½ tsp. parsley, garlic, ½ tsp. chili powder, ¼ tsp. cumin, chilies and salt and pepper. Add corn, tomato, sour cream and ½ cup tomato sauce. Cook for 15 minutes.

Combine remaining ingredients, except for tortillas, to make sauce.

Fill tortillas with beef mixture. Cover with sauce and top with cheese.

Bake, covered, at 350 degrees F for 45 minutes.

Serves 6.

— Diane Schoemperlen
Banff, Alberta

CABBAGE ROLLS WITH SOUR CREAM

1 large cabbage
1 cup raw rice
1 lb. ground beef

1 large onion, chopped
8-oz. can stewed tomatoes
1 pint sour cream

Peel leaves from cabbage and place in boiling water until limp. Drain and remove centre vein.

Mix together rice, ground beef and chopped onion. Place about 2 Tbsp. of mixture on each cabbage leaf and roll up, envelope fashion. Line baking dish with remaining leaves. Place cabbage rolls in layers and pour the stewed tomatoes over them. Add tomato juice, if necessary, to cover.

Bake at 350 degrees F for approximately 2 hours. Remove from oven and spread sour cream over rolls. Return dish to oven for 5 minutes, then serve.

Serves 4 to 6.

— Paula Gustafson
Abbotsford, B.C.

SHEPHERD'S PIE

1 lb. ground beef or 3 cups leftover meat
¼ cup chopped green pepper
¼ cup chopped onion
1 Tbsp. shortening
1 Tbsp. flour
1 tsp. salt
½ tsp. chili powder
Dash pepper

½ cup tomato sauce, page 204
1 cup water
½ cup cooked carrots
½ cup peas
½ cup cooked celery
½ cup chopped mushrooms
3 cups seasoned hot mashed potatoes
Paprika

Sauté ground beef, green pepper and onion in shortening until meat is browned and pepper tender. Drain off any excess fat. Sprinkle next four ingredients in. Stir in tomato sauce, water, carrots, peas, celery and mushrooms. Combine well and cook until mixture thickens.

Place mixture in 2-quart casserole dish. Top with potatoes and sprinkle with paprika. Place under broiler to brown, or bake at 425 degrees F for 15 minutes.

Serves 6.

— *Mrs. W. Atkins*
Agincourt, Ontario

BEEF NOODLE BAKE

1 lb. ground beef
¼ cup butter
2 onions, thinly sliced
1 stalk celery, chopped
1 clove garlic
1½ tsp. salt
⅛ tsp. pepper

1½ tsp. chili powder
6-oz. can tomato paste
1 cup tomato sauce, page 204
2 cups water
2 cups uncooked noodles
1½ cups shredded Cheddar cheese

Brown meat in butter, then add onions, celery and garlic. Fry until onions are translucent. Add remaining ingredients except for noodles and cheese. Cover and simmer for 30 minutes. Remove garlic.

In a greased 2-quart casserole dish, layer the ingredients: first, half the noodles, then half the meat mixture, and finally one-third of the cheese. Repeat.

Bake at 325 degrees F for 30 to 35 minutes. Sprinkle with remaining cheese and brown under broiler.

Serves 4 to 6.

— *Maud Doerksen*
Oak Bluff, Manitoba

CRUSTLESS PIZZA

1 lb. minced beef
¼ cup bread crumbs
½ tsp. garlic salt
¼ tsp. pepper
⅔ cup milk

⅓ cup minced onion
1½ cups tomato sauce, page 204
¼ tsp. oregano
¾ cup sliced mushrooms
1½ cups grated cheese

Combine minced beef, bread crumbs, garlic salt, pepper, milk and onion. Flatten mixture into a greased 9-inch square pan. Cover with tomato sauce. Sprinkle with oregano. Distribute mushrooms evenly over sauce, then top with grated cheese.

Bake at 400 degrees F for 30 to 45 minutes.

— *Heather Rochon*
Fleurimont, Quebec

CHINESE MEATBALLS

1½ lbs. ground beef	2 Tbsp. brown sugar
½ cup chopped onion	1 tsp. soya sauce
Salt & pepper	2 Tbsp. vinegar
3 Tbsp. soya sauce	1 Tbsp. cornstarch dissolved in
2 Tbsp. cornstarch	⅔ cup water
½ cup pineapple juice	1 cup pineapple chunks

Combine beef, onion, salt, pepper, 3 Tbsp. soya sauce and 2 Tbsp. cornstarch and shape into balls.

Fry until brown, remove from pan and set aside. Discard all but 2 Tbsp. of drippings.

To drippings add pineapple juice, brown sugar, 1 tsp. soya sauce and vinegar. Thicken with cornstarch mixture. Add pineapple and meatballs and cook until heated through.

Serves 4.

— *Velma Hughes*
Brantford, Ontario

CHEESE STUFFED MEATBALLS

1½ lbs. medium ground beef	1 small onion, minced
¾ cup fine bread crumbs	4 tsp. Worcestershire sauce
1 egg, lightly beaten	¼ lb. Cheddar cheese, cubed
1 tsp. salt	12 slices bacon, cut in half

Combine beef, bread crumbs, egg, salt, onion and Worcestershire sauce. Roll into 24 small balls and push a cube of cheese into the centre of each one. Wrap a bacon slice around each meatball.

Place on a broiler pan and bake at 375 degrees F for 20 to 25 minutes.

— *Margaret Bezanson*
Nepean, Ontario

SAUTEED LEMON LIVER

1 lb. liver, thinly sliced	¼ tsp. salt
½ cup milk	1 peeled & cored apple,
⅓ cup butter	cut in thin wedges
3 onions, sliced	1 green pepper, cut in thin strips
¼ cup flour	½ lemon
¼ tsp. paprika	

Cover liver with milk and refrigerate for at least 2 hours or as long as overnight. Drain.

Melt butter in a large frying pan. Add onions and cook until soft. Remove from pan. Lightly coat liver with a mixture of flour, paprika and salt. Cook in hot butter until lightly browned. Return onions to pan, along with apple and green pepper. Sprinkle lightly with about 1 Tbsp. of lemon juice. Cover and cook for 5 minutes, or until pepper is done as you like it.

Serves 4.

— *Diane Wilson-Meyer*
Saskatoon, Saskatchewan

VENETIAN LIVER

1 Tbsp. flour
1 tsp. salt
¼ tsp. pepper
1 tsp. paprika
1 lb. beef liver, cut in strips
1 Tbsp. vegetable oil

2 medium onions, sliced
1 stalk celery, chopped
1 green pepper, cut in strips
1 tomato, cut in wedges
¾ cup beef stock
¼ tsp. basil

Put flour, salt, pepper and paprika in a bag and coat liver strips by shaking them in the flour mixture. Sauté liver in oil in a large frying pan, about 3 minutes on each side. Remove to serving platter and keep warm in oven.

Sauté onions, celery and green pepper until soft and golden. Add tomato and cook for another 2 minutes. Arrange vegetables on top of liver.

In the frying pan, combine stock and basil, and bring to a boil. Simmer, uncovered, for about 2 minutes. Pour over liver and serve at once.

Serves 4.

— Diane Wilson-Meyer
Saskatoon, Saskatchewan

BAKED LIVER

1 lb. liver, sliced
⅓ cup flour
Salt & pepper
½ tsp. dry mustard

1 large onion, sliced
8-10 slices bacon
1½ cups tomato juice
1 Tbsp. ketchup

Coat liver slices in flour mixed with salt, pepper and mustard. Place in baking dish and cover with sliced onion and bacon. Mix together tomato juice and ketchup and pour over meat. Bake at 300 degrees F for 1 hour.

Serves 3 to 4.

— Albert Sauer
Niagara-on-the-Lake, Ont.

POLYNESIAN LIVER

2 lbs. liver, cut in strips
⅔ cup pineapple juice
4 Tbsp. tomato paste
1 Tbsp. soya sauce
2 Tbsp. brown sugar
½ cup water

1 onion, sliced into rings
2 Tbsp. cornstarch dissolved
  in ¼ cup cold water
1 green pepper, cut in strips
1½ cups pineapple chunks

Combine liver, pineapple juice, tomato paste, soya sauce, brown sugar, water and onion in frying pan. Bring to a boil and simmer for 3 minutes.

Add cornstarch dissolved in water and cook until thickened. Add green pepper and pineapple, cover, lower heat and simmer for 5 minutes.

Serves 4.

— Catherine Cole
Parry Sound, Ontario

BRAISED LIVER WITH VEGETABLES

1 lb. liver, ½ inch thick
¼ cup flour
Salt & pepper
4 Tbsp. cooking oil
1 onion, diced

2 raw carrots, diced
6 raw potatoes, sliced ¼ inch thick
1 cup tomato juice
1 cup water or vegetable stock

Cut liver into 1-inch squares. Roll in flour seasoned with salt and pepper. Heat oil in heavy frying pan and brown liver in it. Add onion and cook briefly. Add carrots, potatoes, tomato juice and water. Cover and simmer gently for 1 hour, adding water if necessary.

Serves 4 to 6.

ORANGE PORK

2 lbs. pork tenderloin,
  cut into 6 pieces
½ cup flour
¼ cup oil or bacon drippings
Salt & pepper

2 large onions, chopped
½ lb. mushrooms, sliced
3 Tbsp. flour
2 cups orange juice

Coat pork with ½ cup flour, then brown in oil. Sprinkle with salt and lots of pepper. Remove to shallow casserole dish, reserving pan drippings.

To pan drippings, add onions and cook lightly. Add mushrooms and stir briefly. Sprinkle with 3 Tbsp. flour and mix. Gradually add orange juice, stirring constantly, to make a smooth sauce. Taste and adjust seasoning. Pour sauce over pork and cover with foil.

Bake at 350 degrees F for 1 hour, checking occasionally. Add more juice if necessary.

Serve, garnished with orange segments, strips of orange rind or fresh mint.

Serves 6.

— Nita Hunton
Cambridge, Ontario

JAGER SCHNITZEL

THIS PORK IN MUSHROOM AND CREAM SAUCE DISH CAN ALSO MAKE USE OF VEAL.

2 10-oz. pork fillets
1 Tbsp. seasoned flour
3 Tbsp. oil
½ cup butter
½ lb. mushrooms, sliced
1 Tbsp. flour

4 Tbsp. chicken stock
4 Tbsp. dry white wine
Pinch grated nutmeg
Salt & pepper
4 Tbsp. whipping cream

Halve each fillet lengthwise, leaving attached at one side. Open out and pound until flat and thin.

Toss in seasoned flour, then fry gently in 2 Tbsp. oil and ¼ cup butter until golden brown.

Meanwhile, gently fry mushrooms in remaining butter and oil. Add flour and cook for 2 minutes. Gradually add stock, wine and seasonings, stirring all the time. Bring to a boil, and cook gently for 2 to 3 minutes, stirring. Remove from heat and stir in cream.

Pour sauce over meat.

Serves 4.

— Sheila Bear
St. John's, Nfld.

APPLE & PORK CHOP BAKE

4-6 pork chops
4-6 apples, cored & chopped
4-6 onions, peeled & thinly sliced
¼ cup brown sugar

2 Tbsp. cinnamon
Water
Butter

Presoak clay baker for 20 minutes. Salt chops, then layer half of each of the following: apples, onions, chops, sugar and cinnamon in baker. Repeat. Pour in ¼ cup water and dot with butter.

Cover and bake at 400 degrees F for 1 hour, then uncover and bake for 10 more minutes.

Serves 4 to 6.

— Dorothy Malone
Nepean, Ontario

ITALIAN PORK CHOPS

1 egg
3 Tbsp. cold water
3 Tbsp. fine bread crumbs

3 Tbsp. grated Parmesan cheese
4 pork chops
Flour, seasoned with salt & pepper

Beat egg with cold water.

Combine bread crumbs and cheese.

Coat chops with flour. Dip them into the egg mixture, then into bread crumbs and cheese. Place on wax paper and let stand for 1 hour.

Cook in oil, 10 minutes on each side.

Serves 2 to 4.

— Helen Potts
Tilden Lake, Ontario

BARBECUED LOIN PORK CHOPS

4 pork chops
3 Tbsp. seasoned flour
2 Tbsp. oil
¼ cup chopped onion
¼ cup diced celery
2 Tbsp. brown sugar
Juice of half a lemon

½ tsp. salt
⅛ tsp. red pepper
½ tsp. dry mustard
½ tsp. chili powder
½ cup water
1 cup tomato sauce

Coat chops in seasoned flour and brown in oil. Place in ovenproof dish. Mix remaining ingredients together and pour over meat. Cover and bake at 350 degrees F for 1 hour, basting occasionally.

— Maud Doerksen
Oak Bluff, Manitoba

PORK CHOP & POTATO CASSEROLE

4 shoulder pork chops
3 cups sliced potatoes
½ onion, sliced
4 tsp. flour

1 tsp. salt
¼ tsp. pepper
1¼ cups milk

Brown chops in frying pan. Arrange potatoes and onion in layers in greased casserole dish. Sprinkle with flour and seasonings. Top with chops, add milk and cover.

Bake at 350 degrees F for 45 minutes, or until tender. Uncover and continue baking until brown.

Serves 4.

— Maureen Johnson
Pembroke, Ontario

CURRIED PORK WITH PEACHES

4-6 lean loin chops
¼ cup butter
1 medium onion, minced
¼ cup flour
1 tsp. salt

1 tsp. curry powder
2 cups milk
1 cup button mushrooms
3 peaches, halved

Brown chops in small amount of butter. Remove from pan, add remaining butter and sauté onion.

Add flour, salt and curry powder to butter and onions to form a paste. Slowly add milk and stir until smooth. Add mushrooms and simmer 2 minutes over low heat.

Arrange pork in large shallow pan which has a tightly fitting lid. Place half a peach on each chop and pour curried sauce over.

Bake at 350 degrees F, covered, for 45 minutes, then for 15 minutes, uncovered.

Serves 4 to 6.

— Judy Parfitt
Kingston, Ontario

STUFFED PORK CHOPS

HOME BUTCHERED PORK CHOPS ARE IDEAL FOR THIS RECIPE — THEY ARE THICK enough to allow for stuffing.

4 thick loin pork chops
1 cup dry bread crumbs
¾ cup finely chopped apple
½ tsp. salt

2 Tbsp. minced onion
¼ tsp. sage
2 Tbsp. melted butter
Salt & pepper

Combine all ingredients except chops and moisten slightly with a little water. With a sharp knife, cut pockets in the pork chops. Fill loosely with stuffing, then fasten with toothpicks.

Flour the chops and brown well in hot fat in a skillet. Sprinkle each side with salt and pepper. Add ¼ cup water, cover the pan tightly and simmer over low heat until very tender, abut 1½ hours.

Serves 4.

— Sherrie Dick
Quesnel, B.C.

PORK CHOPS & OLIVES MARSALA

¼ cup flour
1 tsp. salt
¼ tsp. pepper
4 shoulder pork chops
1 clove garlic, halved

3 Tbsp. olive oil
½ cup water
½ cup Marsala wine
½ cup sliced pimento stuffed olives

Combine flour, salt and pepper. Rub pork chops with garlic and dredge in flour mixture.

Heat oil in a skillet. Brown chops well on both sides. Pour water over meat. Reduce heat, cover tightly and simmer 30 minutes. Add the wine and olives and continue cooking for another 30 minutes.

Serves 4.

— Dee Lowe
Meacham, Sask.

PORK & SNOW PEAS

1 tsp. sugar
1 Tbsp. cornstarch
2 Tbsp. soya sauce
3 Tbsp. water
3 Tbsp. oil
1 clove garlic, minced

2 slices candied ginger
Dash salt
1 lb. pork loin, sliced
⅓ lb. snow peas
2 Tbsp. dry sherry
½ cup chicken broth

In a small bowl combine sugar, cornstarch, soya sauce and water and set aside.

Heat 1 Tbsp. oil in wok, add garlic, ginger and salt. Cook, stirring, until garlic is golden. Add pork. Stir-fry until lightly browned and cooked through. Remove to a bowl.

Reheat wok. Add 2 Tbsp. oil, then snow peas and stir-fry until peas turn darker green, about 1 minute. Add meat, sherry and broth. Stir in soya sauce mixture. Cook just until broth is thickened.

Serves 4.

— *Barbara J. Spangler*
Sylacauga, Alabama

PORK STEW WITH APPLES & POTATOES

1 lb. lean pork, cut into 1-inch cubes
2 Tbsp. butter
½ tsp. paprika
¼ tsp. pepper
2 tsp. salt
Dash sage
1 clove garlic, crushed

2 Tbsp. flour
3 onions, sliced
4 large potatoes, cubed
2 apples, cored & cut up
2 Tbsp. dry sherry
1½ cups chicken stock

Brown pork in heavy pot with butter. Add paprika, pepper, salt, sage and garlic and stir well. Sprinkle with flour and add onions, potatoes, apples, sherry and stock.

Cover and simmer 40 minutes.

Serves 4.

— *Bryanna Clark*
Union Bay, B.C.

SCRAPPLE

SCRAPPLE, A MEATLOAF ORIGINALLY MADE WITH PORK TRIMMINGS AND SCRAPS, CAN BE served hot with vegetables as a main course, or cold in a sandwich.

1½ lbs. fresh pork shoulder
4 cups cold water
1 tsp. salt
½ tsp. black pepper
1¼ cups corn meal

⅓ cup flour
1 tsp. or more crushed sage
Dash oregano
Dash cayenne pepper

Simmer the pork in the water for about 2 hours. Remove meat from the stock, shred it and set aside.

Strain stock, reserve 1 cup and set aside. Continue to boil the rest of the stock.

In a bowl, combine the rest of the ingredients, then add the cup of reserved stock slowly, while stirring rapidly to avoid lumps.

Add corn meal mixture and shredded meat to the boiling stock. Simmer over low heat for 1 hour, stirring now and again, so that it does not stick to the pan.

Pour into a greased loaf pan and chill. Cut into thin slices and brown on both sides in bacon drippings.

Makes 2 pounds.

— *Cary Elizabeth Marshall*
Thunder Bay, Ontario

QUEBEC TOURTIERE

In French Canadian families, this traditional meat pie is eaten hot after midnight mass on Christmas Eve.

Lard pastry for double-crust 9-inch pie
1 lb. lean ground pork
1 medium onion, chopped
Salt & pepper

½ tsp. savory
Pinch ground cloves
¼ cup boiling water

Mix meat, onions and spices in a saucepan. Add boiling water. Simmer, uncovered, for 20 minutes, stirring occasionally. Skim off any fat.

Roll out half the pastry and line a 9-inch pie plate. Place filling in pie plate and cover with the remaining pastry. Prick with a fork. Bake at 375 degrees F for 30 minutes or until golden.

Serve piping hot topped with homemade tomato ketchup or chili sauce.

Serves 4 to 6.

— *Nicole Chartrand*
Aylmer, Quebec

GEFULLTE PAPRIKA

These stuffed peppers may use either green or yellow peppers.

6 green or yellow bell peppers
2 lbs. ground pork
1 cup cooked rice
Salt & pepper
Marjoram

Paprika
¼ cup chopped onion
¼ cup shortening
¼ cup flour
48-oz. can tomato juice

Hollow out peppers and rinse. Mix ground pork with rice, salt, pepper, herbs and onion. Stuff meat mixture into peppers and set aside.

In large, heavy pot, melt shortening and stir in flour until thick. Add tomato juice and cook and stir until thickened and smooth.

Add peppers. Cover and cook slowly, stirring occasionally, 20 to 30 minutes.

Serves 6.

— *Kris Brown*
Strathroy, Ontario

TERRINE OF PORK

Terrine originally meant the dish in which pates were cooked; it has come to mean the pâté itself.

3-4 strips bacon
1 lb. lean pork, minced
8 oz. pork sausage meat
4 oz. rolled oats
Rind & juice of 1 lemon

Salt & pepper
½ Tbsp. sage
1 grated onion
1 egg, beaten

Stretch bacon to line a loaf pan. Combine remaining ingredients. Press meat mixture into pan and level the top.

Cover with foil, set in a large shallow baking dish containing 1 inch of water and cook 1½ hours at 350 degrees F.

Remove from oven and pour off grease but leave loaf in pan. Weight down the top and leave overnight before removing from pan.

Serve cold, sliced.

— *Wendy Wallace*
Lakefield, Ontario

SWEET & SOUR SPARERIBS

2 lbs. spareribs
⅓ cup flour
1 tsp. dry mustard
⅓ cup soya sauce
1 tsp. vegetable oil
1 clove garlic, crushed

1 inch fresh ginger
⅓ cup vinegar
1½ cups water
½ cup brown sugar
1 tsp. salt
1 small onion, diced

Chop ribs into small pieces. Mix flour, mustard and soya sauce and marinate ribs in this mixture for 30 minutes to 1 hour.

Heat oil. Add crushed garlic and ginger. Brown ribs, add vinegar, water, sugar, salt and onion. Simmer for 1 hour.

Serves 4 to 6.

— *Pieter Timmermans*
Ucluelet, B.C.

STUFFED SPARERIBS

2 racks pork ribs
Garlic powder
½ cup wild rice
¼ cup chopped onion
¼ cup chopped mushrooms

½ apple, peeled & chopped
¼-½ tsp. Worcestershire sauce
¼ tsp. pepper
1 tsp. basil

Roll ribs into a circle, tie with string and sprinkle inside and out with garlic powder. Set aside.

Cook rice in boiling water for 20 minutes. Drain. Add remaining ingredients and mix well. Loosely stuff into ribs.

Bake at 375 degrees F for 1½ hours.

Serves 2.

— *Cheryl Lockhart*
Pickle Lake, Ontario

GARLIC SPARERIBS

2-3 cloves garlic, crushed
2 Tbsp. brown sugar
½ cup honey
¼ cup soya sauce
¼ cup vinegar

6 lbs. pork spareribs,
  cut into 2-inch pieces
1 cup tomato sauce
2 tsp. salt

In a large bowl, combine garlic, sugar, honey, soya sauce and vinegar. Add spareribs and marinate in refrigerator for several hours or overnight, turning meat several times. Drain and reserve marinade.

Combine marinade with tomato sauce and salt in a heavy saucepan. Simmer for 10 minutes.

Bake ribs at 400 degrees F for 30 minutes. Reduce heat to 325 degrees and bake 1 hour, basting frequently with sauce.

Serves 10 to 12.

— *Margaret Silverthorn*
Iona Station, Ontario

TANGY PORK

2 medium onions, finely chopped
2 cups cooked pork, cut in cubes
2 medium carrots, cubed
2 cups tomato juice
½ cup chopped cabbage
2 apples, peeled & chopped
¼ cup brown sugar
¼ cup vinegar
½ tsp. salt
½ tsp. pepper
1 tsp. Worcestershire sauce
1 Tbsp. soya sauce

Fry onions in a small amount of oil until golden. Place in a heavy pot with remaining ingredients. Simmer for 45 minutes on top of stove.

Serves 4.

— *Louise R. Taylor*
Sudbury, Ontario

BAKED COTTAGE ROLL

4 slices cottage roll
4 Tbsp. brown sugar
1 Tbsp. dry mustard
½ cup orange juice

Place slices of meat in baking dish. Combine remaining ingredients and pour over meat. Bake at 350 degrees F for 1 hour, basting once or twice.

Serves 4.

— *Paula Gustafson*
Abbotsford, B.C.

GINGER PORK ROLL

ALTHOUGH THIS DISH REQUIRES A FAIR AMOUNT OF PREPARATION, THE FINAL flavour of pork, crabmeat and seasonings encased in a rich cream cheese pastry makes it all worthwhile.

1 cup butter
4 oz. cream cheese
½ tsp. salt
2 cups flour
1 egg yolk
2 tsp. cream
1 lb. ground pork
½ cup flaked crabmeat
1 tsp. salt
½ cup minced water chestnuts
2 green onions, minced
2 tsp. grated ginger root
2 Tbsp. soya sauce
1 clove garlic, crushed
1 egg
¼ cup fine dry bread crumbs

Beat butter, cheese and salt together until completely smooth. Work in flour to make a smooth dough. Flatten in foil to form an 8" x 6" rectangle. Chill overnight. Remove from refrigerator 10 minutes before rolling. Divide into 4 portions, roll each piece between 2 sheets of floured wax paper to form a 9" x 12" rectangle.

Cook and stir pork until white but not dry. Add remaining ingredients, mix well and cool thoroughly.

Cut each pastry rectangle in half lengthwise and spread with filling. From long side, roll tightly like a jelly roll. Moisten edge and press to seal. Place seam-side down on an ungreased cookie sheet. Chill 1 hour. Bake at 375 degrees F for 30 to 35 minutes. Cool and cut into 1-inch slices. Serve hot or cold.

Makes 8 dozen slices.

— *Irene Simonson*
Seeleys Bay, Ontario

STUFFED PEPPERS

THERE ARE MANY WAYS OF PREPARING STUFFED PEPPERS. THE FILLINGS CAN contain everything from pork, as in this recipe, to beef, lamb or seafood. Methods of preparation also vary — these peppers are cooked on top of the stove, but they may also be baked.

2 Tbsp. shortening	¼ cup raw rice
¼ cup flour	8 green peppers
8-oz. can tomato paste	1 lb. minced pork
2 cups stock	Small bunch fresh parsley
Salt	1 egg
2 small onions, chopped	Salt & pepper
Celery leaves	Marjoram

Heat 1 Tbsp. shortening in a deep saucepan and stir in flour until light brown. Add tomato paste and stir until smooth. Add stock, salt, 1 onion and celery leaves, and bring to a boil. Cook over medium heat, stirring occasionally to keep from burning.

In the meantime, cook rice in boiling water until half done, and cool. Seed and core peppers and wash them thoroughly. Sauté remaining onion in the rest of the shortening. Combine meat, onion, parsley, rice and egg in a bowl. Add salt, pepper and marjoram to taste. Mix well and stuff into peppers.

Place peppers in a large saucepan and pour sauce over them. Bring to a boil, cover and cook over medium heat until done — 25 to 30 minutes.

Serves 4.

— Anton Gross
North Augusta, Ont.

PORK BALLS IN WINE SAUCE

1½ lbs. minced pork	1 cup dry sherry
8 oz. lean bacon, ground	1 cup chicken stock
2 cups fresh bread crumbs	2 Tbsp. wine vinegar
1 large egg	1 Tbsp. sugar
1 tsp. salt	1 tsp. salt
½ tsp. black pepper	4 tsp. cornstarch,
½ tsp. ground allspice	dissolved in 3 Tbsp. water
2 Tbsp. fresh chopped parsley	

In a large mixing bowl, combine the pork, bacon, bread crumbs, egg, salt, pepper, allspice and parsley. Using your hands, knead the ingredients until they are well combined. Shape into 12 balls. Place the balls, in one layer, in a large baking dish. Set aside.

In a small saucepan, combine the sherry, stock, vinegar, sugar and salt over low heat, stirring constantly. When the sugar has dissolved, increase the heat to high and bring the mixture to a boil. Reduce the heat to low and stir in the cornstarch mixture. Cook, stirring constantly, until the sauce has thickened slightly.

Remove pan from heat and pour sauce over meatballs. Place meatballs in the oven and bake for 1½ hours, basting occasionally with sauce.

Serves 4.

— Dolores de Rosario
Hamilton, Ontario

HAM & POTATO CASSEROLE

4 or 5 boiled potatoes
¼ cup butter
¼ cup flour
½ tsp. salt

2 cups milk
½ tsp. Worcestershire sauce
2 cups cubed cooked ham
½ cup grated Cheddar cheese

Slice or dice the potatoes and set aside. In a saucepan, melt the butter and add the flour and salt. Stir until blended. Slowly add the milk, stirring constantly, until smooth and thickened. Stir in Worcestershire sauce, potatoes and ham.

Spoon into 1½-quart baking dish. Sprinkle with cheese. Bake at 350 degrees F for 30 to 40 minutes.

Serves 4 to 5.

— Dianne Orlowski
Stoney Creek, Ontario

STUFFED HAM

12-lb. ham
2 heads cabbage
2 lbs. kale

2 large onions
1½ small red peppers
Salt & pepper

Wash ham. Cut up vegetables, mix and season to taste. Parboil, saving water for cooking ham.

Make deep slits across top and down sides of ham with sharp knife. Stuff vegetables into slits, piling any leftover mixture on top of the ham.

Sew ham in cheesecloth to hold dressing in place and cook slowly in vegetable water until meat is tender.

— Judy Lord
Georgeville, Quebec

HAM & RICE SKILLET

1 cup cooked ham
1 cup sliced mushrooms
½ onion, finely chopped
2 cloves garlic, crushed
⅓ cup chopped raisins
Butter
½ tsp. paprika

½ tsp. Worcestershire sauce
½ tsp. basil
½ tsp. dry mustard
½ tsp. curry powder
Salt & pepper
1 cup cooked rice
2 eggs, slightly beaten

Sauté ham, mushrooms, onion, garlic and raisins in butter until mushrooms are nearly cooked. Add seasonings and rice. Cook over low heat about 10 minutes. Turn up heat, add eggs and stir-fry until eggs are done.

Serves 2.

— Kynda Fenton
Cowansville, Quebec

SAUSAGE, BACON & TOMATO PIE

1 lb. sausages	2 Tbsp. flour
4 slices bacon	Salt & pepper
1 medium onion, chopped	2 lbs. potatoes, cooked
4 tomatoes	Butter & milk

Fry sausages, bacon and onion. Place in greased casserole dish. Fry tomatoes and arrange on top of sausage mixture.

Add flour to remaining fat in pan and cook for a minute or two. Make a thick gravy by adding about 1 cup water. Pour on top of meat and tomatoes.

Mash potatoes, adding milk and butter to taste. Spread on top of casserole and dot with more butter. Bake at 400 degrees F for 20 to 30 minutes until golden brown on top.

Serves 4.

— Sheila Bear
St. John's, Nfld.

CHINESE HOT SAUSAGES

1 lb. pork sausage links	1 Tbsp. soya sauce
1 Tbsp. vegetable oil	1 tsp. Worcestershire sauce
7½-oz. can tomato sauce	¼ tsp. garlic powder
¼ cup brown sugar	Generous pinch of salt

Prick sausage skin in several places. Heat oil in a frying pan just large enough to hold the sausages. Add sausages and brown evenly. Pour off fat.

Stir remaining ingredients together and pour into frying pan. Roll sausages until coated with sauce. Cover, reduce heat to medium-low and simmer for 20 minutes. Stir occasionally. Serve in crusty rolls, or with rice or baked potatoes.

Serves 4.

— Diane Wilson-Meyer
Saskatoon, Saskatchewan

RAGOUT DE PATTES

THIS IS A VERY INEXPENSIVE STEW, USING PORK HOCKS AND ROOT VEGETABLES.

2 pork hocks, washed & scraped	1 small turnip, chopped
to remove hair	Salt & pepper
4 potatoes, chopped	4 Tbsp. flour
4 carrots, chopped	½ cup water

Put meat in a large saucepan, cover with water and simmer until tender, about 1 hour. Then add vegetables and salt and pepper. Simmer for another hour.

Brown flour in frying pan, being careful not to burn it. Add water to flour and mix well. Pour into meat mixture and cook until broth thickens.

Serves 2 to 4.

— Emilia Ouellette
Edmunston, N.B.

HEAD CHEESE

TRADITIONALLY, THIS RECIPE IS MADE USING A WHOLE PIG HEAD. THE SUBSTITUTION of pork hocks provides an easier and tidier method of preparation, but still produces the authentic flavour.

5 pork hocks
2 cloves garlic
3 whole cloves
1 stick cinnamon

2 Tbsp. salt
2 large onions, cut in half
2 large carrots, sliced
½ tsp. pepper

Wash hocks well. Tie in a clean white cotton cloth along with all the remaining ingredients. It is important that the hocks are completely covered by the cloth. Place in a large pot, cover with cold water and bring to a slow boil. Simmer for 3 hours.

Unwrap hocks and discard spices and vegetables. Cut the meat into small pieces or put through a coarse food grinder. Include every piece of meat and skin. Strain the broth, return the meat to it and boil for 10 minutes.

Ladle into straight-sided glass or plastic bowls. Cool and refrigerate. To serve, unmould and garnish with greens. Good with potato salad and coleslaw.

— Aurora Sugden
Argenteuil, Quebec

HERBED LEG OF LAMB

WORK ON THIS DISH MUST BEGIN 24 HOURS BEFORE IT IS TO BE SERVED. ONCE THE marinade is assembled and the lamb placed in it, however, no more labour is required until baking time. The herb combination and the cooking method produce a moist, flavourful leg of lamb.

2 cups red wine
½ cup vinegar
1 cup cooking oil
Parsley
Thyme
4 bay leaves
6 cloves garlic
3 onions, finely chopped
Pinch of nutmeg
2 Tbsp. sugar

1 tsp. salt
6-8 lb. leg of lamb
½ cup finely chopped parsley
1 carrot, finely chopped
1 stalk celery, finely chopped
4 Tbsp. butter
1 cup beef stock
¼ tsp. basil
⅛ tsp. oregano
Salt & pepper

Stir together 1 cup red wine, vinegar, oil, parsley, thyme, bay leaves, 2 cloves garlic (crushed), 2 chopped onions, nutmeg, sugar and salt. Marinate lamb in this mixture for 24 hours, turning frequently.

On day of cooking lamb, make the herb sauce by sautéing parsley, carrot, remaining onion and celery in butter until soft. Place in bottom of roasting pan, along with leftover marinade. Slice remaining garlic into slivers. Pierce the leg of lamb at 3-inch intervals and insert garlic slivers. Roast the lamb at 450 degrees F for 15 minutes. Meanwhile, combine remaining wine, beef stock, basil, oregano, salt and pepper. Pour mixture over lamb, reduce heat to 350 degrees F and continue roasting 15 to 20 minutes per pound. Serve with herb mixture.

Serves 8 to 10.

— Anne Morell
Margaree Valley, N.S.

WEEPING LAMB

6-8 lb. leg of lamb
Cloves of garlic, sliced
Salt & pepper
1 tsp. rosemary

8 potatoes, unpeeled & sliced
Butter
2 large onions, sliced
1 cup chicken stock

Pierce lamb at 2-inch intervals and insert slices of garlic. Rub with salt, pepper and rosemary.

Grease a roasting pan and place one layer of potatoes in it. Dot with butter, add another layer of potatoes and the onion. Dot with butter and add chicken stock.

Place lamb on top of this and roast at 325 degrees F for approximately 2 hours.

Serves 8.

— Mary Reid
Georgeville, Quebec

HUNGARIAN BAKED LAMB CHOPS

6 loin lamp chops, 1½ inches thick
1½ tsp. salt
½ tsp. freshly ground pepper
1 tsp. paprika

2 cups sliced green onions
½ cup sour cream
3 Tbsp. grated Parmesan cheese

Brown chops on both sides in a skillet and pour off fat. Place in a shallow casserole dish and season with salt, pepper and paprika, spread green onions over them and add the sour cream.

Bake at 350 degrees F for 30 minutes. Sprinkle with cheese and bake 30 minutes longer.

Serves 6.

— Brenda Eckstein
Kamloops, B.C.

NAVARIN D'AGNEAU

THIS LAMB STEW USES CARROTS AND TURNIP, BUT OTHER ROOT VEGETABLES MAY BE substituted.

2 lbs. shoulder of lamb, cut into chunks
2 Tbsp. butter
1 large onion, chopped
1½ lbs. carrots, sliced
1 lb. turnip, peeled & diced
1 clove garlic, crushed
1 Tbsp. tomato purée

1 Tbsp. flour
3 cups chicken stock
1 bay leaf
Pinch thyme
Salt & pepper
8 small potatoes, peeled

Fry lamb in butter until golden. Discard all but 1 Tbsp. of fat. Stir in onion, 2 slices carrot, 2 pieces turnip, garlic, tomato purée and flour. Gradually add stock, stirring all the time. Add bay leaf, thyme and seasonings, cover and simmer gently for 1½ hours.

Add remaining vegetables and cook for a further 25 to 30 minutes or until cooked.

Serves 4 to 6.

— Sheila Bear
St. John's, Nfld.

COUSCOUS

THIS IS A TRADITIONAL NORTH AFRICAN STEW MAKING USE OF NATIVE VEGETABLES.

3 cups couscous (semolina)
1½ tsp. salt dissolved in 1½ cups
  cold water
1 Tbsp. oil
½ cup oil
2 lbs. lamb, cut into 2-inch chunks
3 cups finely chopped onion
1½ Tbsp. salt
1 Tbsp. black pepper
¼ tsp. allspice
2 cinnamon sticks

¾ tsp. turmeric
1 tsp. chopped parsley
4-5 tomatoes, quartered
1 cup raw chick peas, cooked
1 lb. carrots
1 lb. turnips
1 lb. zucchini
½ lb. pumpkin
4 potatoes, peeled & quartered
1 chili pepper
Handful raisins

Spread couscous evenly in large, shallow pan. Sprinkle with salted water and 1 Tbsp. oil, then rub grains between fingers, dropping back into pan until water and oil are completely absorbed. Cover with plastic wrap and set aside for 15 minutes.

Meanwhile, in a deep pot, heat ½ cup oil until light haze forms above it. Add meat, onions, salt and pepper. Fry over high heat for 6 to 8 minutes, until browned. Add spices, parsley, tomatoes, chick peas and 3 cups cold water, and stir until mixture boils. Reduce heat to low and simmer, covered, for 1 hour.

Steam couscous in a large sieve over rapidly boiling water for 20 minutes. Do not cover pot, or couscous will get sticky.

Prepare vegetables: scrape carrots and turnips and cut into 1½-inch lengths. Cut zucchini into quarters. Peel and cut pumpkin into 2-inch pieces. After meat broth has cooked for 1 hour, add carrots and turnips and cook 30 minutes more, adding more water if necessary.

Half an hour before serving time, add potatoes, zucchini, pumpkin, chili and raisins to lamb broth, bring to a boil and simmer. Steam couscous another 30 minutes. Serve lamb mixture over couscous.
Serves 6.

— *Ann Simpson*
Ottawa, Ontario

LAMB KORMA

A SPICY LAMB CASSEROLE, THIS DISH IS SIMILAR TO CURRY.

½ tsp. saffron
¼-⅓ cup boiling water
½ cup unsalted cashews
3 green chilies
1½ Tbsp. chopped fresh ginger
1-inch stick cinnamon
½ tsp. cardamom seed
6 cloves
3 cloves garlic
2 tsp. coriander

½ tsp. cumin
1¼ cups water
½ cup ghee (clarified butter)
1 large onion, sliced
1 tsp. salt
1¼ cups yogurt
1 lb. lamb, cut into chunks
1 Tbsp. chopped fresh coriander
2 tsp. lemon juice

Place saffron in a bowl, pour water over it and let sit for 10 minutes. Put cashews, chilies, ginger, cinnamon, cardamom, cloves, garlic, coriander, cumin and water into blender. Blend until smooth — about 2 minutes.

Heat ghee and fry onion until golden. Stir in salt, blended spices and yogurt. Cook gently for 5 minutes, stirring occasionally. Add meat and toss to coat all sides. Add saffron mixture and cook gently, covered, for 20 minutes. Add fresh coriander and cook 10 minutes more. Add lemon juice and serve.

— *Sheila Bear*
St. John's, Nfld.

SPIEDIES

A SHISH KEBOB OF ITALO-AMERICAN ORIGIN, SPIEDIES (PRONOUNCED SPEEDEES) come in varying degrees of spiciness, and this recipe may be altered to suit.

1 lb. beef, lamb or pork
¼ cup red wine vinegar
¼ cup vegetable oil
3 Tbsp. lemon juice
1 Tbsp. oregano

1 Tbsp. minced onion
½ tsp. minced garlic flakes
¼ tsp. dried mint flakes
¼ tsp. salt
⅛ tsp. pepper

Cut meat into bite-sized pieces and set aside.

Combine remaining ingredients and mix well. Let stand for 10 minutes, then pour over meat. Cover and refrigerate overnight.

Thread meat onto metal skewers and broil over hot charcoal fire for about 10 minutes for beef and a little longer for lamb or pork, turning often.

Serve on buttered Italian bread.

Serves 2.

— Melchiore Curatolo
Binghamton, New York

LAMB WITH GREEN PEPPERS

2 lbs. lamb
Salt & pepper
Flour
3 Tbsp. olive oil
2 cloves garlic

1¼ cups white wine
6 green peppers
½ lb. tomatoes
1 bay leaf

Cut meat into 1-inch pieces, sprinkle with salt and pepper and dust with flour.

Heat oil in wide-mouthed casserole dish, crush in peeled garlic, add meat and fry until lightly browned, stirring frequently. Add wine, and boil rapidly until reduced by a third.

Cut peppers lengthwise into quarters, discard seeds and pith and rinse in cold water. Peel and quarter tomatoes. Add peppers, tomatoes and bay leaf to lamb. Cover and simmer gently for about 45 minutes. Check seasoning and serve.

Serves 4.

— Sheila Bear
St. John's, Nfld.

DOLMATHES WITH AUGOLEMONO SAUCE

A GREEK VARIATION OF CABBAGE ROLLS, DOLMATHES TRADITIONALLY MAKE USE OF grape leaves, but maple may be substituted.

48 edible leaves, grape or maple
2 cups cooked rice
1 lb. cooked lamb, finely chopped
Mint
Rosemary

Olive oil
3 large eggs
½ cup lemon juice
1 cup hot chicken stock
Salt & pepper

If using fresh leaves, blanch and cut woody stems off. If using tinned leaves, wash well.

Mix rice, meat and seasonings and add oil to make mixture stick together. Place leaves shiny side down, put 2 Tbsp. stuffing at base and roll, tucking in sides. Place rolls seam-side down in large pot. Add 1 cup water and place a weight on top. Simmer until heated through.

Meanwhile beat eggs until thick and foamy, then add lemon juice slowly. Add hot chicken stock in a steady stream and season with salt and pepper. This sauce will thicken as it is being beaten. Serve over dolmathes.

Serves 6.

— Glenn Countryman
Victoria, B.C.

MASSALE DARH KABABS

THIS IS A SHISH KABAB VARIATION WHICH MAKES USE OF GROUND MEAT AND IS coated with yogurt.

1 Tbsp. green ginger
1 Tbsp. turmeric
1 Tbsp. coriander
3 peppercorns
1 tsp. chili powder
Salt

2 lbs. lamb or beef, ground
3 medium onions, chopped
2 Tbsp. butter
Yogurt
2 Tbsp. rice flour

Grind well all spices and salt. Combine with meat and onions and mix thoroughly. Add half the butter and enough yogurt to moisten. Mix well.

Roll into sausage shapes, powder lightly with flour and dip in yogurt. Fry in remaining butter in a heavy skillet. Handle very gently. When kababs are set, turn them over to brown on the other side.

Serves 4.

— *Betty Ternier Daniels*
Cochin, Sask.

BROWN SUGAR MUSTARD

½ cup lemon juice
¼ cup corn oil
⅛ tsp. Tabasco sauce
½ tsp. coarse salt

¼ tsp. black pepper
¼ tsp. marjoram, crushed
1½ cups well-packed brown sugar
4 oz. dry mustard

Combine lemon juice, oil, Tabasco sauce, salt, pepper, marjoram and brown sugar in blender. Cover and blend at high speed for about 12 seconds, or until the ingredients are thoroughly mixed.

Add about half of the mustard, cover and blend at medium speed for 10 seconds, or until smooth. Repeat with remaining mustard, adding it in 3 parts.

Spoon mustard into jars and seal with plastic wrap.

— *V. Alice Hughes*
Mariatown, Ontario

STEAK SAUCE

6 qts. tomatoes, cooked & strained
2 lbs. brown sugar
1 lb. granulated sugar
1 cup flour
2 tsp. ginger

2 tsp. cinnamon
Cayenne pepper
2 tsp. ground cloves
2 Tbsp. dry mustard
¼ cup salt

Combine all ingredients and mix well. Boil 20 minutes, stirring constantly.

Pack in hot sterilized jars and seal.

Serve with hot or cold meats or as a barbecue marinade.

— *Marilyn Fuller*
Stroud, Ontario

BARBECUE SAUCE

5½-oz. can tomato paste
½ cup vinegar
1½ Tbsp. dry mustard
3 Tbsp. corn syrup
½ tsp. garlic powder

1 tsp. onion powder
½ tsp. celery salt
⅛ tsp. cayenne pepper
½ tsp. salt
1 Tbsp. brown sugar

Mix all ingredients and store in covered container in refrigerator.

— Angela Denholm
Agassiz, B.C.

MEAT COATING

THIS RECIPE PROVIDES A HEALTHY, HOMEMADE ALTERNATIVE TO COMMERCIAL
Shake 'n' Bake.

½ cup wheat germ
½ cup corn meal

1 cup triticale flour
Salt & pepper

Mix until well blended and store in covered container until ready to use.

— Angela Denholm
Agassiz, B.C.

SEASONED FLOUR

PARTICULARLY TASTY FOR COATING PORK CHOPS, THIS COATING CAN BE QUICKLY
assembled and stored for several months.

2 cups flour
2 Tbsp. salt
1 Tbsp. celery salt
1 Tbsp. pepper
2 Tbsp. dry mustard
4 Tbsp. paprika

2 Tbsp. garlic powder or salt
1 tsp. ginger
½ tsp. thyme
½ tsp. sweet basil
½ tsp. oregano

Sift all ingredients together and store in refrigerator. Use to coat pork chops.

Makes 2½ cups.

— J. Hall-Armstrong
Cochrane, Ontario

Pasta

"Lasagne!" he cried, and died with a smile on his face.

— H. Mendoza

One of the world's most unusual museums is located in Italy and is dedicated to that country's most popular food, 62 pounds of which are eaten every year by every citizen. It is called the Museo Storico degli Spaghetti — the pasta museum. Anyone who visits it will see that two histories, those of Italy and pasta, are as intermingled as linguini and tomato sauce.

At the Museo, it becomes evident that Italy's use of the kneaded and pressed product of water and flour, the right flour, predated Marco Polo who, legend had it, brought noodle-making expertise to Europe from the Orient. It is now known that the two cultures independently discovered and developed pasta. In fact, many societies incorporate some noodle variations in their cookery.

But what we usually refer to as pasta is a more specifically defined food, a mixture of plain water and semolina, the flour milled from the hardest of wheats, durum. Pasta may also contain eggs, as noodles do, or oil, but it is the plain water and semolina type that is Italy's staple carbohydrate. Fresh *(pasta fresca)* or dried *(pasta secca),* it comes in scores of shapes — the Italians count more than 600 — most of which are variations on two basic ones, the ribbon and the cylinder. Macaroni and spaghetti are just two of the 600 shapes, which include shells, twists, stars and spheres.

Noodles, which are made with egg and sometimes oil, are the easiest type of pasta to prepare at home. Most easily formed with a hand-crank or electric noodle maker, they can also be pressed and cut by hand. Special cutters and presses are available for forming different types and shapes of pasta. Although the best noodles are made with semolina, they need not be. Noodles may contain all-purpose or even some whole wheat flour, which will taste fine if not traditional, and will cook more quickly than those made with semolina. In health food stores, various types of noodles and pastas are stocked, including ones made with tomato and spinach.

In China and Japan, where noodles have been enjoyed as long as history has been recorded, the second most popular starchy food after rice may be based on the flour of wheat, rice, seaweed, soy, mung beans or buckwheat. Their length symbolizing longevity, noodles are included at Chinese New Year's feasts.

All pasta, from the best ivory-coloured semolina *conchiglie* (giant shells) to whole wheat noodles, must be cooked correctly to retain its distinctive shape while developing in flavour. There is almost as much finesse involved in serving good pasta as in mixing a martini. One will require a big pot, large enough to hold seven quarts of water for every pound of pasta to be cooked. Heat the water to a rolling boil and then add a teaspoon

each of salt and vegetable oil for each pound of pasta. Now pour in the pasta.

Depending upon the size of the pieces, pasta can take from three to eight minutes to cook; fresh, homemade noodles will cook in the shortest time of all. To test for doneness, remove one piece of pasta and bite it. When it is properly cooked, it will be tender while still offering the teeth some resistance — what the Italians call *al dente*.

Recommendations for continuing the process now vary. Some Italian cooks insist that properly cooked pasta need not and should not be rinsed. It can be immediately poured into a colander to drain, thence into a warmed bowl to be served right away. Italians themselves often make use of a special pasta pot which contains a perforated basket to hold pasta, so that draining can be quickly and easily done.

Other cooks insist that pasta should be rinsed to remove some of the starch. This is especially important if the pasta has been cooked in insufficient water. The "Galloping Gourmet" used to suggest that the cooking water be poured off the cooked pasta, which would then be covered at once with cold water, drained and served. Other cooks recommend rinsing pasta under the hot tap to avoid any cooling.

Whether it is rinsed or not, however, is far less important than rapid, non-stop cooking in plenty of water. Anyone who has had pasta cooked over a sputtering woodstove fire can vouch firsthand for the origin of the word pasta — the same as that of paste. Remember it was his feather that Yankee Doodle dubbed "macaroni." Pasta should be light as a feather, not gluey and starchy.

Quite bland in flavour, pasta blends with virtually any sauce or accompaniment. The tomato-and-cheese standby is an honourable one, but by no means the only good way to serve pasta, as the following recipes indicate. The Italians serve pasta with meat, fish, vegetables and even with just a little butter or grated cheese. (If the recipe calls for Parmesan, buy a whole piece from a cheese shop and grate it at home.) The Orientals serve noodles in just as varied a selection of dishes, chow mein (fried noodles) being only one.

While, despite the variety of ways it can be served, few of us who are not Italian are likely to eat pasta twice a day, every day, we can let a little of that Latin expertise influence our meals. The filler at dinner need not always be potatoes, rice or even bulgur. Plain or stuffed or smothered in sauce, pasta in any of its many forms can add variety and nutrition to any meal.

PIZZA

2 Tbsp. yeast
1¼ cups warm water
1 tsp. honey
¼ cup olive oil
1 tsp. salt
3½ cups whole wheat flour
6-8 cups tomato sauce, page 204
3 cups sliced mushrooms

1½ cups chopped green olives
2 green peppers, chopped
1 lb. chopped bacon, cooked to eliminate
  fat but not until crisp
6 cups grated Swiss cheese
6 cups grated mozzarella cheese
3 cups grated Parmesan cheese

To make dough, dissolve yeast and honey in water. Add oil, salt and flour and mix well. Knead until smooth and elastic. Let rise in a warm place until doubled in size — about 1½ hours. Punch down and knead again briefly.

Divide dough into 3 equal portions. Roll each portion out to a 10-inch circle, ⅛ inch thick. Place crust in pizza pan.

Top each crust with about 2 to 2½ cups tomato sauce, then sprinkle vegetables, olives and bacon over this. Top with grated cheeses.

Bake at 425 degrees F for 15 to 20 minutes, until cheese has melted and crust is golden brown.

Makes 3 10-inch pizzas.

GERMAN PIZZA DOUGH

1 cup cottage cheese
2¼ cups flour
2 tsp. baking powder
4 Tbsp. milk
4 Tbsp. oil
1 egg, beaten

Mix cottage cheese, flour and baking powder with pastry blender until crumbly. Combine milk, oil and beaten egg and add to dry ingredients. Stir until well combined and roll out on floured surface to fit pizza pan. Makes two 12-inch pizza crusts. Bake with favourite toppings at 400 degrees F for 35 to 40 minutes.

— *Joann Hudson*
Kingston, N.S.

BASIC TOMATO SAUCE

THIS SAUCE CAN BE USED AS A BASIS FOR SPAGHETTI, LASAGNE, CANNELONI, manicotti or pizza, with or without the addition of ground beef and other vegetables.

¼ cup olive oil
1 clove garlic, minced
2 onions, diced
1 qt. canned tomatoes
½ cup tomato paste
½ cup water
1½ tsp. salt

¼ tsp. pepper
1 tsp. basil
1 tsp. oregano
1 Tbsp. parsley
1 bay leaf
½ cup mushrooms, sliced

Heat olive oil in heavy saucepan. Add other ingredients in order listed. Simmer, uncovered, for 1 to 6 hours.

Add sliced mushrooms for the last 15 minutes.

— *Helen Shepherd*
Brockville, Ontario

EGG NOODLES

Flour
3 large eggs
Olive oil

Mound flour on large, clean working surface. Make a well in the centre of the flour and break eggs into it.

Take ½ eggshell and measure 3 shellfuls of water and 3 of olive oil into the well.

Using a fork, gently beat the liquids to blend and gradually flick flour from the edges into the centre. Keep beating until mixture becomes very stiff.

Sprinkle dough with flour and roll it out, adding flour as necessary to make a very stiff, thin dough. When dough has been rolled as thin as possible, let rest for 10 minutes.

Divide dough into strips 8 inches to 10 inches wide and cut into ¼-inch strips for noodles. Hang over broom handle to dry — 15 to 30 minutes.

To cook, place in boiling water and cook 3 to 7 minutes — until tender.

To store, bag and refrigerate for up to 3 days, or freeze.

— Noni Fidler
Chase, B.C.

MACARONI & CHEESE

THE ADDITION OF TOMATO SAUCE TO THIS TRADITIONAL MACARONI AND CHEESE casserole can provide an interesting variation.

3 Tbsp. butter
3 Tbsp. flour
2 cups milk
½ tsp. salt

Pepper to taste
2 cups grated old Cheddar cheese
2 cups cooked macaroni
¾ cup fine bread crumbs

Melt butter, blend in flour and add milk. Cook and stir over low heat until thick. Add seasonings and 1½ cups cheese. Stir and heat until melted.

Put macaroni in greased baking dish. Pour in sauce and mix well. Mix bread crumbs with remaining ½ cup cheese and sprinkle over top of casserole.

Bake at 350 degrees F for 30 to 40 minutes.

Serves 4.

— Mrs. Bruce Bowden
Dunnville, Ontario

MACARONI SALAD

2 cups uncooked macaroni
1 cup sliced celery
½ cup chopped green onions
¼ cup sliced radishes
1 cup cubed Cheddar cheese

¾ cup mayonnaise
1 Tbsp. vinegar
1 tsp. mustard
1 tsp. salt
Pepper to taste

Cook the macaroni. Drain and rinse with cold water until cool. Toss together the cooked macaroni, vegetables and cheese.

Mix together the mayonnaise, vinegar, mustard, salt and pepper. Toss dressing together with salad. Refrigerate.

Serves 6 to 8.

— Bertha Geddert
Ft. McMurray, Alberta

NOODLE CASSEROLE

3 Tbsp. butter
2 Tbsp. flour
1 cup milk
¼ cup soya grits,
   soaked in ¼ cup water
¼ cup vegetable flakes

½ tsp. salt
½ cup chopped parsley
½ cup grated Cheddar cheese
3-4 cups cooked & drained
   broad egg noodles

Melt butter in heavy saucepan and stir in flour. Cook for 1 minute, then add milk slowly, stirring constantly. Add remaining ingredients except cheese and noodles and simmer for 10 minutes. Mix in cheese, then noodles and place in greased loaf pan.

Bake at 350 degrees F for 30 minutes.

Serves 4 to 6.

— *Shiela Alexandrovich*
Whitehorse, Yukon

COTTAGE CHEESE & NOODLE BAKE

½ cup chopped onion
2 Tbsp. butter
2 Tbsp. flour
1 tsp. salt
Pepper
1 cup milk

1 tsp. mustard
1 cup cottage cheese
½ cup Cheddar cheese, grated
2 Tbsp. lemon juice
8 oz. noodles, cooked
Parsley

Sauté onion in butter until tender. Stir in flour, salt and pepper until smooth. Gradually stir in milk and mustard. Cook until thickened. Stir in cheeses, lemon juice, then noodles.

Pour into a greased casserole dish.

Bake at 350 degrees F for 40 to 45 minutes. Sprinkle with fresh parsley to serve.

Serves 4.

BOUNTIFUL PASTA

1 lb. spaghetti
¼ cup butter
2 Tbsp. vegetable oil
1½ cups whole cherry tomatoes
1 clove garlic, minced
¼ cup chopped green onion
½ tsp. salt

1 tsp. basil
5 cups broccoli, cut into bite-sized pieces
½ cup coarsely chopped walnuts
1 cup chicken broth
½ cup Parmesan cheese
2-4 Tbsp. parsley

Boil spaghetti, drain and set aside.

Melt half the butter in the skillet and combine with oil. Add tomatoes and sauté for 5 minutes until tender. Stir in garlic, onion, salt and basil, and cook for 2 more minutes. Set aside and keep warm.

Meanwhile, steam broccoli until tender. Toast walnuts for 5 minutes and set aside.

Melt remaining butter in a saucepan. Add broth, cheese and parsley and mix well. Add tomatoes, broccoli and spaghetti and toss. Pour onto a warm platter and sprinkle with nuts.

Serves 4.

— *Pat Dicer*
Mission, B.C.

CLAM SAUCE FOR SPAGHETTI

¼ cup butter
5 cloves garlic, peeled & halved
2 Tbsp. whole wheat flour

2 Tbsp. powdered milk
2 5-oz. cans whole baby butter clams
Oregano

Melt butter and slowly sauté garlic for 3 minutes. Do not let butter brown. Remove garlic and add flour and milk. Blend well and remove from heat.

Drain clams and add liquid to flour slowly, beating well with a whisk. Return sauce to medium heat and cook until thick (about 4 minutes). Add clams and oregano and pour over spaghetti.

Serves 2.

— Linda Townsend
Nanaimo, B.C.

WHITE SAUCE FOR SPAGHETTI

2 Tbsp. fresh parsley
2 Tbsp. fresh basil
1 cup butter, melted
⅓ cup grated Parmesan cheese

¼ cup olive oil
2 cloves garlic, mashed
8 oz. cream cheese
⅔ cup boiling water

Mix together parsley, basil and butter. Add cheese, then mix in remaining ingredients. Simmer until well blended. Serve over cooked noodles.

Makes 2½ cups.

— Ken Parejko
Holcombe, Wisconsin

LASAGNE

6 oz. lasagne noodles
2 Tbsp. cooking oil
2 cloves garlic, minced
2 onions, chopped
1 lb. ground beef
½ lb. mushrooms, sliced
2 stalks celery, diced
1 green pepper, diced
12 oz. tomato paste
3 cups stewed tomatoes

1 tsp. salt
¼ tsp. pepper
1 tsp. oregano
1 tsp. basil
2 tsp. parsley
1 bay leaf
1 lb. ricotta cheese
5 oz. spinach
¾ cup Parmesan cheese
1 lb. mozzarella cheese, grated

Cook noodles in boiling water until tender. Drain and set aside.

Heat oil in large heavy frying pan. Add garlic and onions and sauté until onion is soft. Add ground beef and continue to sauté, stirring frequently, until beef begins to lose pink colour. Add mushrooms, celery and green pepper. Continue cooking until meat is well browned. Stir in tomato paste, tomatoes and seasonings. Simmer for at least 1 hour or all day. The longer the sauce simmers, the richer the flavour.

To assemble, mix together ricotta cheese, washed and torn spinach and ½ cup Parmesan cheese.

Pour a very thin layer of meat sauce into a 9" x 13" baking dish. This will prevent the casserole from sticking to the dish. Arrange a layer of cooked noodles over sauce. Top with half of meat sauce, half ricotta-spinach mixture and half grated mozzarella cheese. Repeat layers. Sprinkle remaining ¼ cup of Parmesan cheese over top layer.

Bake at 350 degrees F for 35 to 45 minutes.

Serves 8.

— Wanda Mary Murdock
Willowdale, Ontario

TOFU LASAGNE

THE SUBSTITUTION OF TOFU FOR GROUND BEEF IN THIS RECIPE ALLOWS VEGETARIANS to enjoy a delicious, protein-rich lasagne. Wheat germ adds an additional, slightly nutty flavour.

8-oz. package lasagne noodles
¼ cup butter
½ lb. fresh mushrooms, thinly sliced
3 cloves garlic, finely chopped
½ tsp. salt
⅛ tsp. pepper

3 cups spaghetti sauce
½ cup wheat germ
1 cup mashed tofu
¼ cup grated Parmesan cheese
½ lb. mozzarella cheese, grated
¼ cup chopped fresh parsley

Cook and drain lasagne noodles. Set aside.

Melt butter in large skillet. Add mushrooms, garlic, salt and pepper. Cook until mushrooms are tender. Stir in sauce and wheat germ. Heat through.

Combine tofu and Parmesan cheese in a bowl. Combine mozzarella and parsley in another bowl.

In a 9" x 12" pan, layer half of each of the ingredients: noodles, tofu mixture, sauce and mozzarella mixture. Repeat.

Bake at 350 degrees F for 45 minutes or until hot and bubbly. Let stand for 15 minutes before cutting.

Serves 8 to 10.

— Pat Bredin
Winnipeg, Manitoba

VEGETABLE LASAGNE

ZUCCHINI AND OLIVES PROVIDE ANOTHER INTERESTING VARIATION ON THE STANDARD lasagne flavour. This recipe, like the others, can be frozen with no detraction from the original flavour.

2 Tbsp. oil
1 large clove garlic, minced
1 large onion, chopped
1 green pepper, chopped
2 stalks celery, chopped
½ tsp. oregano
½ tsp. basil
½ tsp. thyme
1 medium zucchini, coarsely grated

1½ cups sliced mushrooms
1½ cups tomato sauce, page 204
5½-oz. can tomato paste
¼ cup grated Parmesan cheese
2 cups cottage cheese, mixed with 1 egg
½ cup chopped black olives
2 cups grated mozzarella cheese
8 oz. lasagne noodles, cooked
10 oz. spinach, torn into 1-inch pieces

Sauté garlic in oil for 1 minute. Add onion, green pepper, celery and herbs and cook for 5 minutes. Add zucchini and cook another 5 minutes. Add mushrooms, tomato sauce and tomato paste. Simmer 20 minutes, remove from heat, add Parmesan cheese and mix well.

Spread a small amount of the sauce in the bottom of a greased, 2-qt. casserole dish. Layer in half of each of the ingredients: noodles, sauce, cottage cheese, spinach, mozzarella and olives. Repeat.

Cover and bake for 1 hour at 350 degrees F. Allow to sit for 10 minutes before serving.

Serves 6 to 8.

— Shan Simpson
Leslieville, Alberta

MANICOTTI

MANICOTTI CAN BE MADE WITH HOMEMADE CREPES, AS THIS RECIPE INDICATES, or with commercial pasta, as in the following recipe. Canneloni noodles may also be used with either of these fillings and do not need to be pre-boiled.

6 eggs
1½ cups flour
¼ tsp. salt
2 lbs. ricotta cheese
½ lb. mozzarella cheese
⅓ cup grated Parmesan cheese

2 eggs
1 tsp. salt
¼ tsp. pepper
1 Tbsp. chopped parsley
¼ cup grated Parmesan cheese
2-3 cups tomato sauce (page 204)

Combine 6 eggs, flour, salt and 1½ cups water in blender. After blending, let stand 30 minutes or longer.

Grease and heat an 8-inch skillet. Pour in 3 Tbsp. of batter, rotating skillet quickly to spread batter evenly. Cook over medium heat until top is dry. Cool on wire rack, then stack with wax paper between them.

For filling, combine all remaining ingredients except the ¼ cup of Parmesan cheese. Beat with a wooden spoon to blend well. Spread about ¼ cup filling down the centre of each manicotti and roll up. Place completed rolls, seam-side down, in a shallow casserole dish, making 2 layers if necessary. Top with homemade tomato sauce and remaining Parmesan cheese.

Bake at 350 degrees F for 30 minutes.

Serves 8.

— *Hazel R. Baker*
Coombs, B.C.

SPINACH BEEF MANICOTTI

2 cups chopped onion
¼ cup butter
¾ lb. fresh spinach
4 cloves garlic, minced
2 tsp. oregano
1 tsp. salt
¼ tsp. pepper
1 lb. ground beef
2 Tbsp. oil

32-oz. can tomatoes
6-oz. can tomato paste
1 Tbsp. basil
1½ tsp. salt
¼ tsp. pepper
12 manicotti shells,
  cooked, drained & cooled
½ cup grated Parmesan cheese

Sauté 1½ cups of the onion in butter for 5 minutes. Tear spinach into 1-inch pieces and add to onion along with 2 cloves garlic, oregano, salt and pepper. Stir-fry 2 to 3 minutes and add ground beef. Cook until beef is thoroughly browned. Set aside.

Sauté remaining onion in oil until soft. Stir in tomatoes, tomato paste, remaining garlic, basil, salt and pepper. Bring to a boil, reduce heat, cover and simmer for 20 minutes.

Stuff noodles with meat filling and place in a shallow baking dish. Cover with tomato sauce and sprinkle with Parmesan cheese.

Bake at 350 degrees F for 30 minutes.

Serves 6.

— *Bryanna Clark*
Union Bay, B.C.

ROTINI & SAUCE

¾ lb. rotini noodles
¾ lb. ground beef
Olive oil
⅔ cup sliced carrots
⅔ cup sliced celery
⅔ cup sliced onion

1½ cups tomato sauce, page 204
Salt & pepper
1 tsp. oregano
Cayenne pepper
1 clove garlic, minced

Cook rotini noodles in boiling, salted water for about 20 minutes, until tender.

Meanwhile, brown beef in a skillet, draining off excess fat.

Sauté carrots, celery and onion in oil on low heat for 5 minutes. Add tomato sauce, seasonings and cooked beef. Simmer, covered, for 10 minutes.

Drain and rinse rotini and top with sauce and Parmesan cheese.

Serves 4.

— Glenn F. McMichael
Goderich, Ontario

SZECHUAN NOODLES

1 lb. spaghetti or Chinese noodles
2 Tbsp. oil
4 green onions, chopped
½ cup minced cooked ham
¼ cup chopped peanuts
⅓ cup sesame seeds

⅓ cup soya sauce
1 Tbsp. cider vinegar
1 tsp. honey
Tabasco sauce
2 Tbsp. ketchup
⅔ cup chopped cucumber or celery

Cook noodles, drain and toss with 1 Tbsp. oil. Set aside.

Stir-fry green onions in remaining oil for 1 minute. Add ham, peanuts, sesame seeds, soya sauce, vinegar, honey, Tabasco and ketchup. Simmer 2 to 3 minutes, add cucumber or celery and cook a few minutes longer.

Add noodles, toss and heat through.

Serves 4.

— Bryanna Clark
Union Bay, B.C.

FETTUCINI ALFREDO

THIS RICH PASTA DISH IS PARTICULARLY DELICIOUS SERVED WITH VEAL COOKED IN A cream sauce or with stuffed zucchini. If spinach noodles are used, the dish will be an attractive green.

½ lb. fettucini noodles
¼ lb. butter
1 cup whipping cream

½ cup grated Parmesan cheese
½ cup chopped parsley
Salt & pepper

Cook noodles in boiling salted water. Drain. Return to pot. Over low heat, stir in butter, cream and cheese and cook, mixing well, until butter is melted and mixture is hot. Stir in parsley and salt and pepper.

Serves 2 as a main dish, 4 as a side dish.

MARSALA LIVER SAUCE FOR PASTA

1 small onion, minced
¼ cup minced parsley
¼ lb. bacon, minced
½ lb. rabbit or chicken livers, quartered
¼ lb. mushrooms, thinly sliced

¼ cup Marsala wine
½ cup tomato paste
½ tsp. ground sage
Salt & pepper

Chop together onion, parsley and bacon to make a paste. Cook for 5 minutes. Add livers and mushrooms and continue cooking until livers are browned.

Add wine, tomato paste and seasonings and simmer for 30 minutes. Serve over spaghetti.

Serves 2.

NOODLE OMELETTE

2 Tbsp. butter
1 Tbsp. oil
1 cup chopped onion
⅔ cup green pepper, sliced into strips

1 cup grated Swiss cheese
8 eggs, beaten
2½ cups cooked noodles
1 tsp. salt

Melt 1 Tbsp. butter and oil in a heavy frying pan. Sauté onion and green pepper until onion browns. Stir in remaining butter and reduce heat to very low.

Combine remaining ingredients and pour over vegetables. Cover and cook over medium-low heat, without stirring, for 15 to 20 minutes. When puffed and browned around the edges, the omelette is cooked.

Serves 8.

Desserts

Promises and pie crust are made to be broken.

Dessert — the applause at the end of a play, the kiss at the end of a date, the reward for one's eating all his liver and spinach. Whether it be baked Alaska, almond cookies, or stewed prunes, desserts have an unmistakably congratulatory aura about them. Well done! You finished your dinner and the crust turned out flaky. After dessert and coffee, one can face the evening, convinced of the sweetness of life.

The sweet tooth, used to entice children to eat their vegetables, and which keeps their parents ever in search of the perfect cheesecake, has been blamed by scientists on an almost instinctive ethic, one that served primitive man well; if it tastes sweet, it's good to eat; if it doesn't, it may be harmful. With everything from ketchup to commercial chicken coating now laced with sugar, the maxim should be reversed, but there it is in any case, resounding in our collective unconscious. Canada's annual "disappearance" of sugar, which includes that used by processors, amounts to 95 pounds per person, and, as the ads say, "it's all energy" — nothing else, simply carbohydrate with not a bit of additional food value.

Europeans, who had only the more nutritious and far scarcer honey as a sweetener since the dawn of civilization, learned of sugar cane after one of

Alexander the Great's men reported the amazing news that Asians were able to obtain honey without bees. Sugar cane travelled with Columbus to the New World, eventually to become an important crop of the Caribbean islands. Not until the advent of the sugar beet industry in the 19th century was Europe's dependence on the tropical sweetener diminished

Almost all of our sweetener is still produced from cane or beets. White sugar, in any of its incarnations as table sugar, berry sugar (a fine grind for sprinkling on berries) or icing sugar, is the least nutritious of all sweeteners, but often the cheapest as well. With the exception of raw icing sugar, it imparts no particular flavour to prepared foods, except that of sweetness. As icing sugar contains cornstarch, any mixture containing it should be heated slightly to dispel its starchy taste; many frosting recipes request the use of boiling water for that reason.

Molasses, the most nutritious by-product of cane sugar, has a distinctive flavour and the dark colour often appreciated in whole wheat breads and cakes. Several types are sold. Blackstrap, usually available only in natural food stores, is very high in nutrients but correspondingly strong, almost bitter, in flavour. Milder in flavour and lower in nutrients are "sulphured" and "unsulphured" or "fancy" molasses. The former is

blackstrap molasses refined with sulphur fumes, the latter, a product of ripened cane that is far less nutritious than blackstrap but still a much better nutritional bet than white sugar.

Although true demerara sugar is raw, cleaned cane sugar, most sold commercially is a sugar/molasses mixture that is "demerara-style." Brown sugars are also composed of white sugar coloured with molasses.

Beyond the cane and beet sugar products are man's oldest sweeteners, still nutritious, tasty and heartily appreciated. Honey is the oldest known sweetener and the only one that is an animal carbohydrate. It is rich in minerals and contains some B vitamins as well as traces of vitamin C, if it is unpasteurized. As individually flavoured as the plants any hive of bees visits, commercial honey is nevertheless usually pale and fairly odourless, pasteurized clover honey. But backyard apiaries produce a fascinating array of raw honeys from the thick, dark and musky to the light and perfumy. For the very best honey, buy it directly from a good beekeeper. Store it in a closed container in a warm, dry place — honey is hygroscopic, it absorbs water from the air. If it cools and becomes granulated, heat it gently over hot water until it is again liquid, but do not allow it to overheat — temperatures over 160 degrees F can change both the colour and flavour.

Maple syrup is a very expensive sweetener for all except those with access to a sugar bush. Darker, lower grade syrups, stronger in flavour than the light ones sold in supermarkets, are preferred by some syrup connoisseurs. Good sugar syrups can also be produced if one boils down the early spring sap of birch trees. As with honey, the most varied syrups can be bought directly from the producer.

While many foods, including milk and beer, also contain sugar, it is in fruits that sweetness is especially appreciated. Fruits contain fructose, the sweetest of all sugars, and so have long been considered among the best of desserts. Drying fruit, concentrating the sugar content, produces morsels as sweet as some candy, but rich in nutrients as well. As an alternative to the desserts described on the next pages, consider fruit for dessert: light, flavourful, nutritious — and sweet.

Many of the dessert recipes which follow in this chapter incorporate both nutrition and good taste — fruits combined with whole grains and dairy products end the meal on a happy note. There are, as well, desserts for those occasions which demand something special.

CATHY'S TRIFLE

2-layer sponge cake
2-3 cups custard
4 cups mixed fresh chopped fruit

1 cup sherry
2 cups whipping cream, whipped
Fresh fruit to garnish

Break cake into 1-inch cubes. Combine with custard, chopped fruit and sherry in a large bowl and mix gently.

Top with whipped cream and fresh fruit.

Serves 8 to 12.

— Cathy Byard
Winnipeg, Manitoba

CHOCOLATE PUDDING

1 cup flour
2 tsp. baking powder
½ tsp. salt
¾ cup sugar
6 Tbsp. cocoa

½ cup milk
4 Tbsp. melted butter
½ tsp. vanilla
1 cup brown sugar
1¾ cups hot water

Combine flour, baking powder, salt, sugar, 2 Tbsp. cocoa, milk, butter and vanilla. Spread in greased 8-inch square pan and sprinkle with brown sugar combined with remaining cocoa. Pour hot water over this. Do not stir. Bake at 350 degrees F for 40 to 45 minutes.

— Rae Anne Huth
Fauquier, B.C.

JERSEY CREAM PUDDING

A LIGHT AND FLUFFY PUDDING, THIS IS DELICIOUS SERVED WITH MOST FRESH FRUITS.

2-3 eggs, separated
3 cups milk
⅓ cup sugar
¼ tsp. salt

2 heaping Tbsp. flour
¼ cup cream
1 tsp. vanilla
Nutmeg

Beat egg whites until stiff and set aside.

Scald together the milk, sugar and salt in a double boiler.

Mix together flour and cream to form a thin batter. Add egg yolks and stir until smooth.

Slowly add hot milk to yolk mixture and stir until smooth. Return to heat, over hot water, and continue cooking and stirring until thick, at least 5 to 10 minutes. Add vanilla, fold in egg whites, pour into a bowl and top with nutmeg.

Serves 4 to 6.

— B. Caldwell
Marysville, B.C.

FRUIT BREAD PUDDING

6 slices bread
1 banana, sliced
½ cup raisins
¼ cup walnuts

1 apple, cored & diced
1 cup brown sugar
⅔ cup water
½ tsp. cinnamon

Toast bread at 325 degrees F for 15 minutes. Cut into cubes and combine with fruit and nuts.

Mix sugar, water and cinnamon together and add to fruit mixture. Toss to coat evenly. Let stand 5 minutes and stir again. Turn into a greased 8-inch square casserole dish.

Bake uncovered at 325 degrees for 30 to 35 minutes.

— Helen Potts
Tilden Lake, Ontario

ORANGE CAKE PUDDING

LEMON JUICE AND RIND CAN BE SUBSTITUTED FOR ORANGE IN THIS DESSERT FOR AN equally delicious pudding.

¼ cup flour	½ cup orange juice
1 cup sugar	2 eggs, separated
¼ tsp. salt	¾ cup milk
1 Tbsp. grated orange rind	

Sift flour, sugar and salt together. Stir in orange rind and juice, egg yolks and milk. Blend well.

Beat egg whites until stiff but not dry. Pour orange mixture over egg whites and fold gently to blend.

Pour into a greased 1-quart baking dish. Set in a pan of hot water. Bake at 350 degrees F for 50 minutes or until a knife inserted into the cake comes out clean.

— *Johanna Vanderheyden*
Strathroy, Ontario

BABA AU RHUM

1 tsp. sugar	2-3 cups flour
1 envelope dry yeast	4 Tbsp. chopped red & green
½ cup lukewarm water	glazed cherries
¼ cup soft butter	2 Tbsp. chopped light raisins
2 cups granulated sugar	½ cup corn syrup
3 eggs	2½ cups apricot nectar
¼ tsp. salt	Grated rind of 1 orange
½ tsp. vanilla	1½ cups light rum
½ tsp. grated lemon rind	

Dissolve 1 tsp. sugar and yeast in water. Let stand until foamy — 10 minutes. Beat together butter, ½ cup sugar and eggs until fluffy. Add salt, vanilla, lemon rind and ½ cup flour. Beat in yeast mixture and enough flour to make a drop-type batter. Add cherries and raisins.

Half-fill 30 small greased muffin tins. Let stand until batter fills tins. Bake at 375 degrees F for 8 to 10 minutes, until golden. Remove from tins when cool.

To make rum sauce, combine in a heavy saucepan the remaining 1½ cups sugar, corn syrup, apricot nectar and orange rind. Bring to a boil and simmer until sugar dissolves — 5 minutes. Remove from heat and stir in rum. Cool.

One hour before serving, place the baba cakes in wide-mouthed jars or deep mixing bowls. Pour the sauce over them slowly, allowing it to soak in. Serve topped with whipped cream or lemon sauce.

Makes 30 baba cakes.

— *Shirley Hill*
Picton, Ontario

MAPLE MOUSSE GLACEE

4 eggs, separated	½ tsp. vanilla
1 cup pure maple syrup	1½ cups whipping cream

Beat egg yolks thoroughly and add maple syrup. Beat well to blend. In a heavy saucepan, cook over very low heat, stirring constantly, until the consistency of a soft custard sauce is reached. Remove from heat, add vanilla and cool thoroughly.

Whip cream and fold in. Beat egg whites until stiff but not dry and fold in. Pour into parfait glasses and freeze until very firm. Let stand a few minutes at room temperature before serving. Garnish with whipped cream and toasted almonds.

Serves 6.

— *Julienne Tardif*
Toronto, Ontario

YOGURT FRUIT MOULD

UNFLAVOURED GELATIN IS A HEALTHFUL ALTERNATIVE TO PREPACKAGED GELATIN mixes. Combined with fruit and yogurt, it provides a light and delicious ending to any meal, especially on a hot summer day.

1 can chunk pineapple (in juice)
1 envelope unflavoured gelatin
2 Tbsp. honey
1 cup apple or orange juice

1 cup plain yogurt
1 banana, sliced
2 oranges, sectioned and seeded

Drain pineapple chunks and place juice in a small saucepan. Sprinkle gelatin over the juice and stir constantly over low heat until gelatin is dissolved — about 5 minutes. Add honey and stir until dissolved.

Pour into a 4-cup mould and add apple or orange juice and yogurt. Stir to mix yogurt evenly.

Let sit in the refrigerator for about 20 minutes or until starting to gel. Add pineapple, banana and orange sections and stir to distribute evenly.

Return to refrigerator until set — about 1 hour. Unmould by placing in a pan of hot water for a few seconds, then inverting on a plate.

— Mikell Billoki
Gore Bay, Ontario

NUTMEG MOUSSE

6 eggs
1½ cups granulated sugar
2 envelopes unflavoured gelatin
½ cup cold water

1 Tbsp. freshly grated nutmeg
1 tsp. vanilla
2 cups whipping cream

Beat eggs until frothy. Gradually beat in sugar and continue beating until satiny and light.

In a small saucepan, sprinkle gelatin over water to soften. Cook over low heat, stirring occasionally, until gelatin is dissolved. Stir into the egg mixture with nutmeg and vanilla.

Whip cream until soft peaks form, and fold into egg mixture. Pour into a 2½-quart mould and chill until firm.

Serves 8 to 10.

— Mary McEwen
Guelph, Ontario

SYLLABUB

THIS OLD ENGLISH DISH IS A FROTHY CHILLED DESSERT WHICH SEPARATES INTO TWO layers.

2 egg whites
½ cup sugar
Juice of ½ lemon

1 cup whipping cream
½ cup white wine

Whip egg whites until stiff, then carefully fold in sugar and lemon juice. Whip cream until peaks form and fold this into the egg whites along with the wine. Pour into individual glasses and chill for 2 hours before serving.

Serves 4.

— Sheila Bear
St. John's, Nfld.

GOOSEBERRY FOOL

THIS DESSERT CAN BE MADE EQUALLY SUCCESSFULLY WITH ALMOST ANY FRUIT.

1 lb. ripe gooseberries
3 Tbsp. water

½ cup sugar
1 cup whipping cream

Top and tail gooseberries. Combine with water and sugar and stew until tender. Press through sieve and chill the purée.

Beat cream until stiff. Carefully fold in gooseberry purée.

Serve in individual dishes with more whipped cream.

Serves 4.

— *Sheila Bear*
St. John's, Nfld.

RASPBERRY BOMBE

MANY BERRY JUICES OTHER THAN RASPBERRY CAN BE USED IN THIS RECIPE.

2 envelopes plain gelatin
3 cups raspberry juice

½ pint whipping cream

Soften gelatin in small amount of cold water. Add ¼ cup boiling water to dissolve. Add gelatin mixture to berry juice. Cool until syrupy, then whip until frothy.

Whip cream until stiff. Add one quarter of juice-gelatin mixture to whipped cream and stir, then add remaining juice.

Pour into a mould or individual serving dishes and refrigerate until set. Serve topped with whipped cream and fresh raspberries.

Serves 4.

— *Signe Nickerson*
Grand Forks, B.C.

YOGURT POPSICLES

1 cup plain yogurt
1 small can frozen orange juice

2 tsp. vanilla

Stir together and freeze in popsicle trays.

— *Kathleen Fitzgerald*
Fort McMurray, Alberta

RASPBERRY SHERBET

½ cup sugar
1 cup water
1 tsp. gelatin
2 Tbsp. water
¾ cup corn syrup

1 pint raspberries, crushed
¼ cup lemon juice
¼ cup orange juice
2 egg whites

Simmer sugar and 1 cup water for 5 minutes. Soften gelatin in 2 Tbsp. water, then dissolve in hot sugar and water. Add corn syrup and cool.

Stir berries and juices into cooled syrup and freeze until firm. Beat until light and fluffy. Beat egg whites, and fold into berry mixture. Spoon into individual serving dishes and freeze.

Serves 8.

— *Elizabeth Vigneault*
Tlell, B.C.

CHOCOLATE CHEESECAKE

THIS CRUSTLESS CHEESECAKE HAS A LIGHT AIRY TEXTURE. THE CHOCOLATE CAN BE omitted and the cake topped with fresh fruit for a different taste.

3 eggs, separated
8 oz. cream cheese, mashed
1 cup sour cream
½ cup sugar

1½ Tbsp. flour
½ tsp. vanilla
1 Tbsp. lemon juice
1 cup chocolate chips

Beat egg yolks and add to cream cheese. Add sour cream, sugar, flour, vanilla and lemon juice. Mix well.

Beat egg whites until stiff peaks form, and gently but thoroughly fold into batter.

Melt chocolate chips in saucepan over low heat. Swirl through batter. Pour into a lightly greased 10-inch springform pan.

Bake at 300 degrees F for 1 hour, turn off heat and leave cake in oven for 1 more hour. Cool cheesecake, then refrigerate until serving time.

Serves 10 to 12.

— *Melissa Eder*
West Long Branch, N.J.

PINEAPPLE UPSIDE-DOWN CAKE

1⅓ cups flour
¾ cup sugar
3 tsp. baking powder
½ tsp. salt
¼ cup shortening

1 egg
¾ cup milk
3 Tbsp. butter
½ cup brown sugar
9 pineapple slices

Combine flour, sugar, baking powder and salt. Cut in shortening. Mix together egg and milk and add to flour mixture.

Meanwhile, melt butter in an 8-inch square pan in oven at 350 degrees F. Sprinkle with brown sugar, then arrange a layer of pineapple slices close together in pan, over butter and sugar. Cover with batter.

Bake at 350 degrees F for 30 minutes.

Turn cake upside down on plate and remove from pan while still warm. Cool before serving.

Serves 9.

— *Shirley Thomlinson*
Carp, Ontario

CANDY NUT ROLL

1 cup sugar
½ cup milk
¼ tsp. salt
1 Tbsp. melted butter

2 cups chopped dates
1 cup walnuts
1 tsp. vanilla
1-2 cups coconut

Boil sugar, milk, salt and butter to the soft ball stage. (When a little of the mixture is placed in a cup of cold water it will form a ball which loses its shape when removed from the water.)

Add the dates and boil for 3 more minutes. Remove from heat, add walnuts and vanilla, and cool to lukewarm.

Knead on a greased cookie sheet until it is no longer sticky. Roll into a long cylinder, then coat with coconut. Wrap in wax paper and chill well. Slice when cold. Keep refrigerated.

— *Signe Nickerson*
Grand Forks, B.C.

LITHUANIAN NAPOLEON TORTE

THIS DELICIOUS TORTE TAKES SOME TIME TO ASSEMBLE, BUT IT IS WELL WORTH THE effort. For variety, melted chocolate, chopped nuts or chopped fruit may be added to the fillings.

Pastry
1 lb. butter, softened
4 cups flour
2 cups sour cream

Filling #1
¾ cup granulated sugar
5 Tbsp. flour
¼ tsp. salt

2 cups milk, scalded
4 egg yolks, beaten
1 tsp. vanilla

Filling #2
2 14-oz. cans sweetened condensed milk
6 egg yolks, beaten
2 tsp. vanilla
½ lb. butter, softened

To make pastry, cut butter into flour until crumbly and blend in sour cream. Form dough into 10 balls. Cover each with wax paper and refrigerate overnight.

Allow dough to stand at room temperature for 15 minutes, then roll each ball into a wafer thin circle on a lightly floured board. Prick all over and bake at 350 degrees F, for 7 to 10 minutes. Cool.

To make filling #1, mix together sugar, flour and salt in top of double boiler. Gradually add hot milk, stirring constantly. Cook and stir until mixture thickens. Pour a small amount over egg yolks, mix thoroughly and pour back into hot mixture. Cook for 2 minutes. Cool, then add vanilla.

To make filling #2, pour milk into top of double boiler and cook, stirring frequently, until thickened — about 30 minutes. Add egg yolks slowly in a thin stream, stirring constantly. Add vanilla. Cook and stir for 10 minutes. Chill. Beat butter until fluffy, then slowly beat in chilled milk mixture.

To assemble torte, place one layer of pastry on a platter and spread with either filling. Continue stacking, alternating fillings, until 1 layer of pastry remains. Frost top and sides with remaining filling. Crush remaining pastry layer and cover torte with crumbs. Refrigerate for several hours.

Serves 30.

— *Diane Cancilla*
Barrie, Ontario

BAKLAVA

¾ lb. butter, cut into ¼-inch pieces
½ cup vegetable oil
40 sheets filo pastry

4 cups walnuts, crushed
¾ cup honey
1 Tbsp. lemon juice

Melt butter over low heat, removing foam as it rises to the surface. Remove from heat, let rest 2 to 3 minutes and spoon off clear butter. Discard milky solids.

Stir oil into butter and coat 9" x 13" baking dish with 1 Tbsp. of mixture, using a pastry brush. Lay a sheet of pastry in baking dish, brush with butter, lay down another sheet and brush with butter. Sprinkle with 3 Tbsp. of walnuts. Repeat this pattern to make 19 layers. Top with 2 remaining sheets of filo and brush with remaining butter.

Score top of pastry with diagonal lines ½-inch deep, 2 inches apart, to form diamond shapes.

Bake at 350 degrees F for 30 minutes, reduce heat to 300 degrees and bake 15 minutes longer, or until top is golden brown.

Remove from oven. Combine honey and lemon juice and pour slowly over baklava. Slice when cool.

— *Carol Gasken*
Winlaw, B.C.

KIFFLE

THESE FILLED CRESCENTS HAVE A RICH, SOUR CREAM DOUGH.

1 envelope dry yeast
1 Tbsp. water
2 cups flour
½ cup butter
2 eggs, separated

½ cup sour cream
Icing sugar
1 cup finely chopped walnuts
½ cup sugar
1 tsp. vanilla

Dissolve yeast in water and let stand for 10 minutes.

Cut butter into flour until crumbly. Combine egg yolks and sour cream and add dissolved yeast. Pour over flour and butter. Mix in and knead for 5 minutes. Form into a ball, place in a greased bowl, cover with wax paper and then a tea towel. Chill for 1 hour.

Divide dough into 3 equal parts. Sprinkle icing sugar onto board, roll each part into a 10-inch circle and cut into 8 wedges.

Combine walnuts, sugar, stiffly beaten egg whites and vanilla. Place some of this filling on each piece of dough and roll up from the wide end in.

Place well apart on greased cookie sheets and bake at 375 degrees F for 25 minutes or until golden brown.

Makes 24.

— Mrs. Ed Stephens
Luskville, Quebec

STREUSEL SQUARES

½ cup butter
1 cup granulated sugar
2 eggs
1 tsp. vanilla
1 cup sour cream or buttermilk
2 cups flour

¼ tsp. salt
1 tsp. baking powder
1 tsp. baking soda
⅓ cup brown sugar
1 tsp. cinnamon
¼ cup chopped walnuts

Cream together butter and granulated sugar. Mix in eggs, one at a time. Add vanilla to sour cream or buttermilk. Sift together flour, salt, baking powder and baking soda. Add dry ingredients to butter mixture gradually, alternating with cream. Combine lightly.

Place half this mixture in 9" x 13" pan. Combine remaining ingredients and sprinkle half over the batter. Spread with remaining batter and top with sugar mixture.

Bake at 350 degrees F for 30 minutes. Cool in pan.

— Nel vanGeest
Weston, Ontario

APPLE-OAT SQUARES

⅓ cup butter
½ cup brown sugar
1 cup flour
½ tsp. baking soda
½ tsp. salt

1 cup rolled oats
2½ cups peeled, sliced tart apples
2 Tbsp. butter
¼-⅓ cup sugar

Cream butter and mix sugar in gradually. Sift flour, add baking soda and salt, and combine with creamed mixture until crumbly. Stir in rolled oats. Spread half the mixture into a greased 8-inch square cake pan. Cover with sliced apples. Dot with butter and sprinkle with sugar (and cinnamon if desired). Spread remainder of crumb mixture on top.

Bake at 350 degrees F for 40 to 45 minutes.

— Johanna Vanderheyden
Strathroy, Ontario

MINCEMEAT SQUARES

1½ cups brown sugar
2 eggs
2 Tbsp. molasses
1 Tbsp. butter
1 tsp. vanilla
2 cups flour
½ tsp. salt
½ tsp. baking soda
1 tsp. cinnamon

1 tsp. cloves
3 Tbsp. hot water
½ cup chopped walnuts
¼ cup raisins
1½ cups mincemeat
1½ cups icing sugar
3 Tbsp. hot milk
½ tsp. vanilla
½ tsp. almond extract

Mix thoroughly brown sugar, eggs, molasses, butter and 1 tsp. vanilla. Add flour, salt, baking soda, cinnamon, cloves, hot water, walnuts, raisins and mincemeat and mix well.

Spread smoothly in 2 well-greased 9" x 13" pans. Bake at 400 degrees F for 12 to 15 minutes.

Combine remaining ingredients and spread over squares while they are still warm.

— *Dawn Livingstone*
Georgetown, Ontario

RHUBARB SQUARES

THIS RECIPE ORIGINATED WITH THE AUTHOR'S GRANDMOTHER, WHO OWNED A BAKERY in Toronto in the 1940s. It has been adapted to make use of whole grains and natural sweeteners.

3 cups chopped rhubarb
¾ cup water
Honey
3 Tbsp. cornstarch
1 cup whole wheat flour
1 cup rolled oats

½ tsp. baking powder
¼ tsp. salt
¼ tsp. nutmeg
½ tsp. cinnamon
2 Tbsp. demerara sugar
½ cup melted butter

Cook rhubarb in ½ cup water, with honey to taste. Mix cornstarch in ¼ cup water and add to stewed rhubarb. Cook, stirring, until thickened, and set aside.

Mix remaining ingredients together. Put half the oat mixture on the bottom of an 8-inch square baking dish. Pat down and fill with rhubarb. Sprinkle remaining oat mixture on top.

Bake 35 minutes at 350 degrees F. Allow to cool for 30 minutes before cutting into squares.

— *Sandra James-Mitchell*
Pickering, Ontario

SCOTCH APPLE PUDDING

2 cups sliced apples
½ cup granulated sugar
¼ tsp. cinnamon
1 egg
½ cup milk
¼ tsp. salt

½ cup brown sugar
½ cup rolled oats
½ cup flour
2 tsp. baking powder
½ tsp. vanilla
⅓ cup butter

Arrange apples in bottom of buttered baking dish. Sprinkle with sugar and cinnamon.

Mix remaining ingredients and pour over apples. Bake at 350 degrees F for 1 hour or until apples are tender.

— *Barb Curtis*
Bowmanville, Ontario

PEACH CRUMBLE

6 medium-sized peaches, peeled,
  pitted & thinly sliced
½ cup brown sugar, firmly packed
Dash mace

1 cup flour
½ tsp. salt
4 Tbsp. butter

Toss peach slices with ¼ cup of the brown sugar and the mace in a buttered 6-cup baking dish.

Mix flour, remaining sugar and salt in a bowl. Cut in butter. Spread over the peaches and pat down lightly. Bake at 350 degrees F for 45 minutes or until golden. Serve warm with cream.

— Erika Johnston
Toronto, Ontario

APPLE BROWN BETTY

1½ cups brown sugar
1¼ cups flour
⅔ cup butter

2 cups thinly sliced apples,
  pared & cored
Cream or milk

Rub flour, sugar and butter together to form a corn meal texture. Press half of mixture into bottom of a 10-inch square pan. Spread apples evenly on top. Cover with rest of flour mixture and pat flat with hand or fork.

Bake 15 to 20 minutes at 350 degrees F until lightly browned and apples are tender. Serve warm with milk or cream.

— Deborah Exner
Delisle, Sask.

BLUEBERRY CRISP

4 cups blueberries
2 Tbsp. tapioca
⅓ cup sugar
1 Tbsp. lemon juice
½ tsp. lemon peel
⅔ cup brown sugar

¾ cup rolled oats
½ cup flour
½ tsp. cinnamon
⅛ tsp. salt
6 Tbsp. butter

Combine blueberries, tapioca, sugar, lemon juice and lemon peel and mix well. Pour into greased 9-inch square baking pan.

Mix together remaining ingredients and place on top of berries.

Bake at 375 degrees F for 40 minutes.

— Ken Parejko
Holcombe, Wisconsin

BLUEBERRY BUCKLE

¼ cup butter
¼ cup honey
1 egg
Salt
1 cup flour
1 tsp. baking soda

⅓ cup buttermilk or yogurt
2 cups blueberries
¼ cup butter
2 Tbsp. honey
⅓ cup flour
½ tsp. cinnamon

Cream together ¼ cup butter, ¼ cup honey, egg and salt. Add 1 cup flour, baking soda, buttermilk or yogurt and mix well. Spread in a greased 8-inch square cake pan. Cover with blueberries.

Combine remaining ingredients and spread over blueberries.

Bake at 350 degrees F for 40 minutes.

— Water Street Co-op
Halifax, N.S.

PEACH KUCHEN

1½ cups flour
½ tsp. salt
¼ tsp. baking powder
2 Tbsp. sugar
⅓ cup butter

4-6 peaches, peeled, pitted & halved
¼ cup sugar
1 tsp. cinnamon
1 egg, beaten
1 cup whipping cream or yogurt

Combine flour, salt, baking powder and sugar. Cut in butter. Pat dough over bottom and sides of 9-inch square pan.

Arrange peaches over pastry and sprinkle with sugar and cinnamon. Bake at 400 degrees F for 15 minutes.

Combine egg and cream or yogurt and pour over peaches. Bake 30 minutes longer. Serve warm or cold.

Serves 9.

— Adele Dueck
Lucky Lake, Sask.

STRAWBERRY SHORTCAKE

THIS SHORTCAKE HAS A MUFFIN-LIKE TEXTURE AND A ROUGH EXTERIOR — ALL THE better to trap the whipped cream and strawberries.

½ tsp. salt
3 cups flour
1 Tbsp. baking powder
4 Tbsp. granulated sugar
1 cup soft shortening

1 egg, slightly beaten with enough
  milk to make 1 cup of liquid
½ tsp. vanilla
1 qt. strawberries, cleaned & hulled
2 cups whipping cream, whipped

Sift together salt, flour, baking powder and sugar. Cut in shortening with pastry blender. When well blended, add egg-milk mixture and vanilla. Mix only until flour is moistened. Spoon into a greased 8-inch square pan, leaving dough in clumps.

Bake at 350 degrees F for 30 to 40 minutes. Cool.

To serve, cut cake into 9 pieces, split each piece open and top with whipped cream and strawberries.

Serves 9.

APPLE PAN CAKE

2 Tbsp. butter
2 apples, quartered & thinly sliced
¼ cup firmly packed brown sugar
¼ tsp. cinnamon
3 eggs

½ cup milk
½ cup flour
¼ tsp. salt
1 Tbsp. brown sugar

Melt butter in a 9-inch round cake pan. Add apples and coat with butter. Sprinkle with ¼ cup brown sugar and cinnamon. Place in 400 degree F oven while preparing batter.

Mix eggs, milk, flour and salt together. Pour over the apples, sprinkle with 1 Tbsp. brown sugar, dot with butter and bake 15 to 20 minutes.

Serves 2.

— Lisa Fainstein
Winnipeg, Manitoba

FRESH APPLE FRITTERS

⅝ cup flour
½ tsp. baking powder
½ tsp. salt
1 egg, separated

3 Tbsp. milk
1 cup chopped apples
Oil for deep frying
Powdered sugar

Combine flour, baking powder and salt and mix well. Beat egg yolk and milk together and stir into dry ingredients. Add apples. Beat egg white until stiff and fold into batter.

Drop by spoonfuls into oil heated to 350 degrees F. Fry until golden brown, drain well and roll in powdered sugar. Serve with maple syrup or honey.

Serves 4 to 6.

— *Janis Huisman*
Springton, P.E.I.

SAUTEED BANANAS

½ cup softened butter
½ cup firmly packed brown sugar
½ tsp. cinnamon
½ tsp. nutmeg

¼ tsp. cloves
Salt
4-6 bananas

Combine all ingredients except bananas and mix well.

Peel and slice the bananas in half lengthwise. To cook each banana, melt 2 Tbsp. butter-sugar mixture and sauté banana over high heat.

Serve with vanilla ice cream.

Serves 4 to 6.

— *Jill den Hertog*
Key Largo, Florida

CUMBERLAND SAUCE

THIS TRADITIONAL SAUCE TO ACCOMPANY HOT OR COLD ROAST MEATS IS ALSO delicious over cheesecake or ice cream.

2 oranges
1 lemon

4 Tbsp. red currant jelly
4 Tbsp. port

Grate rind from fruit, then squeeze for juices. Put rind and juices into heavy saucepan and heat gently until simmering. Add red currant jelly and stir until dissolved. Add port.

Serve warm with hot meats, chill to use with cold meats or desserts.

Makes 1 cup.

— *Sheila Bear*
St. John's, Nfld.

50/50 PASTRY

1 cup whole wheat flour
1 cup pastry flour
1 tsp. salt

¾ cup shortening
2 Tbsp. water

Combine flours and salt, and cut in shortening until crumbly. Stir in water to make pastry form a ball.

Store in refrigerator or freezer until needed. Makes enough pastry for 1 double-crust pie.

— *Jeannette McQuaid*
Belleville, Ontario

PASTRY

5¼ cups flour
1 Tbsp. salt
1 Tbsp. sugar

1 lb. shortening
1 large egg

Sift dry ingredients into a large bowl. Cut in the shortening.

Beat egg and add water to make 1 cup. Pour slowly into flour mixture, stopping to mix with a fork. Add only enough liquid to make pastry form a ball.

Turn out onto a floured board and knead until mixture is smooth. Divide into 4 portions, wrap well and refrigerate or freeze.

Makes enough pastry for 4 double-crust pies.

— Carolyn Hills
Sunderland, Ontario

RASPBERRY FLAN

THIS RECIPE IS FAST AND EASY TO MAKE AND THERE IS NO PASTRY TO ROLL. IT MAKES a wonderful dessert in the winter with frozen berries.

1 cup flour
Salt
2 Tbsp. sugar
½ cup butter

1 Tbsp. vinegar
1 cup sugar
2 Tbsp. flour
3 cups raspberries

Combine 1 cup flour, salt and 2 Tbsp. sugar. Add butter and vinegar and mix well with hands. Press gently into 9-inch pie plate.

Mix together gently 1 cup sugar, 2 Tbsp. flour and 2 cups raspberries. Place in pie plate. Bake at 400 degrees F for 50 to 60 minutes. Sprinkle with remaining berries after removing from oven.

— Donna Gordon
Dorval, Quebec

RASPBERRY SOUR CREAM PIE

Pastry for 9-inch pie shell
2 eggs
1⅓ cups sour cream
1 tsp. vanilla
1 cup sugar
⅓ cup flour

Salt
3 cups fresh raspberries
½ cup loosely packed brown sugar
½ cup flour
½ cup chopped walnuts or pecans
¼ cup chilled butter

Line pie plate with pastry.

Beat eggs and whisk in sour cream and vanilla. Mix sugar, flour and salt and add to egg mixture. Gently stir in raspberries. Pour into pie shell and bake at 400 degrees F for 30 to 35 minutes or until centre is almost set.

Mix brown sugar, flour and nuts. Cut in butter until mixture is crumbly. Sprinkle over pie and return to oven for another 10 to 15 minutes.

— Carol Parry
St. Paul, Minnesota

FRESH RASPBERRY PIE

Pastry for 9-inch double-crust pie
4 cups raspberries
⅔ cup sugar

2 Tbsp. quick-cooking tapioca
1 Tbsp. lemon juice
2 Tbsp. butter

Toss berries lightly with sugar and tapioca. Line a pie dish with pastry and fill with berries. Sprinkle with lemon juice and dot with butter.

Cover with top crust. Slash crust. Bake at 425 degrees F for 20 minutes, then reduce heat to 350 degrees and bake until filling has thickened and pastry is golden, about 40 minutes. Cool before cutting.

— Joan Airey
Rivers, Manitoba

FRESH STRAWBERRY PIE

Baked 8-inch pie shell
1 qt. strawberries, cleaned & hulled
1 cup sugar

⅓ cup cornstarch
1 Tbsp. lemon juice
Whipped cream to garnish

Mix strawberries with sugar and let sit overnight. In morning, drain off juice and add water to make 1¾ cups of liquid.

Blend cornstarch to a paste with ¼ cup liquid in double boiler. Add remaining liquid and cook over direct heat, stirring constantly, until sauce boils and is clear. Place in double boiler, cover and cook another 15 minutes. Remove from heat, add lemon juice and fold in berries.

Cool to lukewarm, then pour into pie shell. Garnish with whipped cream.

— Cindy McMillan
Quesnel, B.C.

STRAWBERRY CHEESE PIE

1½ cups graham cracker crumbs
6 Tbsp. soft butter
½ cup confectioners' sugar
8 oz. cream cheese
1 cup sugar

4 eggs
⅔ pint sour cream
1 tsp. lemon juice
1 pint strawberries
2 Tbsp. cornstarch

Mix together cracker crumbs, butter and confectioners' sugar. Press into a 9-inch pie plate. Chill.

Combine cheese, sugar, eggs, sour cream and lemon juice, and mix well with electric mixer. Pour into pie shell and bake at 350 degrees F for 1 hour.

If using fresh berries, crush, drain and reserve juice. If using frozen berries, drain and reserve juice. Sweeten juice to taste, add cornstarch and cook until thick, for at least 10 minutes. Cool. Add berries and spread over pie.

— Ken Parejko
Holcombe, Wisconsin

BLUEBERRY CHANTILLY PIE

Baked 9-inch pie shell
4 cups blueberries
½ cup honey
½ cup water
2 Tbsp. cornstarch
1 Tbsp. butter

2 Tbsp. Cointreau or Grand Marnier
1 cup whipping cream
2 Tbsp. honey
¼ tsp. almond extract
½ cup sliced almonds

Blend together 1 cup blueberries, honey and water. Add cornstarch and cook until thick. Stir in butter and Cointreau or Grand Marnier. Cool.

Fold in remaining 3 cups of blueberries and pour into baked pie shell.

Whip cream with honey and almond extract. Spoon on top of pie and sprinkle with almonds.

— *David Slabotsky*
Richmond, P.E.I.

OLD-FASHIONED SASKATOON PIE

Pastry for 9-inch double-crust pie
4 cups Saskatoon berries, washed
2 Tbsp. water
2 Tbsp. lemon juice

¾ cup sugar
1½ Tbsp. quick-cooking tapioca
1 Tbsp. butter

Simmer together berries, water and lemon juice, covered, over low heat, for 3 to 4 minutes. Remove from heat and stir in sugar, tapioca and butter. Cool.

Line pie plate with pastry and fill with cooled berry mixture. Cover with top crust, trim and seal edges. Prick top, brush with milk and sprinkle with sugar.

Bake at 450 degrees F for 15 minutes, reduce heat to 350 degrees and bake 30 to 35 minutes longer.

— *Joan Airey*
Rivers, Manitoba

FRESH BLUEBERRY TART

THIS RECIPE PROVIDES A CHANGE FROM THE TRADITIONAL TWO-CRUST FRUIT PIE. THE crust is crispy and slightly sweet, and the whole uncooked berries make the pie taste very fresh.

1½ cups plus 2 Tbsp. flour
Salt
2½ Tbsp. sugar
½ cup unsalted butter
1 egg yolk

2-3 Tbsp. ice water
5 cups blueberries, rinsed
⅓ cup water
½ cup sugar
½-⅔ cup sour cream

Mix flour, salt and 2½ Tbsp. sugar with the butter until crumbly. Stir together the egg yolk and 2 Tbsp. of the ice water. Blend into the flour mixture until dough forms a ball, adding a little more water if necessary. Wrap pastry and chill for at least 1 hour.

Roll out pastry and line a pie plate. Chill for 30 minutes. Weight the pastry with dried peas to keep it from bubbling and bake at 400 degrees F for 6 to 8 minutes. Remove peas, prick pastry lightly and return to oven. Bake another 10 to 15 minutes or until golden. Cool.

Combine 3 cups of blueberries with ⅓ cup water and ½ cup sugar in a heavy saucepan. Bring to a boil over medium heat, stirring constantly. Simmer, still stirring, until mixture thickens to a jam-like consistency — about 15 minutes. Cool.

Spread sour cream in the pie shell. Combine remaining 2 cups of berries with the berry jam. Spread over the cream. Serve at room temperature.

— *Virginia Jamieson*
Swan River, Manitoba

SOUR CREAM PEACH PIE

Pastry for 9-inch pie shell
1 Tbsp. flour
¾ cup sour cream
½ cup granulated sugar

⅓ cup flour
¼ tsp. almond extract
4 cups peeled, sliced peaches
¼ cup brown sugar

Sprinkle pie crust with 1 Tbsp. flour.

Combine sour cream, sugar, ⅓ cup flour and almond extract and stir until smooth. In pie shell, alternate layers of peaches with cream mixture, ending with cream.

Bake at 425 degrees F for 20 minutes, reduce heat to 350 degrees and bake another 35 minutes. Sprinkle with brown sugar and broil until golden.

Cool before serving.

— *Shirley Thomlinson*
Carp, Ontario

SOUR CREAM RAISIN PIE

Baked 9-inch pie shell
1½ cups sour cream
3 egg yolks, well beaten
1 cup sugar
1 tsp. cinnamon

¼ tsp. ground cloves
½ cup raisins
½ cup chopped walnuts
2½ Tbsp. flour

Combine sour cream and egg yolks. Combine remaining ingredients, add to cream-egg mixture and place in a double boiler.

Cook, stirring constantly, until mixture is consistency of heavy cream filling and has turned brown in colour.

Pour into pie shell. Chill before serving.

— *Freda Creber*
Orillia, Ontario

SOUR CREAM APPLE PIE

Pastry for 9-inch pie shell
2 Tbsp. flour
⅛ tsp. salt
¾ cup brown sugar
1 egg
1 cup sour cream
1 tsp. vanilla

½ tsp. nutmeg
2 cups diced tart apples
⅓ cup sugar
⅓ cup flour
1 tsp. cinnamon
¼ cup butter

Sift flour, salt and sugar together. Add egg, sour cream, vanilla and nutmeg. Beat to form a smooth batter. Add apples and pour into pie crust. Bake at 400 degrees F for 15 minutes, reduce heat to 350 degrees and bake another 30 minutes.

Meanwhile, combine remaining ingredients to make topping. Remove pie from oven, sprinkle on topping and return to oven. Bake for 10 minutes at 400 degrees.

— *Leah Patton*
Hamilton, Ontario

APPLE PIE

Pastry for 9-inch double-crust pie
8 cups pared, cored & thinly sliced
  cooking apples
⅓ cup firmly packed brown sugar
⅓ cup granulated sugar
1 Tbsp. cornstarch or 2 Tbsp. flour

1 tsp. cinnamon
¼ tsp. nutmeg
¼ tsp. salt
2 Tbsp. butter
Water or milk
Sugar to sprinkle on top

Place sliced apples in a large bowl. Mix sugars, cornstarch or flour, cinnamon, nutmeg and salt in a small bowl and sprinkle over the apples. Let stand for 10 minutes, until a little juice forms.

Line pie plate with pastry and pile apple mixture into it. Dot with butter and top with pastry. Seal.

Brush top of pastry with a little milk or water and sprinkle lightly with sugar. Slash top.

Bake at 375 degrees F for 40 to 50 minutes or until juice bubbles through slashes and apples are tender.

— *Marva Blackmore*
Vancouver, B.C.

CRABAPPLE PIE

Pastry for 9-inch double-crust pie
4 cups sliced crabapples
¾ cup sugar

1 tsp. cinnamon
1 tsp. nutmeg
1 Tbsp. butter

Line pie plate with pastry and fill with sliced crabapples. Combine sugar and spices and sprinkle over the crabapples. Dot with butter and top with pastry. Crimp edges and slash top.

Bake at 425 degrees F for 15 minutes, reduce heat to 350 degrees and bake 45 minutes longer.

— *Sandra Lloyd*
North Vancouver, B.C.

RHUBARB STRAWBERRY CRUMB PIE

Pastry for 9-inch pie shell
3 cups chopped rhubarb
2 cups strawberries, sliced
1½ cups sugar
⅓ cup flour

1 cup sour cream
½ cup flour
½ cup brown sugar
¼ cup soft butter

Arrange rhubarb and strawberries in unbaked pie shell. Mix sugar and ⅓ cup flour with sour cream and pour evenly over fruit.

Combine ½ cup flour, brown sugar and butter until crumbly and sprinkle over top.

Bake at 450 degrees F for 15 minutes, reduce heat to 350 degrees and bake another 30 minutes, until fruit is tender.

Chill before serving.

— *Margaret Silverthorn*
Iona Station, Ontario

PECAN PIE

9-inch pie shell, baked for 5 minutes
½ cup granulated sugar
3 Tbsp. butter
1 cup corn syrup

3 eggs
1 cup pecan halves
1 tsp. vanilla

Boil together sugar, butter and corn syrup for 2 minutes. Beat eggs and mix with pecans. Pour sugar mixture over eggs and nuts. Add vanilla. Pour mixture into partially baked pie shell and bake at 350 degrees F for 35 to 40 minutes.

— Shirley Hill
Picton, Ontario

BUTTER TARTS

Pastry for 14-16 tart shells
1½ cups brown sugar
2 eggs
1-2 tsp. butter, softened
1 tsp. vanilla

1 tsp. vinegar
½ cup raisins
4 Tbsp. milk
½ cup chopped walnuts

Combine all ingredients except pastry and mix until just blended.

Line tart shells with pastry and fill two-thirds full with mixture. Bake at 350 degrees F for 15 minutes, until filling is firm.

Makes 14 to 16 tarts.

— Mary McEwen
Guelph, Ontario

RHUBARB CUSTARD PIE

Pastry for double-crust 9-inch pie
2 eggs
1 cup granulated sugar

1 Tbsp. melted butter
2 Tbsp. flour
2½ cups rhubarb

Beat together eggs, sugar, flour and butter. Mix in rhubarb and pour into pie shell. Top with upper crust.

Bake at 400 degrees F for 15 minutes, reduce heat to 350 degrees and cook for another 15 minutes.

— Sharron Jansen
Pembroke, Ontario

PUMPKIN PIE

Pastry for 9-inch pie shell
2 eggs, lightly beaten
2¾ cups cooked mashed pumpkin
¾ cup brown sugar
½ tsp. salt

1 tsp. cinnamon
½ tsp. ginger
¼ tsp. cloves
1⅔ cups light cream
Whipped cream to garnish

Combine all ingredients except pastry in order given. Pour into pie shell. Bake at 350 degrees F for 45 minutes or until knife inserted in filling comes out clean. Cool. Top with whipped cream.

— Shirley Morrish
Devlin, Ontario

CUSTARD PIE

Pastry for 9-inch pie shell
1¾ cups milk
3 eggs
⅓ cup honey

½ tsp. salt
⅛ tsp. nutmeg
½ tsp. vanilla

Heat milk until lukewarm. Beat eggs, then add honey, salt, nutmeg, vanilla and milk.. Blend thoroughly and pour into pie shell.

Bake at 450 degrees F for 10 minutes. Reduce heat to 325 degrees and bake until custard is set – 30 to 40 minutes.

— Winona Heasman
Powassan, Ontario

FROZEN YOGURT PIE

¾ cup ground walnuts
½ cup flour
2 Tbsp. oil
1 cup tofu

¾ cup plain yogurt
¼ cup powdered milk
½ cup honey
Almond extract

Combine walnuts, flour and oil. Press into 9-inch pie plate. Bake at 450 degrees F for 10 to 15 minutes, being careful not to burn. Cool.

Thoroughly drain the tofu and combine with yogurt. Stir with a whisk until smooth. Add milk powder 1 Tbsp. at a time. Add honey and almond extract to taste. Mix well.

Pour into pie crust and freeze overnight. Allow to stand at room temperature for 15 minutes before serving.

— Janet Flewelling
Toronto, Ontario

WALNUT CRANBERRY PIE

TANGY, TART AND ATTRACTIVE, THIS PIE, WITH ITS GARNISH OF ORANGE SLICES and whole berries will be a festive addition to the Christmas menu.

Pastry for 9-inch pie shell
3½ cups fresh cranberries
½ cup seedless raisins
1½ cups sugar
2 Tbsp. flour
¼ cup corn syrup

1 tsp. grated orange rind
¼ tsp. salt
1 Tbsp. soft butter
¾ cup walnuts, coarsely chopped
Orange slices & whole cranberries
  to garnish

Grind cranberries and raisins together. Add sugar, flour, corn syrup, orange rind, salt and butter and mix well. Stir in nuts and turn into pie shell.

Bake at 375 degrees F for 40 to 45 minutes. Cool.

Garnish with orange slices and whole cranberries and serve with ice cream.

— Nina Kenzie
Homer, Alaska

FRENCH SILK PIE

Graham cracker crust for 9-inch pie
2 oz. unsweetened chocolate
2 Tbsp. brandy
2 Tbsp. instant coffee
1 cup butter

1 cup sugar
2 eggs
½ cup ground almonds
½ cup ground hazelnuts

Line pie plate with graham cracker crust; refrigerate.

In double boiler, melt chocolate, then stir in brandy and coffee. Cream butter and sugar together. Beat in eggs one at a time. Stir in chocolate mixture and nuts. Pour filling into shell and chill. Serve cold.

— Michael Bruce-Lockhart
Paradise, Nfld.

PUMPKIN CHEESECAKE

1½ cups zwieback crumbs
3 Tbsp. sugar
3 Tbsp. melted butter
16 oz. cream cheese, softened
1 cup light cream
1 cup cooked pumpkin
¾ cup sugar
4 eggs, separated
3 Tbsp. flour

1 tsp. vanilla
1 tsp. ground cinnamon
½ tsp. ground ginger
½ tsp. ground nutmeg
¼ tsp. salt
1 cup sour cream
2 Tbsp. sugar
½ tsp. vanilla

Combine crumbs, 3 Tbsp. sugar and melted butter. Press into bottom and 2 inches up the sides of a 9-inch spring pan. Bake for 5 minutes at 325 degrees F.

Combine cream cheese, cream, pumpkin, ¾ cup sugar, egg yolks, flour, vanilla, spices and salt. Fold in stiffly beaten egg whites and turn into crust. Bake at 325 degrees F for 1 hour.

Combine sour cream, 2 Tbsp. sugar and vanilla. Spread over cheesecake and return to oven for 5 more minutes. Chill before serving.

— Elizabeth Clayton
Nepean, Ontario

TOFU SOUR CREAM CHEESECAKE

1½ cups ground granola, without fruit
½ cup wheat germ
½ cup flour
¼ cup demerara sugar
⅔ cup melted butter
5 cakes tofu
3 cups cottage cheese (small curd)
4 cups sour cream
6 eggs
2 Tbsp. lemon juice

¼ cup maple syrup
¼ cup honey
½ tsp. sea salt
¼ tsp. ground nutmeg
¼ tsp. ground cloves
¼ tsp. ground coriander
½ Tbsp. cinnamon
1 Tbsp. ground ginger
2 tsp. vanilla
2 Tbsp. honey

Combine thoroughly granola, wheat germ, flour, sugar and butter. Press into the bottoms of two 10-inch spring pans. Chill.

Drain tofu. Blend together tofu, cottage cheese, 2 cups sour cream, eggs, lemon juice, maple syrup, ¼ cup honey, salt and spices. Pour over crusts in pans and bake for 40 minutes at 375 degrees F. Allow to cool.

Combine 2 cups sour cream, vanilla and 2 Tbsp. honey, and pour over cooled cheesecakes. Bake for 10 minutes at 425 degrees F. Chill before serving.

Makes 2 large cheesecakes.

— Sunflower Restaurant
Kingston, Ontario

Chinese Beef and Broccoli in Oyster Sauce, page 178

Manicotti, page 209

Fresh Raspberry Pie, page 226; Fresh Blueberry Tart, page 227; Pecan Pie, page 230

Raspberry Bombe, page 217

Blueberry Muffins, page 250; Poppy Seed Muffins, page 249

Raspberry Bars, page 282; Chocolate Chip Cookies, page 274; Oatmeal Chocolate Chip Cookies, page 273

Hot Cranberry Wine Cup, page 290

Assorted Preserves, pages 296-311

RHUBARB CHEESE PIE

1¾ cups graham cracker crumbs
¼ cup brown sugar
⅓ cup melted butter
¼ tsp. cinnamon
¼ tsp. nutmeg
3 cups diced rhubarb
1 cup honey

2 envelopes gelatin
1 cup cold orange juice
½ lb. cottage cheese
Grated rind of 1 lemon
¼ cup raisins
2 bananas, sliced

Combine cracker crumbs, brown sugar, butter, cinnamon and nutmeg and press into 2 7-inch pie plates. Chill.

Stew together rhubarb and honey until rhubarb is just tender but not mushy. Soften gelatin in ½ cup orange juice, then add to hot rhubarb, stirring gently until dissolved.

Stir remaining ½ cup of orange juice into cottage cheese, a little at a time. Then add to rhubarb mixture along with lemon rind and raisins. Place in freezer until mixture begins to thicken − 10 to 15 minutes − then pour into pie shells and garnish with banana slices.

— *Rosande Bellaar Spruyt*
Alcove, Quebec

LEMON MERINGUE PIE

LEMON MERINGUE PIE IS A PARTICULARLY FASCINATING DESSERT AS IT CAN TURN OUT wretchedly − gelatinous and oversweet (as it is served in most restaurants) − or, if made properly, can be a creamy ambrosia of lemony custard, delicate crust and fluffy meringue. This recipe will produce the gourmet result. It takes more time than opening a package of lemon filling, but the result is incomparable.

Baked 9-inch pie shell
1 cup sugar
6 Tbsp. cornstarch
¼ tsp. salt
2 cups milk
3 eggs, separated

3 Tbsp. butter
⅓ cup lemon juice
1 Tbsp. grated lemon rind
¼ tsp. cream of tartar
3 Tbsp. sugar
½ tsp. vanilla

Combine the sugar, cornstarch and salt in the top of a double boiler. Slowly add the milk, stirring constantly. Cook and stir these ingredients over hot water until the mixture thickens − about 15 minutes. Cover the pan and allow to cook 10 minutes longer. Stir occasionally. Remove from heat. Beat the egg yolks in a separate bowl and add about ½ cup of the thickened milk. Then stir this mixture back into the double boiler. Cook and stir over boiling water for 5 to 6 minutes. Remove from heat and stir in butter, lemon juice and lemon rind. Cool this custard, stirring gently every 10 minutes or so. When cool, pour into pie shell.

For the meringue, beat egg whites with cream of tartar until they are stiff but not dry. Beat in sugar, ½ tsp. at a time, followed by vanilla. Heap onto pie and spread with spatula so that meringue goes all the way out to the crust, around the whole pie. Use a light back-and-forth motion of the spatula to make decorative waves in the meringue. Bake at 350 degrees F for 12 to 15 minutes until the meringue is delicately browned on top.

Serves 6.

— *Alice O'Connell*
Centreville, Ontario

Baking

Bake me a cake as fast as you can.

— Anonymous

"With good bread the coarsest fare is tolerable; without it, the most luxurious table is not comfortable," Mary Cornelius writes in *The Young Housekeeper's Friend* of 1845. While food may have been coarser and bread far more plentiful in Cornelius' day than it is in our own — eating a pound of bread a day was not unusual then, and it accompanied most meals — good bread is still a source of great pleasure to us. It is all the more appreciated for its rarity in an age in which "baking" too often means the use of packaged cake mixes, frozen rolls or white, airy loaves that should really be called "bread substitute."

Baking, the type now referred to as being "from scratch," involves mixtures of flour, liquid and other ingredients, usually leavened, and then, of course, baked in the oven. The most commonly used flour for baking is rightly termed "all-purpose," a mixture of hard and soft wheats that will suffice in any recipe, but will be perfect for none. Hard flours contain the highest proportion of gluten, a protein that becomes elastic when wetted and kneaded, retaining the gas bubbles produced by the leavener and so enabling the baked product to rise.

All-purpose flour may be bleached or unbleached, but in Canada it is always "enriched"; that is a few of the nutrients removed in milling have been artificially replaced. Cake flour is white flour made from soft wheat, producing crumbly, finely textured cakes. Gluten flour, on the other hand, is made by washing the starch off high-protein wheat flour, and packaging what remains, a high gluten white flour that is sometimes added to impart extra lightness to whole grain breads.

Besides flour and some type of liquid, leaveners are the most important ingredients in most baking. Baker's yeast should be bought in small quantities and stored in a closed container in the refrigerator or another cool spot. It will die if it is exposed to heat over 140 degrees F, but will multiply rapidly, producing the real leavener, carbon dioxide, at temperatures between 75 and 110 degrees F. All ingredients added to a mixture containing yeast should be warm, never hot.

As yeast ages, it gradually loses its potency. Any baker who doubts the virility of his yeast should check it by adding a pinch to a half cup of warm water, allowing the mixture to sit for about 10 minutes in a warm spot. If, after that time, no foam or bubbles have formed, discard the yeast and buy a new supply. Bread cannot be better than the quality of yeast used to make it. One foil package of yeast equals a tablespoon of bulk yeast, which can be bought in most health food

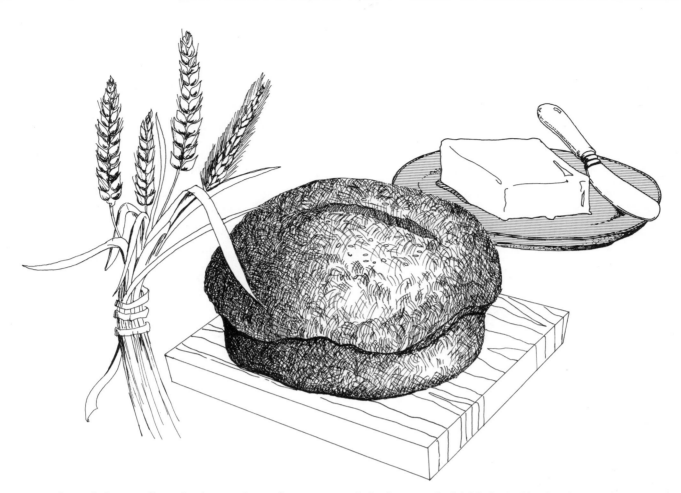

stores where it is usually a far better bargain.

Among chemical leaveners, baking powder is the most popular, although its healthfulness is disputable. It is a mixture of sodium aluminum phosphate and calcium acid phosphate, an alkali and an acid that react to form carbon dioxide when dampened and warmed.

The more benign baking soda is bicarbonate of soda, an alkali that will produce carbon dioxide when it comes in contact with an acid such as sour milk. Baking soda and baking powder are the ususal leaveners in "quick breads," so-called because they do not need to be kneaded and allowed to rise before baking as must the yeasted "slow breads."

Kneading, the process that develops the gluten in such breads, is quite a soothing, rhythmic activity that some cooks include among the attributes of home baked bread. As soon as the bread mixture has incorporated sufficient flour so that it is no longer runny, it should be turned onto a counter or table on which a heavy coating of flour has been dusted. At first, the mixture will be little more than a thick batter, and the cook can sprinkle flour on any wet part that is exposed as he turns and folds the mixture. Keep sprinkling flour on the board as well, so that it will not stick. As the mixture stiffens, smaller quantities of flour should be added. Press on the lump of dough until

it is flattened, fold it in half, give it a quarter turn and press it flat again, continuing this process while incorporating just enough flour to keep it from sticking to fingers and board.

Kneading is usually continued for 10 or 15 minutes, after which the dough should spring back to its original shape when lightly pressed. It is then formed into a ball and placed in a greased bowl, covered, in a warm spot for rising. After it has risen to twice its original size, a process whose duration will depend on both room temperature and the type of bread being made, punch it down all over with the fists. Now cut the dough into loaf-sized portions, which will about half-fill the bread pans and place each section in a greased pan. Cover the loaves, return to the warm spot and, when they have risen above the pan rim, place them in a prewarmed oven to bake. They are done when golden brown on top and bottom.

Whether quick or slow, nothing says economy, flavour − and yes, loving − like something homemade, steaming and fresh from the oven.

ORANGE DATE NUT BREAD

1 cup boiling water
¼ cup orange juice
1 cup chopped dates
1½ cups flour
¼ tsp. cinnamon
¼ tsp. nutmeg
Ground cloves

1½ tsp. baking soda
½ tsp. salt
¼ cup shortening
¾ cup brown sugar
1 egg
1 cup chopped walnuts
2 tsp. grated orange peel

Mix together boiling water, orange juice and chopped dates. Set aside until cooled to room temperature.

Sift together flour, cinnamon, nutmeg, cloves, baking soda and salt and set aside.

Cream together shortening and brown sugar. Add egg, beat well and stir in date mixture. Add dry ingredients and stir batter until moistened. Fold in walnuts and orange peel.

Pour into a greased loaf pan and bake at 325 degrees F for 65 to 70 minutes. Cool bread in pan for 10 minutes, remove and cool completely before slicing.

Makes 1 loaf.

— *Kathy & Rhett Hagerty*
Aldergrove, B.C.

POPPY SEED LEMON BREAD

4 eggs
1½ cups oil
1½ cups light cream
1 tsp. vanilla
½ cup poppy seeds
3 cups flour

2¼ cups sugar
1 tsp. salt
1½ tsp. baking soda
2 tsp. baking powder
Rind & juice of 1 lemon

Combine eggs, oil, cream, vanilla and poppy seeds. Mix together flour, 2 cups sugar, salt, baking soda, baking powder and lemon rind.

Add dry ingredients to egg-cream mixture and blend well. Pour into 2 greased loaf pans and bake at 325 degrees F for 70 minutes.

Meanwhile, mix lemon juice and rind with remaining ¼ cup sugar. Pour over bread while hot and still in pan.

Makes 2 loaves.

— *Audrey Moroso*
Puslinch, Ontario

BLUEBERRY QUICK BREAD

2½ cups flour
¾ cup sugar
1 Tbsp. baking powder
½ tsp. salt
6 Tbsp. butter

¾ cup chopped walnuts
2 eggs
1 cup milk
1 tsp. vanilla
1½ cups blueberries

In large bowl, mix flour, sugar, baking powder and salt. Cut in butter until fine. Stir in walnuts.

In small bowl, beat eggs lightly and stir in milk and vanilla. Stir into flour just until flour is moistened. Gently stir blueberries into batter.

Spoon batter into greased and floured loaf pan. Bake at 350 degrees F for 1 hour and 20 minutes or until toothpick inserted into centre of loaf comes out clean.

Makes 1 loaf.

PUMPKIN BREAD

4 eggs
2 cups granulated sugar
1¼ cups oil
2 cups cooked & mashed pumpkin
1 tsp. salt
3 cups flour

2 tsp. baking powder
2 tsp. baking soda
2 tsp. cinnamon
½ cup chopped walnuts
1 cup seedless raisins

Beat eggs and add sugar, oil and pumpkin. Mix dry ingredients together and add to egg mixture. Stir in nuts and raisins. Bake at 350 degrees F for one hour.

Makes 2 large loaves.

— *Irene P. Simonson*
Seeleys Bay, Ontario

BANANA NUT BREAD

2 cups flour
2 tsp. baking powder
1 tsp. baking soda
¾ tsp. salt
½ cup shortening

1 cup sugar
2 eggs, well beaten
1 cup mashed bananas
1 cup chopped walnuts

Sift together flour, baking powder, baking soda and salt. Cream together shortening, sugar and eggs.

Add bananas to creamed mixture alternately with dry ingredients, combining well after each addition. Stir in walnuts.

Spoon into greased loaf pan and bake at 350 degrees F for 1 to 1¼ hours or until straw inserted into centre comes out clean.

Makes 1 loaf.

— *Janice Clynick*
Clinton, Ontario

ORANGE RAISIN BREAD

1 large orange, unpeeled
¾ cup boiling water
1 egg
¼ cup vegetable oil
2 cups flour
2 tsp. baking powder

1 tsp. baking soda
½ tsp. salt
¾ cup lightly packed brown sugar
¾ cup raisins
½ cup chopped nuts

Cut orange into pieces and remove seeds. Combine in blender with boiling water and blend until almost smooth. Add egg and oil and blend for a few seconds.

Combine remaining ingredients. Add orange mixture and stir just until well blended. Pour into greased loaf pan. Bake at 350 degrees F for 45 to 55 minutes.

Makes 1 loaf.

— *Margaret Butler*
Newcastle, Ontario

CINNAMON BREAD

2 Tbsp. brown sugar
1 Tbsp. cinnamon
½ cup butter
1 cup granulated sugar
2 eggs

2 cups flour
2 tsp. baking powder
½ tsp. salt
1 cup milk
1 tsp. vanilla

Mix together brown sugar and cinnamon and set aside.

Cream butter, granulated sugar and eggs. Combine dry ingredients and add to creamed mixture alternately with milk. Stir in vanilla.

Layer batter and brown sugar-cinnamon mixture in a greased loaf pan, ending with batter.

Bake at 350 degrees F for 1 hour.

Makes 1 loaf.

— Karen Carter
Shoal Harbour, Nfld.

DATE & NUT LOAF

1 cup walnuts
1 cup chopped dates
1½ tsp. baking soda
½ tsp. salt
3 Tbsp. shortening

¾ cup boiling water
2 eggs
1 tsp. vanilla
1 cup granulated sugar
1½ cups flour

Combine walnuts, dates, baking soda, salt, shortening and boiling water. Set aside for 20 minutes.

Beat eggs with a fork and add vanilla, sugar and flour. Add to date mixture and blend.

Pour into a greased bread pan and bake at 350 degrees F for 1 hour.

Makes 1 loaf.

— Joyce Marshall
Whitby, Ontario

LEMON BREAD

1 cup butter
1½ cups sugar
3 eggs
1½ cups flour
1 tsp. baking powder

Salt
½ cup milk
½ cup chopped walnuts
Grated rind & juice of 1 lemon

Cream together butter and 1 cup sugar. Beat in eggs. Combine flour, baking powder and salt. Add to creamed mixture alternately with milk and mix well. Stir in walnuts and lemon rind.

Pour into greased loaf pan and bake at 350 degrees F for 1 hour or until firm on top.

Meanwhile, combine remaining ½ cup sugar with lemon juice. When loaf is baked, spoon lemon sugar over top.

Makes 1 loaf.

— Lily Andrews
Windsor, Ontario

CARROT BREAD

½ cup oil
1 cup sugar
2 eggs, beaten
1 cup shredded carrots
1½ cups flour

1 tsp. baking powder
1 tsp. baking soda
¼ tsp. salt
1 tsp. cinnamon
½ cup milk

Mix oil and sugar. Add beaten eggs and stir in carrots. Sift flour, baking powder, baking soda, salt and cinnamon.

Add small amounts of dry ingredients to sugar mixture alternately with milk. Bake in greased loaf pan for 55 minutes at 350 degrees F.

Makes 1 loaf.

— Patricia A. Leahy
Regina, Sask.

ZUCCHINI LOAF

2 eggs
1 cup sugar
½ cup oil
1½ cups flour
½ tsp. salt
1 tsp. baking powder

½ tsp. baking soda
1 tsp. cinnamon
1 tsp. vanilla
1 cup finely grated raw zucchini
½ cup chopped walnuts

Beat eggs until light and add sugar and oil. Stir together flour, salt, baking powder, baking soda and cinnamon. Add to egg mixture, beating until blended. Mix in vanilla, zucchini and nuts.

Turn into a greased loaf pan and bake at 350 degrees F for 1 hour or until a toothpick inserted in centre comes out clean.

Makes 1 loaf.

— Carolyn Hills
Sunderland, Ontario

DILL BREAD

1 pkg. dry yeast
¼ cup warm water
1 cup cottage cheese
2 tsp. dill weed
2 tsp. salt
¼ tsp. baking soda

1 egg
1 Tbsp. melted butter
1½ tsp. minced onion
2 Tbsp. sugar
2¼-2½ cups flour

Dissolve yeast in water and set aside. Combine in a large bowl, cottage cheese, dill weed, salt, baking soda, egg, butter, onion and sugar. Stir in yeast mixture and then flour.

Knead for 5 to 10 minutes on a floured board. Let rise in a greased bowl until doubled in size — about 1 hour. Punch down. Place in 2 greased loaf pans and let rise for 45 minutes.

Bake at 350 degrees F for 30 minutes. Remove from pans and brush with melted butter.

Makes 1 loaf.

— Pat Bredin
Winnipeg, Man.

WHEAT GERM LOAF

1 cup lukewarm water
1 Tbsp. honey
Salt
1 Tbsp. yeast
2 eggs
1 Tbsp. vegetable oil

⅓ cup soya flour
⅓ cup rice polishings
2 cups bran
3 cups wheat germ
1½ cups water

Combine lukewarm water, honey, salt and yeast and let stand for 20 minutes. Add eggs, oil, soya flour, rice polishings, bran and wheat germ. Mix well and add enough water to make a stiff batter.

Place in a greased loaf pan and let rise in a warm place for 1 hour.

Bake at 325 degrees F for 1¼ to 1½ hours.

Makes 1 loaf.

— Gail Miller
Whitehorse, Yukon

DUTCH PUMPERNICKEL BREAD

2 Tbsp. molasses
3 cups hot water
3 cups Red River cereal

1 cup whole wheat flour
2 tsp. baking soda
1 tsp. salt

In large mixing bowl, combine water and molasses. Add remaining ingredients. Beat at high speed for 2 minutes. Cover with cloth towel and let stand overnight, then pour into greased loaf pan and smooth top.

Bake at 275 degrees F for 1 hour, reduce heat to 250 degrees and bake 1 hour longer. Store in refrigerator for one day before slicing.

Makes 1 loaf.

— Sandra Binnington
Oshawa, Ontario

BRAN BREAD

½ cup brown sugar
2 cups bran
1 cup whole wheat flour
1 cup unbleached white flour

2 Tbsp. wheat germ
1 tsp. salt
2 tsp. baking soda
2 cups buttermilk

Combine dry ingredients. Stir in buttermilk. Spoon into a greased pan and bake at 350 degrees F for 1 hour.

Makes 1 loaf.

— Johanna Genge
Cavan, Ontario

BUTTERMILK CHEESE LOAF

1 cup unbleached white flour
1 cup whole wheat flour
1½ tsp. baking powder
½ tsp. baking soda
2 tsp. dry mustard
1 tsp. salt

1 cup grated Cheddar cheese
1 cup buttermilk
¼ cup oil
2 eggs
2 Tbsp. minced onion

Combine flours, baking powder, baking soda, mustard, salt and cheese. Beat together buttermilk, oil, eggs and onion. Add to dry mixture and stir until moist.

Pour into greased loaf pan and bake at 375 degrees F for 45 to 50 minutes. Cool for 10 minutes, then remove from pan.

Makes 1 loaf.

— Pat Dicer
Mission, B.C.

GOUGERE

A RICH BREAD OF FRENCH ORIGIN, THIS IS TASTY SERVED WARM AS AN accompaniment to soup or stew.

½ cup unsalted butter
1 cup water
½ tsp. salt
1½ cups pastry flour

4 eggs
Any chopped fresh herb
4 oz. Gruyère cheese, grated

Combine butter, water and salt in a saucepan and bring to a boil. Remove from heat and stir in the flour. Return to heat for a few minutes, stirring constantly, until mixture is slightly thickened.

Remove from heat and stir in the eggs one at a time. Then beat in herb and all but a little of the cheese.

Drop seven heaping spoonfuls of the mixture onto a greased cookie sheet in the shape of a ring, each mound of batter touching the rest. Sprinkle the remaining cheese on top and bake at 375 degrees F for 40 to 45 minutes, until golden brown.

Serve hot or cold.

— N. Burk
Ste. Anne de la Rochelle, Quebec

POPPY SEED MUFFINS

2 eggs
2 Tbsp. soft butter
¾ cup sugar
½ cup poppy seeds

1 cup sour cream
2 cups flour
½ tsp. baking soda
2 tsp. baking powder

Cream together eggs, butter and sugar. Add poppy seeds and sour cream. Sift together dry ingredients and stir into creamed mixture until just blended.

Pour into greased muffin tins, filling each two-thirds full. Bake at 425 degrees F for 20 minutes.

Makes 12 large muffins.

— Sheri Israels
West Vancouver, B.C.

BLUEBERRY MUFFINS

1 cup fresh blueberries
1¾ cups flour
¾ tsp. salt
3 tsp. baking powder

2 eggs, well beaten
3 Tbsp. melted butter
¾ cup milk
¼ cup granulated sugar

Mix blueberries and 1 Tbsp. flour. Sift together remaining flour, salt and baking powder.

Combine beaten eggs, melted butter, milk and sugar. Beat until foamy. Add dry ingredients all at once and stir quickly.

Fill greased muffin tins one-third full with batter. Put blueberries on top and cover with remaining batter until tins are two-thirds full.

Bake at 400 degrees F for 15 to 20 minutes.

Makes 12 large muffins.

— Janet Young
Black River Bridge, N.B.

BANANA MUFFINS

½ cup shortening
1 cup granulated sugar
1 egg, slightly beaten
1 cup mashed ripe bananas

1 tsp. baking soda
2 Tbsp. hot water
½ tsp. salt
1½ cups flour

Cream shortening and sugar together, blend in egg and mashed bananas. Dissolve soda in hot water and add to creamed mixture.

Combine dry ingredients and stir into creamed mixture until just blended.

Pour into greased muffin tins and bake at 375 degrees F for 20 minutes.

Makes 12 muffins.

— Helen Potts
Tilden Lake, Ontario

APPLE MUFFINS

4 eggs
2 cups milk
4 Tbsp. melted butter
1⅓ cups sugar
4 cups flour
1 tsp. salt

8 tsp. baking powder
1 tsp. cinnamon
½ tsp. nutmeg
4 medium apples, peeled, cored & chopped

Beat together eggs, milk, butter and ⅔ cup sugar. Combine flour, salt, baking powder, ½ tsp. cinnamon and nutmeg. Add to egg mixture and fold in apples.

Spoon into greased muffin tins until two-thirds full. Combine remaining ⅔ cup sugar and ½ tsp. cinnamon and sprinkle over muffins. Bake at 375 degrees F for 30 minutes.

Makes 24 large muffins.

APPLE HONEY MUFFINS

¼ cup honey
1 egg
¼ cup oil
1 cup apple sauce
⅓ cup orange juice

¾ cup rolled oats
1 cup flour
1 Tbsp. baking powder
½ tsp. cinnamon

In a small bowl, mix honey, egg, oil, apple sauce and orange juice until well combined.

Mix dry ingredients in a large bowl. Make a well in the centre and pour in liquid ingredients, then stir just to moisten.

Spoon into greased muffin tins and bake at 400 degrees F for 25 to 30 minutes.

Makes 12 muffins.

— *Carol A. Frost*
Chilliwack, B.C.

ORANGE OATMEAL MUFFINS

1 whole orange, unpeeled
1 cup rolled oats
½ cup boiling water
½ cup orange juice
½ cup butter
½ cup brown sugar
½ cup granulated sugar

2 eggs, beaten
1 cup flour
1 tsp. baking powder
1 tsp. baking soda
½ tsp. salt
1 tsp. vanilla
½ cup raisins

Place whole orange in blender and purée. Mix with oats, water and orange juice and set aside.

Cream together butter and sugars and add eggs. Combine dry ingredients and add to creamed mixture. Add rolled oat/orange mixture, vanilla and raisins, and stir well.

Bake in greased muffin tins at 350 degrees F for 15 to 20 minutes.

Makes 18 muffins.

— *M. Heggison*
Franklin Centre, Quebec

OATMEAL MUFFINS

1 cup oatmeal
1 cup buttermilk
1 egg
½ cup brown sugar
½ cup oil

1 cup flour
½ tsp. salt
1 tsp. baking powder
½ tsp. soda

Soak oatmeal in buttermilk for 1 hour. Add egg, sugar and oil, and beat well. Combine dry ingredients and stir into oatmeal mixture.

Fill greased muffin tins and bake at 400 degrees F for 15 to 20 minutes.

Makes 12 large muffins.

— *Kass Bennett*
Cranbrook, B.C.

CARDAMOM MUFFINS

1½ cups raisins
¼ tsp. mace
2 Tbsp. brandy
2 tsp. grated orange rind
Orange juice to cover raisins
¼ cup sunflower oil
½ cup honey
2 eggs
¾ cup milk

½ cup wheat germ
¼ cup bran
1¾ cups flour
1½ tsp. baking powder
½ tsp. baking soda
½ tsp. salt
1 tsp. cardamom
⅛ tsp. allspice

Cover raisins with mace, brandy, orange rind and orange juice and let sit overnight.

Mix oil and honey, add eggs and milk and stir well. Combine remaining ingredients and add to egg mixture. Fold drained raisins into batter.

Spoon into greased muffin tins and bake at 400 degrees F for 15 to 20 minutes.

Makes 24 muffins.

— *Jody Schwindt*
Burlington, Ontario

BUTTERMILK BRAN MUFFINS

1 cup bran
1 cup wheat germ
2 cups boiling water
1 cup oil
2 cups granulated or brown sugar
4 eggs, beaten

5 cups flour
5 tsp. baking soda
1½ Tbsp. salt
4 cups milk
4 cups bran flakes
1-1½ cups raisins

Stir together bran, wheat germ and boiling water. Set aside to cool.

Combine remaining ingredients and mix well. Stir in bran mixture. Let sit for 24 hours before using.

Spoon into well greased muffin tins and bake at 400 degrees F for 15 to 20 minutes. Batter will keep up to a week in the refrigerator.

Makes 4 to 5 dozen muffins.

— *Dawn Livingstone*
Georgetown, Ontario

DELICIOUS MUFFINS

¼ cup butter
½ cup brown sugar
¼ tsp. salt
¼ cup molasses
2 eggs
1 cup milk

½ tsp. baking soda
1 tsp. vanilla
1 cup flour
2 tsp. baking powder
1½ cups bran
2-3 Tbsp. wheat germ

Cream together butter, sugar, salt and molasses. Beat in eggs. Add milk, baking soda and vanilla. Mix slightly.

Sift flour and baking powder into creamed mixture, stirring only a little. Add bran and wheat germ. Mix only until all ingredients are moist.

Fill greased muffin tins three-quarters full. Bake at 325 to 350 degrees F for 20 to 25 minutes.

Makes 12 large muffins.

— *Donna Wallis*
Newcastle, Ontario

QUICK MUFFINS

4 eggs
1½ cups milk
¾ cup oil
1 tsp. orange juice
2 cups white flour

2 cups rye flour
1 cup sugar
2 Tbsp. baking powder
Salt
Cinnamon & nutmeg

Combine liquid ingredients well, add flours, sugar, baking powder, salt and spices and mix until just moist.

Bake in greased muffin tins at 400 degrees F for 20 minutes.

Makes 18 muffins.

— C. Majewski
Pansy, Manitoba

CORN MUFFINS

1 cup milk
1 egg
3 Tbsp. oil
¾ cup flour

1 Tbsp. baking powder
3 Tbsp. sugar
1¼ cups corn meal

Beat together milk, egg and oil. Sift together dry ingredients and stir into milk mixture until moist.

Pour into greased muffin tins and bake at 425 degrees F for 20 minutes.

Makes 12 muffins.

— Sheri Israels
West Vancouver, B.C.

CORN MEAL RAISIN MUFFINS

1 cup raisins
Boiling water
2 cups corn meal
3 cups buttermilk
2⅔ cups flour
2 tsp. baking powder

1 tsp. salt
2 tsp. baking soda
2 eggs
1 cup oil
1 cup honey

Scald raisins with boiling water and drain well. Combine corn meal and 2 cups buttermilk and set aside.

Mix together flour, baking powder, salt and baking soda. Beat eggs and add oil, honey and remaining 1 cup buttermilk. Add to corn-meal-buttermilk mixture and then to flour mixture. Add raisins.

Place in greased muffin tins and bake at 400 degrees F for 20 minutes.

Makes 24 muffins.

— Adella Bragg
New Denver, B.C.

CARROT PINEAPPLE MUFFINS

1½ cups flour
1 cup sugar
1 tsp. baking powder
1 tsp. baking soda
1 tsp. cinnamon
½ tsp. salt

⅔ cup salad oil
2 eggs
1 cup finely grated raw carrot
½ cup crushed pineapple, with juice
1 tsp. vanilla

Sift flour, sugar, baking powder, baking soda, cinnamon and salt together in large bowl. Add oil, eggs, carrot, pineapple and vanilla.

Blend on low speed until all is moist, then beat for 2 minutes at medium speed. Half fill greased muffin tins and bake at 350 degrees F for 25 minutes.

Makes 24 muffins.

— *Mrs. W. Atkins*
Agincourt, Ontario

WHEAT GERM MUFFINS

1 Tbsp. butter
¾ cup granulated sugar
1 egg
1 cup wheat germ

¾ cup whole wheat flour
¼ cup unbleached white flour
1 tsp. baking soda
1 cup buttermilk

Cream butter and sugar and add egg. Mix dry ingredients and add alternately with buttermilk to creamed mixture.

Pour into greased muffin tins and bake at 350 degrees F for 15 to 20 minutes.

Makes 12 muffins.

— *Audrey Moroso*
Puslinch, Ontario

ENERGY MUFFINS

2 cups finely grated carrots
1 cup chopped walnuts
¾ cup chopped dates
¾ cup raisins, softened in water & drained
3 cups flour
¼ cup soya flour
½ cup wheat germ
1 cup rolled oats
1 cup coconut
1 tsp. salt

3 tsp. baking powder
2 tsp. mace
2 tsp. cinnamon
1 tsp. nutmeg
3 eggs, beaten
½ cup safflower oil
½ cup honey
¼ cup molasses
2 cups milk or buttermilk

Combine carrots, walnuts, dates and raisins and set aside. Mix together in large bowl flours, wheat germ, oats, coconut, salt, baking powder, mace, cinnamon and nutmeg. Combine remaining ingredients.

Make a well in the centre of flour mixture and add liquid mixture gradually. If not moist enough, add a small amount of water. Add vegetable mixture and stir in.

Bake in greased muffin tins at 350 degrees F for 25 minutes.

Makes 3 dozen muffins.

— *Laura Poitras*
Kemptville, Ontario

FLAKY BISCUITS

1 cup whole wheat flour
1 cup unbleached white flour
1 Tbsp. baking powder
½ tsp. salt

½ cup butter
2 eggs, beaten
½ cup milk

Sift dry ingredients together. Cut in butter until mixture is the texture of small peas. Combine eggs and milk and add to the flour mixture, stirring until moistened.

Turn dough onto a floured board. Roll out to ½-inch thickness. Fold in thirds and roll out again. Repeat 5 times.

Cut into 2-inch rounds. Place on a lightly greased cookie sheet and bake at 400 degrees F for 8 to 10 minutes.

Makes 12 to 15 biscuits.

— Jan Post
West River Stn., N.S.

SCOTCH SODA SCONES

THESE SWEET SCONES ARE COOKED ON TOP OF THE STOVE RATHER THAN IN THE OVEN. Quickly assembled, they are especially delicious served warm with butter, fresh strawberries and whipped cream.

1½ cups flour
½ tsp. baking soda
½ tsp. cream of tartar
¼ cup granulated sugar

Salt
¼ cup lard
½ cup sour milk

? Try

Combine flour, baking soda, cream of tartar, sugar and a pinch of salt. Cut in lard until mixture resembles coarse meal. Add milk and mix with a fork until dough forms a ball.

Divide dough in half. Form each half into a ball, pat down and divide into quarters. Pat into biscuit shape.

Wipe heavy frying pan gently with lard. Fry biscuits on very low heat approximately 15 to 20 minutes per side, turning once.

Makes 8 biscuits.

— Donna Gordon
Dorval, Quebec

WHOLE WHEAT DILL BISCUITS

2 cups flour
1½ tsp. baking soda
1½ tsp. salt
2 tsp. chopped fresh dill

¼ cup butter
1 egg
⅓ cup light cream
Melted butter

Sift 1⅓ cups flour, baking soda and salt into a bowl. Add remaining ⅔ cup flour and dill. Cut butter into dry ingredients until it resembles coarse meal.

Lightly beat egg and add cream. Stir into flour mixture to form a smooth, soft dough.

Turn out onto a lightly floured board and knead for 30 seconds. Roll out to ½-inch thickness with 1½-inch round cutter.

Bake on lightly greased cookie sheets at 425 degrees F for 10 to 15 minutes. Remove and brush tops with melted butter.

Makes 24 biscuits.

— Katherine Dunster
Golden, B.C.

SESAME CHEESE STRIPS

¼ cup sesame seeds
1 cup flour
½ tsp. salt
½ tsp. sugar
½ tsp. ginger

1 cup grated Cheddar cheese
1 egg yolk, beaten
⅓ cup melted butter
1 Tbsp. water
½ tsp. Worcestershire sauce

Toast sesame seeds at 300 degrees F until golden, stirring often. Cool.

Sift flour, salt, sugar and ginger into bowl. Add cheese and sesame seeds and mix lightly with a fork. Combine egg yolk, butter, water and Worcestershire sauce. Add to flour mixture and stir lightly to blend. Shape dough into a ball and roll out to ⅛-inch thickness. Cut into strips.

Bake at 350 degrees F for 10 minutes.

Makes 4 dozen strips.

CHEESE SNAPS

1½ cups flour
½ tsp. salt
½ tsp. cayenne

¼ lb. Cheddar cheese, grated
¼ lb. butter
1-2 Tbsp. ice water, to moisten

Combine flour, salt, cayenne and cheese. Cut in butter until mixture resembles coarse meal. Add enough water to moisten dough to rolling consistency.

Roll to a ¼-inch thickness and cut into 1-inch strips. Mark 1-inch lengths on strips.

Bake at 375 degrees F for 10 minutes. When cool, cut into squares, following markings made before baking.

Makes 5 dozen cheese snaps.

— Stephanie James
Ruskin, B.C.

CHEESE CRISPS

½ cup butter, at room temperature
2 cups grated Swiss cheese

1½ cups flour
½ tsp. salt

Cream together butter and cheese. Add flour and salt and mix well. Form into 1-inch balls. Place on a cookie sheet and flatten with a floured fork.

Bake at 350 degrees F for 12 to 15 minutes, or until pale gold around edges.

Makes 5 dozen biscuits.

— Eileen Deeley
Kamloops, B.C.

CHAPATIS

THIS IS A THIN UNLEAVENED BREAD OF INDIAN ORIGIN.

4 cups flour
1 tsp. salt
3 Tbsp. melted butter
1-1⅔ cups warm water

Combine flour, salt and melted butter. Add enough water to make a dough that is soft but not wet. Knead for 10 minutes, divide into 24 pieces and roll each into a thin circle. Fry in oil until lightly browned on both sides. Serve warm with curried dishes.

Makes 24 chapatis.

CHALLAH

THIS TRADITIONAL JEWISH EGG BREAD CAN MAKE A BEAUTIFUL GIFT.

1½ cups milk
¼ cup sugar
3 tsp. salt
⅓ cup butter
3 eggs

2 pkgs. dry yeast
½ cup warm water
7½ cups flour
Poppy seeds

Combine milk, sugar, salt and butter. Heat until butter melts, then cool to lukewarm.

Beat eggs and reserve 3 Tbsp. for glazing. Soften yeast in the warm water in a large bowl. Stir in the eggs and milk mixture. Beat in 4 cups of the flour until smooth. Beat in enough of the remaining flour to make a smooth dough. Turn out and knead on floured surface until smooth and elastic — 15 minutes.

Place in a bowl, cover and let rise for 1½ hours. Punch down and let rise for another 30 minutes. Punch down and turn out onto board. Divide the dough into six equal portions. Form two braids and place them on two greased cookie sheets.

Let rise for one hour. Brush with the reserved egg, to which a tablespoon of water has been added. Sprinkle with poppy seeds.

Bake at 350 degrees F for 30 minutes.

Makes 2 braids.

— Ruth E. Geddes
Camden East, Ontario

CRUSTY FRENCH BREAD

1 heaping Tbsp. butter
1 heaping Tbsp. salt
1 heaping Tbsp. sugar
2 cups boiling water
1 Tbsp. dry yeast

⅔ cup lukewarm water
1 tsp. sugar
6-6½ cups unbleached white flour
Yellow corn meal

In a large mixing bowl, combine the butter, salt, sugar and boiling water. Stir as it dissolves.

Sprinkle the yeast over the ⅔ cup lukewarm water and 1 tsp. sugar. Let rest 10 to 15 minutes in a warm, but turned-off, oven.

When the butter mixture is lukewarm, add yeast mixture and mix well. Start adding the flour, one cup at a time, mixing well after each addition. When 4 cups have been added, beat vigorously for about 10 minutes with a wooden spoon. Gradually add remaining flour. When it becomes too stiff to mix with the spoon, turn out onto a floured board and knead, adding flour as necessary, until it is satiny smooth and very elastic.

Form into a ball, put it in a large greased bowl, cover and let rise until doubled in size — 1½ hours. Punch it down and let rise again until doubled — about 1 hour.

Prepare the baking sheet by buttering it and sprinkling yellow corn meal lightly over the butter.

Divide the dough into 3 parts and shape into very long, very slender loaves as follows. Roll each part into a rectangle about 14 to 15 inches long and 8 to 10 inches wide. Roll up the long side of the rectangle tightly until it is a narrow, even loaf about 1½ inches wide. Seal the seam and the ends by pinching, and place on the baking sheet. Cover and let rise until double in size. Brush tops of the loaves with cold water. Bake at 375 degrees F for about 1 hour, brushing with cold water every 15 or 20 minutes.

Makes 3 loaves.

— Nicole Chartrand
Aylmer, Quebec

THE BEST CHEESE BREAD

7-8 cups flour
⅓ cup honey
1 Tbsp. salt
2 Tbsp. yeast

2 cups water
⅔ cup milk
3 cups grated old Cheddar cheese

In large warm bowl, mix together 2 cups flour, honey, salt and yeast.

Combine water and milk in a saucepan and heat to 120 to 130 degrees F.

Gradually add liquid to yeast mixture and beat for 2 minutes. Add grated cheese and ½ cup flour, beating until smooth. Gradually stir in enough of the remaining flour to make a stiff dough.

Turn onto a floured board, knead for 10 minutes and form into a ball. Place in a greased bowl and cover with wax paper and a damp tea towel. Place in an oven that has been heated by a pan of hot water and let rise for 1½ hours. Punch down and let rest for 10 minutes.

Shape dough into 3 equal-sized loaves and place in greased loaf pans, cover with wax paper and let rise for 1 hour. Bake at 375 degrees F for 40 minutes.

Makes 3 loaves.

— Anne Millage
Lakefield, Ontario

HEALTH BREAD

2½ cups scalded milk
½ cup oil
½ cup molasses
4 tsp. salt
1 cup rolled oats
½ cup sesame seeds

1 cup wheat germ
2 Tbsp. yeast
2 Tbsp. brown sugar
1½ cups warm water
5-7 cups unbleached white flour
3-5 cups whole wheat flour

Combine scalded milk, oil, molasses and salt. Mix together rolled oats, sesame seeds and wheat germ. Pour scalded milk mixture over rolled oats mixture.

Dissolve yeast and brown sugar in warm water. When milk-oats mixture has cooled to lukewarm, add yeast to it. Stir in flour and knead into a soft dough.

Let rise in a warm place for 1 hour. Punch down and place dough in 3 greased loaf pans. Let rise for 1 to 1¼ hours. Bake at 350 degrees F for 45 to 60 minutes.

Makes 3 loaves.

— Carol Frost
Chilliwack, B.C.

HERB LOAF

2 Tbsp. sugar
2 pkgs. dry yeast
2 cups warm water
2 tsp. salt

2 Tbsp. butter
½ cup & 1 Tbsp. grated Parmesan cheese
4½ cups flour
1½ Tbsp. dried oregano

Dissolve sugar and yeast in warm water in a large bowl. Add salt, butter, ½ cup cheese, 3 cups flour and oregano. Beat on low speed of electric mixer until blended, then on medium speed for 2 minutes. Add balance of flour by hand until well blended.

Cover and let rise for 45 minutes. Stir down and beat for 30 seconds. Turn into greased 1½-quart casserole dish, sprinkle with 1 Tbsp. Parmesan cheese and bake at 375 degrees F for 55 minutes.

Makes 1 loaf.

— Shirley Hill
Picton, Ontario

OLD-FASHIONED HONEY WHEAT BREAD

1½ cups water
1 cup cream-style cottage cheese
½ cup honey
¼ cup butter
2 cups unbleached white flour

2 Tbsp. brown sugar
3 tsp. salt
2 pkgs. yeast
1 egg, beaten
5½-6 cups whole wheat flour

Heat water, cottage cheese, honey and butter until very warm — 120 to 130 degrees F. Combine with white flour, sugar, salt, yeast and egg and beat for 2 minutes with electric mixer at medium speed. Stir in remaining flour by hand to make a stiff dough.

Knead well and place in a greased bowl. Cover and let rise 45 to 60 minutes — until double in size.

Punch down dough, divide into 2 pieces, shape and place in greased loaf pans. Let rise again for 45 to 60 minutes. Bake at 350 degrees F for 40 to 50 minutes.

Makes 2 loaves.

— *Laura Poitras*
Kemptville, Ontario

RICHARD'S RAISIN BREAD

1 cup warm water
3 Tbsp. yeast
1 tsp. sugar
4 cups sour milk
⅔ cup oil
4 eggs, beaten
2 cups sugar

2 tsp. salt
3½ cups raisins
1 cup cracked wheat
1 cup soya flour
9 cups whole wheat flour
4½ cups unbleached white flour

In large bowl, combine water, yeast and 1 tsp. sugar and let stand for 5 minutes. Add sour milk, oil, eggs, sugar and salt to yeast mixture and stir gently. Add raisins. Gradually add flour, beating well after each addition.

When dough is thick enough to knead, turn onto lightly floured board. Keep adding flour, kneading well after each addition, until smooth and elastic.

Place in bowl, cover and let rise in a warm place for 30 minutes or until almost doubled. Punch down, divide into 4 equal parts and place in greased loaf pans. Let rise until double — about 1 hour. Bake at 350 degrees F for 45 to 55 minutes.

Makes 4 loaves.

— *Richard Domsy*
Ruthren, Ontario

SWEDISH RYE BREAD

½ cup water
¼ cup butter
¼ cup brown sugar
2 tsp. salt
1 Tbsp. caraway seeds
1 Tbsp. dry yeast

1 tsp. sugar
½ cup lukewarm water
1½ cups buttermilk
2 cups rye flour
4-6 cups unbleached white flour

Boil together ½ cup water, butter, brown sugar, salt and caraway seeds for 5 minutes. Let cool.

Combine yeast, sugar and warm water and let sit for 10 minutes. Add to boiled mixture along with buttermilk. Add rye flour and mix well. Add white flour until dough is stiff enough to be turned onto floured board.

Knead for 10 minutes, place in bowl, cover and let rise until doubled. Form into 2 round loaves on cookie sheet and let rise until doubled. Bake at 400 degrees F for 25 minutes.

Makes 2 loaves.

— *Judy Wuest*
Cross Creek, N.B.

SPROUTED EIGHT-GRAIN BREAD

6 cups whole wheat kernels
2½ cups assorted whole grains (1 cup
   whole rye & ¼ cup each whole corn,
   brown rice, soy beans, barley, millet &
   rolled oats)
¼ cup honey

1½ Tbsp. baker's yeast
¼ cup gluten flour
½ cup raisins blended with ¼ cup water
1 tsp. salt
½ cup oil

Soak grains, except oats, overnight. Rinse and drain. Return grains to bowl, cover, and let sit for 24 hours. Rinse and drain well again. Continue this until kernels of whole wheat are just starting to sprout — about 3 days.

Grind the sprouting grains very finely. Add remaining ingredients and knead for about 10 minutes. Place in a bowl, cover and let rise until double — about 1 hour.

Divide into 4 pieces, place in greased loaf pans and let rise until doubled. Bake at 350 degrees F for 35 to 40 minutes.

Makes 4 loaves.

— *David Slabotsky*
Richmond, P.E.I.

SUNFLOWER WHEAT GERM BREAD

4 Tbsp. dry yeast
¾ cup warm water
4 Tbsp. honey
1¼ cups milk

4½-5 cups flour
2 tsp. salt
½ cup wheat germ
½ cup sunflower seeds

Dissolve yeast in warm water and add honey. Stir and let sit for 10 minutes. Add milk and stir. Stir in flour one cup at a time until dough can be kneaded. Work in salt.

Knead dough in bowl for 2 minutes or until smooth and elastic. Knead in wheat germ and sunflower seeds and continue to knead for 5 minutes.

Cover with a damp towel and let rise in a warm spot until double — about 1 hour. Punch down, knead for a minute and let rest for 5 to 10 minutes.

Line 2 loaf pans with foil and grease lightly. Shape dough into 2 loaves and place in pans. Let rise, uncovered, until double. Bake at 375 degrees F for 30 to 45 minutes. Cover with foil after 10 minutes to prevent over-browning.

Makes 2 loaves.

— *Cheryl Suckling*
Athens, Georgia

CRACKED WHEAT BREAD

1 tsp. sugar
1 cup warm water
2 pkgs. yeast
2 cups scalded milk
¼ cup butter

¼ cup sugar
1 Tbsp. salt
2 cups cracked wheat
2 cups cold water
9-10 cups flour

Dissolve 1 tsp. sugar in warm water and add yeast. Let stand for 10 minutes.

To hot milk, add butter, ¼ cup sugar, salt, cracked wheat and cold water. Stir yeast liquid and add milk mixture to it. Add approximately 4 cups flour and beat in. Mix in additional flour until dough leaves sides of bowl — about 5 cups.

Turn dough onto floured counter and knead. Place in greased bowl, cover and let rise until doubled. Punch down, turn out onto floured counter and cut into 4 equal pieces. Round each piece, cover and let rest for 10 minutes.

Shape into 4 loaves and place in greased loaf pans. Brush with melted butter, cover and let rise until dough is higher than pan edge. Bake at 400 degrees F for 35 to 40 minutes.

Makes 4 loaves.

— *Cecilia Roy*
Merrickville, Ontario

FINNISH COFFEE BRAID

THIS MOIST COFFEE BREAD, RICH ENOUGH TO SERVE WITHOUT BUTTER, WAS invented by the contributor's grandmother.

2 Tbsp. yeast
½ cup warm water
½ tsp. sugar
1 cup warm milk
1 cup warm water
1 tsp. crushed cardamom

8 cups flour
1½ cups sugar
1 tsp. salt
3 eggs
¼ cup melted butter

Combine yeast, water and ½ tsp. sugar. Let stand for 10 minutes. Stir in warm milk, warm water, cardamom and 2½ cups flour. Let stand until foamy – 2 to 2½ hours.

In another dish, combine 1½ cups sugar, salt, eggs and melted butter. Add to yeast-flour mixture and mix well. Add 5½ cups flour. Let rise until double in bulk and punch down.

Form dough into 12 round strips, 2 inches in diameter. Work into 4 braids and place in loaf pans. Let rise until double. Brush tops with a mixture of egg and milk and sprinkle with sugar.

Bake at 350 degrees F for 35 minutes, or until golden brown.

Makes 4 loaves.

— A.E. Koivu
Thunder Bay, Ontario

ORANGE BREAD

2 tsp. yeast
¼ cup water
Grated rind of 1 orange
¾ cup orange juice
3 Tbsp. honey

½ cup cooked soy grits
½ cup tofu
2 Tbsp. oil
2 cups flour

Dissolve yeast in water. Heat together orange rind, orange juice and 1 Tbsp. honey and simmer for 5 minutes. Stir in soy grits and remove from heat.

Cream tofu and 2 Tbsp. honey until well blended. Add orange juice mixture and yeast and mix well. Stir in oil and flour. Pour into a greased loaf pan and let rise for 1 hour. Bake at 350 degrees F for 45 to 60 minutes.

— Sheri Nelson
Horsefly. B.C.

CARAWAY SEED BREAD

1½ tsp. dry yeast
¼ cup warm water
1½ cups hot water
¼ cup brown sugar
¼ cup molasses

1 Tbsp. salt
2 Tbsp. shortening
3 Tbsp. caraway seeds
2½ cups medium rye flour
3½-4 cups unbleached white flour

Combine yeast and warm water and let sit for 10 minutes. In a large bowl, mix hot water, sugar, molasses, salt and shortening. Stir in yeast mixture and caraway seeds. Add flours, mix well, cover and let rest for 10 minutes.

Knead dough for 5 to 10 minutes or until elastic. Let rise in a covered bowl in a warm spot for 1½ to 2 hours. Punch down and divide into 2 balls. Flatten balls on a greased cookie sheet and let rise 1 to 1½ hours. Bake at 375 degrees F for 30 minutes.

Makes 2 loaves.

— Lynne Hawkes
Sackville, N.B.

ROSEMARY BREAD

7⅓ cups unbleached white flour
2 Tbsp. rosemary leaves
1 Tbsp. salt

4 tsp. dry yeast
1 Tbsp. soft butter
2½ cups hot water

Mix together 2⅓ cups flour, rosemary, salt and yeast. Add butter and hot water. Beat for 2 minutes on medium speed of electric mixer. Mix in 1 cup flour by hand, then beat with electric mixer on high speed for 2 minutes. Add 3 to 4 cups flour, mixing with a spoon. Let rise for 1 hour in bowl.

Divide dough into 6 pieces. Roll into 6 ropes of equal length and make 2 braids. Let rise for 1 hour on a greased cookie sheet. Bake at 450 degrees F for 25 minutes.

Makes 2 braids.

— *Lynne Hawkes*
Sackville, N.B.

YOGURT GRANOLA BREAD

2 tsp. honey
2 cups warm water
2 Tbsp. yeast
¾ cup plain yogurt
¼ cup honey

¼ cup oil
1 Tbsp. salt
4½-6 cups unbleached flour
2 cups granola

Dissolve 2 tsp. honey in warm water. Sprinkle yeast into water and let stand for 10 minutes. Add yogurt, ¼ cup honey, oil, salt and 3 cups of flour and beat with an electric mixer for 2 minutes. Add granola and mix well. Gradually add the rest of the flour.

Cover and let rise for 1 hour until doubled. Punch down and divide into 2 greased loaf pans. Let rise for 45 minutes, then bake at 375 degrees F for 45 minutes.

— *Mary Giesz*
Winfield, B.C.

MILLIE TAYLOR'S WHOLE WHEAT SUNFLOWER BREAD

2 tsp. honey
½ cup lukewarm water
1 heaping Tbsp. yeast
2 cups milk
⅓ cup honey
5 tsp. salt

⅓ cup oil
2 cups cold water
2 eggs
10-16 cups whole wheat flour
1 cup sunflower seeds

Combine honey and lukewarm water and add yeast. Let sit for 15 minutes.

Scald milk and add honey, salt, oil, cold water and eggs. Let cool to lukewarm, then add yeast and stir.

Add 10 to 13 cups of flour and sunflower seeds. Stir and knead, working in 2 additional cups of flour, until dough is smooth.

Place dough in large bowl, coat with oil, cover and let rise until doubled. Punch down and divide dough into 5 equal parts. Cover with dish towel and let sit for 15 minutes.

Shape into loaves and place in greased pans. Cover and let rise until doubled. Bake at 400 degrees F for 20 minutes, reduce heat to 350 degrees for another 20 minutes. Turn out of pans to cool.

Makes 5 loaves.

— *Paddy & Daryl Taylor*
Estevan, Sask.

ANADAMA HEALTH BREAD

2 cups water
1 cup milk
1 cup corn meal
1 cup unflavoured yogurt
4 Tbsp. shortening
1 cup molasses
3 tsp. salt
2 envelopes yeast

1 cup lukewarm water
1 tsp. sugar
1 cup wheat germ
1 cup rolled oats
1 cup granola
4½ cups whole wheat flour
4½ cups unbleached white flour

Heat water and milk until boiling. Gradually add corn meal, stirring constantly. Allow to thicken slightly, remove from heat and add yogurt, shortening, molasses and salt, stirring until blended. Cool to lukewarm.

Soften yeast in lukewarm water with sugar. Allow to sit for 10 minutes.

In a large bowl, combine corn meal mixture with yeast mixture. Add wheat germ, oats and granola, beating after each addition. Add whole wheat flour and stir until blended. Add white flour gradually and turn onto floured bread board. Knead for 10 minutes then form dough into a large ball, place in a greased bowl, cover and let rise until double. Punch down and divide into 5 pieces. Shape into balls and let rise for 10 minutes.

Shape into loaves and place in greased loaf pans, brush tops with melted butter, cover and let rise again. Bake at 375 degrees F for 45 minutes.

Makes 5 loaves.

— Sandra Lloyd
North Vancouver, B.C.

WHOLE WHEAT BREAD

3 Tbsp. yeast
1 Tbsp. honey
1½ cups warm water
7½ cups hot water
1-2 cups powdered milk
½ cup vegetable oil

½ cup molasses
1½ Tbsp. salt
3 cups rolled oats
10 cups whole wheat flour
10-12 cups unbleached white flour

Dissolve yeast and honey in 1½ cups water and let sit for 10 minutes.

Combine 7½ cups water and milk powder in bowl and stir to dissolve. Add oil, molasses and salt and stir to dissolve. Stir in oats, then stir mixture into yeast combination. Add whole wheat flour 3 cups at a time, stirring well after each addition. Add white flour until dough is stiff enough to turn onto a lightly floured bread board.

Knead flour into dough until it is bouncy and no longer sticky. Place in a large bowl, cover and let rise in a warm spot for 1 hour, or until doubled. Punch down, let rest 10 minutes and divide into 6 parts.

Knead each piece lightly, roll out to form an 8" x 11" rectangle and roll up like a jelly roll. Pinch seam closed. With seam-side down, tuck ends under and place in an oiled loaf pan.

Cover and let rise in a warm spot until double. Bake at 375 degrees F for 30 minutes, or until pans sound hollow when rapped on the bottom. Remove from pans to cool.

Makes 6 loaves.

— Susan Burke
Appin, Ontario

UKRAINIAN EASTER BREAD

2 pkgs. yeast
2 cups milk, scalded & cooled to lukewarm
8 cups flour
5 egg yolks, beaten

1 cup sugar
½ cup melted butter
1 cup currants
1 Tbsp. vanilla

Dissolve yeast in milk, add 3 cups flour and let stand in a warm place overnight.

In the morning, add egg yolks, sugar, butter, currants, vanilla and enough flour to make a light dough. Let rise until doubled.

Turn onto a floured board and knead well, adding flour if necessary. Shape into 2 loaves and place in greased loaf pans. Let rise until doubled. Bake at 400 degrees F for 10 minutes, reduce heat to 350 degrees F and bake for 50 minutes.

Makes 2 loaves.

— Donna Petryshyn
Westlock, Alberta

SWEET DOUGH CINNAMON ROLLS

1½ cups milk
½ cup butter
1 pkg. yeast
1 tsp. sugar
3 eggs
1 cup sugar
½ cup sour cream

½ tsp. salt
4-5 cups flour
Oil
Brown sugar
Raisins
Nuts
Cinnamon

Warm milk, add butter and dissolve yeast and 1 tsp. sugar in it. Beat eggs, add remaining sugar, sour cream and yeast-milk mixture and blend well. Add salt and enough flour to make a manageable dough.

Knead well, place in a large bowl and let rise until double.

Roll out to a ¼-inch thick circle and spread with oil and desired fillings. Cut circle into pie-shaped pieces and roll up from wide end to form crescents. Place on cookie sheets and let rise. Bake at 325 degrees F for 15 to 25 minutes.

Makes 12 rolls.

— Irene Simonson
Seeleys Bay, Ontario

ONION ROLLS

4½ cups warm water
1 cup powdered milk
4 Tbsp. sugar
4 Tbsp. oil
2 Tbsp. mustard

2 tsp. salt
2 eggs
1 onion, finely chopped
5-8 cups flour
2 Tbsp. yeast

Combine water, powdered milk, sugar, oil, mustard, salt, eggs and onion and mix well.

In large bowl, combine 5 cups flour and yeast. Add warm water mixture and beat well with mixer until smooth. Add enough flour to make a stiff dough. Knead until smooth and elastic. Place in a greased bowl, and let rise until doubled in bulk. Punch down.

Shape into rolls, place on greased cookie sheets, cover and let rise again until double. Bake at 350 degrees F for 20 to 30 minutes.

Makes 3 dozen rolls.

— Marion Destaunis
Calumet, Quebec

PITA BREAD

THIS MIDDLE EASTERN BREAD FORMS A POCKET IN THE CENTRE AS IT BAKES, WHICH can be split open and filled for sandwiches.

2¼-2¾ cups lukewarm water
2 pkgs. dry yeast
Pinch sugar
8 cups flour

2 tsp. salt
¼ cup olive oil
1 cup corn meal or flour

Pour ¼ cup of water into a small bowl and sprinkle with yeast and sugar. Let rest 2 to 3 minutes, then stir to dissolve completely. Set bowl in warm place for 5 minutes or until mixture has doubled in volume.

Combine flour and salt, make a well in the centre and pour in the yeast mixture, oil and 2 cups of lukewarm water.

Gently stir until well combined. Add up to ½ cup more water until dough forms a ball. Knead for 20 minutes, then let rise 45 minutes or until doubled.

Punch down and divide into 8 pieces. Roll into balls and let rest for 30 minutes.

Sprinkle 2 cookie sheets with corn meal or flour. Roll balls into round, flat loaves about 8 inches in diameter and ⅛-inch thick. Arrange 2 to 3 inches apart on sheets and let rise 30 minutes longer.

Bake at 500 degrees F for about 10 minutes until they are brown and puffy in the centre.

Makes 8.

— *Nina Kenzie*
Homer, Alaska

DINNER ROLLS

2 Tbsp. yeast
½ cup warm water
1 tsp. sugar
3 eggs

½ cup oil
2 tsp. salt
2-3 cups warm water
7½-8 cups flour

Dissolve yeast and sugar in ½ cup warm water. Mix together eggs, oil, salt and warm water. Add yeast and enough flour to make dough soft.

Allow dough to double, punch down and allow to rise again. Shape into rolls and let rise until doubled. Bake at 375 degrees F for 15 minutes.

— *Delia Schlesinger*
Calgary, Alberta

VIENNA COFFEE CAKE

¼ cup lukewarm water
1 pkg. dry yeast
½ tsp. granulated sugar
1 cup milk
½ cup white sugar
¼ cup butter
Salt

1 egg
3 cups flour
⅓ cup sugar
¼ tsp. cinnamon
¼ cup chopped walnuts

Combine water, yeast and ½ tsp. sugar and let sit for 10 minutes. Scald milk and add ½ cup sugar, butter and pinch of salt. Cool to lukewarm and add to yeast mixture. Mix well. Add egg and 1 cup flour and beat well. Add remaining flour and beat for 3 minutes. Place in a greased tube pan.

Combine ⅓ cup sugar, cinnamon and nuts and sprinkle over cake. Let rise in a warm place until doubled in bulk. Bake at 375 degrees F for 35 minutes.

— *Dorothy Hett*
Kitchener, Ontario

SPICY YOGURT RAISIN CAKE

½ cup butter
1 cup granulated sugar
3 eggs
2 cups flour
2 tsp. baking powder
1 tsp. salt
1 cup unflavoured yogurt

1 tsp. baking soda
1 tsp. vanilla
¾ cup raisins
1 tsp. cinnamon
½ tsp. nutmeg
¼ tsp. cloves
½ cup chopped walnuts

Cream butter and sugar together. Add eggs one at a time, beating well after each addition.

Sift flour with baking powder and salt and add gradually to butter mixture. Combine yogurt and baking soda and add to butter a few tablespoons at a time, along with the vanilla.

Combine raisins, spices and walnuts. Pour half the batter into a 9-inch square pan. Sprinkle raisin mixture over top and pour on remaining batter.

Bake at 350 degrees F for 40 minutes.

— *Christine Ferris*
Lasqueti Island, B.C.

COFFEE CAKE

THIS DESSERT IS SERVED DAILY IN THE BELL TELEPHONE CAFETERIA AT THE HEAD office in Toronto. My aunt, an employee, requested the recipe, and the chef scaled it down to household proportions.

½ cup butter
1¼ cups sugar
2 eggs
1 tsp. baking soda
1 cup sour cream
1½ cups flour (half whole wheat)

½ tsp. salt
1½ tsp. baking powder
1 tsp. vanilla
1 Tbsp. cinnamon
2 Tbsp. chopped nuts

Cream butter. Add 1 cup sugar gradually, creaming well. Add eggs one at a time, beating until light after each. Stir baking soda into the sour cream. Sift together flour, salt and baking powder. Add sour cream and flour mixtures alternately to the creamed mixture, beating well. Stir in vanilla.

For topping, mix together the ¼ cup sugar, cinnamon and nuts. Spoon half the batter into an 8-inch square pan. Sprinkle with half the topping. Smooth on the remaining batter, then sprinkle on the rest of the topping. Bake at 350 degrees F for 45 minutes. Serve warm.

— *Merilyn Mohr*
Astorville, Ontario

FRESH RASPBERRY CAKE

½ cup butter
¾ cup honey
2 eggs, well beaten
2 cups unbleached flour

¼ tsp. salt
2 tsp. baking powder
2 Tbsp. milk or cream
1 cup fresh raspberries

Cream butter and honey. Add eggs and mix until light and fluffy. Sift together dry ingredients and add to creamed mixture alternately with milk. Fold in berries.

Bake in a greased and floured 8-inch square pan at 350 degrees F for 40 to 50 minutes. Serve with whipped cream or ice cream.

— *Mary Giesz*
Winfield, B.C.

RHUBARB CAKE

2½ cups flour
¼ tsp. salt
1 tsp. baking powder
½ cup butter
1 egg

1½ cups sugar
4 cups cooked chopped rhubarb
½ cup melted butter
2 eggs, beaten

Combine 2 cups flour, salt and baking powder. Cut in butter until mixture is crumbly, then stir in 1 egg. Reserve 1 cup of mixture for topping and flatten remainder in greased 8-inch square pan.

Mix together remaining ½ cup flour, sugar, rhubarb, butter and beaten eggs. Pour into pan and top with reserved pastry.

Bake at 350 degrees F for 1 hour.

— Marie Sadoway
Saskatoon, Sask.

APPLE SPICE CAKE

3 cups flour
1½ cups sugar
1½ tsp. baking soda
½ tsp. salt
1 tsp. cinnamon
½ tsp. allspice
½ tsp. cloves

¾ cup shortening
1½ cups apple sauce
2 eggs
1 tsp. vanilla
1 cup raisins
½ cup chopped walnuts

Sift flour, sugar, baking soda, salt, cinnamon, allspice and cloves into a large bowl. Add shortening and apple sauce. Beat with electric mixer on medium speed for 2 minutes. Add eggs and vanilla and beat for 1 more minute. Stir in raisins and nuts and blend well.

Pour into greased and floured tube pan. Bake at 350 degrees F for 70 minutes. Cool in pan for 10 minutes, loosen with a knife and turn onto wire rack to finish cooling.

PUMPKIN SPICE CAKE

1¾ cups ground pumpkin flesh
2 cups flour
6 tsp. baking powder
1½ tsp. salt
2 tsp. cinnamon
1 tsp. ginger

½ tsp. nutmeg
¼ tsp. cloves
⅔ cup shortening
1½ cups honey
4 eggs
2 tsp. vanilla

ICE WITH
CREAM CHEESE ICING

Combine pumpkin, flour, baking powder, salt, cinnamon, ginger, nutmeg and cloves and mix well.

Cream shortening, honey, eggs and vanilla. Add flour mixture and mix well.

Bake at 350 degrees F in a 9" x 13" pan for 50 to 60 minutes.

MOVE RACK UP 1 NOTCH FROM CENTER

— Wayne Gochee
Vermilion, Alberta

OLD-FASHIONED RAISIN CAKE

1 cup brown sugar
1 cup & 3 Tbsp. water
2 cups raisins
½ tsp. salt
1 tsp. cinnamon
½ tsp. ground cloves

¼ tsp. mace
¼ tsp. nutmeg
⅓ cup shortening
2 cups flour
1 tsp. baking soda
½ tsp. baking powder

Place sugar, water, raisins, salt and spices in a pan and bring to a boil. Cool. Stir in shortening and remaining ingredients.

Pour batter into greased and floured 9-inch square pan. Bake at 325 degrees F for 1 hour or until top springs back when touched.

— Patty Robinson
Colville, Washington

CARROT CAKE

3 cups flour
2 tsp. baking soda
1½ tsp. baking powder
2 tsp. cinnamon
1 cup honey

1 cup oil
4 eggs
2 cups grated carrot
1 cup raisins or chopped nuts

Measure flour, baking soda, baking powder and cinnamon into bowl. Stir and add honey, oil and eggs. Beat hard by hand for 1 minute. Add carrot and nuts or raisins and beat to mix.

Pour into greased 9" x 13" pan and bake at 350 degrees F for 35 minutes.

— Lynn Hill
Ilderton, Ontario

POPPY SEED CAKE

¼ cup poppy seeds
1 cup buttermilk
1 cup butter
1½ cups brown sugar
4 eggs, separated
1 tsp. vanilla

2½ cups flour
2 tsp. baking powder
1 tsp. baking soda
½ tsp. salt
4 tsp. brown sugar
3 tsp. cinnamon

Soak poppy seeds in buttermilk for 20 minutes. Cream butter and 1½ cups sugar, then mix in egg yolks and vanilla.

Sift together flour, baking powder, baking soda and salt. Add flour mixture and buttermilk mixture alternately to creamed ingredients. Fold in stiffly beaten egg whites.

Pour half of batter into greased tube pan. Combine 4 tsp. brown sugar with cinnamon and sprinkle half on batter. Repeat. Bake at 350 degrees F for 45 to 50 minutes.

— Donna Blair
Victoria, B.C.

DATE OATMEAL CAKE

THIS SPICY SNACKING CAKE IS SO RICH AND MOIST THAT THERE IS NO NEED FOR ICING.

½ cup flour
1 tsp. baking soda
1 tsp. cinnamon
1 tsp. cloves
1 cup boiling water
2 cups rolled oats

¾ cup butter
2 cups brown sugar
2 eggs
1½ cups finely chopped dates
1 cup chopped walnuts

Sift together flour, baking soda, cinnamon and cloves into a large bowl.

Pour boiling water over oats, mix well, cool slightly and blend in remaining ingredients.

Pour oatmeal mixture into dry ingredients and mix well. Bake in an 8-inch square pan at 350 degrees F for 45 minutes.

— *Margaret Butler*
Newcastle, Ontario

PRINCESS ELIZABETH CAKE

1 cup boiling water
1 cup chopped dates
1 cup brown sugar
½ cup butter
1 egg
1½ cups flour
1 tsp. baking powder
1 tsp. baking soda

Salt
1 tsp. vanilla
5 Tbsp. brown sugar
1 Tbsp. butter
3 Tbsp. cream
½ cup coconut
¾ cup chopped walnuts

Pour boiling water over dates. Add 1 cup brown sugar, ½ cup butter and egg. Mix well and let cool. Add flour, baking powder, baking soda, salt and vanilla. Mix well, place in greased 8-inch square pan and bake at 350 degrees F for 5 minutes.

Meanwhile, combine remaining ingredients in a saucepan and bring to a boil. Spread topping over cake, return to oven and bake for 30 to 40 minutes.

— *Eileen Caldwell*
Newburgh, Ontario

WHITE CAKE

2¼ cups flour
4 tsp. baking powder
¾ tsp. salt
1½ cups granulated sugar

½ cup shortening
1 cup milk
1 tsp. salt
3 eggs

Sift together flour, baking powder, salt and sugar. Add shortening, ¾ cup milk and salt. Beat for 1 minute, then add ¼ cup milk and eggs. Beat for 2 more minutes.

Pour into 2 greased 8-inch round pans and bake at 350 degrees F for 35 to 40 minutes or until cake springs back when lightly touched.

— *Shirley Morrish*
Devlin, Ontario

CHOCOLATE BUTTERMILK CAKE

1⅔ cups flour
1 cup sugar
½ cup cocoa
1 tsp. baking soda

½ tsp. salt
1 cup buttermilk
½ cup melted shortening
1½ tsp. vanilla

Mix together flour, sugar, cocoa, baking soda and salt. Beat in buttermilk, shortening and vanilla. Stir until smooth.

Spread into a greased 9" x 13" pan and bake at 375 degrees F for 30 minutes.

— *Ruby McDonald*
Oshawa, Ontario

MARMORKUCHEN

THIS GERMAN MARBLE CAKE MAKES AN EYE-CATCHING DESSERT. FOR ADDED appeal, cocoa icing, page 273, may be dribbled over the top while the cake is still warm.

1½ cups granulated sugar
1 cup unsalted butter
6 eggs, separated
1½ cups flour

1½ tsp. baking powder
Grated rind & juice of 1 lemon
¾ cup cocoa powder

Cream butter and sugar until smooth. Beat in egg yolks.

Mix flour and baking powder and add slowly to creamed mixture. Add lemon rind and juice. Beat egg whites until stiff. Fold into cake mixture until just blended.

Divide dough in half. Add cocoa to one half and leave the other half white.

In the bottom of a greased bundt pan, place blobs of some of the chocolate batter then fill in the gaps with white batter. Continue alternating chocolate and white until all the batter is used up.

Bake at 350 degrees F for 45 minutes.

— *Kris Brown*
Strathroy, Ontario

GRANDMA'S POUND CAKE

2 cups flour
1 cup butter
1⅔ cups granulated sugar

5 large eggs
1 tsp. almond extract

Sift flour, measure and then sift 5 times. Cream butter until frothy and pale, then add sugar gradually and mix until fluffy. Add eggs, one at a time, beating after each addition until well blended. After last egg is added, beat for 5 minutes. Fold in flour slowly by hand. Add almond extract and pour into a well greased tube pan.

Bake at 300 degrees F for 1½ hours.

— *Mrs. R. F. Kempf*
Burlington, Ontario

CHOCOLATE ZUCCHINI CAKE

2½ cups flour
½ cup cocoa
2½ tsp. baking powder
1½ tsp. baking soda
1 tsp. salt
1 tsp. cinnamon
¾ cup butter
2 cups sugar

3 eggs
2½ tsp. grated orange rind
2 tsp. vanilla
2 cups grated zucchini
½ cup milk
1 cup ground nuts
¾ cup icing sugar, sifted
1 Tbsp. orange juice

Combine flour, cocoa, baking powder, baking soda, salt and cinnamon.

In a large bowl, combine butter and sugar, then beat in eggs. Stir in 2 tsp. orange rind, vanilla and zucchini.

Stir in dry ingredients, alternating with milk and nuts. Pour into greased bundt pan and bake at 350 degrees F for 1 hour.

Combine icing sugar with orange juice and ½ tsp. orange rind and spread over warm cake.

— Elizabeth Eder
Baltimore, Maryland

WACKY CAKE

THE SIMPLICITY OF THIS CAKE IS HARD TO BEAT. IT IS ASSEMBLED IN THE BAKING PAN and contains no eggs, yet produces a moist cake with a delicious chocolate flavour.

Try

1½ cups flour
1 tsp. baking powder
1 cup granulated sugar
½ tsp. cinnamon
1 tsp. baking soda
½ tsp. salt

3 Tbsp. cocoa
1 tsp. vanilla
1 Tbsp. vinegar
5 Tbsp. melted butter
1 cup lukewarm water

Combine dry ingredients in an 8-inch square pan. Add remaining ingredients, mix well and bake at 350 degrees F for 30 minutes.

— Sharon Steele
Burns Lake, B.C.

CREAM CHEESE ICING

8 oz. cream cheese
4 Tbsp. butter
3½ cups icing sugar

Salt
2 tsp. vanilla

Cream cheese with a fork, blend in butter, add sugar and salt, mix until smooth and spread.

— Cary Elizabeth Marshall
Thunder Bay, Ontario

BUTTER ICING

½ cup soft butter
1 cup less 2 Tbsp. sifted icing sugar
¼ cup cold milk

¼ cup boiling water
1 tsp. vanilla

Cream butter and add sugar. Beat until thick and creamy. Add milk and blend. Gradually beat in hot water, then add vanilla.

— Catherine Rupke
Kettleby, Ontario

LEMON HONEY FROSTING

½ cup butter
½ cup honey
8 oz. cream cheese

1 tsp. vanilla
2 Tbsp. lemon juice
2 cups instant milk powder

Cream the butter and add honey and cream cheese. Beat until smooth. Stir in the vanilla and lemon juice and work in the milk powder, mixing until thick and creamy.

— Cary Elizabeth Marshall
Thunder Bay, Ontario

CHOCOLATE ICING

½ cup sugar
1½ Tbsp. cornstarch
2-3 Tbsp. cocoa
Dash salt

½ cup boiling water
1½ Tbsp. butter
½ tsp. vanilla

Mix sugar and cornstarch together. Add cocoa and salt. Add water and cook until thick. Remove from heat and stir in butter and vanilla. Spread while hot.

— Barbara Davis
Mississauga, Ontario

WHITE WHITE ICING

THE AMOUNT OF ICING SUGAR IN THIS RECIPE MAY BE VARIED TO make a soft icing for spreading or a stiffer icing for decorating.

1 lb. shortening
½ tsp. peppermint flavouring
¼ tsp. salt

1 lb. icing sugar
7 Tbsp. milk

Cream softened shortening with electric mixer. Add flavouring and salt. Beat in sugar one cup at a time with a little milk, blending well after each addition. Beat at high speed until light and fluffy.

— Shanon Cooper
Mayo, Yukon

COCOA ICING

⅓ cup cocoa
2 cups icing sugar
2 Tbsp. butter

1 tsp. vanilla
Hot water

Melt cocoa and add sugar, butter and vanilla. Blend in hot water until mixture will spread smoothly.

— *Roxanne Kistler*
Plymouth, Michigan

OATMEAL COOKIES

1 cup butter
½ cup granulated sugar
1 cup brown sugar
1 egg
1 tsp. vanilla
3 Tbsp. milk

1½ cups flour
1½ cups rolled oats
¾ cup coconut
1 tsp. baking powder
1 tsp. baking soda
⅛ tsp. salt

Cream together butter and sugar, then beat in egg, vanilla and milk. Combine dry ingredients and add to creamed mixture.

Drop by spoonfuls onto greased cookie sheets and bake at 375 degrees F for 15 to 20 minutes or until golden brown.

Makes 5 to 6 dozen cookies.

— *Andrea Stuart*
Winnipeg, Manitoba

TASTY OAT COOKIES

1 cup sunflower oil
1½ cups honey
2 tsp. vanilla
½ tsp. salt
2½ cups flour

½ cup water
4 cups large flake rolled oats
½ cup chopped walnuts
¼ cup sunflower seeds
1½ tsp. cinnamon

Cream together oil, honey, vanilla and salt. Add flour and water gradually, stirring until well mixed. When smooth, add oats, nuts, seeds and cinnamon. Mix well.

Spoon onto greased cookie sheets and bake at 350 degrees F for 25 minutes or until golden brown.

Makes 8 to 9 dozen cookies.

— *Vickie Johnson-Munn*
Summerland, B.C.

OATMEAL CHOCOLATE CHIP COOKIES

1 cup butter
1½ cups brown sugar
2 eggs
1 tsp. vanilla
1½ cups flour

2⅓ cups rolled oats
2 tsp. baking soda
1 tsp. salt
12-oz. pkg. chocolate chips
1½ cups chopped nuts

Cream butter and sugar. Beat in eggs and vanilla. Add flour, oats, baking soda and salt. Mix well and stir in chips and nuts.

Drop by spoonfuls onto greased cookie sheets and bake at 350 degrees F for 12 to 15 minutes.

Makes 6 to 8 dozen cookies.

— *Sandra Lloyd*
North Vancouver, B.C.

CHOCOLATE CHIP COOKIES

1 cup butter
1 cup brown sugar
1 cup granulated sugar
2 eggs
1 tsp. vanilla

2¼ cups flour
3 tsp. baking powder
1 tsp. salt
1 cup chopped walnuts
12-oz. pkg. chocolate chips

Cream butter, sugars, eggs and vanilla. Add remaining ingredients in order listed. Mix well.

Drop by spoonfuls onto greased cookie sheet with 2 inches between cookies. Bake at 375 degrees F for 8 to 10 minutes.

Makes 6 dozen cookies.

— *Shirley Morrish*
Devlin, Ontario

DAD'S COOKIES

1 cup butter
1 cup granulated sugar
½ cup brown sugar
1 egg
1 cup flour

1 tsp. baking powder
1 tsp. baking soda
1 cup bran flakes
1 cup rolled oats
1 cup fine coconut

Cream butter, add sugars and then the egg. Beat until light and creamy.

Sift together flour, baking powder and baking soda. Add bran flakes, oats and coconut. Stir into creamed mixture and mix well.

Drop by teaspoonfuls onto greased cookie sheets. Press down with a fork and bake at 350 degrees F for 10 minutes or until cookies are light brown.

Makes 6 to 8 dozen cookies.

— *Christine Davidson*
Wingham, Ontario

HERMITS

2 cups flour
½ tsp. baking soda
½ tsp. salt
½ tsp. cinnamon
½ tsp. nutmeg
¾ cup shortening

1 cup brown sugar
1 egg
¼ cup cold strong coffee
½ cup raisins
½ cup chopped walnuts

Combine flour, baking soda, salt, cinnamon and nutmeg. Cream shortening and sugar and add egg. Add dry ingredients to creamed mixture alternately with coffee. Stir in raisins and nuts.

Drop by teaspoonfuls onto greased cookie sheet and bake at 400 degrees F for 6 to 8 minutes.

Makes 3 to 4 dozen cookies.

— *Audrey Moroso*
Puslinch, Ontario

SCHOOL BUS COOKIES

1½ cups butter
2 cups brown sugar
2 eggs
1½ cups flour
2 tsp. baking powder
¼ tsp. baking soda

1 tsp. salt
¾ cup bran
1½ cups rolled oats
½ cup dates
¾ cup wheat germ

Cream butter, sugar and eggs. Sift in flour, baking powder, baking soda and salt, then stir in bran, oats, dates and wheat germ.

Mix well and drop by small spoonfuls onto a cookie sheet. Bake at 375 degrees F for 10 to 12 minutes.

Makes 5 to 6 dozen cookies.

— *Janet Stevenson*
Fredericton, N.B.

AUNTIE SUSIE'S PEANUT BUTTER COOKIES

½ cup shortening
1 cup peanut butter
½ cup white sugar
½ cup brown sugar
1 egg

1½ cups flour
1 tsp. baking soda
½ tsp. baking powder
½ tsp. vanilla

Cream shortening and peanut butter. Gradually add sugars. Add egg and beat well. Sift dry ingredients together. Gradually add to creamed mixture. Stir in vanilla.

Roll batter into small balls, place on ungreased cookie sheet and flatten with a fork. Bake at 375 degrees F for 10 to 15 minutes. Cool on a rack.

Makes 4 dozen cookies.

— *Patricia Forrest*
Rosemont, Ontario

SUGAR COOKIES

¾ cup butter
1 cup sugar
1 egg
1 tsp. baking soda
1 tsp. cream of tartar

2 cups flour
Salt
½ cup milk
½ tsp. vanilla

Cream butter and sugar together. Stir in egg. Combine dry ingredients and add to creamed mixture alternately with milk. Stir in vanilla.

Roll out dough and cut into shapes. Bake on greased cookie sheets at 375 degrees F for 10 to 12 minutes.

Makes 3 to 4 dozen cookies.

— *Goldie Connell*
Prescott, Ontario

SHORTBREAD

½ lb. butter
½ cup cornstarch

½ cup icing sugar
1 cup flour

Beat butter until light and add remaining ingredients one at a time, beating well after each addition. Roll into small balls and flatten with fork.

Bake at 300 degrees F for 30 minutes.

Makes 3 dozen.

— *Shirley Hill*
Picton, Ontario

DIGESTIVE COOKIES

½ cup whole wheat flour
½ cup unbleached white flour
½ cup wheat germ
¼ cup sugar
¼ cup sesame seeds
½ tsp. salt

½ tsp. baking powder
1 cup rolled oats
½ cup butter
½ cup cold water
1 tsp. vanilla

Mix together dry ingredients. Cut in butter, then add water mixed with vanilla to form an easily handled dough.

Roll to ¼-inch thickness. Cut out cookies with floured glass. Place on greased cookie sheets and bake at 350 degrees F for 10 to 12 minutes.

Makes 3 to 4 dozen cookies.

— *Brigitte Wolf*
Lucknow, Ontario

BUTTERSCOTCH COOKIES

1 cup butter
2 cups brown sugar
2 eggs
1 cup walnuts

1 tsp. vanilla
1 tsp. cream of tartar
4 cups flour

Cream butter and sugar and add eggs, walnuts and vanilla. Mix cream of tartar and flour and combine with creamed mixture.

Pack into loaf pan or wrap in rolls in wax paper and chill overnight. Remove from pan and cut into thin slices. Bake at 350 degrees F for 10 to 15 minutes.

Makes 8 dozen cookies.

— *Pat McCormack*
Whitehorse, Yukon

CARDAMOM COOKIES

2½ cups flour
2 tsp. ground cardamom
3½ tsp. cinnamon

1¼ cups butter, softened
½ cup white sugar

Combine flour, cardamom and cinnamon in a bowl. In another bowl, cream together sugar and butter. Gradually add flour and spices, mixing until texture resembles coarse sand.

Form dough into ¾-inch-diameter rolls and chill until stiff — at least 1 hour. Cut into ¾-inch-thick slices and place on lightly greased cookie sheets. Bake at 350 degrees F for 12 to 15 minutes — until very lightly browned.

Makes 4 dozen.

— *Janet Jokinen*
Cobourg, Ontario

SESAME SEED COOKIES

2 cups flour
¼ cup wheat germ
1½ tsp. baking powder
¼ tsp. salt
⅓ cup honey

¾ cup butter
2 egg yolks
¼ cup milk
1 tsp. vanilla
Sesame seeds

Mix together flour, wheat germ, baking powder and salt. Add honey and butter. When crumbly, add egg yolks, milk and vanilla.

Knead until smooth. For each cookie, shape a rounded tablespoon of dough into an oval loaf. Roll in sesame seeds.

Bake on greased cookie sheets at 375 degrees F for 15 to 20 minutes.

Makes 4 dozen cookies.

— *Bryanna Clark*
Union Bay, B.C.

RAISIN SESAME COOKIES

1¼ cups flour
½ tsp. baking soda
½ tsp. salt
1 tsp. cinnamon
¾ cup raisins
½ cup oil

1 cup sugar
1 egg, beaten
1¼ cups rolled oats
1 cup sesame seeds
¼ cup milk

Sift flour with baking soda, salt and cinnamon. Stir in raisins.

Beat together oil, sugar and egg. Add rolled oats, sesame seeds and milk. Gradually beat in flour mixture and stir dough until thoroughly blended.

Drop dough by heaping teaspoonfuls onto a greased cookie sheet, allowing room for cookies to spread. Bake at 375 degrees F for 10 to 15 minutes.

Makes 4 dozen cookies.

— *Holly McNally*
Fredericton, N.B.

RAISIN COOKIES

1 cup water
2 cups raisins
1 cup shortening
2 cups sugar
3 eggs
1 tsp. vanilla
1 cup chopped walnuts

4 cups flour
1 tsp. baking powder
1 tsp. baking soda
2 tsp. salt
1½ tsp. cinnamon
¼ tsp. nutmeg
¼ tsp. allspice

Combine water and raisins, boil for 5 minutes and cool.

Cream shortening and add sugar, eggs, vanilla, cooled raisins and walnuts.

Combine remaining ingredients, add to creamed mixture and blend well. Drop by teaspoonfuls onto greased cookie sheets and bake at 350 degrees F for 12 to 15 minutes.

Makes 10 dozen cookies.

— *Mrs. Jack Stacey*
Harrowsmith, Ontario

BUTTERHORN COOKIES

1 cup butter
1 egg yolk
¾ cup sour cream
2 cups flour

¾ cup sugar
1 tsp. cinnamon
¾ cup raisins

Cream the butter and yolk and add the sour cream and flour. Blend well and chill for 1 hour.

Roll out dough to ¼-inch thickness. Combine the sugar, cinnamon and raisins and sprinkle evenly over dough.

Cut dough into triangles. Roll triangles up from large end and curve to form a semi-circle. Place on ungreased cookie sheets. Bake at 375 degrees F for 30 minutes.

Makes 2 to 3 dozen.

— Sheri Israels
West Vancouver, B.C.

BANANA DATE COOKIES

3 ripe bananas
1 cup chopped dates
⅓ cup oil

2 cups oatmeal
½ cup sunflower seeds
1 tsp. vanilla

Mash the bananas and combine with chopped dates and oil. Add remaining ingredients and mix well.

Drop by spoonfuls onto a greased cookie sheet and flatten with a fork. Bake at 375 degrees F for about 15 minutes.

Makes 24.

— Heather Struckett
London, Ontario

SPICY TOFU COOKIES

1½ cups flour
½ cup raisins
½ cup finely chopped walnuts
½ cup chopped dates
½ tsp. baking soda
½ cup butter
⅔ cup honey

1 egg
8 oz. tofu
1 tsp. ginger
1 tsp. cinnamon
½ tsp. nutmeg
½ tsp. salt
1 tsp. vanilla

Mix together first 5 ingredients. Blend remaining ingredients and add to flour mixture. Combine well and drop by spoonfuls onto greased cookie sheets.

Bake at 400 degrees F for 10 to 15 minutes.

— Renate Manthei
Toronto, Ontario

CREAM CHEESE COOKIES

½ lb. butter
8-oz. pkg. cream cheese
2 cups flour

3 Tbsp. sugar
2 tsp. salt
Grape jelly

Cream butter and cheese and add flour, sugar and salt. Chill thoroughly in refrigerator. Roll out dough, using plenty of flour, and cut half into circles and half into strips. Place 1 tsp. grape jelly in centre of each circle and top with strips in the shape of an X. Press edges together.

Bake at 350 degrees F until golden.

— *Shirley Hill*
Picton, Ontario

APPLE SAUCE OATMEAL COOKIES

½ cup shortening
1 cup sugar
1 egg
1 cup unsweetened apple sauce
1 tsp. baking soda
1¾ cups flour

½ tsp. salt
1 tsp. cinnamon
½ tsp. nutmeg
1 cup raisins
1 cup oatmeal

Cream together shortening, sugar and egg. Mix apple sauce and baking soda, and sift together the flour, salt and spices. Add apple sauce and dry ingredients to creamed mixture. Mix in raisins and oatmeal.

Drop by spoonfuls onto greased cookie sheet. Bake at 350 degrees F for 10 minutes.

Makes 3 dozen.

— *Audrey Moroso*
Puslinch, Ontario

BANANA OAT BARS

¾ cup butter
1 cup packed brown sugar
1 egg
½ tsp. salt
1½ cups mashed ripe bananas (4-5 medium)

4 cups uncooked oats
½ cup coconut
1 cup chocolate chips

Cream butter and sugar until fluffy. Beat in egg, salt and bananas. Stir in remaining ingredients. Turn into greased 9" x 13" pan.

Bake at 350 degrees F for 1 hour or until golden brown and toothpick comes clean.

Cool and cut into 2-inch bars. Store in refrigerator until needed.

— *Jan Gibbs*
Rocky Mountain House, Alberta

POPPY SEED COOKIES

½ cup butter
⅓ cup sugar
1 egg
1 cup flour

⅓ tsp. salt
½ tsp. vanilla
¼ tsp. grated lemon rind
2 Tbsp. poppy seeds

Cream butter and mix in sugar and egg. Combine flour and salt and add to butter along with vanilla, lemon rind and poppy seeds. Mix well.

Roll into balls and flatten on greased baking sheets. Bake at 350 degrees F for 10 to 12 minutes.

Makes 2 dozen cookies.

— *Shirley Morrish*
Devlin, Ontario

MAPLE SUGAR COOKIES

½ cup butter
½ cup maple sugar
1 egg
½ cup milk

1 cup whole wheat flour
¾ cup unbleached white flour
½ tsp. salt
½ cup raisins

Cream together butter and maple sugar. Add egg and milk and beat. Mix in flours, salt and raisins.

Drop by teaspoonfuls onto greased cookie sheets. Bake at 325 degrees F for 10 minutes or until browned around edges.

Makes 40 cookies.

— *Andra Hughes*
Apsley, Ontario

SOFT MOLASSES COOKIES

1 cup granulated sugar
1 cup molasses
1 cup shortening, melted
4 cups flour
2 tsp. baking soda

1 egg
1 cup cold water
1 tsp. cinnamon
½ tsp. ground cloves
1 tsp. salt

Cream together sugar, molasses and shortening. Stir in 1 cup flour, baking soda, egg and water.

Sift together remaining 3 cups flour, cinnamon, cloves and salt. Stir into creamed mixture.

Refrigerate for 1 hour, then drop by teaspoonfuls onto cookie sheet. Bake at 375 degrees F for 12 to 15 minutes.

Makes 8 dozen cookies.

— *Janice Touesnard*
River Bourgeois, N.S.

KISLINGS

These are rich Christmas-time cookies.

1 cup butter
¼ cup granulated sugar
2 cups sifted flour
¼ tsp. salt

½ cup well drained, sliced maraschino
  cherries
½ cup chopped walnuts
Confectioners' sugar

Cream butter, add sugar and mix until fluffy. Add remaining ingredients and mix well. Form dough into small balls and place on ungreased cookie sheet.

Bake at 300 degrees F for 30 to 40 minutes or until bottoms are golden.

Roll in confectioners' sugar.

Makes 3 dozen cookies.

— *Bonnie Byrnes*
Verdun, Quebec

GINGER SNAPS

These cookies, accompanied with hot cocoa, have been served to overnight guests at Marshlands Inn every evening since the inn opened in 1935.

1 cup melted shortening
½ cup granulated sugar
1½ cups molasses
2 heaping tsp. baking soda

2 heaping tsp. ginger
2 heaping tsp. salt
4½ cups flour

Combine shortening, sugar and molasses. Sift baking soda, ginger and salt with flour, and stir into creamed mixture.

Shape into rectangular logs and chill overnight. Slice very thinly and bake at 350 degrees F for 7 to 8 minutes.

Makes 10 dozen cookies.

— *Marshlands Inn*
Sackville, N.B.

DATE SQUARES

1 lb. dates
¾ cup hot water
Salt
1 tsp. vanilla
1½ cups flour

½ tsp. baking soda
1½ cups rolled oats
1½ cups brown sugar
1 cup butter

Combine dates, hot water and salt in a saucepan. Cook over medium heat until dates are soft and water is absorbed. Add vanilla and let cool.

Stir flour and baking soda together. Add oats and brown sugar and mix well. Work in butter with fork until mixture is crumbly.

Spread half the mixture in the bottom of a 9-inch square pan and pat down. Cover with date filling and pat remaining mixture on top.

Bake at 350 degrees F for 20 to 25 minutes.

— *Mrs. Fred Smith*
Mountain Grove, Ontario

LEMON SQUARES

1 cup butter
½ cup icing sugar
2 cups flour
4 eggs
1½ cups sugar

Pinch salt
4 Tbsp. flour
1 tsp. baking powder
8 Tbsp. lemon juice

Stir butter, icing sugar and flour together and press into a 9" x 13" pan. Bake at 350 degrees F for 10 minutes.

Beat eggs and add remaining ingredients. Pour over cookie base and bake 25 minutes longer.

Cut into bars while hot, and sprinkle with icing sugar when cool.

— Mrs. W. Atkins
Agincourt, Ontario

JAM BARS

½ cup shortening
½ cup sugar
½ tsp. vanilla
½ tsp. almond extract
1 egg
1½ cups flour

1 tsp. baking powder
½ tsp. cinnamon
¼ tsp. ground cloves
½ tsp. salt
Jam or marmalade

Cream together shortening, sugar, vanilla and almond extract. Stir in egg. Sift together dry ingredients, add to creamed mixture and blend well.

Spread half the dough in a greased 8-inch square pan, cover with jam or marmalade and top with remaining dough.

Bake at 400 degrees F for 25 minutes. Cool, then cut into bars.

Makes 20 bars.

— Donna Jubb
Fenelon Falls, Ontario

RASPBERRY BARS

1 cup butter, softened
⅓ cup sugar
2 egg yolks
2 cups flour

1 cup raspberry jam
4 Tbsp. confectioners' sugar
½ cup chopped walnuts

Cream butter and sugar. Beat in egg yolks, then stir in flour, half a cup at a time.

Press half the dough into a 9-inch square baking pan. Spread with jam and top with remaining dough. Sprinkle with confectioners' sugar and walnuts.

Bake at 375 degrees F for 35 minutes. When cool, cut into bars.

Makes 27 bars.

ANNA LIEB'S BROWNIES

MY GRANDMOTHER, WHO LIVED WITH US UNTIL I WAS 17 YEARS OLD, WAS AN excellent cook with a pronounced Old-World style. In order to preserve her recipes, I tried following her around the kitchen making notes on quantities used and steps followed. This worked for a few uncomplicated treats, but was unsuccessful for her more intricate creations. One recipe which we have managed to duplicate is her brownies. Always moist and rich, they are my idea of what brownies should be.

1 cup butter	1 Tbsp. baking powder
2 cups sugar	1 tsp. salt
4 eggs	2 tsp. vanilla
4 squares unsweetened chocolate, melted	1 cup chopped walnuts or slivered
2 cups flour	almonds

Cream together butter and sugar until light. Beat in eggs. Add melted chocolate and beat again. Mix in flour, baking powder, salt and vanilla.

Spread mixture in a greased 9" x 13" baking pan and sprinkle liberally with nuts. Bake at 350 degrees F for 35 minutes. When cool, cut in squares.

Makes 2 dozen brownies.

— Alice O'Connell
Centreville, Ontario

SESAME SEED BARS

2 cups hulled, raw sesame seeds
1¼ cups honey

Brown sesame seeds lightly in a heavy preheated skillet.

Combine seeds with honey in a saucepan and cook to hard ball stage (265 degrees F), stirring frequently with a wooden spoon.

Pour onto an oiled cookie sheet and spread to ⅛-inch thickness. Score into 1¾ x 1½ inch bars while still warm. Cool and break into pieces.

Place on cake rack for one day for crispier, less sticky bars. If storing bars, place wax paper between layers.

— N. Kariel
St. John's, Nfld.

LYNN'S GRANOLA BARS

1 cup butter	½ cup powdered milk
1 cup brown sugar	1½ cups rolled oats
2 eggs	¾ cup wheat germ
¼ cup molasses	¾ cup coconut
1 tsp. vanilla	¾ cup sunflower seeds
1¾ cups flour	¾ cup chopped dried fruit
½ tsp. baking soda	⅓ cup sesame seeds
½ tsp. salt	

Cream together butter, brown sugar, eggs, molasses and vanilla. Sift together flour, baking soda, salt and powdered milk, add to creamed mixture and blend well. Add remaining ingredients and mix well.

Spread in a 9" x 13" pan and bake at 350 degrees F for 20 to 25 minutes or until golden.

— Judy Wuest
Cross Creek, B.C.

Beverages

Let us wet our whistles.

— Petronius
Satyricon

More than half the human body is composed of plain water, H_2O. No wonder that, next to air, water is our most pressing physical need; every day we lose up to two quarts of water as urine and another quart or so in perspiration and exhalation.

Not all of this water is replenished by beverages; like the human body, most foods have an astonishingly high water content. A slice of bologna is more than half water, oysters are 85 per cent water, broccoli is 91 per cent water, and a pared cucumber is 96 per cent water. And then there are watery dishes like yogurt, soups and stews. If we watch our diets closely, we might get by without drinking at all.

But beverages are an important part of most diets, a matter of custom and habit as much as thirst, which could, of course, be satisfied with plain water alone. Nevertheless, some of us get by day after day without ever letting the stuff touch our lips; we choose instead drinks that speed us up, drinks that slow us down, drinks that make us act funny, drinks that are fashionable, drinks that have a nice colour or a nice flavour, or make our mouths tingle.

All that doesn't mean that we take beverages lightly. Cocoa was so prized a drink among the Aztecs that they used cacao beans as currency; the American revolution was sparked by a tax on tea; a tenth of all the sugar consumed in the United States goes to the Coca-Cola company.

As milk is surpassed by pop in North American consumption, one thing becomes clear: Little of our drinking is done with nutrition in mind. Latest figures indicate that every American drinks about 36 gallons of soft drinks a year, a figure that has trebled in 20 years. And, except for the sodas that include vitamin C, all of it comes without any nutrient other than carbohydrate (sugar). A can of lemon pop that advertises "natural lemon flavour" turns out to contain no lemon at all. The drink manufacturer doesn't mean the flavour is lemon because the drink has natural lemons in it; he means it has flavouring in it that resembles that of a lemon. Nutritional doublespeak.

Here follow a number of recipes that promise exactly what they deliver, satisfying ways to keep one's body liquids replenished while ingesting a few nutrients along the way. Perhaps we can start another revolution.

GINGER TEA

2½ cups water
2 inches fresh green ginger,
  coarsely grated
4 tsp. honey or brown sugar
½ lemon, sliced

Combine ingredients and boil, uncovered, for 10 to 15 minutes. Strain and serve in mugs.

Serves 2.

— Cary Elizabeth Marshall
Thunder Bay, Ontario

RHUBARB PUNCH

3 lbs. fresh rhubarb
16 cups water
6 cloves

1½ cups honey
Juice & pulp of 3 oranges &
  1½ lemons

Combine rhubarb, water and cloves and simmer for 10 minutes. Strain. Add honey, oranges and lemons. Serve chilled.

Serves 20.

— David Slabotsky
Richmond, P.E.I.

TOMATO-VEGETABLE COCKTAIL

THIS EASILY MADE TOMATO DRINK IS FAR MORE FLAVOURFUL AND LESS EXPENSIVE than similar commercial beverages. It can be cooked for a longer or shorter time than that suggested, depending upon the thickness desired.

16 large ripe tomatoes
½ cup carrots, chopped
½ cup celery, chopped
½ cup onion, chopped

2 tsp. salt
2 Tbsp. lemon juice
1 tsp. Worcestershire sauce
Dash Tabasco sauce

Wash, core and chop tomatoes. Combine with remaining ingredients in a heavy saucepan. Bring to a boil, lower heat slightly and cook rapidly until vegetables are tender. Press through a strainer or food mill.

To store, ladle into quart jars leaving ¼-inch headroom. Seal and process 15 minutes in water bath.

Shake well before using.

Makes 2 quarts.

— *Debbie Walker*
Delta, Ontario

VEGETABLE-FRUIT JUICE I

1 large carrot, cleaned & cut in chunks
1 small apple, cored & cut in chunks
1 small orange, peeled, seeded & cut in chunks
Apple juice

Using an electric blender liquify orange, apple and carrot with 2 cups apple juice until fruit particles are as small as possible. Fill the blender with more apple juice and blend for a few more seconds.

Makes 4 glasses.

— *Maria Gosse*
Botwood, Nfld.

VEGETABLE-FRUIT JUICE II

1 small raw beet,
  peeled & cut in chunks
1 small apple, cored & cut in chunks

1½ cups orange juice
Apple juice

Using an electric blender, liquify beet, apple and orange juice until fruit particles are as small as possible. Fill the blender with apple juice and blend again for a few seconds.

Makes 4 glasses.

— *Maria Gosse*
Botwood, Nfld.

PAPAYA COOLER

6 oz. papaya juice
3 oz. strawberries

⅓ banana
1 Tbsp. raw sugar or honey

Mix all ingredients in a blender with 1 cup of crushed ice. Serve in tall frosted glass.

— *Kattie Murphy*
Gagetown, N.B.

FRUIT SMOOTHY

1 orange
1 banana
2 apples

2 cups milk
½ cup sesame seeds
1 tsp. cinnamon

Combine all ingredients in a blender and mix until smooth. This can be served as a drink, or frozen for a cool dessert.

Serves 2 to 4.

— Sheri Nelson
Horsefly, B.C.

CRANBERRY TEA

THIS MAY BE SERVED EITHER HOT OR COLD, BUT IS ESPECIALLY DELICIOUS IN THE winter, served as a hot appetizer.

1 qt. cranberries
1 qt. water
2 sticks cinnamon

6 oranges
3 lemons
2 cups sugar

Cook together the cranberries, water and cinnamon. Mash and put through a sieve. Add sugar and the juice from the oranges and lemons. To increase quantity, 1 large can frozen orange juice and 1 small can frozen lemonade may be added, with additional water to taste.

Basic recipe serves 6.

— Anne Erb
State College, Pennsylvania

LEMONADE CONCENTRATE

2 Tbsp. grated lemon rind
¾ cup fresh lemon juice
1 oz. citric acid

3 cups granulated sugar
2 cups boiling water

Combine all ingredients and stir until completely dissolved. Store in refrigerator and mix with water to make desired strength.

— Jane Cuthbert
Prescott, Ontario

CAROB-BANANA MILKSHAKE

1 medium banana
1 egg
1½ Tbsp. honey

½ tsp. vanilla extract
2 Tbsp. carob powder
3½ cups whole milk

Blend all ingredients using an electric blender.

Makes 4 glasses.

— Maria Gosse
Botwood, Nfld.

VANILLA MILKSHAKE

THIS RECIPE AND THE EIGHT THAT FOLLOW, SENT IN BY MARIA GOSSE OF BOTWOOD, Nfld., can be made into popsicles by freezing in ice cube or popsicle trays.

1 egg
2½ Tbsp. honey
½ tsp. vanilla extract

½ cup milk powder
3½ cups whole milk

Blend all ingredients using an electric blender.

Makes 4 glasses.

APPLE MILKSHAKE

1 large apple, peeled, cored & quartered
1 egg
2 Tbsp. honey

½ tsp. cinnamon
½ cup milk
3 cups plain yogurt

Liquify in an electric blender first 5 ingredients. Then buzz blender again for a second to blend in the yogurt.

Makes 4 glasses.

PEACH OR APRICOT MILKSHAKE

4 peaches or apricots, fresh or
  frozen, peeled
1 egg
2 Tbsp. honey

A few drops almond extract
½ cup milk
1½ cups plain yogurt

Liquify together in an electric blender first 5 ingredients. Then buzz blender again for just a second to blend in the yogurt.

Makes 4 glasses.

ORANGE-BANANA MILKSHAKE

1 medium-sized banana
3 Tbsp. frozen undiluted orange juice
2 Tbsp. honey
1 egg

½ tsp. vanilla extract
½ cup milk
2 cups plain yogurt

Liquify together in an electric blender first 6 ingredients. Then buzz blender again for just a second to blend in the yogurt.

Makes 4 glasses.

GRAPE MILKSHAKE

6 oz. frozen undiluted grape juice
1 egg

1½ Tbsp. honey
3 cups plain yogurt

In an electric blender, liquify first 3 ingredients. Then buzz blender again for a second to blend in the yogurt, until milkshake is thoroughly mixed.

Makes 4 glasses.

BANANA MILKSHAKE

2 medium bananas
1 egg
2 Tbsp. honey

½ tsp. vanilla
½ cup milk
1½ cups plain yogurt

Liquify together first 5 ingredients using electric blender. Then buzz blender again for just a second to blend in the yogurt.

Makes 4 glasses.

PINEAPPLE MILKSHAKE

1 14-oz. can pineapple chunks
1 Tbsp. honey

1 egg
2 cups plain yogurt

Liquify together first 3 ingredients and ½ cup of the yogurt in an electric blender. Then buzz blender again for just a second to add remaining 1½ cups yogurt.

Makes 4 glasses.

PEANUT BUTTER MILKSHAKE

4 Tbsp. peanut butter
1 egg
½ tsp. vanilla extract

2 Tbsp. honey
½ cup milk
2½ cups plain yogurt

Liquify together in electric blender first 5 ingredients. Then buzz blender again for just a second, to blend in the yogurt.

Makes 4 glasses.

STRAWBERRY MILKSHAKE

1 cup fresh or frozen strawberries
 (do not thaw if frozen)
1 egg
2 Tbsp. honey

½ cup milk
Few drops almond extract
1½ cups plain yogurt

Liquify together first 5 ingredients using electric blender. Then buzz in blender again for just a second to blend in the yogurt.

Makes 4 glasses.

HOT CIDER

3 qts. apple cider
⅔ cup brown sugar
¼ tsp. salt
1 tsp. whole allspice

1 tsp. whole cloves
4 cinnamon sticks
¼ tsp. nutmeg

Heat 2 cups cider with sugar and salt, stirring until sugar dissolves. Pour into slow cooker with remaining cider. Tie spices in cloth bag and drop into cider. Cover and simmer for 2 to 3 hours. Remove spices at serving time.

— *Mary Lou Ross*
Tavistock, Ontario

MULLED CIDER

1 orange
1 lemon
1 lime
1 cup sugar
1 egg, beaten until frothy

72-oz. can apple cider
½ tsp. allspice
3-4 cinnamon sticks
3-4 whole cloves

Combine juices of orange, lemon and lime. Simmer together with sugar and egg. Add remaining ingredients, simmer 15 minutes longer and serve hot.

— Pat McCormack
Whitehorse, Yukon

MULLED WINE

½ cup water
¼ cup orange juice
¼ cup sugar
1 cinnamon stick

2 cloves
½ lemon, thinly sliced
1½ cups wine
2 oz. brandy

Boil water, orange juice, sugar, cinnamon and cloves for 5 minutes. Add lemon slices and let stand for 10 minutes. Add wine and heat gradually, but do not boil. Add brandy at serving time.

Serves 2.

— Cheryl Suckling
Athens, Georgia

HOT CRANBERRY WINE CUP

4 cups cranberry juice
2 cups water
½ cup honey
1 cinnamon stick
12 cloves

1 lemon, sliced
2 bottles Burgundy wine
1¼ cup lemon juice
Nutmeg

Combine in a large non-aluminum pot, the cranberry juice, water, honey, cinnamon, cloves and lemon. Bring to a boil, stirring, and continue cooking until honey is dissolved. Add wine and lemon juice. Heat gently and serve in preheated mugs, sprinkled with nutmeg.

— Bryanna Clark
Union Bay, B.C.

SUMMER SPRITZER

2 cups sugar
7 cups water
12 oz. frozen orange juice

12 oz. frozen lemonade
2 cups vodka, rum or gin

Boil together sugar and water until sugar is dissolved. Chill. Add remaining ingredients, mix well and freeze.

To serve, put 1 scoop in tall glass and fill with mineral water.

— Eileen Deeley
Kamloops, B.C.

COFFEE LIQUEUR

2 cups granulated sugar
1½ cups water
2 Tbsp. coffee

1 Tbsp. vanilla
26-oz. bottle alcool

Combine all ingredients except alcohol in heavy sauce pan. Bring to a rolling boil. Let cool and strain. Add alcohol, and bottle.

— L. Howson
Peterborough, Ontario

SANGRIA

THIS COOL SUMMER PUNCH OF SPANISH ORIGIN IS EASILY EXPANDED TO SERVE A CROWD. Wine may simply be poured into the pitcher or punch bowl as it is needed, and additional soda, ice and fruit slices stirred in.

2 bottles red wine
1 bottle club soda
1 cup brandy

2 cups orange juice
Lemon, orange & lime slices
Ice cubes

Mix red wine, club soda, brandy and orange juice. Add enough ice cubes to chill thoroughly. Top with lemon, orange and lime slices.

Serves 8.

RUMPLE

CREATED AS A HOT PICK-ME-UP AFTER A LONG WINTER'S DAY OF OUTDOOR ACTIVITY, rumple can be made to serve two or 20.

5 cups apple juice
6 oz. maple syrup or honey
6 oz. rum
6 cinnamon sticks

Heat apple juice until steaming and add sweetener. Pour into 6 mugs with rum. Add cinnamon stick and serve immediately.

Serves 6.

— Christine Campbell
Elginburg, Ontario

LEMON BEER

2 lemons
1 lb. brown sugar
1 lb. granulated sugar
½ cup thick syrup

8 quarts water
¼ tsp. dry yeast
Handful raisins

Grate rind from lemon and set aside. Cut lemons into ¼-inch slices.

Combine sugars, syrup and lemon rind in a pail. Boil 2 quarts water and pour over sugar mixture. Add remaining cold water and lemon slices. Add yeast, cover and let sit overnight.

Strain through cheesecloth and pour into bottles. Add ¼ tsp. sugar and a few raisins to each bottle. Cap tightly and store in a cool place for at least 7 days before using.

Makes about 8 quarts.

— Iris White
Prince George, B.C.

RASPBERRY PUNCH

16 oz. raspberry cordial
6 oz. frozen lemonade concentrate
6 oz. frozen orange juice concentrate
20 oz. pineapple juice

2 qts. water
26 oz. sparkling mineral water
1 bottle white rum

Combine all ingredients in a punch bowl. Add ice cubes just before serving.

— Cheryl Suckling
Athens, Georgia

IRISH COFFEE

2 jiggers Irish whiskey
2 tsp. demerara sugar
Fresh hot coffee

Warm whiskey and sugar together and pour into 2 coffee cups. Fill cups about three-quarters full with coffee and top with whipped cream.

Serves 2.

— Mary Patton
Kingston, Ontario

MAY BOWL

Sweet woodruff sprigs
1¼ cups icing sugar
4 bottles Moselle wine
1 cup brandy

1 qt. soda water or champagne
Orange slices
Fresh pineapple sticks
Strawberries

Combine 12 sprigs woodruff, sugar, 1 bottle Moselle and brandy. Cover and let sit for 30 minutes. Remove woodruff. Stir and pour over a block of ice in a punch bowl. Add remaining ingredients.

— Cary Elizabeth Marshall
Thunder Bay, Ontario

CAFE BRULOT

FOR THOSE WITH A FLAIR FOR THE DRAMATIC (AND SOME SKILL), THIS CAN BE prepared at the table in a chafing dish, adding a flaming spoonful of brandy before stirring in the coffee.

1 tsp. whole allspice
3 sticks cinnamon, broken
Grated rind of 2 oranges & 1 lemon

5 Tbsp. sugar
1 cup brandy or cognac
5 cups strong, fresh, hot coffee

Warm together spices, orange and lemon rind, sugar and brandy, but do not boil. Stir to dissolve sugar. Add coffee. Strain into cups and serve.

Serves 6.

— Cary Elizabeth Marshall
Thunder Bay, Ontario

CRANBERRY PUNCH

2 cups sugar
1 cup water
2 bottles gin

2 48-oz. tins grapefruit juice
1 bottle cranberry juice
2 cups cold tea

Boil sugar and water together and cool. Combine in punch bowl with remaining ingredients. Add ice cubes just before serving.

BRUNCH PUNCH

THIS IS A VARIATION OF A TRADITIONAL WEDDING BREAKFAST PUNCH IN WHICH champagne is used in place of white wine.

4 bottles dry white wine
2 qts. orange juice
1 bottle club soda
Orange slices

Combine all ingredients in a punch bowl and add ice cubes just before serving.

Preserves

How camest thou in this pickle?

**— William Shakespeare
The Tempest**

Modern legend has it that a couple living in a big Canadian city built a bookshelf in their living room that wasn't meant to hold a single book. Decked shelf upon shelf with home canned dills, corn relish, strawberry jam, lemon marmalade, peaches, brandied pears, apple pie filling and spaghetti sauce, it was, the couple thought, far more beautiful in its appearance and its promise than the posters or pictures that would otherwise have covered the wall. It was good taste in three dimensions. Storage conditions were not the best — such jars should really be kept in a cool, dark place for best maintenance of colour and nutrients — but in their apartment, no such spot could be found. So the couple displayed the produce of their balcony cucumbers and pick-your-own strawberries and top-of-the-season, market tomatoes for all to share in its colourful delights. Their guests were impressed first by the wall, then by dinner.

The story may be apocryphal, but the trend is real enough. Canadians are rediscovering the possibilities of home preserving: that it can save them money (though it won't necessarily do so) while enabling them to produce custom-made jams, jellies and pickles, many of which cannot be found on store shelves, even those of specialty shops.

Although freezing and drying are widely used methods of preserving, canning is the one chiefly treated in the following recipes. It still depends upon the same principle as always: Food is sterilized and kept sterile in sealed containers from which air is excluded. "Processing," the sterilization technique, kills spoilage organisms so that foods will not become rancid or toxic during storage.

While the canning of high acid foods is quite straightforward — fruits, tomatoes and pickles can be adequately and quite quickly processed in rapidly boiling water — low acid foods such as meat, fish and vegetables must be processed at high temperatures in a pressure canner, or for long periods of time in boiling water.

The basic piece of equipment one requires for most home canning is a boiling water processor, a large, deep pot with a rack to support the jars. The pot or bath is filled with sufficient boiling water to cover the filled jars as they are lowered into it, and the lid is then placed on top. As soon as the water resumes boiling, the processing time given in the recipe is calculated.

The only other essential pieces of equipment are jars and their lids. Available in many hardware and grocery stores, the jars come in half pint, pint, quart and two-quart sizes with two sizes of neck openings, "standard" and "wide mouth."

Purchased jars come with a supply of fitted metal lids and screw bands, but for future use the cook will have to buy replacement lids.

In preparing any canned food, follow the recommended processing time exactly. It is dependent upon the ingredients in the jar, and one cannot be altered without changing the other. Food that is insufficiently acidic or too briefly processed can not only spoil, but worse, may harbour botulism toxins that can be lethal. Pickle recipes, especially, should not be tampered with. Some popular pickle ingredients such as cucumbers or corn are low in acid and require the correct amount of vinegar to be rendered safe. Jams, fruit syrups and jellies allow the cook more leeway. These high-acid items are safe enough that some cooks do not process them at all, simply topping sterilized, filled jars with melted paraffin — a method definitely second best to sealing with a metal or glass lid, as paraffin often separates from the rim of the jar, allowing mould to grow on the preserve. If the recipe does not demand that the preserve be processed, metal lids or glass lids and rubber rings can be screwed tightly onto the sterilized, filled jars.

A jar that hisses after processing is likely one that has not sealed. Test all jars when cool by removing the retaining screw ring and pressing against the side of the sealed lid. Gentle pressure should not move it. Metal lids that are sealed will appear indented; some fruits and tomatoes, when sealed, will rise in the jar, leaving a layer of juice in the bottom.

If, upon opening a jar of preserves, the cook notices that the seal is loose, the food effervesces or appears or smells strange, the jar's contents should be discarded. Do not taste food that seems suspicious. For specific details about canning, write for Agriculture Canada's free booklet, "Canning Canadian Fruits and Vegetables," available from the Information Division, Agriculture Canada, Ottawa, Ontario K1A 0C7.

A variety of home preserved foods that are obviously sound and properly sealed are the cook's grocery store, insurance and supply of personal, exclusive gifts. A small investment in some decorator labels and pretty ribbon will ensure that Uncle Stan need never receive another hand-painted tie.

DILL PICKLES

4 lbs. small cucumbers
Fresh dill
8 cloves garlic

3 cups water
3 cups white vinegar
5 Tbsp. pickling salt

Scrub cucumbers and soak overnight in ice water. Drain and pack into 4 hot, sterilized quart jars. Place sprays of dill and garlic cloves on top of cucumbers.

Combine remaining ingredients and bring to a boil. Pour over cucumbers and seal jars. Store for 1 month before eating.

Makes 4 quarts.

— Sheila Couture
Trenton, Ontario

DILLED ZUCCHINI

6 lbs. zucchini, trimmed & thinly sliced
2 cups thinly sliced celery
2 large onions, chopped
⅓ cup salt
Ice cubes

2 cups sugar
2 Tbsp. dill seeds
2 cups white vinegar
6 cloves garlic, halved

Combine zucchini, celery, onions and salt in large bowl, place a layer of ice on top, cover and let stand for 3 hours. Drain well.

Combine sugar, dill seeds and vinegar in a saucepan and bring to a boil, stirring constantly. Stir in vegetables, and heat, stirring several times, just to a full boil. Ladle into hot, sterilized jars, place 1 to 2 pieces of garlic in each and seal.

Makes 8 to 10 pints.

— Laura Poitras
Kemptville, Ontario

DILLED GREEN TOMATOES

15 medium-sized green tomatoes
Fresh dill
5 cloves garlic
5 whole cloves

2½ tsp. cayenne pepper
1 qt. vinegar
1 qt. water
⅓ cup pickling salt

Wash tomatoes and slice if necessary. Pack into 5 quart jars. Add 3 heads dill, 1 clove garlic, 1 whole clove and ½ tsp. cayenne to each jar.

Boil vinegar, water and salt for 5 minutes. Pour over tomatoes and process for 20 minutes in a boiling water bath.

Makes 5 quarts.

— E. V. Estey
Faro, Yukon

DILLED BEAN PICKLES

3 lbs. fresh green beans
½ cup chopped fresh dill
2 cloves garlic, peeled & halved
2 cups water

4 Tbsp. salt
2 cups white vinegar
4 tsp. sugar
½ tsp. cayenne pepper

Parboil beans in unsalted water until tender — 5 to 10 minutes. Pack upright in sterile jars and add dill and garlic.

Heat water, salt, vinegar, sugar and cayenne to a boil. Pour over beans. Seal jars and let stand for 6 weeks.

Makes 4 to 5 pints.

— E. Evans
Toronto, Ontario

DILLED CARROTS

6 cups cold water
2 cups white vinegar
½ cup pickling salt
¼ tsp. cream of tartar

6 lbs. baby carrots
6-7 cloves garlic, slivered
6-7 large sprigs fresh dill

Combine water, vinegar, salt and cream of tartar, stirring until salt is dissolved.

Scrape and trim carrots. Put a slivered clove of garlic in each of 6 or 7 pint jars. Add a dill sprig to each, then pack in carrots upright. Pour vinegar mixture over carrots to fill jars.

Process for 10 minutes in a boiling water bath and store in a cool place for 3 weeks.

Makes 6 to 7 pints.

— *Kathee Roy*
Toronto, Ontario

PICKLED CARROTS ROSEMARY

2 hot peppers
4 cloves garlic
1 tsp. rosemary
2 lbs. carrots, peeled & cut
  into 4-inch long strips

2 cups water
2 cups white vinegar
3 Tbsp. pickling salt
3 Tbsp. sugar

Cut peppers into quarters lengthwise. Place 2 strips pepper and 1 clove garlic into each of 4 pint jars. Add ¼ tsp. rosemary to each jar. Pack tightly with carrot sticks.

Bring water, vinegar, salt and sugar to a boil, reduce heat and simmer, uncovered, for 5 minutes. Pour over carrots, seal and process for 10 minutes in boiling water bath.

Let pickles age for 1 month before eating.

Makes 4 pints.

— *Lynn Hill*
Ilderton, Ontario

SWISS CHARD PICKLES

4 qts. Swiss chard, cut into 1-inch pieces
8 medium onions, sliced
Pickling salt
White vinegar
4 cups white sugar
2 Tbsp. celery seed

3 Tbsp. mustard seed
½ cup cornstarch
2 Tbsp. dry mustard
1 Tbsp. curry powder
2 tsp. turmeric

Layer Swiss chard and onions in large pickling kettle and sprinkle with salt. Let stand for 1 hour. Drain and add vinegar to cover.

Stir in sugar, celery seed and mustard seed and cook until tender. Add cornstarch, mustard, curry powder and turmeric.

Seal in sterilized jars.

Makes 12 pints.

— *Dorothy Hall*
Norwood, Ontario

CHUNKY MUSTARD PICKLES

1 medium cauliflower
1 qt. large cucumbers
3 sweet red peppers
3 green peppers
1 qt. small cucumbers
1 qt. onions, chopped
1 qt. pickling onions
1 cup pickling salt
3 qts. water

5 cups sugar
½ cup water
4½ cups vinegar
¼ oz. celery seed
¼ oz. mustard seed
¼ cup dry mustard
¾ cup flour
1 Tbsp. turmeric

Chop cauliflower, large cucumbers and peppers into chunks. Add small cucumbers, onions and pickling onions. Cover with a brine made of the pickling salt and 3 quarts water and leave overnight. In the morning, rinse and drain well.

Combine with sugar, ½ cup water, vinegar, celery seed and mustard seed and bring to a boil. When boiling, take some of the liquid and mix to a smooth paste with dry mustard, flour and turmeric. Stir back into pickles and cook for 5 minutes. Bottle and seal.

Makes 6 to 8 quarts.

— Beth Hopkins
Courtenay, B.C.

PICCALILLI

6 green peppers
6 red peppers
8 cucumbers
8 cups chopped green tomatoes
6 large onions
1 cup pickling salt

5 cups vinegar
2 lbs. brown sugar
2 tsp. dry mustard
2 Tbsp. mixed pickling spice,
    tied in cheesecloth

Wash peppers, cut in half and remove seeds. Peel cucumbers, cut stem ends from tomatoes and peel onions.

Put peppers, onions and cucumbers through coarse setting of meat grinder. Score tomatoes and cut into small cubes.

Measure 8 cups of tomatoes into bowl. Put ground and chopped vegetables in layers in large pot, sprinkling each layer with salt, using 1 cup salt in all. Let stand overnight.

Strain vegetables through fine-holed colander. Remove as much liquid as possible and replace vegetables in pot. Add vinegar, brown sugar, mustard and pickling spice. Cook until sauce becomes clear — about 35 minutes — stirring occasionally.

Remove pickling spice and place piccalilli in hot, sterilized jars and seal.

Makes 8 to 10 pints.

— Mrs. W. Atkins
Agincourt, Ontario

PETER PIPER'S PICKLED PEPPERS

10 lbs. sweet green peppers
Pickling salt
24 ice cubes
3 cloves garlic, sliced
3 cups vinegar

5 cups sugar
½ tsp. celery seed
½ tsp. turmeric
2 Tbsp. mustard seed

Slice peppers and sprinkle lightly with pickling salt. Mix in ice cubes and garlic and chill for 3 hours.

Remove garlic and drain peppers. Combine remaining ingredients in a heavy saucepan and add peppers. Bring to a boil, then place in hot jars and seal.

Makes 6 to 8 quarts.

— Dee Lowe
Meacham, Sask.

CURRY PICKLE

Zucchini & onions to fill 4 or 5 quart
  jars, thinly sliced
Salt brine to cover zucchini & onion
6 cups vinegar
6 cups sugar
2 Tbsp. celery seed

2 Tbsp. dry mustard
4 Tbsp. hot curry powder
2 Tbsp. turmeric
6 whole cloves
8-10 slices ginger root
1 tsp. Tabasco sauce

Soak zucchini and onion slices in salt brine overnight. Drain and pack in jars.

Combine remaining ingredients, bring to a boil and pour over vegetables. Seal jars and let stand a few weeks before eating.

Makes 4 to 5 quarts.

— Brigitte Wolf
Lucknow, Ontario

SWEET PICKLES

6 qts. cucumbers
¾ cup pickling salt
Boiling water
1 plum
3 pints white vinegar

4 Tbsp. white sugar
4 Tbsp. pickling salt
4 Tbsp. mustard seed & ½ cup
  mixed pickling spice tied in a bag
11-12 cups white sugar

Cut cucumbers into chunks and place in a large crock with ¾ cup pickling salt. Cover with boiling water and let sit overnight. In the morning, drain and wipe each piece dry. Return to crock with plum.

Heat vinegar, 4 Tbsp. sugar, 4 Tbsp. pickling salt, mustard seed and pickling spice together and add to cucumber. Cover with a plate.

Add 1 cup sugar each day for 11 to 12 days. Mix with a wooden spoon.

After 12 days, drain cucumbers and heat syrup. Place cucumbers in jars, pour syrup over and seal.

Makes 6 quarts.

— Hilda Jackson
Clinton, Ontario

WATERMELON PICKLE

4 qts. watermelon rind
4 Tbsp. salt
3 Tbsp. alum
11 cups sugar

2 cups white vinegar
1½ tsp. whole cloves
3 sticks cinnamon

Cut rind into 1-inch cubes, place in pot and add salt. Cover with water and add alum. Bring to a boil, reduce heat and simmer for 30 minutes. Drain and rinse.

Simmer in 4 more quarts of water (or enough to cover) until tender. Add sugar and cook until transparent. Add vinegar and cook another 25 minutes. Toss in cloves and cinnamon and cook 5 minutes. Pack in 6 jars, with syrup and spices. Seal. Let sit for 2 weeks before eating.

Makes 6 pints.

— Cary Elizabeth Marshall
Thunder Bay, Ontario

HONEY PICKLED BEETS

2 qts. beets
1½ cups white vinegar
1 cup honey
1 cup water
1 tsp. salt

1 tsp. allspice
2 cups onion rings
2 tsp. each whole cloves, mustard seed &
  2 cinnamon sticks placed in a spice bag

Cook the beets and slip off the skins. Combine the vinegar, honey and water in a large saucepan and add to this the salt and allspice. Drop the spice bag in and simmer for 5 minutes.

Add the beets and onion rings and simmer gently for 20 minutes.

Pack into hot sterile jars, cover with liquid and seal.

Makes 4 pints.

— Ruth E. Geddes
Camden East, Ontario

PICKLED MUSHROOMS

THIS TRADITIONAL RUSSIAN RECIPE CAN BE USED WITH BOTH DOMESTIC AND WILD mushrooms and is especially suited to shaggy manes and the honey mushroom.

1 cup red wine vinegar
2 whole cloves
½ cup cold water
5 whole peppercorns
1 bay leaf

2 tsp. salt
2 cloves garlic, crushed
1 lb. mushrooms
1 Tbsp. vegetable oil

Combine vinegar, cloves, water, peppercorns, bay leaf, salt and garlic in a 2-quart enamelled saucepan. Bring to a boil, add mushrooms and reduce heat. Simmer, uncovered, for 10 minutes, stirring occasionally.

Cool to room temperature. Pour into 1-quart jar and slowly pour oil on top. Secure top with plastic wrap, cover tightly and let sit for at least 1 week.

Makes 1 quart.

— Sandra Kapral
Prince George, B.C.

PICKLED ONIONS

Boiling water
4 lbs. pickling onions
2½ cups pickling salt
3 qts. cold water
3 cups white vinegar

1 cup water
3 cups sugar
2 Tbsp. mixed pickling spice,
  tied in a bag

Pour boiling water over onions and let stand 5 minutes. Drain and plunge into ice water. Drain and peel off skins.

Dissolve pickling salt in 3 quarts cold water and pour over onions. Let stand overnight. Drain and rinse several times under cold running water.

Bring vinegar, 1 cup water, sugar and spices to a boil. Reduce heat and simmer for 15 minutes. Remove spices, add onions and bring back to a boil.

Ladle into sterilized jars and fill with vinegar syrup. Seal.

Makes 5 pints.

— Linda Forsyth
Winnipeg, Manitoba

CHILI SAUCE

30 ripe tomatoes, peeled & diced
8 onions, diced
3 sweet red peppers, diced
3 green peppers, diced

2 cups diced celery
2½ cups brown sugar
3 cups vinegar
3 Tbsp. pickling salt

Combine all ingredients in a large pot and mix well. Simmer, uncovered, until thick — 4½ hours.

Seal into jars while hot.

Makes 5 pints.

— Karen Herder
Lindsay, Ontario

SAUERKRAUT

2 lbs. cabbage
4 tsp. pickling salt

Remove loose outer leaves of cabbage. Wash and drain inner head, cut into quarters and remove core. Shred or cut into ⅛-inch strips. Mix thoroughly with 3 tsp. salt by hand.

Tightly pack cabbage into clean, hot jars. Press down with fingers and cover with a piece of clean cheesecloth. Cross 2 wooden sticks on top of the cheesecloth below the neck of the jar, place lid on loosely and set in a shallow pan to catch any overflow of brine.

Store for 2 to 3 weeks at 70 degrees F. When fermentation has stopped, wipe jars clean and remove sticks and cheesecloth. Press cabbage down firmly to release the last of the air bubbles. Combine 1 quart water with remaining 1 tsp. salt and pour over cabbage. Place lid on jar and process for 10 minutes in boiling water bath.

Makes 1 quart.

— Mary Dzielak
Calumet, Quebec

HORSERADISH

2 cups grated horseradish
1 cup white vinegar

½ tsp. salt

Place horseradish in sterilized 1-quart jar. Combine vinegar and salt and pour over horseradish. Seal jar and store in a cool place.

Makes 1 quart.

— Shirley Morrish
Devlin, Ontario

KETCHUP

1½ tsp. whole cloves
1 stick cinnamon
1 tsp. celery seed
1 tsp. allspice
1 cup white vinegar
8 lbs. ripe tomatoes

2 medium onions, chopped
¼ tsp. red pepper
6 apples, cut in eighths (optional)
1 cup sugar
4 tsp. salt

Add spices to vinegar and bring to a boil. Cover, turn off heat and let stand.

Mash tomatoes in a pot, add onion, pepper and apples. Heat to a boil and cook for 15 minutes. Put through a sieve. Add sugar to tomato juice and reheat to a boil. Skim. Cook down to half the original volume.

Strain vinegar mixture and add to juice with salt. Simmer, stirring frequently, for 30 minutes.

Fill hot, sterilized jars and seal.

Makes 4 to 5 pints.

— Kathy MacRow
Kingston, Ontario

TOMATO JUICE

12 very large ripe tomatoes,
  cut in thin wedges
1 large green pepper, diced
3 medium onions, chopped

1 celery stalk, diced
⅓ cup sugar
1 Tbsp. salt

Place all ingredients in a large heavy pot. Bring to a boil, lower heat, cover and simmer for 35 minutes, stirring occasionally.

Put mixture through a food mill, strain, return juice to pot and bring to a boil. Pour into 3 hot sterilized quart jars, leaving ¼-inch head room. Screw lids on, then process in a boiling water bath for 15 minutes.

Makes 3 quarts.

— Gwen Steinbusch
Winnipeg, Manitoba

HOT TAMALE SAUCE

THIS SAUCE IS DELICIOUS WITH MEXICAN COOKING AND ALMOST ANY BEAN OR MEAT dishes.

15 large ripe tomatoes
4 large peaches
3 large tart apples
4 pears
6 medium onions
3 cups diced celery

3 Tbsp. mixed pickling spice
4 tsp. salt
1½ cups cider vinegar
1 cup honey
12 small chili peppers

Blanch, peel and slice tomatoes and peaches. Core and slice apples and pears. Peel and thinly slice onions. Cut celery into small pieces. Tie pickling spice in a cheesecloth bag.

Combine all ingredients in a large pot and cook slowly until honey is dissolved and fruit is well mixed. Boil steadily, stirring occasionally, until sauce is thickened — about 40 minutes.

Turn into hot, sterile jars and seal.

Makes 3 to 4 quarts.

— Betty Ternier Daniels
Cochin, Sask.

CORN RELISH

6 cups corn
4 onions
½ large cabbage
2½ cups vinegar
1 Tbsp. salt

2½ cups sugar
3 Tbsp. flour
1 Tbsp. mustard
1 Tbsp. celery seed
½ tsp. turmeric

Combine corn, onions, cabbage and vinegar. Bring to a boil and simmer for 30 minutes. Add salt and sugar.

Blend together flour, mustard, celery seed and turmeric. Wet, then thin, with vinegar. Add to vegetables. Cook for 15 minutes.

Seal in sterilized jars.

Makes 3 to 4 quarts.

— Mrs. Fred Smith
Mountain Grove, Ontario

RHUBARB RELISH

2 qts. rhubarb, chopped
  into 1-inch lengths
1 qt. onions, thinly sliced
2 cups vinegar
2 cups sugar

1 Tbsp. salt
1 tsp. cloves
1 tsp. allspice
1 tsp. cinnamon
1 tsp. pepper

Place all ingredients in a large pot and mix well. Cook slowly until rhubarb is soft, then boil for 1 hour.

Seal in sterilized jars.

Makes 4 pints.

—Shirley Gilbert
Calgary, Alberta

ZUCCHINI RELISH

10 cups zucchini
4 cups onions
5 Tbsp. pickling salt
1 red pepper
1 green pepper
2¼ cups vinegar
3 cups sugar

1 tsp. nutmeg
1 tsp. dry mustard
1 tsp. turmeric
1 tsp. cornstarch
2 Tbsp. celery seed
½ tsp. pepper

Grind zucchini, onions and salt and let stand overnight. Drain and rinse twice in cold water to remove salt.

Grind red and green peppers together. Add to zucchini with remaining ingredients. Cook for 30 minutes.

Ladle while hot into sterile jars and seal.

Makes 5 to 6 pints.

— Gail Berg
Kispiox Valley, B.C.

PATTY'S MINT RELISH

1 cup packed mint leaves
6 medium onions
2 green peppers
2 lbs. apples
3 pears

¾ lb. raisins
1 oz. mustard seed
2 Tbsp. salt
2½ lbs. white sugar
1 qt. cider vinegar

Put mint, onions, green peppers, apples, pears and raisins through a meat chopper, then place in a crock.

Boil together remaining ingredients and pour over mint mixture. Let stand 1 week, bottle in sterile jars and seal.

Makes about 4 pints.

— Mary Reid
Georgeville, Quebec

BLACK CURRANT JAM

4 cups black currants
2 cups boiling water

6 cups granulated sugar
Butter

Wash and drain the currants. Add boiling water, bring to a boil and cook for 8 minutes.

Meanwhile, warm sugar slowly in a large pan in the oven. Add to currants, mix thoroughly and bring to a boil, stirring occasionally. Boil hard for 4 minutes. Remove from heat and add small piece of butter. Skim jam and pour into sterilized jars. Seal with melted paraffin wax.

Makes 8 jelly glasses.

— *Kathy Turner*
Ottawa, Ontario

BLUEBERRY JAM

2 cups blueberries
1 cup sugar

In a 2-quart saucepan, combine blueberries and 3 Tbsp. water. Bring to a boil and cook, uncovered, for 10 minutes. Add sugar and boil, uncovered, to jam stage — about 10 minutes. Carefully pour the jam into jars.

Makes 1½ cups.

— *Glenna Keating*
Dorval, Quebec

RED PLUM JAM

2 lbs. red plums
1 cup water

6 cups sugar
1 Tbsp. butter

Pit and cut up the plums. Cook, covered with water, until soft. Remove from heat, mash, and add sugar, stirring until it is completely dissolved. Cook over medium heat, stirring to prevent sticking.

Boil the mixture until candy thermometer registers 220 degrees F. Remove from heat, skim the froth and stir in the butter. Place in jars and cap.

Makes 9 jelly jars.

— *Mary Dzielak*
Calumet, Quebec

MOM'S STRAWBERRY JAM

4 cups strawberries
1 Tbsp. vinegar

3 cups white sugar

Wash and hull the strawberries. Add vinegar and bring to a boil, cover and boil for 1 minute. Add sugar and boil 20 minutes uncovered, stirring occasionally.

Pour into a large bowl and let stand overnight. Pour into sterilized jars, cover with melted paraffin wax, cool and put lids on.

Makes about 1 quart.

— *Joan Bridgeman Hoepner*
Norway House, Man.

FOUR BERRY JAM

3 cups raspberries
1 cup strawberries
2 cups blueberries

2 cups Saskatoon berries
4 cups honey
2 pkgs. powdered pectin

In a large pot, bring the berries and the honey to a rolling boil and simmer for about 15 minutes. Add the 2 packages of pectin, bring back to a rolling boil and boil for 2 minutes.

Pour into hot sterilized jars and seal.

Makes 6 pints.

— *Cary Elizabeth Marshall*
Thunder Bay, Ontario

APRICOT JAM AMANDINE

1 lb. dried apricots
6 cups water
⅓ cup lemon juice

8 cups sugar
1 Tbsp. butter
2 oz. slivered almonds

Cut up the apricots and soak in water overnight. Cook gently, covered, until tender — about 20 minutes. Remove from heat, mash and stir in lemon juice and sugar until completely dissolved.

Return to heat and boil until it reaches 220 degrees F. Remove from heat, skim the froth, and stir in the butter and almonds. Fill and cap jars.

Makes 9 jelly jars.

— *Mary Dzielak*
Calumet, Quebec

RASPBERRY OR BLACKBERRY JAM

6 cups berries
6 cups sugar

Place berries in flat-bottomed pan and mash with potato masher as they heat. Bring to a full boil and boil for 2 minutes. Add sugar and boil for 1 minute.

Remove from heat and beat with electric mixer for 4 minutes. Pour jam into hot, clean jars and pour hot wax over to seal.

Makes about 3 pints.

— *Beth Hopkins*
Courtenay, B.C.

BLACKBERRY & APPLE JAM

3 lbs. green apples
2 cups water
2½ lbs. blackberries

9 cups sugar
½ cup lemon juice
1 Tbsp. butter

Peel, core and slice the apples. Place in a pot with water and cook until soft — about 10 to 15 minutes. Remove from heat and mash. Add the blackberries, mix thoroughly, then add the sugar and lemon juice and stir until the sugar is completely dissolved. Boil the mixture until the candy thermometer registers 220 degrees F.

Remove from heat and skim the froth off the top of the jam with a large metal spoon. Stir in the butter. Pour into hot, sterilized jars and cap immediately.

Makes 10 jelly jars.

— *Mary Dzielak*
Calumet, Quebec

PARADISE JELLY

6 cups washed & cubed quince
6 cups quartered crabapples
3 cups cranberries

Granulated sugar
Rose geranium leaves

Boil quince in just enough water to cover. When it begins to soften, add apples and then cranberries. When all are soft, place in a jelly bag and drain into a bowl. Add a scant cup of sugar to each cup of fruit juice. Boil for about 20 minutes or until mixture gels when dropped onto a plate.

Pour into glasses, put a rose geranium leaf in each glass, and seal with paraffin.

Makes 6 pints.

— Cary Elizabeth Marshall
Thunder Bay, Ontario

WILD ROSE JELLY

2 cups apple juice
3 cups tightly-packed
  fresh wild rose petals

3 cups white sugar
½ bottle Certo

Heat apple juice to the boiling point. Place washed and drained rose petals in large saucepan and pour apple juice over them. Bring to a boil and boil for 20 minutes. Strain juice into another large saucepan. Add sugar, stir, bring to a boil and stir in Certo. Boil for 1 minute. Pour into sterile jelly glasses and seal with wax.

Makes 6 jelly glasses.

— Shirley Morrish
Devlin, Ontario

APPLE JELLY

4 lbs. green apples
½ cup lemon juice

3 cups water
Sugar

Wash and cut up apples without peeling or coring. Add lemon juice and water and boil until tender.

Remove from heat, mash and strain through jelly bag. Measure the juice and add 1 cup sugar for each cup of juice. Boil until juice reaches 220 degrees F, remove from heat and skim the froth. Place in jars and cap.

— Mary Dzielak
Calumet, Quebec

MINT JELLY

1 cup packed fresh mint leaves
½ cup vinegar

1¼ cups water
1½ lbs. sugar

Wash the mint, chop finely and bring to a boil with water and vinegar. Remove from heat and let stand for a few minutes. Add sugar and bring back to a boil. Boil for 20 minutes or until jelled.

Place in jar.

— C. Majewski
Pansy, Manitoba

ROWANBERRY JELLY

ROWANBERRY IS KNOWN AS MOUNTAIN ASH IN CENTRAL CANADA. THE BERRIES should be gathered after frost and should taste tart, but not so bitter that your mouth puckers.

4 qts. ripe rowanberries　　　　8 cups sugar
1 qt. water　　　　　　　　　　1 pkg. pectin

Simmer the berries in water until soft. Mash, then strain the juice through a cloth. Bring juice to a boil and add sugar. Add pectin when sugar is dissolved and boil for 1 or 2 minutes or until it tests done. Seal with ¼ inch paraffin wax.

Makes 2 pints.

—Cary Elizabeth Marshall
Thunder Bay, Ontario

ELDERBERRY JELLY

3 cups elderberry juice　　　　7½ cups sugar
½ cup lemon juice　　　　　　　1 bottle Certo

Boil juices and sugar, then add the Certo. Bring to a full rolling boil and cook for 1 minute. Remove from the stove, stir and skim off the foam. Pour into jars and seal.

Makes 4 to 6 jelly glasses.

— Joanne Ramsy
Aylmer, Ontario

PINEAPPLE JELLY

1 qt. pineapple juice　　　　　6 cups sugar
1 qt. tart apple juice

Bring combined juices to a boil, stir in sugar and boil rapidly until syrup sheets. Pour into sterile jars and seal.

Makes 4 to 6 pints.

— Janice Touesnard
River Bourgeois, Nova Scotia

PEACHSTONE JELLY

Skins, peach stones & overripe peaches　　7¼ cups sugar
1¼ cups strained lemon juice　　　　　　1 bottle Certo

Place peaches, stones and skins in a large pot and barely cover with water. Bring to a boil and simmer, covered, for 10 minutes. Place in a strainer and squeeze out juice to make 3½ cups.

Add the lemon juice and sugar and mix well. Place over high heat and bring to a boil, stirring constantly. Stir in Certo, bring to a full rolling boil and boil hard for 1 minute, stirring constantly.

Remove from heat, skim off foam and pour into jars. Cover with hot paraffin.

Makes 5 to 6 pints.

— Ruth Anne Laverty
Listowel, Ontario

COLONEL GREY'S CHUTNEY

CHUTNEYS, WHICH ORIGINATED IN INDIA AS ACCOMPANIMENTS TO CURRIED DISHES, are now as varied as the different cultures that have adopted them. Spicy, flavourful and exotic, they add a piquant touch to chicken, pork, lamb and curries.

1 qt. vinegar
4 lbs. demerara sugar
5 lbs. Granny Smith apples
4 oz. ginger root
2 cloves garlic

1 oz. red chilies in muslin bag
1 tsp. cayenne pepper
2 tsp. salt
½ lb. seedless raisins

Heat vinegar and sugar until sugar is dissolved. Peel and slice apples. Scrape and grate ginger. Peel and crush garlic.

Combine all ingredients in a heavy saucepan. Cook until thick and dark, removing chilies after 5 minutes. Place in jars and seal.
Makes 2 to 3 quarts.

— Eileen Deeley
Kamloops, B.C.

PEACH CHUTNEY

6 cups peeled, chopped peaches
4 cups peeled, chopped apples
2 cups raisins
4 cups brown sugar
1½ cups cider or malt vinegar

2 tsp. cinnamon
1 tsp. cloves
1 tsp. allspice
2 tsp. salt
⅛ tsp. black pepper

Combine all ingredients and cook slowly, stirring frequently, until thick — about 1 hour. Pour into hot sterilized jars and seal.

Makes 4 to 5 pints.

— Carolyn Hills
Sunderland, Ontario

BANANA CHUTNEY

2 onions, finely chopped
1 lb. very ripe bananas, mashed
1 lb. pitted dates
1 cup cider vinegar
¾ cup brown sugar
½ cup molasses
4 cloves garlic, crushed
1-inch slice fresh ginger, crushed

1 Tbsp. cinnamon
½ Tbsp. nutmeg
½ Tbsp. ground cloves
½ Tbsp. ground cardamom
½ Tbsp. ground coriander
1 tsp. fenugreek
1 tsp. cumin
1 tsp. turmeric

Combine onions, bananas, dates, vinegar, sugar and molasses in a heavy saucepan. Crush all the spices, mix together and stir into banana-date mixture.

Heat quickly to a boil and stir, while boiling, for 5 minutes. Reduce heat and simmer for 20 minutes. Let cool and pour into jars. Seal.

Makes 1 quart.

— Ingrid Birker
Toronto, Ontario

TOMATO CHUTNEY

4 lbs. tomatoes
1 lb. chopped apples
3 onions, finely chopped
2 cups vinegar
2 Tbsp. salt
½ tsp. allspice
2 cloves garlic

2 cups honey
1 cup raisins
1 tsp. cinnamon
1 Tbsp. dry mustard
1 tsp. cayenne
1 tsp. cloves

Chop tomatoes and add remaining ingredients. Cook until thick and clear, stirring occasionally.

Seal in hot sterilized jars.

Makes 5 pints.

— *Lisa Brownstone*
Avonhurst, Sask.

TOMATO BUTTER

6-qt. basket ripe tomatoes
1 Tbsp. salt
4 cups white sugar

2 cups white vinegar
2 Tbsp. mixed pickling spice,
  tied in a bag

Peel and cut up tomatoes. Sprinkle with salt and let stand overnight. In the morning, pour off the juice.

Add remaining ingredients to tomatoes, place in a large heavy pot and simmer until thick — about 2 hours.

Bottle in sterile jars.

Makes 4 to 6 quarts.

— *Alice Wires*
Kirkfield, Ontario

LEMON BUTTER

THIS PRESERVE IS DELICIOUS SPREAD ON TOAST FOR EVERYDAY USE, OR ON Christmas pudding for a special treat.

8 eggs, well beaten
4 cups sugar
1 cup butter

¼ cup grated lemon rind
1 cup lemon juice

Combine eggs and sugar in a double boiler. Add butter, lemon rind and lemon juice. Cook over gently boiling water, stirring frequently, until it thickens. Bottle and cool.

Makes eight 8-ounce jelly glasses.

— *Kathy Turner*
Ottawa, Ontario

WINNIFRED'S APPLE BUTTER

10 lbs. apples, sliced
5 cups water
4 cups sugar

1 cup corn syrup
2 tsp. cinnamon
1 tsp. allspice

Place apple slices in Dutch oven and add water. Boil and cook down for 1 hour. Sieve or put through a blender and add sugar and syrup. Return to heat and cook down until desired thickness is reached — 2 to 3 hours. Add spices and pack into jars.

Makes about 4 quarts.

— *Debbie Winder*
Watford, Ontario

RHUBARB MARMALADE

6 large oranges
6 cups finely chopped rhubarb

1 cup water
9 cups sugar

Peel and section 4 oranges. Chop pulp into small pieces, discarding rinds. Wash the other 2 oranges and cut up coarsely. Put through fine blade of food chopper.

Combine rhubarb, orange pieces and ground orange in a kettle. Add water, cover, and bring to a boil. Uncover, add sugar and stir until sugar is dissolved. Boil hard, uncovered, until mixture thickens — 20 to 30 minutes.

Skim and ladle into sterilized jars. Top with thin layer of paraffin.

Makes about ten 8-oz. jars.

— Joanne Kellog
Barrie, Ontario

SCOTCH ORANGE MARMALADE

6 navel oranges
10 cups water
10 cups sugar

1 cup lemon juice
1 Tbsp. butter
½ cup Scotch whiskey

Shred the oranges, discarding the tough centre fibre. Put them in a pan with the water and soak overnight. The next day, cook, covered, until tender.

Let cool, then stir in the sugar and lemon juice until dissolved. Boil until mixture reaches 220 degrees F. Remove from heat, skim the froth and stir in the butter and whiskey. Pour into jars and seal.

Makes 12 jelly glasses.

— Mary Dzielak
Calumet, Quebec

PEACH MARMALADE

1 orange
2 lemons
1 cup water

2 lbs. ripe peaches
5 cups sugar
½ bottle liquid pectin

Grind orange and 1 lemon in blender with water. Put into a small pot and add juice from the other lemon. Boil, covered, for 20 minutes.

Peel, pit and chop peaches finely. Put in large pot with citrus mixture and sugar. Boil hard for 2 minutes. Add pectin and boil until jelly thermometer reaches 221 degrees F. Remove from heat and stir and skim foam for about 10 minutes. Pour into sterile jars and seal.

Makes 2 pints.

— Judy Wuest
Cross Creek, N.B.

YELLOW TOMATO MARMALADE

3¼ cups peeled & chopped
  yellow tomatoes
Rind of 1 large lemon, grated

¼ cup lemon juice
6 cups sugar
1 bottle Certo

Cook tomatoes, covered, for 10 minutes without any water. Add lemon rind, lemon juice and sugar. Bring to a boil over moderate heat, stirring constantly, and boil hard for 1 minute. Turn off heat. Add Certo and stir vigorously for 5 minutes. Bottle in sterile jars.

Makes 1½ pints.

— Mary Reid
Georgeville, Quebec

BRANDIED CHERRIES

2 lbs. sweet cherries
2 cups sugar

2 cups water
Brandy

Place unpitted cherries in a large bowl and cover with ice cold water. Let them stand for 30 to 40 minutes. Drain.

Dissolve sugar in 2 cups water, stirring all the time, and bring to a full boil. Boil rapidly for 5 minutes. Add the cherries and bring once more to a rolling boil. Remove from heat, wait until the boiling stops and repeat operation twice more, stirring gently with a wooden spoon.

Fill sterilized jars three-quarters full with fruit and syrup, place covers loosely on jars and let stand until cool, then fill each jar with brandy. Stir with a silver or wooden spoon. Seal. Turn jars upside down overnight, then store in a cool, dark place right side up, for at least 3 months before using.

Makes 4 pints.

— Kathleen Fitzgerald
Fort McMurray, Alta.

Index